MW01042894

WINDOWS INTO THE
HISTORY & PHILOSOPHY
OF EDUCATION

SAMUEL JAMES SMITH

Liberty University

Kendall Hunt
publishing company

Cover image © Shutterstock, Inc.

www.kendallhunt.com
Send all inquiries to:
4050 Westmark Drive
Dubuque, IA 52004-1840

Copyright © 2020 by Kendall Hunt Publishing Company

ISBN 978-1-7924-2463-2

All rights reserved. No part of this publication may be reproduced,
stored in a retrieval system, or transmitted, in any form or by any means,
electronic, mechanical, photocopying, recording, or otherwise,
without the prior written permission of the copyright owner.

Published in the United States of America

TABLE OF CONTENTS

# DEDICATION

This book is dedicated both to a group and to an individual. First, the group is made up of second-career teachers, career switchers who have chosen teaching as their profession after exploring at least one other vocation. I have been blessed to meet hundreds of them on their journey to the schoolhouse from their service in the military or as firefighters, nurses, ministers, secretaries, realtors, law enforcement officers, soldiers, chefs, missionaries, and a wide variety of other vocations. You may be among them. If so, thank you for fulfilling what Nancy Pearcey in her book *Total Truth* (2008) refers to as your "cultural mandate" to serve others. As you look in the mirror, know that your previous service to humanity has been holy, whether you mopped floors, brokered stocks, or defended our country. As you look through the window into the field of education, be assured that your future service will also be holy as you step into the role of educator, and remember to take on the challenge of Colossians 3:23—"Whatever you do, work at it with all your heart, as working for the Lord, not for men" (New International Version).

The individual to whom I dedicate this book was my daughter and greatest teacher. For over thirteen years she taught our family what it meant to be patient, joyful, loving, and considerate of others—despite her circumstances. Emily Kate Smith (1994-2007) danced, laughed, sang, and teased as she taught us the greatest lessons of life. Despite her Down syndrome, heart disease, and leukemia, she persevered, and even now she continues to teach us.

ACKNOWLEDGMENTS

The patience and love of my wife, Sonja, has helped me to navigate through life while taking on projects such as this book. Above all, she has listened to me tell the stories before I wrote them. Her ear helped me to solidify thoughts before they reached the page. She visited museums with me when she would much rather have been on the beach, and she watched historical documentaries when she would have preferred romantic comedies.

Colleagues at Liberty University have been invaluable in this project, especially faculty who teach history, law, sociology, and theology. Many of them have pored over these pages, offering valuable feedback and guidance along the way. I am especially appreciative of the assistance of Ken Cleaver, Jeffrey Hodge, and Christiana Link. Grant Knaus applied his exceptional videography skills to record guest presenters Ken Cleaver, Donna Donald, John S. Knox, Rena Lindevaldsen, and Roger Schultz, all of whom contributed their expertise in an engaging format.

Twenty-five years ago, God planted in me the thought of writing a book with my students in mind. The project was deferred so often that I began to doubt whether I would have the time to conduct the required research and to write the manuscript. God, however, is faithful and—through a number of unexpected circumstances—He provided the resources, time, energy, and people that it took to bring the idea to fruition. I thank Him for the promise found in Psalm 32:8, "I will instruct you and teach you in the way you should go; I will counsel you with my loving eye on you" (New International Version).

INTRODUCTION

Windows, lenses, and mirrors provide different functions, but all three serve to enhance vision. Windows provide a snapshot into time and space. Viewers on one side of the glass attempt to obtain an accurate outlook of what is on the other side. If the view is incomplete, observers may position themselves differently to alter the angle of their vision. If the view is distorted, the glass may be cleaned to ensure that objects and events are perceived as they truly are—at least to the degree that accuracy is possible. Yet, no matter how many angles viewers consider and despite how clear the glass may be, the view is limited by the window frame and by the surrounding walls. Lenses are chosen either to magnify or to change a perspective by refraction of light; as the light is changed, observers see something different and must take into account how the lens has changed the view. Mirrors are different from windows and lenses in that, instead of looking outward to some-

© Janez Habjanic/Shutterstock.com

thing exterior, they reflect on the observers. One cannot look directly into a mirror without seeing oneself.

History as Windows and Lenses

Historians realize that their research into events of the past is similar to one's attempt to maximize a view through a window. The goal is to increase the accuracy and understanding of a limited space in time. A major difference, however, is that historians look through their windows vicariously—through documents, artifacts, journals, letters, photographs, etc.—all of which provide limited perspectives of the events through another person's eyes. Just about the time the point of saturation is reached or a supposed exhaustive work is published on a particular historical topic, new evidence is discovered that provides a clearer view. New evidence may appear in the form of recently discovered journals, letters, or other artifacts that may serve to increase understanding. These artifacts may introduce the observer to new characters or events in the narrative or to a different way of perceiving those events. The artifacts themselves may not be new, but attention drawn to them in a novel context may provide a fresh look through the same window.

The title of this book, *Windows into the History and Philosophy of Education*, is just that—a series of windows with limited perspectives, of views positioned from various angles. It is not intended to be exhaustive and is not fully presented chronologically. It is neither an introduction nor an overview, as it assumes the reader already has developed an understanding to some degree of the general history of education and the philosophies that have motivated educators of the past. For readers less familiar with historical and philosophical foundations of education, the appendices provide a list of significant educational thinkers of the past (Appendix A), an overview of select educational theories (Appendix B), and strategies for formulating one's personal philosophy of education (Appendix C).

Students of educational foundations often inquire about the place of religion historically in the field. Some are surprised to find that not only philosophers and psychologists but also many theologians played a significant role in how current ideas about teaching and learning developed over time. Readers who are devoutly religious themselves might wonder about the degree to which it is appropriate, legal, or ethical to incorporate religious topics into the public school classroom. Appendix D addresses this issue.

The primary intent of the book, however, is to take the views that have already been explored by those interested in the foundations of education and to bring a richer perspective to them. Windows into the history of education, especially in America, have included familiar individuals such as Horace Mann and John Dewey, and rightly so. It is assumed that the reader has gotten a good view of these two men and other people who have dominated the literature on the history of education. This book acknowledges these figures but also introduces readers to other less well-known characters such as Rebecca Protten, Judith Sargent Murray, Horace Bushnell, Margaret Douglass, General Oliver Otis Howard, and Susan Miller Dorsey. These individuals are contextualized in such a way as to situate them within the larger scenario so that readers will recognize a familiar view while at the same time comprehending the view in a fresh way.

In actuality, a window is simply an opening in a wall, the frame through which to see the landscape. The glass is a type of lens. For accuracy, viewers desire the glass to be as transparent and as inconspicuous as possible. As the glass becomes less noticeable, the view becomes clearer. While historians indeed value objectivity, they often apply different lenses through which to interpret the landscape. Some prominent current lenses include Marxism, critical feminist theory, and postmodernism. Other lenses have included American exceptionalism, ethnohistory, utopianism, and revisionist history. It would be disingenuous for me to deny that I applied a lens in writing this book. I indeed did so, and—in what qualitative research refers to as *situation to self*, *reflexivity*, and *bracketing*—I will disclose potential bias by explaining my experiences and perspectives that served as the context of the book.

 A Personal Lens: Situation to Self

I am a descendent of Heinrich Schmidt, a German who migrated in the 1760s to Virginia. His son, Henry Smith, was a blacksmith who fought in the Revolutionary War. This information was retrieved from records kept by the Moravian Church, so I assume that Henry was a Moravian. The record cites Northern Neck Land Grants as indicating that Henry owned 237 acres in 1788. In 1823, he and his family moved to the mountains of what is now Wayne County—colloquially known as "Out Wayne" by locals—near Huntington, West Virginia, where I was born 139 years later in 1962.

My mother's side of the family was involved in the Primitive Baptist Church, also known as Old Regular, Hard Shell, and Foot Washing Baptists. My maternal grandfather, whom we called PawPaw, was a moderator of the church. PawPaw held a great deal of influence within the church and often participated in tag-team preaching in which two or more preachers would deliver impromptu sermons during a lengthy

© eyepark/Shutterstock.com

worship service. In these services, my mother typically was one of many who would shout, wave hankies, and sometimes run the aisles. Emotionalism in worship was highly valued, and the dichotomy between the head and the heart was an oft-repeated theme. As a teenager, I visited a different church where I prayed the sinner's prayer and began the journey of my born-again salvation experience. Two years later, after deciding to attend a Bible college in Houston, Texas, I visited my PawPaw to say goodbye. He cautioned me one last time about studying man's ideas in books other than the Bible and reminded me that the Bible alone was worthy of study.

Later in life, I continued to grapple with this heart–mind dichotomy but eventually made some sense of it through professors, mentors, and books. God used people such as Prof. Jack Eitelbuss, who initially taught me history and philosophy of education. God also used Dr. Roy W. Lowrie, Jr., whose books taught me the practical application of God's truth even before I personally met him years later and sat under his teaching. Three key books that shaped my thought regarding the nature and application of truth were Francis Schaeffer's *How Should We Then Live: The Rise and Decline of Western Thought and Culture* (1976), Nancy Pearcey's *Total Truth: Liberating Christianity from Its Cultural Captivity* (2005), and Vishal Mangalwadi's *The Book that Made Your World: How the Bible Created the Soul of Western Civilization* (2011).

My interests in literature, history, theology, and education were cultivated through coursework at both private and public universities, and in 1994—while working on a doctorate at Oklahoma State University—I was given my first opportunity to teach the history and philosophy of education at a nearby Christian university. This experience sparked my passion for the "why" behind the "what" and the "how" of education. While honing my own philosophy of education, I found great satisfaction in introducing students to the various "whys" that drove educational thinkers of the past, in making connections with current events, and in coaching students as they developed their own philosophies of education. This continues to be my primary passion to this day.

As a person of strong beliefs and convictions, I have found navigating my teaching in higher education to be a challenge sometimes. On the one hand, I feel a strong desire to persuade students to embrace the same philosophies of life and education that I hold. On the other hand, part of my philosophy of education is that students must critically evaluate all ideas, including mine, and choose for themselves what they perceive to be the ultimate purpose of life and of learning. This challenge came to a peak as I taught a World Religions course for a secular university. To maintain my integrity as an instructor, I taught all religions equally, yet I cannot deny that my hidden curriculum was for students to see the superiority of Christianity and to decide to follow Christ after comparing the various religions of the world. In the capstone assignment, some students wrote of how the course led them to return to the church of their childhood while others shared how exploration of Buddhism drove them to reject Christianity and to follow what they perceived as a more enlightened way. The former lifted me to the heights of gratification while the latter sunk me to the depths of disappointment. Had I failed in presenting biblical truth? Was I not carrying out what I perceived to be my ultimate calling as a Christian teacher?

The above reflections are an attempt at *reflexivity*, the process researchers use to state and evaluate their experiences and beliefs. Readers may consider reflexivity as a form of full disclosure so that they understand the potential biases the author may reveal. Researchers consider reflexivity a practice of owning their potential biases in an effort to bracket them. *Bracketing*, also known as *epoché*, is the author's attempt to set aside possible biases that arise from experiences and beliefs and to inhibit them from interfering with the research at hand. The goal of reflexivity and bracketing is to present the research as it is with minimized distortion from the author's biases. In addition to practicing reflexivity and bracketing during the writing process of this book, I presented each chapter to historians and theologians with the expertise to review and critique the work.

That said, more needs to be discussed about bias. In the news media, bias begins the moment an editor or producer decides to hype one story or to cut another. The selection process alone reveals a measure of bias. In this book, I selected particular individuals and events to highlight based on what I had come to perceive as important in the history and philosophy of education. This selection was undeniably influenced by a biblical worldview lens. The decision of what topics to write about and how to present them was also informed by a desire to represent the scholarly literature on the history and philosophy of education as a field of study. Therefore, it is not biased to emphasize theologians such as Augustine, Thomas Aquinas, Martin Luther, and John Calvin—all of whom are acknowledged in secular research as having profoundly transformed education. Neither is it biased to highlight the faith of individuals who were motivated by their beliefs to bring about social reform, as in the instances of Jesuit and Moravian missionaries, Benjamin Rush, the Beecher family, William McGuffey, and many others. These selections are supported by the body of knowledge in the field.

 Overview

Each chapter of this book is a window into a period of time. Some chapters highlight a particular individual while others focus more on educational developments during that time. **Chapter 1** provides an overview of the philosophical milieu of Ancient Athens. Why Athens? Our starting point could have been with Confucianism in China or with the Fertile Crescent of Mesopotamia. This work, however, focuses on educational developments in the Western World and, therefore, begins with the birthplace of Western philosophy. This is not to imply that China or the Middle East would not have been good starting points, but—as discussed above—these chapters are windows with limited views and are not intended to represent a comprehensive global perspective.

The medieval era is represented by **Chapters 2 and 3** on Augustine from the Early Middle Ages and Thomas Aquinas from the High Middle Ages. The focus is on how the medieval Roman Catholic Church gave prominence early on to Augustine's Christoplatonism and how the revival of Aristotelian ideas in scholasticism served as a pilot light for the coming Scientific Revolution. **Chapter 5** revisits Augustine's ideas and their revival by Christian Humanists of the Protestant Reformation so that there was a return to the primary sources and original languages of the Bible and other classical works.

Chapters 4, 6, and 7 provide slices of history from the Atlantic World. Atlantic history explores the colliding cultures of Europe, Africa, and the Americas. It considers how the migration of people and how their exchange of ideas, material goods, and customs were synthesized to form new ways of perceiving and living in the world. Transcending the typical study of isolated governments, Atlantic history focuses on interactions of cultures surrounding the Atlantic Ocean. This field of study came about by the mid-twentieth century as historians realized that research on the era of exploration had been saturated. Some new information was still being added but what was needed was more integration of themes and a holistic look at interactions rather than so many isolated narratives and simple comparisons. History of the Atlantic World explores geographic zones that transcend political boundaries, states in relation with other states, and states in relation to the whole Atlantic area. This relatively new field of study implements terms, such as *cross-fertilized histories*, *methodological pluralism*, and *expanded horizons* to express how Atlantic history is different from traditional approaches to history.[1] Three themes are found in Atlantic studies: (1) European expansion, (2) creative and adaptive interactions among cultures, and (3) the beginning and end of Atlantic history. The notion that Atlantic history may have an end is controversial. Some believe it ended with political revolutions, while others claim that its conclusion coincided with the demise of the slave trade. Still, there are historians who point to ongoing interactions of cultures around the Atlantic Ocean as evidence that research in this field should continue.[2]

Chapters 8, 9, 10, and 11 narrow the attention mostly to educational developments in America and follow a traditional sequence through colonial, revolutionary, early national, and civil war eras. Attention is given to the theories and practices of some well-known personages as well as to those of perhaps unfamiliar but nevertheless significant individuals. Some names that may be new to readers are Judith Sargent Murray, Horace Bushnell, Margaret Douglass, and General Oliver Otis Howard. A section subtitled "Meanwhile, Back in Europe" explores Johann Heinrich Pestalozzi, who is worth a trip back across the Atlantic to become acquainted with the man known as the "Father of Modern Education" and as the "Father of Pedagogy."

The chronological sequence begins to break down in Chapters 12 and 15 for the sake of tracing important topics in an isolated manner so as to offer them the attention they deserve. **Chapter 12** follows the history and philosophy of Native American education from the pre-Columbian era to the late twentieth century. **Chapter 15** outlines educational reforms in the United States, especially through presidential politics from Thomas Jefferson to Barack Obama.

Chapter 13 takes a look at the Progressive Era by focusing on an important but relatively obscure woman, Susan Miller Dorsey, who served as superintendent of schools in Los Angeles, California.

Chapter 14 accomplishes something rare in Foundations of Education textbooks. It provides a limited tour of educational conditions in select countries during World War II in Eastern and Western Europe and in the United States. Readers will catch a glimpse through a number of windows into the experiences of children, school administrators, and former soldiers in Poland, Finland, England, and the United States.

The final two chapters explore two philosophical approaches to education that have made significant inroads into the postmodern curriculum and instruction. **Chapter 16** returns the reader to nineteenth-century Europe where Danish philosopher and theologian Søren Kierkegaard articulated his existentialist philosophy. This chapter is intentionally placed out of chronological order because Kierkegaard's influence was not prominent in the field of education until long after his lifetime. It was not until the twentieth and twenty-first centuries that existentialism began to be embraced in any meaningful way by educational theorists, often in the form of postmodernism or synthesized with Marxist theory in Paulo Freire's critical pedagogy, which is the topic of **Chapter 17**.

 Focus: Key Topics and Terms

While photographers have the feature of autofocus in modern cameras, readers have no such advantage. Readers tend to focus on what connects with their own experiences and interests and may be guided to attend to what is accentuated by the writing style, headings, images, bold font, and other formatting. To facilitate focus in this book, light is drawn to key topics and terms at the beginning of each chapter. Also, selected terms are placed in bold font upon their first occurrence within the chapter.

© Niels Hariot/Shutterstock.com

Mirrors: Reflections into One's Own Beliefs

At the end of each chapter is a list of questions for reflection. They serve to review content from the chapter itself and to encourage exploration into supplementary sources for further research. The deeper purpose of these questions, however, is to guide readers in looking back at themselves as they would in a mirror. The view in a mirror typically captures an image of the one looking into it, and it also captures the context surrounding the individual. Readers are challenged to capitalize on this opportunity to evaluate their own "why" behind the "what" and the "how" of their own calling.

At the end of each chapter is a list of questions for reflection. They serve to review content from the chapter itself and also to encourage exploration into supplementary sources for further research. The deeper purpose of these questions, however, is to guide readers to look back at themselves as they would in a mirror. The view in a mirror typically captures an image of the one looking into it, and it also captures the context surrounding the individual. Readers are challenged to capitalize on this opportunity to evaluate their own 'why' behind the 'what' and the 'how' of their own calling.

Which beliefs conveyed in this book resonate most with you? Which ones do you embrace and which do you reject? Do you find an educational thinker within the covers of this book worthy of emulation? If so, why? What is the long-range impact you desire to make on individuals and on society through your own work in the field of education?

As you articulate your responses to the questions above, especially to the last one, and as you consider the questions at the end of each chapter, you will begin to formulate your own philosophy of education. Doing so may mean that you incorporate new vocabulary—such as *epistemology*, *ontology*, or *metaphysics*—into your reflections about teaching and learning. Even more importantly, however, when the alarm goes off in the morning, your "why" for getting out of bed and for doing what you do each day might be a bit more solidified than it was previously.

 Go to www.khlearn.com to watch an introduction video.

ENDNOTES

1. David Armitage, "The Varieties of Atlantic History," in *Major Problems in Atlantic History*, eds. Alison Games and Adam Rothman (Boston: Houghton Mifflin, 2008), 16-23.
2. Thomas Benjamin, *The Atlantic World: Europeans, Africans, Indians and Their Shared History, 1400-1900* (Cambridge: Cambridge University Press, 2009), xxiii-xxvi.

CHAPTER 1

ANCIENT ATHENS: BIRTHPLACE OF WESTERN PHILOSOPHY

Plato and Aristotle as portrayed by Raphael in the fresco entitled The School of Athens *as found at the Vatican*

© serato/Shutterstock.com

FOCUS: KEY TOPICS AND TERMS

Aristotle
Epicureans
Idealism
Plato

Realism
Skeptics
Socrates
Socratic method

Sophists
Stoics

"Know Thyself! The unexamined Life is not worth Living" (Socrates).

Whether people agree or not with Socrates' claim that "the unexamined life is not worth living," they cannot refute that Socrates, this ancient Athenian who lived four centuries before Christ, made a significant impact on the fields of philosophy and of education. Known primarily for his teaching method, Socrates was accused of corrupting the youth of his time. When people challenge others to think differently from the traditional ways that have been passed down, they sometimes upset the apple cart, the power structure, the political system—and that is exactly what Socrates did.

This description of Socrates sounds somewhat like another man who was also known as a great philosopher, does it not? Both Socrates and Jesus were accused of being troublemakers. Both were known for using strategic questioning strategies to challenge the thinking of their disciples, and both were unjustly condemned to death—Jesus by the cross and Socrates by taking hemlock. Neither of them wrote any books, so what we know of them is derived primarily from the writings of their students. Now, before we discuss Socrates' influence on his students and how that influence has trickled down through the millennia, let us take a closer look at the philosophical milieu that existed in ancient Athens.

 Philosophical Milieu of Ancient Athens

In the seventeenth chapter of the book of Acts, Luke portrays the philosophical tone in ancient Athens. Granted, Paul was there approximately five hundred years after **Socrates**, **Plato**, and **Aristotle**, but the same schools of philosophy continued to dominate academic thought in Athens.

Paul began his day in the synagogue discussing theology with the Jews and God-fearing Greeks, but he left the synagogue to go to the marketplace, called the *agora*. The word *agora* is the merger of two Greek words that mean "I shop" and "I speak in public." Athenians did not go to the marketplace just to buy fish and bread; they went there to hear what the latest ideas were—to find out what merchants were learning from other parts of the world.

STOICS

Built around the agora (the marketplace) were porches with beautiful columns, sculptures, and paintings. Because of these features, they called these public spaces *stoas*, or painted porches. On the *stoas*, politicians, philosophers, and poets gathered to share their ideas. Some of the more frequent 'street preachers,' as they might be known today, became known as *Stoics* because they were some of the most outspoken and dogmatic speakers on the *stoas*. What did Stoics believe? Generally, they believed in the supernatural—that the gods were real and that these gods determined the human world. They believed people should seek truth but that there was something blocking them from reaching that truth. Similar to the Buddhist belief regarding Nirvana, Stoics taught that truth could not fully be reached until passion and desire were removed. Passion, desire, and emotions distracted learners and distorted truth, so true learning must diminish these distractions. Thus, the term *stoic expression*.

EPICUREANS

Acts 17 describes how Paul left the synagogue and went to the marketplace later that same day, he reasoned "with those who happened to be there." This group of people included the Stoics, but it also included a group of philosophers called Epicureans, named after their founder, Epicurus. Unlike the Stoics, Epicureans did not believe in the supernatural. They were materialists, hedonists, who did agree with Stoics on one particular point—that one could pursue truth and know it. A major difference, however, is that it was not passion and desire that kept learners from truth; it was pain, sorrow, and suffering. Epicureans would call the pursuit of truth the "pursuit of happiness," which is the source of Thomas Jefferson's third unalienable right in the Declaration of Independence after having borrowed the first two—life and liberty—from John Locke.

SKEPTICS AND SOPHISTS

SKEPTICS. Acts 17 mentions specifically that Stoics and Epicureans began to debate with Paul, but—more than likely—there were other philosophical groups at the marketplace that day. It would have been common for Skeptics to be present on the stoa. The Skeptics were followers of Pyrrho, whose beliefs were in reaction to the radically polar views of the Stoics and Epicureans. They believed that all sources of truth were flawed. The senses often perceived reality incorrectly, and flawed human reason could result in incorrect conclusions. Truth could not be known, and it was therefore futile to make any truth claims.

One can imagine the Skeptics in the marketplace as they listened to the Stoics and Epicureans argue. The response of the Skeptics might be found in some of their most common expressions:

- "Every saying has its corresponding opposite."
- "Not more one thing than another."
- "We determine nothing."

And determining nothing was truly what they were all about. They taught that, since truth cannot be known, Skeptics would teach people to withhold judgment, suspend belief, and refrain from making any truth claims.

SOPHISTS. Now, in addition to the Stoics, Epicureans, and Skeptics, there was at least one more group that Paul most likely confronted in the marketplace—the Sophists. Sophists were different from the others in that they were compensated as educators. In order to understand the Sophists as educators, one must know who their students were, what their curriculum focused on, and why they taught their students.

Who were their students? Sophists tutored wealthy male citizens of Athens.

What was their curriculum? Relativism and rhetoric were central to the content of their instruction. Sophists perceived truth as relative, dependent on circumstances. They held skills as more valuable than content because content (or truth) could change, but skills were valuable in any context. Of all skills, why did they place so much emphasis on rhetoric? This emphasis related to the motivation, or the "why," of their teaching.

Why? Athens was the birthplace of democracy, but it was not a representative democracy in which representatives voted for legislation on behalf of their constituents. It was a direct democracy whereby every adult male qualifying as a citizen could vote on legislation. Because of this, skills of persuasion were paramount. He who could persuade others held a great deal of power and could also protect his wealth. Since

Acropolis in Athens, Greece

there was no income tax system as exists today, many laws indicated who would be responsible to pay for construction of a bridge or to pay expenses for a festival to the gods. Citizens with old wealth battled against those with new wealth over who would fund such projects. Who truly had the most wealth? Sophists were not so much concerned with which citizens actually had more wealth. Their concern was more to ensure that their clients were able to persuade voters that someone else should pay. Critics often portray Sophists similarly to how some might view a defense attorney. This perspective of the Sophists was held among their contemporaries and is currently held among many historians. The negative connotations applied to words such as *sophistry* and *sophomoric* reveal the type of reputation the Sophists had.

Protagoras was credited as originating the role of the Sophist in Athenian society. The word *protagonist* is derived from his name. A protagonist is an actor, a lead character. For a plot to develop, however, every protagonist needs an antagonist, and Protagoras's antagonist was his teacher—Socrates. How fitting! Socrates was certainly antagonistic to Protagoras's ideas that "Man is the measure of all things" and that there is no absolute truth. The **Socratic method** itself may even be described as somewhat antagonistic with its questioning, probing, and requiring students to defend their rationale.

 ## Plato's Idealism

Under the tutelage of Socrates, Protagoras had a fellow pupil who is far more renowned than he—Plato. It is through Plato's writings that the world has learned about their mentor Socrates, and it is also through these same sources that the world was introduced to the philosophy of **idealism**. To understand the central principle of idealism, one might consider what it means to be in a strictly platonic relationship. Such a relationship values the emotional and spiritual aspects of friendship rather than the physical.

Plato illustrated through his Allegory of the Cave how ultimate reality is not in the shadows of this physical world but instead is outside the cave. Real meaning is not in the cave at all, where people are captives chained so that they see only the shadows cast on the back of the cave wall. The captives may come to believe the shadows are all that exist, but—Plato argues—if the captives could be released and enter the world outside the cave, they would experience the ideas and ideals behind the shadows themselves. For example, justice and freedom are abstract ideals that should be taught and for which all society should strive. How common it is, though, to hear someone declare, "Life's not fair!" And as Jean-Jacque Rousseau (1712-1778) observed, "Man is born free but is everywhere in chains." Do these observations about justice and freedom make those ideals not real? Because they may be attained only to a limited degree in this world, does this make them irrelevant? Not at all, claimed Plato! According to him, abstract ideals of justice, freedom, beauty, goodness, and virtue are the most important concepts to teach.

 ## Aristotle's Realism

It has been said that all philosophy is a footnote to Plato. The point of that statement is that various philosophies either agree or disagree with Plato to some extent. The disagreement started with his own student—Aristotle. Raphael's Renaissance fresco entitled *School of Athens* illustrates the difference between Plato and Aristotle by picturing Plato pointing upward while holding a book down by his side. This gesture symbolizes Plato's idea that ultimate truth is out there beyond the cave for people to aspire to and that observations of this physical world, while they certainly exist and hold some practical value, are shadows in comparison with the ideals, virtues, and abstract concepts that make people distinctly human. In contrast, Aristotle is pictured holding a book outward in one hand while gesturing to it with the other. Aristotle's eyes are looking directly into his teacher Plato's as if to indicate some sort of face-off between the two. While they both agreed that there were universal absolute truths, Aristotle held that ultimate reality is found in natural law—observations about the physical world and how it worked. Therefore, Aristotle was considered the father of natural **realism**.

Engraving on a Greek banknote of the Apostle Paul's sermon to the Areopagus

© vkilikov/Shutterstock.com

With this brief snapshot of philosophy in ancient Athens, consider how educational arguments have played out in more recent times. Why do some embrace common core curriculum and others reject it? Why do some parents enroll their children in a private classical school or prefer a magnet or charter school that emphasizes technology? Why do some teachers, such as Rafe Esquith, spend hours memorizing and performing Shakespearean plays with elementary students while others focus on literature perceived as more relevant to contemporary student experiences?[1] It may be—as in the difference between Plato and Aristotle or between the Stoics and the Epicureans—that they see meaning, purpose, and ultimate reality in different ways.

In Acts 17, Paul began his day in the synagogue and then progressed to the marketplace where he interacted with Stoics, Epicureans, Skeptics, and Sophists. People in the marketplace were so intrigued by the strange newness of Paul's message compared to all the other philosophies that they took him to the meeting of the Areopagus where the council made judicial decisions. It was there, on Mars Hill, more commonly known as the Acropolis, where Paul gave his famous sermon that transformed lives of men and women that day by introducing them to the Way, the Truth, and the Life in the person of Jesus Christ. This passage may challenge readers to consider their own "marketplace" and how they might engage culture to impact it in a similar manner as did Paul.[2]

 Go to www.khlearn.com to watch a video about the birthplace of Western philosophy.

 Reflection

For personal reflection, content review, and further research:

1. What type of impact did Socrates and Jesus have on their students and on society?
2. The Stoics and Epicureans had starkly different epistemological perspectives. What barriers did each believe the learner must overcome in order to know truth?
3. How were the learning outcomes different for the Stoics, Epicureans, Skeptics, and Sophists? What was their goal for their students?
4. What did the Sophists mean by "man is the measure of all things"? How might this perspective be observed in current worldviews?
5. Which philosophical thought resonates most with you: Plato's idealism or Aristotle's realism? Why?
6. Some Christian theologians warn against Christoplatonism—the tendency for Christians to see Plato's idealism as representing biblical truth. Though there is some evidence that Plato may have been influenced by Hebraic thinking, what might be some problems with perceiving Plato as being more closely aligned to biblical truth than Aristotelian realism?
7. Are there universal absolute truths? If so, can they be known? Compare how each of the following might respond to these questions: Stoics, Epicureans, Skeptics, Sophists Idealists, and Realists. Evaluate the degree to which their answers would align with a biblical worldview.
8. After reading Acts 17, reflect on how Paul addresses issues of metaphysics, cosmology, ontology, anthropology, and teleology. What evidence do you see that he understood the diversity of Athenian culture?

ENDNOTES

1. Rafe Esquith, *Teach Like Your Hair's on Fire: The Methods and Madness Inside Room 56* (New York: Penguin Books, 2007).

2. See Sheila G. Dunn, *Philosophical Foundations of Education: Connecting Philosophy to Theory and Practice* (Upper Saddle River, NJ: Pearson, 2005); Gerald L. Gutek, *A History of the Western Educational Experience*, 2nd ed. (Long Grove, IL: Waveland Press, 1995); Gerald L. Gutek, *Historical and Philosophical Foundations of Education: A Biographical Introduction* (Upper Saddle River, NJ: Pearson, 2011); Gerald L. Gutek, *Philosophical, Ideological, and Theoretical Perspectives on Education*, 2nd ed. (Boston: Pearson, 2014); George R. Knight, *Philosophy & Education: An Introduction in Christian Perspective* (Berrien Springs, MI: Andrews University Press, 2006); D. Bruce Lockerbie, *A Passion for Learning: A History of Christian Thought on Education* (Colorado Spring: Purposeful Design Publications, 2007); J. P. Moreland and William Lane Craig, *Philosophical Foundations for a Christian Worldview* (Downers Grove, IL: Intervarsity Press, 2003); Allan C. Ornstein, Daniel U. Levine, Gerald L. Gutek, and David E. Vocke, *Foundations of Education* (Boston: Cengage Learning, 2017); Janice B. Tehie, *Historical Foundations of Education: Bridges from the Ancient World to the Present* (Upper Saddle River, NJ: Pearson, 2007).

CHAPTER 2

AUGUSTINE: IDEALISM THROUGH A CHRISTIAN LENS

© eldeiv/Shutterstock.com

Augustine of Hippo statue in Victoria, Gozo, on the island of Malta

FOCUS: KEY TOPICS AND TERMS

Allegory
Cicero
Dialogue
Forms
Illumination

Liberal arts
Manichaeism
Neoplatonism
Quadrivium
Reminiscence

Rhetoric
Trivium
Virgil

If all Western philosophy is a footnote to Plato, it might also be legitimate to suppose that all Christian philosophy of education is a footnote to Augustine. After all, Augustine was one of the earliest and most prominent theologians to offer a systematic synthesis of ancient philosophy with biblical truth, and—as Aristotle's realism was a response to Plato's idealism—Thomas Aquinas's scholasticism was similarly a response to Augustine's Christian **liberal arts**. Though it has been nearly two millennia since this North African monk and bishop wrote and established his order of learning communities, Augustine's writings and life example continue to provide a relevant model for educators both theoretically and practically.

 ## Background and Context

Augustine (354-430) was born in the North African town of Tagaste to Patricius, a pagan father, and Monica, a Christian mother. Patricius was an unfaithful husband and a distant, abrasive father. Monica's persistent Christian testimony, however, influenced Patricius to convert late in life and eventually played a role in her son's spiritual journey.[1] Canonized by the Roman Catholic Church as a saint, Monica displayed many of the dispositions that were later incorporated into communities of Augustinian monks. For instance, as an example of virtue, Monica refused to participate in gossip. She was a listener, peacemaker, prayer warrior, and devotee to the church. Though a loving supporter of her son, she unhesitatingly stood for truth, often in opposition to him—warning him of the dangers of a promiscuous lifestyle and even ejecting him from their home when he converted to Manichaeism.[2] Though Augustine was thirty-one years of age when he finally converted to Christianity, the early lessons taught and the decades of prayer offered by Monica lingered with him throughout his search for meaning and truth. To a different extent, the same could be said about the paganism of his father. Surely, Augustine reflected on both parents' beliefs as he experimented with **Manichaeism**, skepticism, and **Neoplatonism**, and—though limited information is available regarding Patricius' specific beliefs—Augustine wrote much regarding his own ultimate rejection of paganism while at the same time integrating Platonic language and concepts as tools to express Christian truths.

Reflecting on his boyhood education in Tagaste, Augustine described it as a "miserable experience" that served only to prepare him for the hardships of adult life. His teacher frequently beat him as punishment for performing poorly in arithmetic, his weakest subject. He excelled, however, at verbal skills, such as spelling, grammar, vocabulary, and memorization, but his education came to a temporary halt at the age of sixteen because of limited finances. After Patricius' death, Monica arranged for Augustine to continue his education in nearby Carthage. It was there that Augustine received the best available classical education with an emphasis on **Cicero's** style of **rhetoric** and where he honed his skills to become a renowned orator. At the same time as he was developing himself intellectually, Augustine was also indulging his sexual passions in promiscuous living and beginning to pursue spiritual truth through the sect of Manichaeism, which espoused skepticism and a duality of soul and body, light and darkness, and good and evil forces.[3]

In Carthage and then back in his hometown of Tagaste, Augustine's career developed as an orator and a teacher of rhetoric. He took on a concubine with whom he had a son, Adeodatus, and—although he eventually ended his relationship with his concubine—he stayed close to his son until Adeodatus' untimely death. In his role as father, he was intentional about developing a closer relationship with his son than he had experienced with Patricius. It is telling that the meaning of his son's name was "gift of god." The two were later baptized on the same Easter Sunday and shared many experiences together, including a seven-month monastic-style retreat and many travels through Italy and back to Africa where Adeodatus suddenly died not long after Monica's death. However, while Adeodatus was still young and Augustine was in his twenties, Augustine persisted in Manichaeism.[4] Until becoming disillusioned by what he perceived as the superficiality and shallowness of Manichaeism, he continued in the cult until he shifted his focus to the philosophy of Neoplatonism.

Having left North Africa for professional opportunities in Rome, Augustine was soon presented with an even more prestigious position in Milan, which he anxiously pursued. It was in Milan where his life would be dramatically transformed. Monica, having joined Augustine there, began worshiping at the basilica of Bishop Ambrose and encouraged Augustine to go hear this skillful orator preach. Out of curiosity, he did so, and his intellectual conversion had begun. He found himself surprised at how intellectually appealing Ambrose's gospel message seemed in comparison with his earlier impressions of Christianity.[5] Later, in *Confessions*, he would acknowledge that God had led him to Ambrose so that Ambrose might lead him to God. At the time, however, Augustine was steeped in Neoplatonic philosophy, but Ambrose used philosophical language and concepts as a bridge to convey theological truths of the gospel. Even more important than demonstrating that it was possible to be both an intellectual and a Christian, Ambrose demonstrated a father's love, something Augustine had never experienced from his own father. Augustine wrote, "I began to feel affection for him, not at first as a teacher of truth…, but simply as a man who was kind to me."[6] Later, Augustine integrated into his own teaching and mentoring the same allegorical hermeneutic of biblical interpretation and the importance of love in the student–teacher relationship.

Simplicianus, one of Bishop Ambrose's presbyters, also played a significant role in Augustine's intellectual conversion. Simplicianus began to mentor him and teach him theology. He told Augustine of Marius Victorinus, a former Neoplatonist who had converted to Christianity.[7] In *Confessions*, Augustine wrote, "When this man of yours, Simplicianus, told me all this about Victorinus, I was on fire to be like him." Yet, Augustine hesitated. He believed he had found the "pearl of great price," but he could not yet fully surrender. This was not the first time he had held back from complete spiritual surrender. In his youth, he had prayed, "Make me chaste and continent, but not yet."[8]

His moral, or spiritual, conversion would come after a visit from a Christian layman named Ponticianus, who witnessed to Augustine and his friend Alypius. Ponticianus shared about Antony's monastic life and read selections to them from a book of Paul's letters, which he noticed they already had a copy in their possession. The Holy Spirit convicted the hearts of both Augustine and his friend during this conversation. After Ponticianus left, Augustine emotionally asked Alypius, "What is wrong with us?.... Look at us!" He left Alypius to go deeper into the garden alone. In that moment, he underwent a multi-sensory experience of sights, sounds, and involuntary physical reactions that he described as "an absurdity." Upon hearing a child possibly playing a game in a nearby house sing out, "Take it and read it. Take it and read it," he was reminded that Antony had opened the Scriptures to heed the first passage he would read. Augustine believed this was what God intended him to do in response to hearing the child's voice.[9]

He then returned to Alypius where he saw the book of Paul's letters sitting on a nearby bench. It appears Alypius had been reading and reflecting on the Scriptures during the same time that Augustine was deep in the garden. Augustine randomly turned to the thirteenth chapter of Romans where he read Paul's exhortation not to live in debauchery but to "clothe yourself with the Lord Jesus Christ." The two men discussed this and other passages together and then went immediately to share the good news of their conversion with Monica.[10]

Learning in Community

Augustine, his "heart's brother" Alypius, and his son Adeo-datus committed to being baptized together on Easter Sunday; however, that would be seven months away. So—in the meantime—they, Monica, and a small intimate group of his brother, cousins, and students went on retreat to the countryside. This group of less than a dozen friends and family lived in what might be considered a "pre-monastic" community of learners. A teacher by both career and passion, Augustine naturally led the group as they sought "knowledge of God and soul." Together they worked, prayed, studied the Bible, and read the works of **Virgil** and Cicero. As a newly converted Christian, Augustine began trends he would continue throughout his life—learning in community and acknowledging truth, wherever it may be found, as God's truth.[11]

After Augustine, Adeodatus, and Alypius were baptized by Ambrose, their small entourage began to journey back to North Africa, but they were delayed near the port in Italy where Monica died. During this delay, Augustine used the time to observe several monasteries in the region.[12] He had been intrigued with monastic life from the time just prior to his conversion when he heard from Ponticianus about the Egyptian hermit Antony. The example of Antony and other ascetics convinced Augustine that he could achieve victory

Nineteenth-century fresco by Pietro Gagliardi of the death of Monica, mother of Augustine

over his sexual lust and ambitious desires.[13] Another example that influenced his thoughts about learning in community was Marius Victorinus. Since hearing from Presbyter Simplicianus about Victorinus—a teacher of Rhetoric in Rome who had converted from Neoplatonism to Christianity—Augustine was determined to be like him.[14] Eventually, he would synthesize his interest in theology, philosophy, and asceticism into a unique form of monasticism known as the Augustinian order. First, however, he would experiment further with a prototype in his hometown.

Still grieving the death of his mother, Augustine returned to his North African hometown to experience shortly thereafter the sudden death of his teenage son Adeodatus. It was in this context that Augustine, Alypius, and other friends and family developed a proto-monastic community on his family's property in Tagaste. Though still not a monastery in the proper sense, the Tagaste community was a more formal experience and was longer in duration than his previous retreat. The Tagaste group was much more focused on spiritual growth than the seven-month community in Italy, but they too included a great deal of philosophical study. Additionally, they were more ascetic and systematic about their schedule of prayer, fasting, and service. Having left his books behind in Italy, Augustine approached extra-biblical content quite differently in this second community. This too reflected his focus on the process of contemplation and divine **illumination** to arrive at truth rather than a reliance on specific content, such as the liberal arts of the **trivium** (grammar, rhetoric, and dialectic) and the **quadrivium** (astronomy, music, geometry, and arithmetic). Augustine led the community until he and Alypius left for Hippo three years later. The community continued,

© Renata Sedmakova/Shutterstock.com

however, until Alypius returned to serve as the bishop of Tagaste and to develop it into a more formalized monastery.[15]

Expecting to live the remainder of his life as an ascetic monk, Augustine was reluctant to be ordained as a presbyter but was convinced to do so by Bishop Valerius of Hippo. Valerius—sensitive to Augustine's skills as an orator, mentor, teacher, philosopher, and leader—assigned him responsibilities that best fit his skill set. For instance, even though the role of preaching to the congregation was typically that of the bishop, Valerius surrendered this role to Augustine. Valerius also understood the importance of monastic life to Augustine and therefore designated a plot of land in the church garden for that purpose. The garden monastery included Augustine's core group of friends who joined him from Tagaste, but it also drew an extremely diverse group of men from various socioeconomic levels, geographic regions, and age groups. As a learning community, they made for a diverse group of students, most of whom were not prepared for the expectations to interpret Scripture, to teach it, and to engage in philosophic and apologetic arguments.[16]

For those who would be ordained into the clergy, Augustine—after he had become bishop of Hippo—established a second more rigorous monastery in the bishop's house. In this advanced learning community, Augustine took three main approaches to educate clergy. First, he trained them in a hermeneutic process of interpreting Scripture so that they would be well prepared to teach the Bible to others. Second, he provided intellectual training in apologetics, theology, and the liberal arts. Finally, he engaged them in dialogue both formally and informally. Dialogues might take a variety of forms but, for Augustine, the process of engaging reflective speculation was important because it provided opportunities for divine illumination. Dialogues might be centered on the reading and discussion of spiritually inspiring books, theological questions, or practical issues regarding the ministry.[17]

 ## Augustine's Philosophy of Education

Augustine is most popularly known for having written *Confessions* and *City of God*. In *Confessions*, he did what was uncommon in autobiographical literature of the time. In the context of a prayerful narrative directed to God, he revealed intimate details of himself—even those that were unflattering—and disclosed his most private thoughts. Though typical in memoirs of today, this type of self-effacing, tell-all memoir was an innovative genre in Augustine's day.[18] In *City of God*, Augustine presented an apologetic work against paganism and an exposition on the Christian philosophy of history. It was written after the Goths sacked Rome (the "city of man") in 410 AD and in response to accusations that, because Christians were perceived as poor citizens, they were somehow to blame for this calamity. Therefore, in a series of sermons, letters, and other writings, Augustine took to defending the *City of God*.

Though these two works provide a valuable context for Augustine's life experiences and theological thoughts—certainly relevant to his philosophy of education—it is in three other works that he more specifically conveys educational theories and practical applications. First is *The Teacher* (*De Magistro*), written in the form of a dialogue between Augustine and his teenage son Adeodatus, shortly before Adeodatus' death in Tagaste. *The Teacher* addresses the issue of communication between teachers and students, critically analyzing language itself and how words are used as signs to convey universal realities. It explores the process of knowledge acquisition through reflective contemplation and divine illumination. The second, *On Christian Doctrine*, appears to be a theological work, but it is more so a guidebook for teachers and is a proposal for Christian curriculum based on the liberal arts. The third is *On Catechizing of the Uninstructed*, also known as *Instructing the Unlearned*. The most practical of three, it was written in response to a deacon's question about how best to teach those who desire to learn more about the Christian faith but who lack a fundamental knowledge base. Even today's teacher can relate to its descriptions of diverse learners and the problems of engaging them in the classroom.[19] These three works most clearly convey Augustine's philosophy of education.

AUGUSTINE'S EPISTEMOLOGY

According to Augustine, "wherever truth may be found, it belongs to the Master."[20] All truth, therefore, is God's truth—whether it is proclaimed by a Christian believer or by a pagan. To be clear, Augustine was not syncretizing paganism with Christianity. He did, however, acknowledge points at which extra-biblical truth, particularly Neoplatonism (i.e., Idealism), was compatible with Christian doctrine, and he drew upon that truth to enhance learning. Since it was believed by some church fathers that the ancient Greeks had been exposed to the writings of Moses, had been enlightened by the Holy Spirit to understand some divine truths, or that Plato while in Egypt may have interacted with the prophet Jeremiah, it is reasonable to consider that Augustine was reclaiming truths that the ancients had drawn from the Hebrews. Nevertheless, if truth claims are compatible with biblical doctrine, per Augustine, they are from the mind of God. It is in the mind of God where divine ideas (i.e., concepts or **forms**) reside; therefore, apart from Him, concepts, propositions, and properties cannot exist.[21]

How then does one come to know and understand truth? Augustine's theory of knowledge acquisition is based upon reflective contemplation and divine illumination. Since God is the cause of all things and also the cause of anyone knowing those things, He is the illuminator of all truth. Learners experience this illumination through reflective contemplation, which is the process of learning. Plato referred to this process as "**reminiscence**," which is similar to retrieving thoughts from long-term memory. Plato's theory, however, involved the notion of reincarnation: that thoughts, or forms, could have been retained in memory from a previous life and could later be retrieved through reminiscence. Augustine, though rejecting reincarnation, did agree with Plato that there are two realms of knowledge: in the upper story are ideas and forms, and in the lower story are senses and matter. This parallels Augustine's two-city theory and might be understood as "knowledge in the City of God" in the upper story and "knowledge in the City of Man" in the lower story. Augustine and Plato would agree that the lower story is inferior because sensory knowledge can be unreliable and fleeting. The upper story, however, consists of absolute truth, and Augustine would add that Scripture is the superior and ultimate source for acquiring such truth.[22]

There is the perennial question of the roles of faith and reason in learning, and Augustine grappled with this as would the later scholastics and Thomas Aquinas. Augustine's "spiritual idealism," sometimes referred to as "Christianized Neoplatonism," would prevail throughout the Middle Ages until reimagined with Aristotelianism in the twelfth and thirteenth centuries. Augustine's explanation was that both faith and reason were required for true learning.[23] Since, however, something must first be known in order for there to be faith in that knowledge, reason is essential to faith. Augustine conceded that there are some issues that cannot yet be known by reason but that someday will. Until then, with some concepts, faith must temporarily precede reason—especially in matters relating to the doctrine of salvation. In the end, however, reason will precede faith.[24] After all, God gave reason to mankind that they may understand concepts, including the concept of God himself. Through reason it is possible to know truth without reliance on sensory experience.[25] Therefore, in Augustine's epistemology, God and His Word are the source of truth. Reason through reflective contemplation is the practice of seeking truth, and divine illumination is the required condition to arrive at truth.

The social aspect of Augustine's theory of learning cannot be ignored. Though a monk, he most certainly was not hermitic. He lived and learned in community both prior to and after his conversion. For him, solitude was only a temporary choice for specific purposes, but it was not an ideal condition for seeking truth, because truth belonged to no one individual. Reflective contemplation was ignited by dialogue that involved challenging questions and answers.[26]

AUGUSTINE'S CURRICULUM AND INSTRUCTION

Before addressing the question of what content Augustine believed was most valuable to include in the curriculum, one must consider what he envisioned to be the ultimate purpose of education. In Book I of *Confessions*, he wrote, "Our hearts are restless until they can find peace in you."[27] Augustine saw the search for truth, unity, and happiness as synonymous with the search for God. This search must also involve self-reflective inquiry of seeing oneself clearly so that there is an understanding of the need for redemption. Therefore, Scripture provides the best content to accomplish this, while the liberal arts serve as a bridge to understanding spiritual truths within Scripture. Though Augustine wrote much about the value of the liberal arts, it was the act of contemplation itself that was more valuable than the trivium and quadrivium.[28] In fact, he often warned his students to approach the liberal arts with caution. Through the lenses of Scripture and church tradition (i.e., creeds), classical studies may contribute to increased understanding of universal truths. Outside those parameters, however, such study may lead to vanity.[29]

Perhaps the most practical and interesting source for Augustine's methods of instruction was provided in his discussions regarding challenging students—those who lacked skills, motivation, or interest. The garden monastery in Hippo was certainly not the first time Augustine had faced challenging students. One reason he had left North Africa for Rome in his early career was to seek students who were more motivated to learn and more appreciative of what he had to offer. The challenges of the garden monastery students, however, far surpassed the typical lackadaisical students he had encountered earlier. His students had arrived in Hippo with diverse life experiences and levels of learning. Below are suggestions he offered to other instructors:

READINESS TO LEARN. All other instructional factors are contingent upon student readiness to learn. If students are not yet found to be friendly or attentive, instructors are responsible for making them so.[30]

ENVIRONMENT. The environment must be pleasant and cheerful with attention given to the student's physical comfort. Though class sessions in Augustine's day required students to remain standing, he recommended offering them a seat if this would be more conducive to their learning.[31]

CLEAR EXPECTATIONS. Instructors should be careful not to assume that students are aware of what is expected of them and should, therefore, communicate clear expectations so that there is no doubt what students should do.[32]

STUDENT INTEREST AND MOTIVATION. Students may become disinterested with lessons covering information they already know; therefore, develop procedures to discover their level of understanding prior to instruction. They may also become bored by an overwhelming amount of content at one time;

to avoid this, break down the content into manageable units. Another source of student boredom is the requirement to memorize unreasonably lengthy passages.[33] Rather than by the memorization of facts, students are motivated by the discovery of the truth behind those facts; therefore, learning should focus on finding meaning in the content. Intrinsic motivation is crucial to learning and—since God through divine illumination is the ultimate teacher—the instructor can only use words to stimulate contemplation; students must want to learn.[34]

METHODS OF INSTRUCTION. To keep students from missing key elements of a lesson, provide an overview beforehand and a summary afterward.[35] Thought should be given to the appropriate style of presentation, which is a vital condition before learners can be receptive to content.[36] Rhetorical skills of the instructor should move students emotionally; instructors should observe student expressions and physical movements to monitor indicators of their emotional engagement. Methods of instruction should be adjusted according to the size of the class and to the diversity of students; for instance, instruction should be different if students are homogeneously grouped with all having similar educational backgrounds or heterogeneously grouped with a variety of educational levels. Methods should also be differentiated if students are "city-bred, rustics, or a mixture of both.... The same medicine is not to be given to all."[37] **Allegory** and **dialogue** are generally the most effective methods of instruction. Because a text has layers of meaning (i.e., literal, moral, and spiritual), allegory is an effective tool to reach the higher, more abstract levels of meaning.[38] Dialogue, however, was Augustine's preferred method—both formally and informally. In his *Soliloquies*, he wrote, "There is no better way of seeking truth than by the method of question and answer."[39]

STUDENT–TEACHER RELATIONSHIP. Relationship and reciprocity were extremely important to Augustine and his teaching style. Students often became his friends, involved intimately with his family circle. "We should try to meet our pupils with a brother's, a father's and a mother's love," Augustine wrote, "... for so great is the power of a sympathetic disposition of mind that our hearers are affected while we are speaking and we are affected while they are learning."[40] At times when it appears that the educational process is waning, the solution may be to improve the student–teacher relationship; this may be accomplished by using gentle encouragement to drive out fear, making a joke, telling a story, or making the content relevant to the student's everyday life. Never should a teacher embarrass a student but should instead "win him over by our friendly tone."[41]

Augustine's legacy is represented by the rich literary works he left behind: nearly a thousand sermons, hundreds of letters, and 117 books. Through them, he demonstrated, as Ambrose and others had modeled for him, that faith and reason

Church window in the Dom of Cologne, Germany, depicting Saint Augustinus

© jorisvo/Shutterstock.com

are not only compatible but that one enriches and informs the other. His philosophy of education and its practical application continue to resonate with those who seek inspiration in their pursuit to teach from a Christian worldview.

 Go to www.khlearn.com to watch a video about Augustine.

 Reflection

For personal reflection, content review, and further research:

1. Albert Bandura's theory of social cognitive learning places great significance on role models in learning. What positive and negative role models influenced Augustine? How did he later in life serve as a mentor and role model for others?

2. In what way did Augustine practice group learning in communities? How did his practices align with what is now known as "professional learning communities" or PLCs?

3. What curriculum made up Augustine's liberal arts? What did Augustine see as the purpose of the liberal arts?

4. In Hippo, Augustine's students were much more diverse than in previous settings. How so? How did this challenge Augustine's teaching and how did he differentiate his instruction? Later, he wrote *Instructing the Unlearned*. What advice did he share for teachers who have classrooms including diverse learners? Which piece of advice do you see as most relevant for teachers today and why?

5. In *De Magistro*, Augustine discussed the importance of signs in teaching. What were these signs? How did Augustine draw from Plato's idealism in this concept of teaching by using signs?

6. The statement "All truth is God's truth" has been attributed to Augustine as well as to many others. What did Augustine mean by this statement? What other interpretations might there be for this phrase?

7. Explain Augustine's theory of knowledge acquisition. How was it similar to and different from Plato's theory?

8. Some biblical worldview proponents (e.g., Nancy Pearcey, Francis Schaeffer, J. P. Moreland, and others) are critics of the upper story and lower story perspective of Plato and Augustine. Do you see it as a helpful or harmful model to understand knowledge and truth?

9. Paraphrase Augustine's perspective on faith and reason. Do you agree? If so, why? If not, how do you see the two differently than he did?

10. What did Augustine consider to be the ultimate purpose of education?

11. Was Augustine ahead of his time in his pedagogical theory? Why or why not?

ENDNOTES

1. Lockerbie, *A Passion for Learning*, 54.
2. Edward L. Smither, *Augustine as Mentor: A Model for Preparing Spiritual Leaders* (Nashville, TN: B&H Academic, 2008), 93-98.
3. Madonna. M. Murphy, *The History and Philosophy of Education: Voices of Educational Pioneers* (Upper Saddle River, NJ: Pearson Prentice Hall, 2006), 79-80.
4. Ibid..
5. Everett Ferguson, *Church History: The Rise and Growth of the Church in Its Cultural, Intellectual, and Political Contexts*, vol. 1 (Grand Rapids, MI: Zondervan, 2013), 1:270.
6. Smither, *Augustine as Mentor*, 103-4.
7. Ferguson, *Church History*, 270.
8. Augustine, "Confessions," in *Christian Apologetics: Past & Present*, vol. 1, ed. William Edgar and K. Scott Oliphint (Wheaton, IL: Crossway, 2009), 241-9.
9. Ibid., 246-56.
10. Ibid.
11. Smither, *Augustine as Mentor*, 100-1, 136-8.
12. Ibid., 139.
13. Avery Cardinal Dulles, *A History of Apologetics* (San Francisco, CA: Ignatius Press, 2005), 78.
14. Augustine, "Confessions," 241-3.
15. Smither, *Augustine as Mentor*, 139-44.
16. Ibid., 145-6.
17. Ibid., 148-53.
18. Murphy, *The History and Philosophy*, 79.
19. See Lockerbie, A Passion for Learning, 56; Murphy, The History and Philosophy, 81.
20. Augustine, "On Christian Doctrine," in *A Passion for Learning*, ed. D. Bruce Lockerbie (Colorado Springs, CO: Purposeful Design Publications, 2007), 57.
21. J. P. Moreland and William Lane Craig, *Philosophical Foundations for a Christian Worldview* (Downers Grove, IL: Intervarsity Press, 2003), 505-6.
22. Dunn, Philosophical *Foundations of Education*, 67-9.
23. Ibid., 70.
24. Rodney Stark, *For the Glory of God: How Monotheism Led to Reformations, Science, Witch-hunts, and the End of Slavery* (Princeton: Princeton University Press, 2003), 148-9.
25. C. B. Eavey, *History of Christian Education* (Chicago: Moody Press, 1964), 96.
26. Henry Chadwick, *Augustin of Hippo: A Life* (Oxford: Oxford University Press, 2009), 30-1.
27. Augustine, "Confessions," 210.
28. Eric Kenyon, "Augustine and the Liberal Arts," *Arts & Humanity in Higher Education* 12, no. 1 (2012): 107-11.
29. Ryan N. S. Topping, "Augustine on Liberal Education: Defender and Defensive," *The Heythrop Journal* 51, no. 3 (2010): 385.
30. Augustine, *On Christian Doctrine*, 58.
31. See John Immerwahr, "Augustine's Advice for College Teachers: Ever Ancient, Ever New," *Metaphilosophy* 39, no. 4 (2008): 662; Murphy, *The History and Philosophy*, 82.
32. Augustine, *On Christian Doctrine*, 59.
33. Lockerbie, *A Passion for Learning*, 55.
34. Murphy, *The History and Philosophy*, 82.
35. Lockerbie, *A Passion for Learning*, 55.
36. Augustine, *On Christian Doctrine*, 58.
37. Augustine, "Instruction on the Uninstructed," in *The History and Philosophy of Education: Voices of Educational Pioneers*, Madonna Murphy (Upper Saddle River, NJ: Pearson Prentice Hall, 2006), 83-5.
38. Edward L. Smither, "Augustine: Teacher as Mentor," in *A Legacy of Religious Educators: Historical and Theological Introductions*, ed. Elmer L. Towns and Benjamin K. Forrest (Lynchburg, VA: Liberty University Press, 2017), 25.
39. Smither, *Augustine as Mentor*, 138-9.
40. Augustine, *Instruction on the Uninstructed*, 84.
41. Immerwahr, "Augustine's Advice," 662.

CHAPTER 3

THOMAS AQUINAS: REALISM THROUGH A CHRISTIAN LENS

Thomas Aquinas

FOCUS: KEY TOPICS AND TERMS

Abstractions
Analytic truths
Averroës
Dichotomy
Empirical science
Faith

First cause
Liberal arts
Neo-scholasticism
Platonic
Quadrivium
Realism

Scholasticism
Sensory perception
Synthetic truths
Thomistic
Trivium
Unmoved mover

Though Thomas Aquinas's theory of knowledge experienced a resurgence in **neo-scholasticism**—especially in traditional Catholic and in Protestant classical schools—its educational influence is currently minimal, limited to isolated pockets of educational traditionalism. Why is this so? An answer may be considered by examining the following issues:

- The historical contexts of Aquinas and of **scholasticism**
- Aquinas's epistemological arguments related to the nature and acquisition of truth
- Interplay of faith and reason in Aquinas's theological arguments
- Assessment of Aquinas in light of current perspectives

Such exploration will show that the ideas of Aquinas—though not popularly embraced by current educational theorists—continue to be implemented in schools that value classical curriculum and in traditional Catholic schools.

Background and Context

The work of Thomas Aquinas (1225-1274) impacted not only the fields of philosophy, theology, and apologetics but also the field of educational foundations, which primarily addresses historical and philosophical foundations of education. Educational theory and practice are driven by epistemological understandings, and—because Aquinas's epistemology has been so influential—it is integral to understanding educational developments in the West. **Epistemology** is "the branch of philosophy which studies the nature, sources, and validity of knowledge."[1] It addresses the reliability of knowledge and valid means of arriving at truth. Aquinas proposed answers to epistemological questions that impacted education in the Middle Ages and beyond, but context is needed prior to exploring further how he answered these questions.

With a count and countess as parents, Thomas was born into a noble family related to both Italian and French royalty. At the age of five, he was sent to a Benedictine monastic school, and as a teenager, he entered the university at Naples. When he was eighteen, to his parents' dismay, he announced that he sensed a calling to enter the mendicant order of the preaching Dominicans. Fearful of how Thomas' vow of poverty might reflect negatively on the family, they locked him away as a prisoner in their home for over a year in the hope of convincing him otherwise, but he remained undeterred.[2] As a tall young man with a quiet, serious personality lent to prayer and reflective thinking, Thomas was well-suited to the intellectually oriented Dominicans. He studied at the University of Paris, lectured at the University of Cologne, and at twenty-five years old, became ordained as a priest. At thirty-one, he was assigned as professor of theology, which involved commenting on the works of great authors, disputing ideas in a debate format, and teaching. His students knew him as a humble, kind, devoted professor who worked hard and was at times absent-minded. On his journey to visit Pope Gregory X, Thomas fell ill and died at the age of forty-nine before arriving at the Vatican.[3]

Thomas' writings were by far the most impactful of the Middle Ages.[4] His *Summa Theologica* became his most important work and quickly became, along with the Bible and Peter Lombard's writings, one of the principal sources studied in theology courses at the University of Paris.[5] In this work, he used the philosophy of ancient Greek philosophers, especially Aristotle, to explain key doctrines of Christian faith.[6] In his *Summa Contra Gentiles*, Thomas provided an apologetic guide for Christian missionaries to Muslims in Spain, and in *De Magistro* he presented a theory of teaching and learning.[7]

The Dominicans produced a number of scholars, such as Aquinas and Abelard, who became so popular that thousands of students traveled to hear them lecture, contributing to the rise of the university.[8] The university had emerged from cathedral schools that had originated to train Benedictine and Augustinian monks,[9] and as cathedral schools experienced decline, the universities—affiliated with the mendicant Franciscan and Dominican orders—grew in number and in popularity.[10] This growth coincided with and was stimulated by other factors, including a revival in European commerce and the reintroduction of Aristotelianism through Arabic scholars.[11]

As the crusades came to an end, Arabic culture and philosophy began to spread throughout Western Europe. One example of this was through a Spanish Arab by the name of **Averroës** (1126-1198). Within three decades after his death, Averroës' commentaries on Aristotle became widely disseminated throughout both Islamic and Christian academia but were controversial on both sides. Among Muslims, Averroës was considered an unorthodox heretic. Among Christians, there was the conundrum of addressing significant contradictions to biblical doctrine while employing valid Aristotelian logic to advance the gospel. Troublesome in Averroistic Aristotelianism was the claim that the world is eternal and absolutely necessary. According to Averroës, the only immortal aspect in humanity is the "agent intellect, which each individual shares in common with the entire human species."[12] His teachings also clashed with Christian ideas regarding human nature, origins, eschatology, God's providence, and redemption. Motivated by the desire to correct Averroës' distortions and to evaluate Aristotle through the lens of biblical truth, Aquinas developed his philosophical system.

Though Aquinas may be the most renowned name affiliated with scholasticism, this educational method had already been impacting Europe for nearly two centuries prior to Aquinas.[13] The scholastic movement had been displayed in the works of Anselm (1033-1109), Peter Abelard (1079-1142), and others.[14] After Averroës, however, the method was used to fortify Christian faith by organizing revealed truths using an Aristotelian system of deductive logic. Aquinas, then, became the leading scholar in this effort. In his synthesis of Aristotle and Christianity, he taught that reason should be the primary means of acquiring knowledge. For knowledge beyond the realm of reason, however, people must rely on faith. This form of scholasticism, known as Thomism, became the official philosophical position of the Roman Catholic Church.[15]

Thomas Aquinas teaching pupils as shown on a German stamp (ca. 1974)

 Epistemological Arguments Related to the Nature and Acquisition of Truth

As Aquinas integrated Aristotle and Christian theology, he built his epistemology on a strong foundation of metaphysical support. He identified three methods of scientific inquiry: natural science, mathematics, and metaphysics. Of the three, metaphysics is the "first philosophy" and is different from the first two in that it exists and can be understood apart from matter. Examples of abstract concepts that can exist without matter would include theological concepts of God and angels, and other **abstractions**, such as number sense— for example, the concepts of one, many, less, or half. Although these concepts may exist in matter, matter is not required for their existence; the concept of these abstractions can exist in and of themselves. How does one come to know abstract concepts of being? Aquinas's answer was through the means of analogy, and this leads us to his epistemological theory.[16]

Theories of knowledge address three questions: Is it possible to know anything? If so, what can we know? And how can we know it? Answers to these questions are threads woven throughout Aquinas's writings and were inspired by Aristotle. According to Aristotle, knowledge is "the actualization of the general concepts in the intellect, based on the data from the external world reported by the senses."[17] Though Aquinas agreed with Aristotle on the value of **sensory perception**, he expounded this learning theory to include the supernatural.

Truth for Aquinas was acquired through both faith and reason. Humans are the only rational animals; therefore, they are the only creatures who naturally think. What do they think about? Above all, they contemplate their purpose. They do this as they perceive through their senses the universe and observe that there is design and order, cause and effect. Aristotle claimed that these observations would lead to the deduction of a **First Cause**, an **Unmoved Mover**. Aquinas agreed with Aristotle and considered this Mover to be God, and—because God was pure reason—rational beings have the capacity to understand Him and the rational world He created. This leads to a **dichotomy**: a natural world that is known through reason, and a supernatural realm that is known through faith.[18]

Another dichotomy is extended to types of truth: **analytic truths** and **synthetic truths**. Analytic truths are self-evident and may be conveyed through statements such as "God is good" or "If A = B and B = C, then A = C." These statements do not depend upon experience but may be declared as true by logic and intuition. Conversely, synthetic truths do rely on experience and must be tested by **empirical science**. For example, to know that "The church is five miles from city hall," one must measure the distance from one point to the other. In a departure from Aristotle, Aquinas held that, of the two types of truth, analytic truths were superior because they formulated first principles:

> Wherefore the intellect naturally knows natures which exist only in individual matter; not as they are in such individual matter, but according as they are abstracted therefrom by the considering act of the intellect, hence it follows that through the intellect, we can understand these objects as universal; and this is beyond the power of sense.[19]

Though truth may be known through both faith and reason, those truths arrived at through faith hold supremacy, and—when the two paths overlap—they still lead to the same conclusions, whether by faith, by reason, or by a combination of the two.[20] An example of this overlap may be found in Aquinas's *Summa Theologica* in which he outlines the *Quinque Viæ*, his five ways of reasoning for the existence of God through arguments for motion, causality, necessity, contingency, and design.[21]

In his *Compendium of Theology* Aquinas presented the dichotomy intellect: potential and active. He denied the **Platonic** idea that knowledge was caused passively by a "sharing in, or influx of, some intrinsically subsisting actually intelligible forms."[22] Instead, it is through the senses that particular forms of things are perceived. These particular forms, however, are only potentially intelligible; they essentially do not become intelligible until something active brings them to actuality in the universal sense. Aquinas used the analogy of light and color to illustrate this concept. Color is a particular thing that is potentially knowable. However, it cannot be known in a universal sense until light acts upon the particular color. Then it can be known and understood. Particular forms are only potentially known, but they are actually known when the active intellect casts light on them, perceiving them in a universal sense. "We would not need to posit [an active intellect]," Aquinas alleged, "if the forms of things were actually intelligible, as the Platonists held."[23] In order for anything to be known, learners first need to engage their sensory perception, which is their potential intellect. Secondly, they need to engage their active intellect, which brings light to the perceived thing and makes it understood. These dichotomies of faith and reason, analytic and synthetic truths, and potential and active intellect hold clear implications for Aquinas's theory of teaching and learning.

Aquinas's Theory Applied to Curriculum and Instruction

The curriculum and instruction of scholasticism were so integrated that it is difficult to discuss one apart from the other. They included four main elements: commentaries, disputed questions, sermons, and theological synthesis. Commentaries were writings and lectures on established works acknowledged by the Roman Catholic Church. A candidate for the master's degree was required, for instance, to read and comment publicly on Peter Lombard's *Sentences*. Therefore, the commentary itself was both a form of curriculum and instruction at the medieval university.[24]

Disputed questions were conducted for the purpose of both teaching content and of training in rhetorical and persuasive communication skills. At the University of Paris, the Dominicans and Franciscans often debated one another. One of their key points of contention was disagreement on what the highest power of the soul was. The Franciscans believed that it was will, which in essence was love, and that it was this will, or love, that was the means whereby humans could relate with God. In contrast, the Dominicans alleged that it was the intellect that allowed people to know God. Scholars were expected to engage regularly in these debates of *quaestiones diputatea* in front of the student body, and this practice laid the foundation for how debates continue to be held today.[25] Debates comprised a list of pros and cons, arguments in support of and objections against particular theological issues. These disputes began with the objections first, which were then followed by the replies intended to reject the objections. Though conducted orally, disputed questions were also a written theological genre that is exemplified in *Summa Theologica*. Question 27, for example is "Of the Cause of Love" and includes four points of inquiry. The first of which is "Whether good is the only cause of love?" Three objections are presented, one of them which states, "The Philosopher says that 'we love those who acknowledge their evils.' Therefore it seems that evil is the cause of love." The corresponding reply rejects the objection by stating, "Those who acknowledge their evils, are beloved, not for their evils, but because they acknowledge them, for it is a good thing to acknowledge one's faults, in so far as it excludes insincerity or hypocrisy."[26]

Disputed questions were also practiced in debates between the liberal arts faculty and the theology faculty. The two faculties often clashed because the **liberal arts**—based on the ***trivium*** of grammar, logic, and rhetoric and on the ***quadrivium*** of arithmetic, geometry, music, and astronomy—relied heavily on classical Greek and Latin writings. Such writings were often studied based on the commentaries of the Arabic Averroës, whose worldview, as noted earlier, conflicted with the Christian perspective held by those on the faculty of theology. Two examples of Aquinas's contribution to these debates included his *On There Being Only One Intellect: Against the Averroists* and *On the Eternity of the World*.[27]

Sermons comprised another form of both written curriculum and oral instruction. Preaching, especially for the Dominicans, was considered a teaching activity. Those who had earned the status of "master" preached to current university candidates for the master of theology degree. A series of sermons would make up a conference. Unfortunately, only relatively few of Aquinas's sermons have survived as examples of this genre—two of which are "On the Child Jesus" and "On the Parable of the Sower."[28]

Theological syntheses make up the final theological genre that also served as a means of curriculum and instruction. These were catechisms and systematic theologies presenting various doctrines of the church. Examples from Aquinas's writings include *Summa Theologica*, the *Compendium of Theology*, and *Summa contra Gentiles*. All of Aquinas's theological syntheses began with the transcendence of God and ended with an application to practical life.[29] All of these theological genres represent applications of Aquinas's epistemological theories.

In addition to the theological genres listed above, the instructional method of discovery should also be noted as being integral to Aquinas's teaching and learning theory. Some assumptions are required, however, before discovery can be acknowledged as a valid means of knowledge acquisition. First, there must be an assumption of Christian personalism—that human beings are individuals endowed by God with a personal intellect. This idea is in direct contradiction with Averroës' concept of the "oneness of the intellect"—that there is only one single intellect that is shared with all humanity. Individual personhood requires a distinct intellect; otherwise, there would be no separate self to do the discovering. There must be two distinct individuals: a teacher and a learner. Second, there must be an assumption that rejects Plato's notion that truth has been deposited in the human soul and that learning is simply an act of remembering what the soul already knew before it became a physical being. Therefore, in order for discovery learning to occur, there must be a separate intellect for each person and that intellect must not have entered the world already having truth deposited in it.[30]

Although knowledge itself has not been implanted in the human soul, according to Aquinas, the "seeds of knowledge" are already in the soul. The seeds make up the potency, or potential intellect, discussed above. Discovery learning occurs when actualization is brought about by a double cause: an inner cause and an outer cause. The inner cause is the agent intellect in each individual person. The outer cause is sensible reality, the tangible world. Without these assumptions, the "seeds of knowledge, and the double cause, discovery learning could not be possible."[31]

The theological genres and discovery learning as outlined above were all **Thomistic** methods of formal instruction. Aquinas, however, distinguished between formal schooling, *disciplina*, and informal education, *educatio*. While formal schooling focuses on *scientia*, specific subject matters that make up bodies of knowledge, informal education develops a person into one who is good and virtuous.[32]

Whether in formal or informal settings, who serves as the teacher? What is the role of the teacher? Unlike the current popular learning theory of constructivism that emphasizes autonomous learning, Aquinas rejected the theory that individuals could teach themselves or could independently construct knowledge, truth, and reality. For Aquinas, God, angels, and other humans could serve as teachers. God's presence in the soul as *magister* is not a supernatural phenomenon. It is part of natural revelation that God would teach people by bringing light to the "seeds of knowledge" in the agent intellect. Angels, too, can be teachers, but—being lower than God—they cannot provide universal concepts or truths that serve as foundational for further rational thought. Only God can do that. Neither can angels do what human teachers do, which is to actualize potential knowledge by modeling the rational process. What angels can do, however, is to reinforce the light of human intellect.[33]

Aquinas's view of the human teacher's role was influenced by the Dominican integration of faith and learning. Teachers serve dual roles: that of theoretician and that of practitioner. In the first role, teachers are philosophers, researchers, and reflective scholars. In the second, they are instructors engaged with their students—planning, organizing, and delivering the content.[34] This interaction of theory and practice would be embraced by current-day proponents of critical pedagogy who encourage teachers to integrate theory and practice. They would reject, however, the central role Aquinas espoused for teachers as deliverers of content who held an authoritative role in matters of curriculum and instruction.

Critical theorists would also reject Aquinas's perspectives regarding the discipline of young children. In line with other scholastics of his day, Aquinas encouraged external discipline. External control was necessary until sufficient growth had occurred for children to practice self-control or self-discipline. Once the external discipline was internalized, the child's intellect would then control the will.[35] For current-day educational theorists, this approach appears far too similar to that of B. F. Skinner's behavioristic theory of operant conditioning to be embraced by a post-Freudian era.

Through Time and Other Lenses

Today, university students in teacher preparation programs study only token passages of Thomas Aquinas's epistemological ideas. Other than connecting him to scholasticism, neo-scholasticism, traditional Catholic schools, and the classical education movement, they know little else of his theory or his impact. In this closing section, a brief overview through time and other people's lenses will help to formulate a fuller view of his impact and what critical perspectives have been presented of his ideas.

Nearly three centuries after Aquinas taught at the University of Paris, Ignatius Loyola studied at this same university where he was exposed to the *Summa Theologica*. Ignatius was so impacted by the Dominican teaching of Thomism that he required Aquinas to be taught in all Jesuit theology classes and that Aristotelian principles be taught in all teaching of metaphysics.[36] Others, however, such as the Christian Humanists of the same era as Ignatius, were not as appreciative of Aquinas. They criticized his views and portrayed his theological ideas as substandard. Though some of this criticism was because of his implementation of Aristotelian logic, much of it was simply because they did not believe his use of Latin was as refined as it should be. Rodney Stark judged, however, that "In fact, Aquinas, wrote excellent Latin. But it was not the flowery, poetic style prized by Valla and other Humanists."[37]

Diarmaid MacCulloch pointed out that, along with the Christian Humanists of the sixteenth century, Reformation leaders also attacked scholastic theologians. Martin Luther, for example, believed that Thomists were intentionally conspiring with pagan Aristotelians to destroy the truth,[38] and he criticized the nominalist scholasticism that had permeated university theology faculties for nearly two centuries. In Spain, however, a revival of Thomism prevailed, and when the Spanish began committing injustices against natives in the New World, it was the Thomist worldview rather than Humanism that motivated the Dominicans to intervene. Thomists helped to drive the Counter-Reformation, and they capitalized on the printing press as much as the Humanists did.[39]

In the foreword to Harry Lee Poe's *Christianity in the Academy: Teaching at the Intersection of Faith and Learning*, Dallas Willard discussed "the unceasing human problem" regarding faith versus reason, and he therein commends the work of Aquinas for illustrating how the two processes interact to reveal truth. Through Aquinas's influence,

> human capacities for thought and study were accepted as good and necessary things, though limited in what they could provide in the way of knowledge about reality and about human well-being and well-doing. They were to be encouraged and cultivated, but only in proper subordination to the contents of the tradition of revealed truths—God-told truths.[40]

Later in the book, Poe references Aquinas in the problem of applying biblical truth to academic curricular issues. As instructors may grapple with how to accomplish this, Poe simply declared, "Faith's most appropriate place in a discipline is where it already is."[41] He went on to applaud Aquinas for encouraging people to research what was possible and to be motivated by the knowledge that a Creator God existed.

Poe offered a comparison of the times in which Aquinas lived to the twenty-first century, especially relating to how the typical medieval person perceived order and how a typical modern person perceives it. In the Middle Ages, there was an assumption by the vast majority of people that the universe contained order, meaning, and purpose and that this was attributed to a sovereign Creator God. There is no such assumption of order in the twenty-first century, Poe observed, and this lack of assumption has serious implications regarding how Christian apologists make their case. For instance, Aquinas's argument "might be turned on its head" and argued in the reverse. Instead of arguing that God must exist because order can be observed in the universe, the argument might be presented that the universe had order and meaning because a Creator God exists.[42] This appears to be a shift to a preference toward presuppositionalism.

Chiding the reader, Poe disparaged those who long for the good old days "when faith and learning were one." Those were the same days, he noted, that were full of superstition, debauchery, and corruption within the church. He also chided C. S. Lewis for blaming Aquinas for "dividing things" because there has always been and always will be a truncation of truth in one way or the other.

Another analysis is offered by David I. Smith and James K. A. Smith. Their context is Christian higher education, in which they observe that there is a common perception that Christian college equals chapel services, strict moral rules, and plenteous prayer. Those areas are where faith resides, but other areas—such as classrooms and research labs—are neutral. They praised Mark Noll for challenging this dualism in his *The Scandal of the Evangelical*

Stained glass window in the Cathedral of Mechelen, Belgium, depicting Thomas Aquinas

© jorisvo/Shutterstock.com

Mind, which makes many of the same points that Nancy Pearcey makes in *Total Truth*. Both Noll and Pearcey question the dichotomy of faith and learning and the treatment of them as parallel rather than as fluid.[43]

For Christian schools and universities that are seriously considering the role of faith and reason in their learning experience, serious conversations are occurring and many current worldview authors inform these discussions. Though the same issues argued by Aquinas are being debated today, most educators are little aware of the man, his teachings, or his tremendous influence in the realm of academia and learning theory. Though in acknowledgment of him or not, his ideas continue to be debated. His instructional methods, however, have mostly gone by the wayside as pragmatist, postmodernist, and constructivist learning theories prevail both in public and private schools. It is only in pockets of educational traditionalism, such as traditional Catholic and Protestant classical schools, where the instructional methods of Thomas Aquinas are widely practiced.

Go to www.khlearn.com to watch a video about Thomas Aquinas.

Reflection

For personal reflection, content review, and further research:

1. Explore the recent movement of classical schools and compare it to nineteenth-century neo-scholasticism and medieval scholasticism. How are they similar and different?
2. What topics are studied in the field of epistemology? Describe Aquinas's epistemological beliefs.
3. Describe the Dominican monastic order, why it appealed to Aquinas, and how his involvement in it influenced his philosophy of education.
4. Explain which Greek philosopher most influenced Aquinas and how he synthesized Christian theology with classical Greek thought.
5. How did Aquinas explain the difference between faith and reason?
6. Of the three scientific methods of inquiry, which did Aquinas perceive as most important. Why?
7. How does Aquinas's explanation of abstract numerical concepts (e.g., one, many, less, or half) compare to the current notion of number sense in constructivist mathematics?
8. What was the role of sensory perception in Aquinas's epistemology? How did he expand on this?
9. How did Aquinas dichotomize truth? Do you believe this dichotomy to be helpful? Why or why not?
10. How did Aquinas use the analogy of light and color to explain his theory of knowledge acquisition?
11. Compare the Franciscan and Dominican orders regarding their views of knowledge acquisition. How did their theological views impact their educational theories?
12. Compare the role of debate in medieval scholasticism to how debate is incorporated into current education.
13. Compare the concept of "Christian personalism" with Islamic Averroës' concept of "oneness of the intellect." What implications do these concepts have regarding discovery learning?
14. How is Aquinas's theory of learning contradictory to modern constructivism?
15. Evaluate Aquinas's thoughts on the discipline of children.

ENDNOTES

1. George R. Knight, *Philosophy & Education: An Introduction in Christian Perspective* (Berrien Springs, MI: Andrews University Press, 2006), 20.
2. Lockerbie, *A Passion for Learning*, 100.
3. Murphy, *The History and Philosophy*, 112-3.
4. William Edgar and K. Scott Oliphint, K. Scott, eds., *Christian Apologetics: Past & Present*, vol. 1. (Wheaton, IL: Crossway, 2009), 395.
5. Gerald. L. Gutek, *A History of the Western Educational Experience*, 2nd ed. (Long Grove, IL: Waveland Press, 1995), 103.
6. Murphy, *The History and Philosophy*, 113.
7. Avery Cardinal Dulles, *A History of Apologetics* (San Francisco, CA: Ignatius Press, 2005), 114.
8. Gutek, *A History*, 98.
9. Stark, *For the Glory*, 62.
10. Dulles, *A History of Apologetics*, 111.
11. Gutek, *A History*, 98.
12. Dulles, *A History of Apologetics*, 112-3.
13. Knight, *Philosophy & Education*, 54.
14. Edgar and Oliphint, *Christian Apologetics*, 311, 337, 365.
15. Knight, *Philosophy & Education*, 55.
16. Edgar and Oliphint, *Christian Apologetics*, 396-7.
17. Daniel Fărcaş, "Thomas Aquinas: Teaching Theology in the Age of Universities," in *A Legacy of Religious Educators: Historical and Theological Introductions*, ed. Elmer L. Towns and Benjamin K. Forrest (Lynchburg, VA: Liberty University Press, 2017), 74.
18. Knight, *Philosophy & Education*, 56-7.
19. Thomas Aquinas, *Summa Theologica*, I, q. 12, art. 4, trans. Dominican Fathers (New York: Christian Classics, 1948), 52.
20. Knight, *Philosophy & Education*, 57-8.
21. Edgar and Oliphint, *Christian Apologetics*, 405-7.
22. Thomas Aquinas, *Compendium of Theology*, trans. Richard J. Regan (Oxford: Oxford University Press, 2009), 62.
23. Aquinas, *Compendium*, 62.
24. Fărcaş, "Thomas Aquinas," 70.
25. Ibid., 68-9.
26. Thomas Aquinas, *St. Thomas Aquinas, Summa Theologica: Vol. 3 of 10.*, trans. Dominican Province (Forgotten Books, 2007), 179-80.
27. Fărcaş, "Thomas Aquinas," 68.
28. Ibid., 72.
29. Ibid., 72-3.
30. Fărcaş, "Thomas Aquinas," 74-5.
31. Ibid., 75-6.
32. Gutek, *A History*, 95.
33. Fărcaş, "Thomas Aquinas," 76-7.
34. Gutek, *A History*, 111.
35. Ibid., 146.
36. Gutek, *A History*, 149-150.
37. Stark, *For the Glory of God*, 384n.222.
38. Diarmaid MacCulloch, *The Reformation: A History* (New York: Penguin Books, 2003), 126.
39. Ibid., 86-7.
40. Harry Lee Poe, *Christianity in the Academy: Teaching at the Intersection of Faith and Learning* (Grand Rapids, MI: Baker Academic, 2004), 9.
41. Ibid., 104.
42. Poe, *Christianity in the Academy*, 111-2.
43. David I. Smith and James K. A. Smith, eds., *Teaching and Christian Practices: Reshaping Faith & Learning* (Grand Rapids, MI: Willam B. Eerdmans, 2011), 1-2.

CHAPTER 4

FIFTEENTH-CENTURY ATLANTIC WORLD

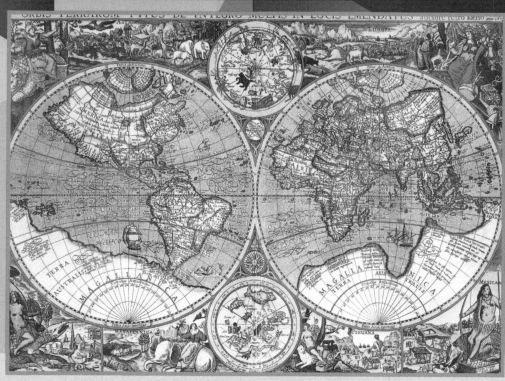

17th century world map designed by Petro Kaerio in 1607

© Joao Virissimo/Shutterstock.com

FOCUS: KEY TOPICS AND TERMS

Africanus
Aztecs
Chavin culture
Copernicus

Ideographs
Inca Empire
Mesoamerica
Mexica Empire

Olmec culture
Phonetic system
Pictographs
Printing press

Sculpture from the ancient Olmec civilization in what is now south-central Mexico

© photoshooter2015/Shutterstock.com

As would be expected in any culture and historical era, there has always been some type of transmission of learning from one generation to the next throughout human history. In the fifteenth century, as Europeans began to explore Africa and the Americas, they learned the languages and social ways of the indigenous people groups. What is briefly explored in this chapter are the processes of education that existed at that time and to what end. Also considered is how interaction with the other cultures progressed, inhibited, or transformed educational practices. As is the case in any culture, religious beliefs and social practices influenced educational structures and the philosophy behind education. This chapter will address the degree to which fifteenth-century Atlantic cultures were literate and the ways in which their literacy was impacted.

 The Americas

People of the **Mexica Empire**, also known as **Aztecs**, lived in the central part of the Valley of Mexico in **Mesoamerica**. The **Inca Empire** stretched along the west coast of South America from what is Quito southward along the Central Andes. Both cultures carried much of their heritage into the fifteenth century from ancient civilization. The Mexica heritage was the ancient **Olmec culture**. For the Inca, it was the **Chavin culture**. They taught religious concepts, values, and practices as well as styles of art and architecture, patterns of governance, and much more. In the Inca Empire, their religious tradition included the sacrifice of children from four to ten years of age. Each year, they sacrificed many thousands in order to satisfy the sun god.[1]

Both Mexica and Inca were expansionist. The Mexica in particular were warlike. The Inca were evangelical in their expansionism in that they believed they were lifting other people up by conquering them and teaching them how to serve their gods properly. Mexica took their war captives to the top of a temple where priests—while the captive was still alive—would cut out the captives beating heart. They would throw the body down the steps of the temple and would then ceremoniously eat the bodies, not so much for food but as to honor them. In their belief, they considered that their captured victim had transformed into a god. Children were also sacrificed because of a belief that their hearts were needed by the rain god.[2]

Though there was limited literacy in the Americas, over 1,200 languages and dialects had developed from 300 diverse language groups. Their isolation from the rest of the world was one of the contributing factors to the limited literacy. Another limitation was that they had no beasts of burden, such as horses and oxen. As a result, they did not develop wheeled vehicles or other inventions that could have saved on human labor. Not having domesticated animals limited their immune system because—unlike people in Eurasia—people in the Americas were not exposed to diseases carried by the animals, which would have helped build their immunities. These factors contributed to Native American delays in developing literacy. Mesoamerica, however, did develop the use of **pictographs**, **ideographs**, and a limited **phonetic system**.[3]

Africa

Africa was not as isolated as the Americas. Traders came with books to the Songhay Empire in the Niger River Valley to trade for grain, kola nuts, ivory, slaves, and gold. One of the trading centers in Songhay was the city of Timbuktu, which had a population of 80,000 and was relatively a wealthy community. There were 180 Koranic schools and even Islamic universities where students wrote and debated. In 1464, Sunni Ali became a tyrant king who persecuted and killed scholars and holy men. According to the description provided by Al-Sa'dis, King Sunni Ali might have been somewhat of a fifteenth-century "Hitler." Al-Sa'dis described him as a "great oppressor and notorious evil-doer ... a despot, and a butcher."[4]

Muslims who lived in the cities were literate in Arabic, but people outside the city, such as common herdsmen, were not. Similar to preliterate people in the Americas, teaching still occurred among preliterate African communities. It did

African warriors, sixteenth-seventeenth century brass plaque

© Everett - Art/Shutterstock.com

not, though, follow a formal curriculum, nor was it founded on a particular theoretical base. Instruction was focused predominantly on the transmission of practical skills and values. Learning was immediately applied to solve practical problems. Because theirs was a top-down traditional culture of acquiescence, the main purpose of values education was to instill the dominant values of the culture. The same was true about religious instruction. Instructional methods relied on oral fables, folklore, legends, myths, and proverbs.[5]

Leo Africanus, a Moor who had been exiled from Spain, visited the Niger Valley Region in the early sixteenth century and recorded his observations. The three quotes below from Africanus' writing indicate that educated men were sponsored at the expense of the king.
- "Here [in Timbuktu] are a great store of doctors, judges, priests, and other learned men that are bountifully maintained at the king's cost and charges …"
- "[In Melli], professours read their lectures onely in the temples, because they have no colleges at all."
- "[Outside of Gago, in the villages and hamlets], they are ignorant and rude people, and you shall scarce finde one learned man in the space of a hundred miles."[6]

In Africanus' quotes referring to Timbuktu and Melli, he indicates that the learned men and professors were not the same as priests. This implies a separation of secular and sacred knowledge, especially in his statement describing how professors in Melli had no colleges to teach in so that they had to teach in the temples. Education was quite different in the villages and hamlets outside of Gago. The outskirts were sparsely populated, and the people who did live there were poor and uneducated.

As noted earlier, the Americas were delayed in educational developments in large part because of isolation from the rest of the world. That was somewhat of a factor for sub-Saharan Africa. They obviously were not as isolated from Eurasia as cultures were in the Americas, but they were isolated from other areas of Africa. This isolation limited the exchange of ideas, commodities, and inventions that could spark growth. Underpopulation also delayed the growth of learning. Death, disease, and slavery were the main reasons that the area was so underpopulated. Diseases—such as sleeping sickness, malaria, and leprosy—weakened the populace, and from 770 to 1,500, over seven million Africans were sold into slavery. Most of these enslaved people were women and children.[7]

 Europe

A shared religion and language serve as cohesive elements in society, resulting in more collaboration, peace, and collective values. In such an environment, learning is more likely to thrive as ideas are shared, challenged, and synthesized. The religious identity of the region was such that the land was known as "Christendom" until Strabo, a Greek geographer, labeled it as "Europa." Europe was certainly not a homogeneous culture. There were several different language groups and ethnic groups, but it was the heritage of ancient Rome that brought the commonality. The language of education, for instance, was Latin, and—although there were concentrations of Jews and Muslims in parts of Europe, there was a shared understanding brought by the predominant religion or Christianity with some shared values across all religions.[8]

Even prior to the 1450 invention of the **printing press**, the number of universities had grown to fifty-six in the early fifteenth century. Once books could be mass produced, the diffusion of knowledge increased all the more. The Bible was printed in 1455, which set the stage for the Protestant Reformation as people could read for themselves what the Bible said and hold church leaders accountable if they strayed from its truth. The availability of reading materials made Europe the most literate culture in the world. Similar to the twenty-first century information revolution with the accessibility of the Internet, the fifteenth-century printing press diffused a much larger amount of information in a faster way than ever had been done before. It was a transformational phenomenon.[9]

As knowledge began to be exchanged, critical review by others brought about an unprecedented amount of analysis and synthesis of

Gutenburg printing press, invented in Germany (c. 1436)

© Everett Historical/Shutterstock.com

information. For example, an explorer who discovered that a map was incorrect or incomplete could correct it and spread the new geographical information out for others to continue the review and correction of the new map. The growth of science was made possible as people like **Copernicus** could access facts to adjust his theories and to develop new ones. Transformational learning continued to explode once contact with other parts of the Atlantic World developed into the engagement and exchange of ideas, commodities, and technologies.[10]

 Go to www.khlearn.com to watch a video about the fifteenth-century Atlantic World.

Reflection

For personal reflection, content review, and further research:
1. How did learning develop differently in the Americas, Africa, and Europe during the fifteenth century?
2. Compare the invention of the printing press to the advent of the Internet. How did each influence the dissemination of knowledge?

ENDNOTES

1. Stan Juneau, *History and Foundation of American Indian Education* (Helena, MT: Montana Office of Public Instruction, 2001), 5.
2. Benjamin, *The Atlantic World*, 12-8.
3. Alberta Yeboah, "Education Among Native Americans in the Periods Before and After Contact with Europeans," (paper presented at the annual National Association of Native American Studies Conference, Houston, Texas, February 14-19, 2005), 3.
4. Benjamin, *The Atlantic World*, 25-7.
5. Dama Mosweunyane, "The African Educational Evolution: From Traditional Training to Formal Education," *Higher Education Studies* 3, no. 4 (2013): 50-4.
6. Alison Games and Adam Rothman, eds., *Major Problems in Atlantic History* (Boston: Houghton Mifflin, 2008), 35-8.
7. Mosweunyane, "The African Educational Evolution," 50-2.
8. Benjamin, *The Atlantic World*, 36.
9. Ibid., 47.
10. Ibid., 48.

CHAPTER 5

REFORMATION AND THE EXPLOSION OF LEARNING

Monument of the Reformer Martin Luther in Erfurt, Germany

© Jonathan Schoeps/Shutterstock.com

FOCUS: KEY TOPICS AND TERMS

Aquinas
Augustine
Calvin, John
Calvinism
Catechisms
Comenius, John Amos
Erasmus, Desiderius
Gutenberg

Humanists
Latin Grammar Schools
Latin Vulgate
Luther, Martin
Melanchthon, Philipp
Natural Philosophy
Natural Science
Ninety-five Theses

Nominalism
Pansophism
Platonic
Priesthood of All Believers
Printing Press
Protestant Reformation
Scholasticism
Wycliffe, John

Students new to the study of educational foundations may be surprised to learn that so many theologians have influenced the history and philosophy of education. Even secular scholars grant prominent positions to Augustine of Hippo, Thomas Aquinas, Martin Luther, John Calvin, and other theologians. Although attention given to these transformational leaders may only be cursory in some introductory studies, the ideas of theologians—particularly those of **Protestant Reformation** leaders—are cited as having impacted the development of literacy and common schools in the West, especially in colonial New England. For example, a reader of Luther's *Three Treatises* will notice references he made to education, schooling, and the role of church and government in society. In *To the Christian Nobility of the German Nation* (1521), Luther wrote, "I would advise no one to send his child where the Holy Scriptures are not supreme. . . . I greatly fear that the universities, unless they teach the Holy Scriptures diligently and impress them on the young students, are wide gates to hell."[1] Such doctrinal and educational beliefs, cultivated during the Reformation, served as underpinnings for the development of universal publicly funded education in the West.

Martin Luther on U.S. stamp (ca. 1983)

© MarkauMark/Shutterstock.com

 Martin Luther's Ideas and Influence on Education

In addition to pointing out corruption in the Roman Catholic Church and issues he had with ecclesiastical authority, Luther voiced concerns he had about the curriculum in universities, monasteries, and convents. Before they became corrupted, Luther complained, the convents and monasteries in particular were more inclusive and were in essence, "Christian schools where Scripture and the Christian life were taught, and where people were trained to rule and to preach."[2] He was critical of universities and called them to a "thorough reformation," noting that they had become a means of spreading sin and false teaching, just as "everything the papacy has instituted and ordered" had done.[3] Other nuances, such as Luther's dislike for Aristotle, must also be understood, especially to appreciate his countercultural thinking in contrast to the predominance of Aristotle's influence in the prevailing scholastic thought. For example, Luther held such disdain for Aristotle's books that he urged they all be discarded from the university curriculum. In his forthright language, Luther referred to Aristotle as a "damned, conceited, rascally heathen" whose teachings misled Christians and should therefore be censored.[4] Such reaction should be considered in the context that Europe was just beginning to experience increased exposure to classical literature, including the works of Aristotle and a number of other Greek philosophers. Luther did concede, however, that the curriculum might benefit from abridged versions of Aristotle's *Logic, Rhetoric,* and *Poetics.* These works would help students learn to speak and preach well, but Aristotle's notes would have to go. Luther also did not hold much regard for the **scholasticism** of Thomas Aquinas. Throughout Luther's works, there are several reverent mentions of **Augustine**, whose philosophy was much more **Platonic**, but there were no admiring comments about **Aquinas**.

 Go to www.khlearn.com to watch a video about the Reformation.

Even prior to Luther's prominence, some communities—such as Nuremberg—were beginning to take action to shift the control and funding of schools from the church to local governments.[5] With the advent of more affordable and available paper and printing, schools began to grow even more, especially in more densely populated areas. With increased curiosity about ancient writings, a heightened emphasis was being placed on the classics, which resulted in "The New Learning,"[6] which was essentially humanism, nominalism, and natural philosophy. Scholasticism, however, had risen to prominence in medieval universities and can be understood as "the formal university method of academic investigation, by a logical system of questioning and listing data from the authorities."[7] The forthcoming Reformation, Renaissance, Enlightenment, and Scientific Revolution would all play a role in challenging scholasticism's instructional system. Arguments would begin to intensify over the best way to come to truth. The scholastics would continue to maintain that logical analysis and propositional arguments were the best learning methods, while humanists would embrace the rhetorical skills of persuasion.

PRINTING AND THE DISSEMINATION OF IDEAS

Gutenberg's introduction of the **printing press** in the mid-fifteenth century was a significant development. Although it was certainly a tool to disseminate ideas, it served more to transform a culture that was not as interested in the written text to one that valued it greatly—especially among those who, until the invention of the press, had little hope of accessing much printed material in their lifetimes. Luther's **Ninety-five Theses** and millions of copies of Luther's other works were distributed throughout Europe because of the printing press. Without the press, these ideas would have been discussed in class the next day without much fanfare, if at all, throughout the rest of Europe. There is no question that the press made the dissemination of ideas much easier, rapid, and more affordable. This accessibility opened the common person's awareness to a wealth of knowledge. Oral and written cultures fused to the point where, in the late Middle Ages, the population was becoming increasingly literate, especially in the cities—explaining why the Reformation spread more rapidly in the cities than in the rural areas.[8] With this accessibility came a democratization of learning. Not only were printed materials more available but they were also more frequently being printed in the language of the home rather than in classical languages, such as Latin. This was liberating to the common person. As Reformers were liberating individuals from abuses of the church, they were also liberating them to possibilities through the printed word.

Reformers were **humanists** who cared about text and how truth could be discovered and conveyed through text. Many different ideas were being disseminated in this era beyond the ideas of Reformers: **nominalism**, **natural science**, **natural philosophy**, and many other ideas were dispersed by this growing medium. Protestantism was "good business for printers.... The increase in Bibles created the Reformation rather than being created by it."[9] There was even concern that the laity might begin spending more time reading than listening to the church's preaching. In preaching, the church could continue to propagate its tradition, while reading the original Word of God would weaken it. Printing eventually transformed Europe's perceptions of learning altogether and made literary skills more desirable. This growing individual empowerment through reading was quite compatible with the empowering doctrine of the **priesthood of all believers**.

PRIESTHOOD OF ALL BELIEVERS: LITERACY AND VOCATION

Luther believed that a works-based salvation placed far too much power in the church and, in essence, manipulated the laity to become subservient to a bureaucratic structure that was driven by greed and corruption. He wrote in *To the Christian Nobility of a German Nation* that there were three walls that needed to be torn down in order to bring about this reform. These walls were ideas and practices: (1) no "temporal power," especially the government, has jurisdiction over the church; (2) the pope is the sole interpreter of the Bible; and (3) only the pope can summon a council.[10] For Luther, to tear down these walls was to build dignity and independence into the individual believer. In reference to Romans 12 and 1 Corinthians 12, Luther stated, "There is no true, basic difference between laymen and priests, princes and bishops, between religious and secular, except for the sake of office and work .... They are all of the spiritual estate, all are truly priests, bishops, and popes. But they do not all have the same work to do."[11] It is this doctrine of the **priesthood of all believers** that drove Luther, Calvin, and others to bring about reform. Steinheuser, in his introduction to Luther's *To the Councilmen of All Cities in Germany That They Establish and Maintain Christian Schools* (1524), noted, "With his conception of the spiritual priesthood of all believers, Luther could not but regard the educational system of the church as antiquated and insufficient."[12]

The rise of modern education, especially for common people, can be attributed to the Reformation belief that all individuals should be able to read the Bible in their own language. An illustration of this may be observed in the stark contrast between southern Italy in the early seventeenth century and the British Isles and northern Europe during the same era. In southern Italy, there were no Bibles available to laypeople in their common language. Pope Paul V had observed that "so much reading of the Scripture ruins the Catholic religion."[13] Bibles were banned and burned, and for over 200 years not a single Bible was printed in the common language on the Italian peninsula. Over a century earlier in England, however, **John Wycliffe** taught that the Bible superseded the tradition of the high church and of papal authority, and his followers translated the ***Latin Vulgate*** into English.[14] These translations found their way into the homes of common English folks—not just for males to read but also for females. Having begun in Germany, this trend of common people reading the Bible in their own language continued to spread throughout other parts of Europe, especially in the north.

Although Luther's perspectives on the education of females reflected the limitations of his time, the doctrine of the priesthood of all believers was extremely liberating for girls and women. Though Luther continued to perceive women in traditional roles of wife, mother, and housekeeper, he extended to females the same basic primary school education that he proposed for boys, and this primary education should be in the language of the home rather than in Latin, as had been customary.[15]

In addition to influencing the spread of literacy education for both boys and girls, the doctrine of the priesthood of all believers began to deconstruct the dichotomy between sacred and secular. The dividing wall between the holy monastic life of devotion and the secular common life of servanthood was gradually being chipped away as Luther placed a great deal of weight on the concepts of calling and vocation. In her book *Total Truth*, Nancy Pearcey pointed out that Martin Luther referred to vocations as "God's masks." She went on to discuss how Lutheran writer Gene Edward Veith explained that, although God might sometimes intervene supernaturally apart from human participation—such as the time He provided manna from heaven—he ordinarily provides through the work of humans. Most people, for instance, are fed not by the miracle of manna but by the processes of "agriculture, transportation, food processing, and retailing." For these human processes, Pearcey used the term "cultural mandate," which refers to the original calling in Genesis for all humans to be fruitful and to subdue the earth. The concept of "cultural mandate" illustrates one of the Reformation legacies as being the Protestant work ethic and the perspective that work is worship—a holy calling. [16]

The elevated view of productive labor and its resulting accumulation of wealth are often credited with the later rise of capitalism. This theory was made popular by German sociologist Max Weber in his 1904 book, *The Protestant Ethic and the Spirit of Capitalism*, and was affirmed two decades later by English Christian socialist R. H. Tawney's *Religion and the Rise of Capitalism* (1926). Such a direct connection between the Reformation and capitalism should be considered only with great caution; the Reformation may not have been a required condition for the development of capitalism but it certainly was an enabler of it.[17] Nevertheless, Luther was more concerned with educating for values and spiritual development than for building economic wealth. He recognized three categories of vocations: (1) religious, (2) political, and (3) economic/domestic—each with "its own dignity, required training, and function."[18]

Two of Luther's manuscripts convey clearly his thoughts on education: *To the Councilmen of All Cities in Germany That They Establish and Maintain Christian Schools* (1524) and *A Sermon on Keeping Children in School* (1530). The first reveals that, although he gave priority to religious teaching, Luther promoted liberal arts as being of value in and of itself. He addressed education for the poor and hinted at making school attendance compulsory. Although the curriculum would be Christian, the responsibility of these schools is that of secular governments. The second work provided talking points to preachers to encourage parishioners to keep their children enrolled in school even after they acquired the ability to "do sums and read."[19] Earning money may be a priority, but it becomes idolatry if it is valued beyond preparing to be preachers and rulers.

INTERSECTION OF LUTHER'S THEOLOGY AND EDUCATIONAL PHILOSOPHY

Throughout Luther's *Three Treatises*, it is evident that he was an Augustinian and leaned toward a Platonic framework. Allusions to Augustine's fifth-century work, *City of God*—in which he describes two cities, one of God and one of man—can be seen throughout Luther's writings, as can references to idealist abstractions. Luther gave preference to words over signs, to testament over sacrament, to spiritual over physical, to promises over commandments, and to faith over works.[20] As Luther discussed both spiritual and temporal issues, he revealed democratic sensibilities, and at times appeared to introduce a measure of contradiction by seemingly preferring the power of man's government over God's church. This, however, may not be so much a contradiction as it was Luther's sense that all institutions and individuals need accountability.

As noted earlier, Luther held contempt for Aristotelian and Thomistic ideas. He was appalled that theologians used Aristotle to rationalize the doctrine of transubstantiation. He decried the influence that Aristotle had on theology and said that Thomas Aquinas "is to be pitied not only for attempting to draw his opinions in matters of faith from Aristotle, but also for attempting to base them upon a man he did not understand."[21] The Holy Spirit, he declared, was greater than Aristotle, and even the very theologians who integrated realism into their teachings admitted that the philosophy eventually broke down. For all of Luther's railing against Aquinas, he had much in common with him. They both embraced faith as a legitimate means to explain concepts such as the Trinity or the deity of Christ.

Other Reformers and Their Influence on Educational Developments

John Amos Comenius (1592-1670) on Czech Republic 200 Korun 1998 Banknote

As noted earlier, Luther and Calvin are the two Reformers typically highlighted in the history and philosophy of education, though often given only superficial attention. There is even less consideration given to other Reformers, though sometimes the names of Melanchthon and Erasmus are mentioned. It is also common for the name **John Amos Comenius**, a Czech Moravian, to be credited as having authored the first illustrated children's book, *Orbis Sensualium Pictus* (1658), which in English means *The Visible World in Pictures*.[22] Unfortunately, his other contributions are generally ignored, such as his theories of *pansophism*, that both natural and supernatural truths should be studied to develop universal wisdom, and his vision of *omnes omnia omnino*, the teaching of "all things to all people with reference to the whole."[23] The basic contributions of Comenius to the field of education are presented here only as an example of the many Reformation-era ideas that are normally overlooked. Before turning to Calvin, consideration is now given to Melanchthon and to Erasmus.

PHILIPP MELANCHTHON

Philipp Melanchthon, the "Teacher of Germany," was a professor at Wittenberg University and a supporter of Luther. For over four decades, Melanchthon served instrumentally to construct a system of education in Germany. He authored a number of student textbooks and handbooks on the development of schools.[24] Despite all of these contributions, he is much less known in the field of education than other popularly studied German educators, such as Friedrich Froebel and Johann Herbart.

In his *Orations on Philosophy and Education*, Melanchthon presented a thoroughly systematic and comprehensive philosophy of education. He addressed topics including the order of learning and the role of schools and dedicated entire chapters to the educational philosophies of Plato, Aristotle, Erasmus, and Luther. Believing that schools were ordained by God, he traced teachers and centers of learning throughout the Bible, including Moses, the Old Testament school of the prophets, Jesus, Paul, and others. Melanchthon perceived the primary purpose of schools "to inculcate, preserve, and pass on the true teachings of the Bible."[25] However, unlike Luther, Melanchthon also valued learning as an end in and of itself. The two also differed in their perspective of the purpose of language. While Luther chiefly saw language as a means to spread the gospel, Melanchthon understood it as an instrument to discover what it means to experience humanity. They agreed, however, on the importance of teaching classical languages in upper levels of education, especially for the purpose of ensuring that posterity would rightly interpret the doctrines of Scripture.[26]

© Sergiy Palamarchuk/Shutterstock.com

Melanchthon's philosophy of education might be summed up in the following quote from his *Orations*:

> Then even more difficult is the defense of religion, in which it is necessary to bear in mind the quarrels of all ages, to reveal the snares, to refute sophisms, to remove the disguise of false convictions and to make clear and fortify the true opinions. No one can do these things without a great variety of skills and without erudition.[27]

DESIDERIUS ERASMUS

A comparison of Luther to **Desiderius Erasmus** provides further insight into Luther's educational ideas. Both men were northern Christian humanists who shared in common a concern that the church had harmed the gospel by distorting Scripture.[28] They were also similar in that they followed the "tradition of internal and communal reformation used earlier by the medieval Cluniac Benedictines and the Franciscans."[29] They both sought to distribute the Bible in its most accurate translation from the original languages, to rescue the church from legalism by humanizing it more, and to diminish papal authority.

Desiderius Erasmus

© Travel Faery/Shutterstock.com

In *The Education of a Christian Prince* (1516), Erasmus shared a philosophical and practical approach to education, including the role of the prince's tutor, the importance of Christian dogma in the teaching of philosophy, and the necessity of the prince to serve as an ethical role model to his subjects. Like Reformers Luther and Calvin and common school proponents Thomas Jefferson and Horace Mann, Erasmus believed that "the main hope of a state lies in the proper education of its youth."[30] In the chapter entitled "The Qualities, Education, and Significance of a Christian Prince," he covered topics such as selecting a proper tutor, early childhood education, learning outcomes, primacy of the state's purposes over that of the parents, and curriculum content, such as fables, myths, analogies, and Christian dogma:

> The teacher should enter at once upon his duties, so as to implant the seeds of good moral conduct while the sense of the prince are still in the tenderness of youth. . . . The teacher's task is always the same, but he must employ one method in one case, and another in another. . . . Therefore, the tutor should first see that his pupil loves and honors virtue as the finest quality of all . . .[31]

As the selection above indicates, Erasmus' ideas were very much in line with the Reformers who stressed the teaching of children from a young age and a curricular emphasis on values education based on biblical and classical literature. Erasmus' concepts that were countercultural for his time include an acknowledgment of childhood stages, developmentally appropriate practice in pedagogy, and differentiated instruction.

JOHN CALVIN

A valuable work revealing the educational theories of John Calvin is his *Catechism of the Church of Geneva: That Is a Plan for Instructing Children in the Doctrine of Christ*. It conveys Calvin's concerns about how the corrupted church had neglected examining children in Christian doctrine and outlines the purpose and importance of **catechisms** in order to accomplish this task:

Bust of John Calvin (1509-1564) at Targu Mures, Romania

© Adriana Iacob/Shutterstock.com

> It has always been a practice and diligent core of the church that children be rightly brought up in Christian doctrine. To do this more conveniently not only were schools formerly opened and individuals enjoined to teach their families properly, but also it was accepted public custom and practice to examine children in the Churches concerning the specific points which should be common and familiar to all Christians. That this be done in order, a formula was written out, called a Catechism or Institute.[32]

Calvin continued to express his anxiety about the threat of barbarism to posterity without intervention from God. This intervention, he concluded, may be in the preservation of the church's written texts. What better record of the church's teachings, he declared, "cannot be observed with clearer evidence than from the Catechisms."[33]

The educational implications of **Calvinism** were much greater than simply the use of catechisms as an instructional method. With its "highly intellectual theology,"[34] Calvinism required not only its ministers to be literate but also its laity. Thus literacy—primarily for the purpose of reading, understanding, and interpreting the Bible—was a priority in Calvinist communities, such as in parts of the Netherlands, Switzerland, England, Scotland, and North America. This literacy, combined with the notion that an outward sign was needed as evidence of one's predestination, contributed both to spiritual and economic development. Therefore, education for the masses became highly valued for eternal and temporal reasons. According to Calvin's doctrine of total human depravity, the nature of students was basically sinful and should be taken into account by teachers as they develop classroom discipline systems. Formal schools then would serve to inculcate disciplined self-control. One means of doing so was by corporal punishment.

Like Luther, Calvin encouraged a school system of two tracks: one for common people and another for the upper classes. Common schools would implement the catechisms, basic academic skills, and literacy in the vernacular language. Whereas, **Latin grammar schools** for the upper class would focus on the classics to prepare students as leaders in the church, government, or community. Puritans brought this system of education with them to New England in 1620 and by 1647 passed the Old Deluder Satan Act, the first compulsory education law in the New World. This law required towns of fifty families or more to provide a teacher for basic academic skills. Towns of one hundred were required to establish a Latin grammar school to prepare boys to attend Harvard College, which had been established just over a decade prior.[35]

As far as many novice students of educational history are concerned, the story of the Common School Movement began with Horace Mann. Yet, individuals and doctrinal beliefs of the Protestant Reformation served as impetus for mass education long before Mann. In an effort to represent the Common School Movement more fully, this chapter has focused specifically on the contributions of a few select Reformation leaders and the ideas they espoused. Most likely, the name Horace Mann will continue to be the most recognized, especially in the United States, for contributing to the idea that all children should be taught in publicly funded schools. However, Reformation leaders and their beliefs were just as influential, if not more so, than Mann's efforts.

 Go to www.khlearn.com to watch a video about reformation and the explosion of learning.

Reflection

For personal reflection, content review, and further research:

1. Why are so many theologians studied in the history and philosophy of education?
2. Both Augustine and Luther rejected much of Aristotelian philosophy, preferring Platonic thought as more of an apologetic tool to defend the Christian faith logically. Why is this so? Compare the two theologians and their reliance on Plato's idealism as opposed to Aristotle's realism.
3. Explain how the printing press served as a transformational tool for literacy and the democratization of knowledge.
4. How did the Reformation serve to further education for females?
5. Consider the dichotomy of knowledge described in the chapter on Thomas Aquinas, and compare it to the deconstruction of that dichotomy discussed in this chapter on the Reformation. How did concepts taught in the Reformation serve to weaken the dichotomy of Thomism?
6. What did Philipp Melanchthon believe about the role of language in learning, and how does this compare to the role of language in the theories of Jean Piaget and Lev Vygotsky?
7. Which Reformers' beliefs about education would be compatible to prominent current theories, and which would be in contradiction to them?
8. How did theological principles of the Reformation serve to drive the notion of mass literacy and thus mass education?
9. How would John Calvin's perception of the nature of the learner be different from Jean-Jacques Rousseau's? What implications would these different concepts hold for education of children?
10. It has been claimed that the Reformation sailed across the Atlantic to impact the New World, especially New England. How might this have been so? Provide examples of how such an influence impacted education in New England.

ENDNOTES

1. Martin Luther, *Three Treatises*, trans. Charles M. Jacobs (Minneapolis: Fortress Press, 1970), 100.
2. Ibid., 63.
3. Ibid., 92.
4. Ibid., 93.
5. MacCulloch, *The Reformation*, 51.
6. Ibid., 75-6.
7. Ibid., 25.
8. Ibid., 70-75.
9. Ibid., 72-73.
10. Martin Luther, "To the Christian Nobility of the German Nation," in *Three Treatises*, trans. Charles M. Jacobs (Minneapolis: Fortress Press, 1970), 10-11.
11. Ibid., 14.
12. Martin Luther, *Works of Martin Luther, Volume 4*, trans. Charles M. Jacobs (Albany, OR: Books for the Ages, 1997), 74.
13. MacCulloch, *The Reformation*, 406.
14. Peter Marshall, "Britain's Reformations," in *The Oxford Illustrated History of the Reformation*, ed. Peter Marshall (Oxford: Oxford University Press, 2015), 194.
15. Gutek, *Historical and Philosophical Foundations*, 111.
16. Nancy Pearcey, *Total Truth: Liberating Christianity from Its Cultural Captivity* (Wheaton, IL: Crossway Books, 2008), 47-50.
17. MacCulloch, *The Reformation*, 604-5.
18. Gerald L. Gutek, *A History of the Western Educational Experience*, 2nd ed. (Long Grove, IL: 1995), 141.
19. Luther, *Works of Martin Luther*, 102.
20. Luther, *Three Treatises*, 162, 278, 282-3, 297.
21. Ibid., 145.
22. Lockerbie, *A Passion for Learning*, 177.
23. David I. Smith and Joan Dudley, "John Amos Comenius: Teaching All Things to All People," in *A Legacy of Religious Educators: Historical and Theological Introductions*, ed. Elmer L. Towns and Benjamin K. Forrest (Lynchburg, VA: Liberty University Press, 2017), 211.
24. Riemer Faber, "Philipp Melanchthon on Reformed Education," *Clarion* 47, no. 18 (September 1998): 428.
25. Ibid., 431.
26. Mihai Androne, "The Influence of the Protestant Reformation on Education," *Procedia – Social and Behavioral Sciences* 137 (July 2014): 85.
27. Philipp Melanchthon, *Melanchthon: Orations on Philosophy and Education*, ed. Sachiko Kusukawa (Cambridge, UK: Cambridge University Press, 1999), 18.
28. MacCulloch, *The Reformation*, 15.
29. Gutek, *A History*, 136.
30. Desiderius Erasmus, *The Education of a Christian Prince*, trans. Lester K. Born (New York: Columbia University Press, 1936), 35.
31. Ibid., 146-148, 212-3.
32. John Calvin, *Calvin: Theological Treatises*, trans. J. K. S. Reid (Philadelphia: The Westminster Press, 1954), 88.
33. Ibid., 90.
34. Gutek, *A History*, 145.
35. Ibid., 146-7.

CHAPTER 6

JESUITS IN THE ATLANTIC WORLD, 1500s-1700s

Jacques Marquette preaching to Indians of New France (1675)

FOCUS: KEY TOPICS AND TERMS

Afonso I
Aldeias
Algonquians
Angola
Aquinas, Thomas

Capuchin Friars
Charles V
Huron
Iroquois
Kongo

Loyola, Ignatius
Montagnais
Scholasticism

Pedro Nunes, a Portuguese cosmographer, wrote in 1537 that explorers had not only discovered "new islands, new lands, new seas, [and] new peoples," but they had also discovered "new sky, new stars." This statement reflects the explosion of new knowledge Europeans were experiencing as they became exposed to previously unknown cultures, animals, plants, and people in the New World. Nunes wrote this as Spain was beginning to enter its Golden Age. Spain's Golden Age was in the sixteenth century when the country gained prominence in the arts, literature, and sciences and also in power and wealth. Part of this Golden Age was an increase in learning, which involved the development of universities, libraries, printing presses, and theaters.[1]

A Catholic priest by the name of **Ignatius Loyola** was a theologian during Spain's Golden Age and was significant in the Catholic Church's Counter-Reformation. Ignatius' greatest desire was to be a soldier in the crusades. He became a commander, but his military career was ended when his legs were crushed by a cannon ball. In 1540, he created a new monastic order known as the Society of Jesus, or the Jesuits. This new order was structured and run in a militaristic style but also had a strong emphasis in evangelism and education. Ignatius—having been influenced by the medieval **scholasticism** of **Thomas Aquinas**—developed a three-part curriculum of classical literature, natural science, and theology. This system of education was intended to teach Catholic doctrine and to help Catholics defend their doctrine apologetically.[2]

 ## The Americas and Jesuit Education

A map of the New World produced by cartographer Diego Gutierrez in 1562 showed a Spanish presence throughout the Caribbean, southwest North America, Central America, and all of South America except for what is now much of Brazil and Argentina. In addition to seeking wealth, the Holy Roman Emperor **Charles V** believed that the religious orders should evangelize indigenous peoples throughout these areas. At first, this responsibility was given to the Franciscans, Dominicans, and the Augustinians. Later, however, the primary responsibility for missions was given to the Jesuits. These were all mendicant orders, which meant that they took a vow of poverty and were committed to helping the poor and feeble. Ironically, in some cases Jesuits gained quite a bit of wealth through the slave trade.[3]

© Zvonimir Atletic/Shutterstock.com

Ignatius of Loyola, altarpiece in the Basilica of the Sacred Heart of Jesus in Zagreb, Croatia

By the late sixteenth century, migration from Spain to the Indies and other parts of the Americas was growing at such a rapid rate that cities were being built, especially in New Spain and Peru. They were built on the Spanish model with a central plaza, churches, and universities to educate wealthy colonists. Spaniards who immigrated to America found opportunities beyond their limited prospects in their home country. They lived in cities with strong economies based on mining and agriculture. Their government buildings, cathedrals, and colleges were architecturally designed of stone and incorporated artistic sculptures. Intellectually, the Spanish colonists considered themselves as superior to the American Indians. They viewed natives similarly to how they viewed children. Indians had the capacity for learning and progressing, but they were not as developed and therefore needed to be treated as a parent would treat a child.[4]

In sixteenth-century Lima, Peru, cities were laid out in a grid style with a central plaza and exquisite architecture displayed in convents, cathedrals, and universities. In 1551, the Spanish founded the University of San Marcos in Lima, and in 1584, a printing press was established there. A sixteenth-century writer described Lima as an "earthly paradise." Another writer in the seventeenth century compared Lima to Rome, Genoa, and other prominent Italian cities with its temples, wealth, and "thriving university and colleges." There were, as early as 1630, religious schools for Indians. Pedro de Leon Portocarrero described a large convent of 400 nuns that were "intelligent women." At the Jesuit College of San Martin, over 500 students studied a curriculum described by Portocorrero as "very elaborate . . . incorporating many branches of learning." The Spanish extended economic and educational opportunities even to the Peruvian Indians, many of whom ran their own haciendas, growing crops using both Indian and African slave labor. These wealthy Indians were welcomed into Spanish colonial society and enrolled their sons into the same Jesuit boarding schools as the colonists did.[5]

In 1531, Portugal's colonization of Brazil began. The king of Portugal stated that his main purpose for colonization was "to settle the land of Brazil . . . in order that the people of that land might be converted to our Holy Catholic Faith." To that end, he sent six Jesuits in 1549 and increased that number within a few decades to 125. Their work, however, was more as conquistadores than as missionaries. Mission villages, known as *aldeias*, were created to house natives who allied themselves with the Portuguese. These villages were run by the Jesuits, who required the natives to assimilate to Spanish religion and customs and to grow food for the *aldeias*.[6]

Along the eastern coast of Brazil, the Indian population drastically declined in the late sixteenth century because of disease and conquest. Most natives withdrew to the interior to avoid the Portuguese settlers. Natives who were conquered or who allied themselves with the Portuguese were gathered into the mission villages where they were taught the Bible and Spanish customs. Both Portuguese slave raiders and Jesuits eventually went into the interior of Brazil where the Jesuits built mission villages while the slave raiders captured Indians. These conflicting interests set the two Portuguese groups at odds. In an effort to keep the raiders from capturing the Indians, Jesuits at times leased out the labor of the mission Indians. To further minimize this conflict, by 1600, the king of Portugal entrusted the Jesuits with the care and protection of the Indians. In Paraguay, the Jesuits set up a theocracy made up of a multitude of mission villages called reductions. This experiment lasted for 150 years until the Jesuits were expelled from Paraguay in 1767. To increase the efficiency of governance, in 1620 Brazil was divided into two states: Estado do Brazil and Estado do Maranhao. The latter was directly controlled by Lisbon, Portugal, rather than Salvador, Brazil. In Estado do Maranho, Lisbon followed the example of Spain by assigning the task of education, health, and welfare to Jesuits and other religious orders, such as the Benedictines, Franciscans, and Carmelites. The

Indians in the Jesuit mission villages were never completely safe from slave raiders, and the tension between the raiders and the Jesuits became increasingly bitter. The Portuguese settlers resented the Jesuits for limiting their source of labor. When the missions were removed from Jesuit control in the eighteenth century, Indians abandoned them.[7]

 Go to www.khlearn.com to watch a video discussing Jesuit influence in Itaugua, Paraguay.

Wilhelm Lamprecht's 1869 painting entitled *Père Marquette and the Indians* is representative of the Jesuits' work in North America. It depicts Jesuit Jacques Marquette preaching in 1675 to Indians of New France. In the early seventeenth century, the French required their native partners to accept evangelization as part of a trading agreement. Therefore, along the St. Lawrence River, Jesuits created mission settlements where the **Algonquians**, **Montagnais**, **Huron**, and **Iroquois** were baptized. Natives—having been weakened by disease—willingly agreed to these arrangements. For those natives who refused to move into the mission settlements, the Jesuits began to conduct 'flying missions,' which were evangelistic expeditions into the Indian towns. The Jesuits learned the native languages and religions in order to be more effective at teaching the Indians. Some Jesuits were martyred, and eventually the Jesuits in New France abandoned their cause, concluding that the natives were savages so corrupt that they could not be redeemed. Jesuits were also discouraged by their observation that Indians who did convert were more likely to die of disease than those who did not. The increased deaths of converted Indians, however, were related to their more frequent interactions with Europeans and their lack of immunity to European diseases than to the fact that they had converted.[8]

 Go to www.khlearn.com to watch a video showing images of the University of Santa Clarita, Stanford University, and San Jose State College in 1948.

 ## Africa and Jesuit Education

In the early sixteenth century, Portuguese Jesuits arrived in the **Kongo** at the request of the Christian King **Afonso I** who had been baptized along with his father upon initial contact with the Portuguese. Although Afonso was a Christian, his subjects were not; they remained pagan. He had solicited assistance from the Jesuits to evangelize them, but after his death, the Jesuits sided with a political faction that was favorable to the slave trade. Their efforts then turned from building churches to trading in slaves, which led to the demise of the mission. Upon arrival in sixteenth-century **Angola**, the Jesuits were met with resistance. They concluded that peaceful conversion of Angolans to Christianity was impossible, so a forceful military approach would be taken. Early in the seventeenth century, the Portuguese Jesuit missionary efforts along the coast of Angola were largely unsuccessful at reaching the Luso-Africans, who were a mix of Portuguese and African descent but who spoke Portuguese. This population was only nominally Christian and was generally not open to the efforts of the Jesuits. Therefore, the Jesuits turned their attention to accumulating wealth through the slave trade. Rather than impacting Angola with the gospel or education, Jesuits unfortunately came to be known more for their involvement in the slave trade. Later, **Capuchin friars** arrived in Angola as missionaries in the mid-seventeenth century. The number of churches began to grow rapidly as Capuchin friars were active in educating both Africans and Portuguese colonists in Angola. The Catholic Church in Angola, however, was also involved in the slave trade with Jesuits owning ships that took enslaved people from Africa to Brazil.[9]

Statue of San Pedro Claver, a Spanish Jesuit priest and missionary devoted his life and work to the African slaves of Cartagena

 Go to www.khlearn.com to watch a video about Jesuits in the Atlantic World.

 Reflection

For personal reflection, content review, and further research:

1. Discuss the influence of Aquinas on Ignatius and how that paralleled the influence of Augustine on Luther and other Protestant Reformers. How did these influences affect the development of education by the Protestants as compared to Catholic education?

2. Describe early Spanish and Portuguese efforts to educate the Indians and how their education of the natives compared to the education offered to colonial children.

3. What was the source of conflict between Portuguese slave raiders in Brazil and the Jesuits? Why did the Portuguese settlers grow to resent the Jesuits, and how did this influence the Jesuit mission work?

4. Compare Jesuit missionary efforts in North America, South America, and Africa. Evaluate their successes and failures.

ENDNOTES

1. Benjamin, *The Atlantic World*, 162.
2. See Gutek, *A History*, 149-52; Murphy, *The History and Philosophy*, 126; John D. Woodbridge and Frank A. James III, *Church History. Vol. 2, From Pre-Reformation to the Present Day* (Grand Rapids: Zondervan, 2013), 205-8.
3. Benjamin, *The Atlantic World*, 173.
4. Ibid., 175-6.
5. Ibid., 178-9, 295.
6. Ibid., 153-6.
7. Ibid., 199, 203-4, 308-10.
8. Ibid., 309-10.
9. Benjamin, *The Atlantic World*, 115-95.

CHAPTER 7

SLAVERY IN THE NEW WORLD

Eighteenth-century plantation

FOCUS: KEY TOPICS AND TERMS

Atlantic Creoles
Carter, Robert "King"
Du Bois, W. E. B.
Fort Christiansborg
Moravian Church

Mulattos
Pidgin
Plantation system
Protten, Rebecca
Provision grounds

Society for the
    Propagation of the
    Gospel (SPG)
Stono Rebellion

Any consideration of slave culture in North America should begin by examining the people themselves who became enslaved. They were not a homogeneous demographic group. Their languages and experiences differed, and—as they joined with others—they adapted to survive. They created new languages and made difficult decisions regarding the degree to which they would assimilate or resist. Since most North American slaves worked on plantations, it is important to explore the types of labor systems they experienced, living conditions, and incentives used to motivate productivity. Also, it is key to understand how slaves navigated their individual autonomy and cultivation of family structures.

 ## Demographics and Assimilation of North American Enslaved People

A significant demographic among North American slaves were the **Atlantic Creoles**. Historians have referred to them as "the charter generations, whose experience, knowledge, and attitude were more akin to that of confident, sophisticated natives than of vulnerable newcomers." Atlantic Creoles included both Africans and those of mixed race, referred to at that time as **mulattos**. Some were transported directly from the African Atlantic coast, but others had spent time in Iberia or other regions of Europe or the Caribbean before arriving in North America. Atlantic Creoles had diverse cultural experiences by nature of their mixed parentage, from travel, or from both. Because of their exposure to various languages and cultures, Atlantic Creoles were savvier in their interactions than most other enslaved people. Some of them served as translators between plantation owners and slaves. Also, because of their mixed ethnicity, they could at times conveniently identify with the culture that best suited their purposes at the moment. Atlantic Creoles were typically religious—often practicing Roman Catholicism—and entered into traditional marriages, which is contrary to their reputation as being promiscuous rabble rousers.[1]

Slave Quarters at Boone Hall Plantation, Mt Pleasant, South Carolina (photo, 2019)

An example of how Creoles were distinguished from other slave groups may be observed in South Carolina, where Creoles were perceived differently from recent arrivals, the Carolina-born, and the country-born. For instance, Creoles who had recently arrived in America were viewed by their masters as a less threatening group than other recent arrivals. Creole slaves took less time to assimilate to the new culture and to learn English. Because of this, they served as effective mediators between the other Africans and the plantation owners. Almost as nonthreatening as the Creoles were the Carolina-born, who were valued for their ability to understand the local culture and to communicate well with the plantation family. The country-born were born elsewhere in America and, though not quite as threatening as new arrivals, were viewed with suspicion and careful supervision until they had settled into the new location.[2]

The assimilation process at **Robert "King" Carter's** plantation in Williamsburg, Virginia, illustrates what a typical arrival would have been like in eighteenth-century North America. "King Carter" was the richest planter in the colony in 1727 when he purchased a number of slaves from a trading ship that had docked in Chesapeake. He inspected their bodies, chose the healthiest, and then gave them new names. Most names were either those typically used with children (e.g., Moll, Nan) or farm animals (e.g., Jumper). Periodically, a majestic name would be assigned—perhaps of a mythical god (e.g., Hercules)—as if to mock the subjugation of such strength. Though slaves answered to their newly assigned names, they continued to use their African names in secret.[3]

 Living, Working, and Learning Environments

Very few slaves, approximately five to ten percent, worked outside of a plantation environment. These few were owned by townspeople and served them as domestic slaves. Plantations designated a plot of land as quarters for the slaves, with some elements of these quarters reminiscent of African villages. Cabin floors

© Lost_in_the_Midwest/Shutterstock.com

were made of packed dirt. Storage pits were dug in the ground around the cabins where personal items were kept. The Carter plantation in Williamsburg was an example of how the slave quarters resembled an African village, especially in how slaves held various types of ceremonies and celebrations, including dances, weddings, and funerals.[4]

Plantations typically had more male than female slaves simply because more males were brought to America on the slave ships. This made it challenging for slave families to meet the European expectations of a husband, wife, and children. Harsh conditions decreased fertility and increased infant mortality. Also, husbands and wives were sometimes sold to different plantations. Because of the shortage of children, a steady stream of new slaves was imported to maintain the labor force. Beginning in the mid-eighteenth century, however, slaves began to have an increased number of births so that there was a larger number of Black and mulatto children.[5]

With such constant challenges to the family structure, an academic education was rare for the slave population. Exceptions existed in isolated instances. Literate slaves secretly taught one another how to read. Planters sometimes taught reading and basic math to trusted slaves so that they could then use those skills to help operate the plantation. Missionaries taught the gospel, most often verbally but at times with the written word. In the early eighteenth century, Rev. Alexander Garden was a prominent Anglican Church leader in the Carolinas, Georgia, and the Bahamas. Garden worked with the **Society for the Propagation of the Gospel** (SPG). In his letters to London SPG leaders, he wrote of his concern to evangelize slaves in the region. Believing that it was easier to make progress with those born in America than with those born elsewhere, Garden targeted the country-born slaves under ten years of age. Additionally, Rev. Garden proposed that—because slaves appeared to respond better to other slaves than to White missionaries—home-born slaves should be trained to do the evangelizing of the children. In a 1740 letter, he wrote, "They are, as 'twere, a Nation within a Nation."[6]

Owners wanted their newly arrived slaves to understand and speak English as soon as possible to maximize their ability to follow directions. Slaves continued, however, to speak their African languages as long as they could. Many of them spoke Creole languages, also known as **pidgin**, which blended European languages with their native African tongues. There were at least twenty-five Creole languages spoken in the British Atlantic World. Most Creole dialects were based on African grammatical structures with a European-language vocabulary. Some Creole languages, however, created new grammatical structures. These pidgin languages were practical in that they provided a common language for slaves from different African tribes. Creole languages also served as a communication tool to support resistance efforts among slaves.[7]

Planters typically chose a system of labor that was organized by gangs, tasks, or a combination of the two. In the gang system, slaves were divided into groups by age, health, and sometimes sex. The "great gang" comprised the vigorous able-bodied young men and women who would do the most difficult jobs of field work, building construction, and ditch-digging. Older and less able workers were placed in a second group who would conduct less rigorous work, such as fertilizing the crop. Children made up the third gang and would handle simpler jobs, such as weeding. In the task system, individual slaves were assigned a task for each day. Once that task was completed, the rest of the day was left for the slaves to do as they pleased. They might choose to use this time for recreation or for cultivating their own family garden. If any academic instruction were to occur at all, it would most likely be during the free time available under the task labor system.[8]

Over time, the plantation system became an increasingly harsh environment for slaves. As more slaves were imported, their value decreased, and they were treated more severely. This shift in treatment corresponded to higher incidents of death, disease, suicide, and infanticide. In the mid-eighteenth century, there was a trend toward less punitive conditions to encourage more slave births. More births would be less costly than purchasing African slaves, so there was a degree of improvement in food, clothing, and health care. Small plots of lands called **provision grounds** were provided as incentives to slaves. On this land, they could grow crops for their family or to sell at the market. To have more control over the amount of money slaves earned from this, some planters required slaves to sell all of their produce to the planter for a set amount. One problem with the provision grounds was that slaves might sell enough of their own produce to gain an amount of money to fund resistance or to purchase themselves out of slavery. To avoid such problems, some planters implemented an allowance system whereby they purchased and kept in stock extra food and clothing to give to the slaves as a regular allowance. The allowances were intentionally minimal so as to strengthen dependency of slaves on the **plantation system**.[9]

Slaves resisted in a number of ways, but open rebellion was problematic because it led to a brutal response that usually made conditions worse. One of the most notable rebellions in North America was the unsuccessful **Stono Rebellion**, in which a group of a hundred slaves ran in 1739 from South Carolina to Florida, fighting along the way. Resistance was typically carried out by slowing down productivity, damaging tools, or even committing suicide. One method of resistance involved eating so much dirt that the result was a painful death. Escaping was an option for resisters, but—as with rebellion—it too risked the possibility of capture and a brutal response. In North America, runaways were not as common as elsewhere. There were, however, groups that formed runaway communities in Florida, Louisiana, and the southeast.[10]

 ## Rebecca Protten: From Slave to Educator and Missionary on Both Sides of the Atlantic

Many examples could be highlighted of individuals among the slave population who made an impact in the education and well-being of other slaves and people of African heritage. **Rebecca Protten** is one who stands out because of her transatlantic influence on three continents, her actions to increase literacy among slaves, and her success in Christian evangelism. In 1718, Rebecca was born into slavery in Antigua. At a young age, she was kidnapped and sold to a planter on the nearby island of St. Thomas. Her owners were Christians, and were pleased when, as an adolescent, she converted to Christianity and began to excel at reading the Bible and other books. They were so impressed by her progress that they granted Rebecca her freedom and offered her a paid job as a house servant, which she accepted.

Rebecca partnered with the **Moravian Church** in St. Thomas to teach and evangelize slaves. These actions were viewed as subversive to many of the planters. News of violent slave rebellions in nearby islands and in North and South America caused planters to fear that literacy and Christianity might lead slaves to unite in revolt. Rebecca's work was so successful that she became the first African American woman to be ordained as a Christian minister and has been called the Mother of Modern Missions.

"Context is everything" is more than an axiom in relation to Rebecca Protten's life. Rebecca's life wove a web across the Atlantic World, connecting movements of religion, rebellion, and race from the Caribbean, to Europe, and finally to Africa. At the end of her life, what prevailed was the context through which she navigated the worlds of slavery and religious faith in the eighteenth century. Her story serves as a mirror on a larger narrative—the origins of the Black church itself.[11] Rebecca and her missionary cohorts were harbingers of what was to come after them—an international evangelistic movement.[12]

Rebecca's intriguing biography came about as pieces of a puzzle were collected from personal letters, church records, and legal documents from both sides of the Atlantic—from the West Indies, Denmark, Germany, Africa, Pennsylvania, and elsewhere. These documents were in various languages requiring translation. One key source was Christian Oldendorp's 1777 *History of the Mission of the Evangelical Brethren on the Caribbean Islands of St. Thomas, St. Croix, and St John.* Oldendorp could not have known certain facts about Rebecca unless she told him directly or had told someone else that he eventually interviewed.[13] Though he did not arrive at St. Thomas until after Rebecca had left for Europe, both she and Oldendorp had been in the Moravian city of Herrnhaag, Germany, in 1740, where they most likely met for the first time.[14] From stories he had collected from the Caribbean, Oldendorp already knew that Rebecca's pre-baptism name was Shelly, that she was a mulatto born in Antigua, and that at approximately the age of six she had been kidnapped and sold as a domestic slave on the island of St. Thomas. Oldendorp's objectivity is sometimes uncertain because of his proslavery sentiments and also because one of his purposes for writing about Rebecca was to persuade planters to allow missionary work on their plantations. Oldendorp most likely skewed his writings about Rebecca to make her efforts and the work of similar missionaries acceptable to slave owners. In plantation societies, such as St. Thomas, missionaries who sought to educate and evangelize slaves were at the mercy of planters who would permit missionary presence only if it assured increased docility and productivity of their slaves. Missionary efforts were shut down if planters suspected that they might lead to rebellion.

Such deliberately guarded writing can also be seen by Rebecca's own pen. A letter of testimony she wrote from St. Thomas to the Moravian sisters in Herrnhut, Germany, serves as an example. She wrote of her vision to preach among enslaved plantation workers and to cultivate a Black Christian community in America. She neglected to mention, however, her desire to see them freed. Yet, her goals, as a woman of color, were ambitiously countercultural—especially considering societal limitations on women like her at the time.[15]

In addition to letters, church documents, and biographical manuscripts, a number of paintings serve to tell Rebecca's story. Several of these were painted by Johann Haidt, a lay preacher and artist for the Moravian Church both in Germany and in Bethlehem, Pennsylvania. Haidt's painting entitled *First Fruits* serves as evidence of Rebecca's prominence within the Moravian Church. It depicts Jesus in Heaven surrounded by ethnically diverse Christians who had joined the church through Moravian missions and who had already died. Rebecca's daughter Anna Maria, who had died at the age of four, is included in the arms of a woman named Catherine. Still alive at the time, Rebecca was not in the painting, but the inclusion of her daughter along with just twenty others is an indication that her status as a leader in the church was considerable.[16] Another Haidt painting is a family portrait of Rebecca with her husband and their young daughter.

After the death of their daughter, Rebecca and her husband spent their final days as educators and missionaries in **Fort Christiansborg**, in the Accra region of the Gold Coast of Africa, which is modern day Ghana—also the final home of African-American scholar and social activist **W. E. B. Du Bois**. Little is known of Rebecca's final years as a widow and teacher in West Africa, where she died in obscurity. There is no account of how she spent her last days, no details about her death, and no gravesite to mark her memory. This may be fitting in that her legacy, much like her life, does not draw attention to herself but to the impact she made in education and evangelism.

In a biography entitled *Rebecca's Revival*, author Jon R. Sensbach bookended the narrative with two contrasting slave rebellions. The first, which occurred when Rebecca was just a teenager, was the violent 1733 St. John rebellion in which a magistrate and his daughter were gruesomely slaughtered. The rebellion lasted for months before being squelched.[17] This opening scene serves multiple purposes—to contextualize the cruel subjugation of slavery, to explain complex tribal relationships that transferred from Africa across the Atlantic, and to imply the value of missions to slaves, their masters, and society at large. In many places, Sensbach explicitly evaluated missionary practices in the context of slavery. Regarding the rebellion at the close of the book, however, he chose to allow the reader to infer much of the impact that a century of missions work had accomplished. In 1848, more than five decades after Rebecca's death, 8,000 slaves marched on the St. Croix fort and peacefully demanded their freedom. It was a "bloodless" event, and "the government, remarkably, capitulated instead of shooting them."[18] The implication is that Rebecca's revival had changed the hearts, minds, and motives of both slaves and slave owners. Literate slaves had read in the Bible of their identity in Christ and had developed the empowered community of which Rebecca alluded to in her letters.

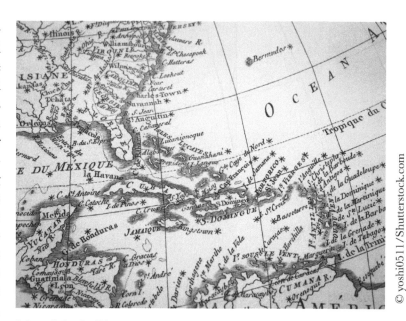

Map of the Caribbean

Christianborg Castle on the Gold Coast of Africa (now Ghana)

Johann Haidt's painting entitled First Fruits *(1747) depicting Rebecca Protten's deceased daughter in Heaven[19]*

© yoshi0511/Shutterstock.com

© Everett Historical/Shutterstock.com

© Museum Het Hernhutter Huis, Zeist, Netherlands, photo Fred Manschot/Mel Boas

Go to www.khlearn.com to watch a video about slavery in the New World.

Reflection

For personal reflection, content review, and further research:

1. In the discussion of the education of enslaved people in North America, why is it important to consider the diversity of their demographics and life experiences?
2. What circumstances hindered the ability for adult and child slaves to receive an academic education?
3. Explain the conditions under which a slave might be taught to read.
4. How did the use of language among slaves serve as an expression of resistance?
5. Which of the three labor systems was most conducive to family time and therefore to educational endeavors?
6. In what ways did slaves resist the plantation system?
7. How does the life of Rebecca Protten serve as a model of social responsibility for educators?

ENDNOTES

1. Ira Berlin, "From Creole to African: Atlantic Creoles and the Origins of African-American Society in Mainland North America," *The William and Mary Quarterly* 53, no. 2 (1996): 253-9.
2. Benjamin, *The Atlantic World*, 401-2.
3. Berlin, "From Creole to African," 251.
4. Benjamin, *The Atlantic World*, 402-3.
5. Ibid., 412-3.
6. Shevaun E. Watson, "'Good Will Come of this Evil': Enslaved Teachers and the Transatlantic Politics of Early Black Literacy," *College Composition and Communication 61*, no. 1 (2009): 73-4.
7. Benjamin, *The Atlantic World*, 213-4.
8. Ibid., 403-7.
9. Ibid., 407-12.
10. Ibid., 414-6.
11. Jon F. Sensbach, *Rebecca's Revival: Creating Black Christianity in the Atlantic World* (Boston: Harvard, 2005), 7.
12. Ibid., 241.
13. Ibid., 31.
14. Ibid., 236.
15. Ibid., 63-4.
16. Ibid., 189-91.
17. Ibid., 8-13.
18. Ibid., 246.
19. Johann Haidt, *First Fruits*, 1747, painting, Moravian Church Archives.

CHAPTER 8

COLONIAL NORTH AMERICA

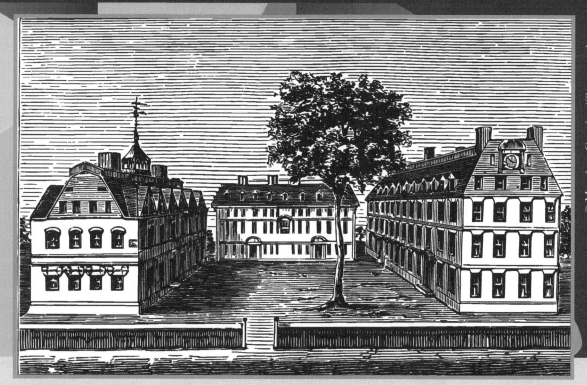

Harvard College (1720)

© Morphart Creation/Shutterstock.com

FOCUS: KEY TOPICS AND TERMS

Agnosticism
Calvinism
Catechisms
Chauncy, Charles
Comenius, John Amos
Davenport, James
Deism
Edwards, Jonathan
Eliot, John
Emotionalism
Enlightenment

Grammar schools
Great Awakening
Harvard College
Hornbooks
Locke, John
Moral education
New Divinity
New England Primer
New Light
Old Deluder Satan Act
Old Lights

Orbis Pictus
Petty schools
Priesthood of all
  believers
Princeton
Puritans
Rationalism
Reason
Republicanism
Romantic
Rousseau, Jean-Jacque

Sensory experience
Stockbridge,
  Massachusetts
Stuyvesant, Peter
Tennent, Gilbert
Tindal, Matthew
Unitarianism
*Westminster Shorter
  Catechism*
Winthrop, John, Jr.
Yale

Settlers in North America brought with them a vast array of ideas from philosophy, politics, and religion that had already made a transformational impact on the Western world. The printing press had made dissemination of a variety of classic and contemporary works increasingly available to common people, and these ideas crossed the Atlantic with the colonists—ideas from Plato, Cicero, Erasmus, Luther, Calvin, and a plethora of others. Settlers had been exposed to the doctrine of the **priesthood of all believers**, the notion of universal education, and the emphasis of piety as being the chief end of education. In colonial America, education was perceived as much broader than strictly the institutional school as conceived today. The process of education began with the family, the church, and popular publications, such as newspapers, almanacs, and pamphlets.

The concept of learning communities was certainly not foreign to colonists. They would soon begin their own such communities similar to those long established in Europe as far back as Plato, Augustine, and Aquinas. The university, however, was an educational construct for adults, while learning for children was largely a matter of the home and sometimes religious and local communities. Theories and practices of education in England, both for children and adults, were transported to the New World. Descriptions of Elizabethan-era **petty schools** and **grammar schools** with their **hornbooks** and **catechisms** were very much like what eventually developed in the American colonies—as was the process for licensing schoolmasters, which began in England in the early twelfth century.

Early educational attempts, such as those in Virginia and New Amsterdam, were delayed, while schools in New England thrived early on. Though the Virginia Company arranged in 1624 for the construction of a free public school in Charles City, the supplies were lost at sea, and the funds were applied instead to build a hospital. Another attempt at a school was made when an anonymous donation of £550 was designated for the cause; instead, it was misapplied to build an ironworks plant. For these and various other reasons, schools continued to be delayed in Virginia. The Company in New Amsterdam created a minimally funded school that suffered from political battles between the city and the Company. **Peter Stuyvesant** solicited increased funds from the city, but they refused unless the Company would give up control of the schools to the city. The delays in Virginia and New Amsterdam contrast with those in New England, where the Plymouth Colony at first left education to the realm of the church and the home. In Boston, however, formal education was begun as early as 1635 with the hiring of a schoolmaster.[1]

How European beliefs and practices were carried to the American colonies and how they were then implemented and adapted with American sensibilities can be seen in the establishment of the American university. The university's origins are found in the eleventh-century medieval era in Bologna, Italy, and Oxford, England. Harvard, Yale, and Princeton mirrored their European counterparts but with distinctly American thrusts of **republicanism** and **Calvinism**. It is interesting to note that **John Winthrop, Jr.**, considered appointing **John Amos Comenius** to the presidency of **Harvard College**. Even the consideration of such a decision indicates the desire for American education to draw from European roots and to build upon Christian foundations.[2]

New England Primer[3]

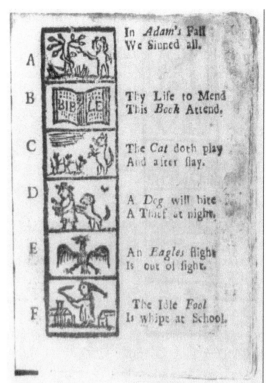

A page from the New England Primer[4]

Source: Library of Congress

For more than 150 years the ***New England Primer***, often called "The Little Bible of New England," served as the principal textbook for millions of colonists and early Americans. First compiled and published *ca.* 1688 by Benjamin Harris, a British journalist who emigrated to Boston, it gained popularity not only in New England but also throughout colonial America and parts of Great Britain with estimates of copies sold from six to eight million by 1830. Less than a hundred pages in length, this early textbook proved significant in both reflecting the norms of Puritan culture and propagating those norms into early American thought. In the *New England Primer*, Harris provided a tool of reform that promoted literacy, proliferated compulsory education, and solidified a Calvinist ethic in colonial America.

The historical milieu in which the primer emerged contributed to its rise to prominence. In 1630, a group of **Puritans** settled the Massachusetts Bay area with the goal of developing a society based on biblical principles as embodied by the English Reformation. The doctrine of the priesthood of all believers motivated Puritans to teach reading to all citizens so that they could know and follow the Christian Scriptures. As early as 1642, Massachusetts law required literacy instruction to all children, servants, and apprentices. The 1647 **Old Deluder Satan Act**—in order to ensure that "learning may not be buried in the grave of our forefathers"—required every township of 50 households to hire a teacher. Towns twice that size were mandated to set up schools that would prepare students for the university, Harvard being the only one existing in colonial America at the time. With only the hornbook and Bible available in most schools, New England was ready for a textbook that would be affordable, portable, and compatible with the predominant worldview.

Borrowing principles from the first illustrated book intended for children—John Amos Comenius's ***Orbis Pictus***— and his own *Protestant Tutor*, Harris incorporated crude woodcut illustrations and religious content to teach reading skills and to encourage rote memorization of Calvinist doctrine. Graduated literacy instruction began with the alphabet, simple letter combinations, and syllables, increasing to complex sentences intended for rote memorization. Themes of sin, death, punishment, salvation, and respect for authority were displayed through alphabetic rhymed couplets, poems, prayers and scriptures. The theme of punishment, for instance, was exhibited in the rhyming couplet for the letter *F*: "The idle fool/Is whipt at school." Such themes for a child's textbook may seem morbid in light of **Jean-Jacque Rousseau's** notions of childhood innocence, but they would not seem so to Puritan families who embraced the doctrine of infant corruption caused by the original sin of Adam.

The primer was reproduced by a variety of publishers, resulting in 450 editions by 1830. Adaptations were printed for various geographic regions and ethnic groups, such as the 1781 *Indian Primer* printed in both the

Mohawk and English languages. With each new edition came content changes, though the core elements of the pictured alphabet and catechism remained constant. The couplet for the letter *A* never changed—"In Adam's fall/We sinned all," but many of the others were modified to reflect evolving political or religious beliefs. For instance, independence from Britain saw the alteration of "Our king the good/No man of blood" to "The British king/Lost states thirteen" and later to "Queens and kings/Are gaudy things." One of the most blatant political alterations was made in 1776 when an image of King George III was simply relabeled with the name of John Hancock.

The influence of the **Great Awakening** brought about several changes to the primer. For example, the couplet for the letter *C* was amended from "The cat does play/And after slay" to "Christ crucify'd/For sinners dy'd." The Great Awakening's influence shifted the primer's emphasis from God's wrath to His love and contributed to the addition of more prayers and hymns, such as Isaac Watts' "Cradle Hymn." As moral education became more secularized, the emphasis on punishment and sin softened. For example, in later versions, consuming fire as a punishment was replaced with the threat of having treats taken away. Literacy as a means to finding eternal salvation was replaced in one 1790 version as a path to financial security, and in an 1819 edition, the rhyme for *K* expressed the value of play—"Tis youth's delight/To fly their kite."

Various adaptations included the Lord's Prayer, Apostles' Creed, Ten Commandments, Westminster Shorter Catechism, John Cotton's *Milk for Babes*, and the common children's prayer "Now I Lay Me Down to Sleep." Also present in some editions was an account of John Rogers' martyrdom accompanied by a woodcut of his burning at the stake while his wife and children watched. The catechetical drill included some of the following questions: "What is the chief end of man?" "What is the first commandment?" "What is faith in Jesus Christ?" Later such secular questions were included as "Who saved America?" and "Who betrayed America?"

Though criticized for depicting children as depraved and for using God as a metaphor to manipulate submission to the political and religious authority of New England, the primer made a lasting impact on the moral landscape of America. Of the millions printed, fewer than 1,500 copies remain, the earliest having been published in 1727. This relatively low number of surviving texts indicates the constant use the primer received and the impact its principles had on the development of American values. The multiple editions of existing copies serve as a valuable record chronicling the changes in early American philosophy of education.[5]

 Jonathan Edwards

Most narratives on **Jonathan Edwards** describe his life experiences, family, education, conversion, ministry, and missions work with the Indians. They identify him as an intellectual, theologian, and scientist. Some accounts note his significance as an apologist, especially as he argued against **Enlightenment** thought, **deism**, and **Unitarianism**. Primarily, he is presented as the

Jonathan Edwards (1703-1758)[6]

From The New York Public Library, https://digitalcollections.nypl.org/items/510d47db-11c9-a3d9-e040-e00a18064a99

famed Great Awakening preacher. There is yet, however, another prominent role Edwards has played, and that is in the field of educational philosophy. Though usually granted only token attention in typical foundations of education studies, Edwards' theory of knowledge and of learning is deserving of much deeper study than it has received. In addition, it is worth considering the notion that Edwards' revivalism was instrumental in propagating the importance of the individual commoner in society and that—because of this—a movement was energized to educate the common person.

BACKGROUND AND CONTEXT

Though Jonathan Edwards is thought of as an American New Englander, he must be perceived primarily as a British citizen in order for his life experiences and ideas to be contextualized properly.[7] He was a child of the Enlightenment, engaging and synthesizing the philosophical arguments of his time. This grappling of ideas can especially be observed in his *Miscellanies* and *Notebooks* that he began writing at age nineteen and continued toward the end of his life. In them, he recorded the development of his thoughts on theology, philosophy, and science. Much of this journaling formed the basis for some of his published works—many of which reveal Edwards' engagement with European ideas of his day.[8]

In addition to his status as a British citizen, Edwards' family context must also be considered. He was born to Esther Stoddard Edwards, the daughter of prominent revivalist pastor Solomon Stoddard. Esther had been well educated and was strong in theological studies. She assisted her husband in teaching all eleven of their children—Jonathan and his ten sisters. Even into her nineties, long after her husband had died, Esther continued to teach.[9]

Jonathan's father, Timothy Edwards, like his father-in-law, was also a revivalist preacher. Timothy served as a war-time military chaplain during Queen Anne's War. Letters home to Esther conveyed his priorities for their children—that they be educated well academically, morally, and spiritually. He reminded Esther to ensure that Jonathan not lag behind in his Latin studies and that he be instructed in morality so as not to become "rude and naughty." Having been a school teacher prior to marrying Esther, Timothy had long held education in high regard. Despite having been expelled from Harvard, Timothy did not let that deter him from returning there to earn both his B.A. and M.A.[10] As a pastor, Timothy set aside a room in the parsonage as a classroom to prepare local boys for entrance to Harvard. He did not, however, teach only boys. He also taught his ten daughters and even tasked the four sisters older than Jonathan with tutoring him in his studies. The girls' education went beyond basic literacy as they taught Jonathan using Latin Bible commentaries and the works of Addison and Steele. Nine of the ten sisters attended Boston finishing school as had their mother.[11]

Jonathan, a precocious child, by age thirteen had written letters that later became scientific articles on his observations related to the flying spider and the rainbow.[12] He entered the Connecticut Collegiate School, which became known as **Yale**. He was three years ahead of most of his contemporaries, who typically enrolled at sixteen. This age difference may have contributed to his struggles socially. In addition to being naturally shy, Jonathan held interests more aligned with those of adults than with his classmates, whose immature and sometimes immoral antics greatly annoyed him.[13]

In 1720, he graduated at the head of his class with his B.A. and in 1721 experienced conversion to salvation in Christ. Shortly after his conversion, he conveyed deep disappointment in his own "proud and self-righteous spirit." To address this, he developed a list of *Resolutions*, some of which required strict discipline in habits related to eating, drinking, sleeping, and speaking.[14] One of the resolutions relayed what was, and continued to be, a central tenet of his philosophy of education: "Resolved, to study the Scriptures so steadily, constantly and frequently, as that I may find and plainly perceive myself to grow in the knowledge of the same."[15]

Between pastoring his first church in what is now lower Manhattan and his second in Bolton, Connecticut, Edwards earned his M.A. at Yale, at which time he was exposed to the writings of Newton and Locke.[16] In 1727, he was ordained, married, and partnered with his grandfather in the ministry at Northampton. Two years later when his grandfather died, Edwards became the pastor where he preached and led a number of renowned revivals for over a span of two decades.[17] Like his parents, Jonathan ensured that both his sons and daughters were educated well at home. Unlike them, however, he did not send his daughters to finishing school in Boston. The development of their souls was his highest concern. In morning devotions, Jonathan quizzed them with age-appropriate questions on their knowledge of the Bible. Each Saturday evening, to bring in the Sabbath, he taught them the ***Westminster Shorter Catechism***. He ensured that they could not only recite it but that they also understood it.[18]

Unfortunately, his Northampton ministry ended in controversy as the congregation dismissed Edwards for attempting to change membership policies. This led him, however, to serve as a missionary to Native Americans in **Stockbridge, Massachusetts**, from 1751 to 1758. It was in his mission work at Stockbridge that he further explicated his philosophy of education and also demonstrated it in practice. Jonathan observed that Indians valued their children and were eager to educate them. He, however, rejected the traditional means by which the English educated not just Indian children but also their own.[19]

After reluctantly accepting the office of president at the College of New Jersey, which later became **Princeton**, he died in 1758 at the age of forty-four from complications from a smallpox vaccination.[20] Edwards' legacy includes many writings that impacted the time in which he lived and continue to be studied today. They include *Religious Affections* (1746), *The Freedom of the Will* (1754), *The Nature of True Virtue* (published posthumously in 1765), the sermon *Sinners in the Hands of an Angry God* (1741), and a biography of David Brainerd (1749).

ENLIGHTENMENT INFLUENCE

As noted earlier, studying Newton and Locke during his M.A. at Yale was formative on Edwards' thinking. He was anxious to read the latest thoughts, to evaluate them through the lens of biblical truth, and to synthesize them into his Calvinistic worldview as was appropriate.[21] After carefully scrutinizing Enlightenment ideas, Edwards was left even more confident that the key to a unified theory of knowledge could only be found in God's Revelation as expressed through Jesus Christ and in the Bible.[22] It was in his notebooks, such as the *Miscellanies* and *The Mind*, that he expressed his synthesis of thoughts from natural philosophy. In his notebooks, Edwards asked a multitude of practical questions, such as "Why is air necessary to preserve a fire?" and

John Locke (1632-1704)

© Georgios Kollidas/Shutterstock.com

"Why are no two trees exactly alike?" He expressed a special interest in both the practical properties and the spiritual dimensions of light. This dual interest in both scientific and theological dimensions of life was common among Edwards' contemporaries, as few of them found any conflict between science and theology. Some, however, such as **Matthew Tindal**, argued for a rational, deistic religion that relegated God's intervention in the natural world as unnecessary.[23] It was this breed of **rationalism** that Edwards opposed in his apologetic works. For example, in Number 1340 of *Miscellanies* entitled "The Insufficiency of Reason as a Substitute for Revelation," he called deism a "gross mistake" of considering "material things the most substantial beings, and spirits more like a shadow."[24]

New England universities were slow to incorporate the natural philosophy, but once they did, it became quite controversial.[25] When Edwards wrote *Thoughts on the Revival* in 1758, he was concerned that Harvard and Yale were "nurturing neither piety nor prophets."[26] Seeing the creeping influence of deism and Unitarianism, Edwards joined his Presbyterian fellow revivalist **Gilbert Tennent** and other Presbyterians to found the College of New Jersey with the intent that it would remain true to its Christian purpose, unlike they believed Harvard and Yale had done.[27] Though Edwards argued for theology to remain the queen of the sciences, he was clear about his support for the natural sciences to be presented in the college curriculum. He was simply being consistent that biblical studies should always be given preeminence over other truth claims. Edwards praised scientists and inventors as "benefactors of the race," and he even pursued his own studies in the medical sciences.[28] Faith and reason were not contradictory for Edwards. He was confident that he could develop a theory of knowledge that would unite faith, reason, and experience under the supremacy of revelation and with a strong affective component.[29]

PHILOSOPHY OF EDUCATION

Edwards was an idealist, an Augustinian, and a Calvinist. These labels are offered strictly as reference points to initiate an exploration of Edwards' general philosophy. The nuances are the results of a unique synthesis as he engaged Enlightenment ideas, particularly those of **John Locke**. Though Edwards did not embrace all of Locke's ideas, he did find in Locke new categories that helped him describe the relationship between ideas and reality.[30] For instance, Edwards valued the use of data to draw scientific conclusions. He believed, however, that sensory perceptions had no existence apart from the mind. Because God is sovereign and the source of all knowledge, truth, and experience, an individual's sensory perceptions do not originate within the individual but with God. Sensations, therefore, are divine ideas that are conveyed to humans by the will of God.[31]

MORAL EDUCATION. Since issues of predestination and God's sovereignty are significant in Calvinism, the question of freedom of the will, or choice, is one that Edwards could not ignore. He and Locke shared the same general perspective—that what moves the mind to a perceived choice is the desire of good. For Edwards, that good was ultimately God. Edwards went on to distinguish between two types of choices: voluntary and involuntary inclinations. To those who may argue that only voluntary inclinations represent freedom of will, Edwards would respond that freedom is not related to the origin of the choice but with the incident of the choice itself. Therefore, whether inclinations are voluntary or involuntary, Edwards insisted that individuals are fully responsible for their choices.[32]

In *The Nature of True Virtue*, which was not published until seven years after his death, Edwards presented a philosophy of social ethics, in which he elaborated on the importance of the freedom of will as exercised through choice. It is the *summum bonum*, the ultimate good, that drives choices. When the *summum bonum* is God, the result is that choices benefit society. When the *summum bonum* is distorted, however, the result is a deterioration of society caused by sin. Therefore, it is important to educate children to love God above the good of self, family, nation, tribe, or race. Failing to do so will result in a society of individuals whose misplaced affections bring fragmentation in society rather than unity.[33]

As foundational as Scripture was to Edwards' philosophy, he chose not to quote the Bible in *The Nature of True Virtue*. He did, however, refer to it as the source for his belief that affections should be directed above all to God. In *Religious Affections*, though, he cited Scripture quite liberally as he emphasized that God is love and that any good action is a display of that love. Again, he underscored the theme of harmony and the unity that comes to society when people love God and also love what God loves. This foundation for **moral education** was contrary to the Enlightenment movement that sought to parallel the new natural science and to establish a science of morality based on self-evident first principles rather than on revealed truth.[34]

If one word were to represent Edwards' philosophy of moral education, it might be the word "relationships." For him, all meaning was discovered and expressed in loving relationships. This included both divine and human relationships. Human relationships could not experience the highest value unless they were subordinated by a proper relationship with God. As important as the material world was to scientific knowledge, it was temporal and was only part of what made a person educated. To Edwards, a truly educated person understood the affections, especially as they were communicated by God, and could respond appropriately to that love in right relationship with God and with others.[35]

THEORY OF KNOWLEDGE AND TRUTH. As in his philosophy of moral education, Edwards' theory of knowledge contained themes of unity and harmony as well. He rejected a dichotomy of reality that was divided into strictly material and spiritual elements; he instead took the extreme opposite view of Thomas Hobbes, who believed that ultimate reality was found in material substance. For Edwards, "nothing has any existence anywhere else but in consciousness," and it was in the divine mind that all the universe existed. He disagreed with Locke who started with experience and also disagreed with Descartes who started with human reason. In and of themselves, neither experience nor reason was a sufficient source of knowledge or a means to arrive at truth. God's sovereignty trumped any of the Enlightenment theories so that all truth was a concept in the mind of God that could be known fully only in a proper relationship with God. **Sensory experience** was valuable—just as it had been for young Edwards in his study of spiders—but it provided a limited view of reality. **Reason** could serve to correct limited experience, but reason too was flawed. Scripture must serve as the foundation of all knowledge and then work in tandem with experience and reason.[36]

Edwards' Platonic leanings are revealed as he described the language God uses to convey truth. Because everything exists as an archetype in the Divine Mind (which is reminiscent of Plato's forms existing in the Absolute Mind), humans can only know reality through God's language of signs and shadows. Where Edwards differed from Plato is that God's language was manifested in the Scripture, in persons (specifically the persons of the Trinity), and in relationships with those persons. These distinctions set Edwards theory of knowledge apart from Platonists and deists. What was true, right, and real could be experienced through harmony—a right relationship—with God. An analogy he often used to illustrate this concept was music. Music required harmony, proportion, and complex relationships for it to be experienced. Music, therefore, played both a theoretical and practical role for Edwards as he implemented it in the homeschooling of his own children and in the mission school to Native Americans.[37]

RATIONALISM VERSUS EMOTIONALISM

Regarding a 1737 Northampton revival, Edwards wrote the following description:

> The Congregation was alive in God's Service, every one earnestly intent on the Publick Worship, every Hearer eager to drink in the Words of the Minister as they came from his Mouth; the Assembly in general were from time to time, in Tears while the Word was preached; some weeping with Sorrow and Distress, others with Joy and Love, others with Pity and Concern for the Souls of their Neighbours.[38]

His wife Sarah Pierrepont Edwards recounted her reaction to the sermon of preacher Samuel Buell in 1742:

> [It] moved me so exceedingly, and drew me so strongly heavenward, that it seemed as it were to draw my body upwards, and I felt as if I must necessarily ascend thither. At length, my strength failed me, and I sunk down; when they took me up and laid me on the bed, where I lay for a considerable time, faint with joy, while contemplating the glories of the heavenly world.[39]

These descriptions by both Jonathan and his wife Sarah, illustrate the **emotionalism** of the Great Awakening. It was, however, much more than just an emotional movement; it was also a grass-roots intellectual movement. The revivals were sparked in New England where, with the exception of Indians and Africans, literacy was already common. As emotions were stirred, **New Light** followers applied their reading ability to deepen their understanding of spiritual matters by studying the Bible, theological works, and devotional materials. This aided in the further development of cognitive skills and the desire to explore a variety of new ideas available in Enlightenment literature. Ironically, while the Great Awakening drew many to submit to God's sovereignty, it may also have sparked some in their intellectual pursuits to follow deism or **agnosticism**.[40]

The **Old Lights** ridiculed what they perceived to be shallow emotionalism: "weeping, crying out, twitching, and falling down during worship."[41] They accused the revivalists of disparaging "humane reason and rational preaching."[42] Edwards acknowledged the increasing emotional expressions and even admitted that extremists had, in some instances, perverted the revival.[43] Nevertheless, he defended the emotionalism as acceptable and even necessary. This was a grass-roots movement in which the common person was central. Despite gender, race, social status, or educational level, a dramatic conversion was available to all. The typical New Englander was at least nominally Christian, attended church, and had a high level of biblical literacy. Therefore, few were in need of an intellectual conversion to the gospel. They were extremely open, however, to a spiritual and emotional conversion—an experience with God that they had not to that point known.[44] In a unique way, the Great Awakening took the Reformation doctrine of the priesthood of all believers to a higher level. The Reformation opened the commoner to the truth of the Scripture; the Great Awakening opened the commoner to an intimate relationship with the Author of that truth.

Various dichotomies thematically reoccur in Edwards' works: head-heart, reason-emotion, thinking-feeling, sensual-spiritual, science-revelation, notional-sensible, and understanding-affections. Critics of the revivalist movement, such as **Charles Chauncy**, accused New Lights of neglecting the former in each of the above pair while overly emphasizing the latter. There may be some legitimacy to the allegation of anti-intellectualism. For example, Gilbert Tennent, an Awakening preacher, encouraged his followers to assume that education weakened a minister's faith. He called educated ministers "Letter-Learned Pharisees" and "Dead

Dogs that cannot Bark."[45] These sentiments, however, were not representative of those espoused by most Awakening proponents—Jonathan Edwards' *via media* being a prime example.

Michael Haykin suggested that Edwards' *via media*—his balance between extreme ways of knowing—may be his greatest contribution to the philosophy of education.[46] Unlike his contemporaries Charles Chauncy and **James Davenport**, who respectively followed extremes of reason and of emotion, Edwards argued in *Religious Affections* that true religion engages the believer holistically—both rationally and emotionally:

> As on the one hand, there must be light in the understanding, as well as an affected fervent heart, where there is heat without light, there can be nothing divine or heavenly in that heart; so on the other hand, where there is a kind of light without heat, a head stored with notions and speculations, with a cold and unaffected heart, there can be nothing divine in that light, that knowledge is not true spiritual knowledge of divine things.[47]

The head and heart are so deeply interrelated that, for there to be true understanding, there must be an experience of holy affections. This was true in his theology, but it was also true in his philosophy and practice of education.

Edwards also expounded on his *via media* in his *Miscellanies*. In his apologetic against Matthew Tindal, he outlined the limitations of reason and experience as valid ways of knowing in and of themselves. He argued that it goes against common sense to claim that reason alone, without the aid of revelation, can be held up as authoritative truth. Reason cannot explain the metaphysical world, nor can it demystify how a physical being can display perception, understanding, thought, volition, love, hatred, etc. Also, human experience cannot be relied upon without the verifying testimony of history, tradition, memories, senses, or the corroboration of other people's experiences.

EDUCATIONAL THEORY INTO PRACTICE

A primary result of the revivalist movement was the salvation and spiritual renewal of the common people. A secondary result was the social reform carried out at the grassroots level by those same transformed people. Reformers were driven by their belief that, by bettering the condition of humanity, they would be ushering in a millennial reign of a utopian society that would precede the return of Christ. Many were convinced that America was the "New Jerusalem" and that they were God's chosen people to bring about this societal transformation.[48] Just as laypeople had become more active in the revivals by initiating prayer meetings, Bible studies, and exhortations, they also became more active in social reform.[49] One of those reforms was education for the common person. Jonathan Edwards advocated for common learning for the poor in his *Thoughts on the Revival*:

> Great things might be done for the advancement of the kingdom of Christ at this day by those who have ability by establishing funds for the support and propagation of religion . . . . by searching out children of promising abilities, and their hearts full of love to Christ, but of poor families (as doubtless there are such now in the land), and bringing them up for the ministry; and by distributing books that are remarkably fitted to promote vital religion and have a great tendency to advance this work. — Or if they would only bear the trouble and expense of sending such books into various parts of the land to be sold, it might be an occasion that ten times so many of

those books should be bought as otherwise would be — by establishing and supporting schools in poor towns and villages; which might be done on such a foundation as not only to bring up children in common learning but also might very much tend to their conviction and conversion and being trained up in vital piety. Doubtless something might be done this way in old towns and more populous places that might have a great tendency to the flourishing of religion in the rising generation.[50]

The quote above supports the argument that, more so than Horace Mann, the seeds planted in both the First and Second Great Awakenings deserve credit for being the impetus behind the common school movement that eventually led to free public schools for all children.

Edwards' interest in education was not strictly theoretical from the pen and the pulpit. He held strong convictions about the practice of teaching and implemented them in his role as tutor at Yale, in the home-schooling of his own children, in his parsonage school for future ministers, and in his Stockbridge mission school to the Indians. He decried the methods of instruction used by the English not just to the Indians but also to English children themselves. Edwards believed they focused far too much on the ability to sound out words rather than on the ideas represented by those words. Understanding was key, and to that end, he advocated for what he called a "familiar" method of teaching. He drew from the Socratic method of questioning and from John Locke's emphasis on the significance of personal experience in the learning process.[51]

In a letter to Sir William Pepperrell, a financial supporter of Stockbridge's Indian mission, Edwards wrote, "Children should never read a lesson without the master or mistress taking a care that the child be made to attend to, and understand, the meaning of the words and sentences which it reads." He believed this could be done through "familiar" questions presented conversationally and through an invitation for students to pose their own questions. This would lead to what he identified as the chief cognitive faculty—understanding. Without understanding, the student could not judge, discern, or speculate. His "familiar" method also featured story-telling, which Edwards began to implement not just in his classroom instruction at Stockbridge but also in his sermons to the Indian congregation.[52]

Edwards' school at Stockbridge was innovative for a number of reasons. He engaged the community in school activities by inviting the public to attend assemblies where students would share what they had learned in class and receive awards for their achievements.[53] He placed great emphasis on the affective aspect of teaching. Because emotions were critical to learning, he proposed that teachers should influence the heart of their students. He perceived students holistically with the mind, will, and heart interacting as one impacted the other. Students are motived by love; therefore, teachers should display sincere affection for them. Students are also motivated by pleasure; therefore, teachers should cultivate a classroom atmosphere that is "pleasant, entertaining, and profitable." Teachers should welcome new knowledge and model for students what it means to be a researcher and a life-long learner.[54] These concepts were not typical for schools in the eighteenth century, and—even today—these ideas would more likely be attributed to **Romantic** European thinkers, such as Jean-Jacque Rousseau, Johann Pestalozzi, and Friedrich Froebel, than to the preacher of *Sinners in the Hands of an Angry God*.

Also innovative for his time was the integrative, holistic aspect of his curriculum. He provided a rich context for the study of the Bible by immersing students in ecclesiastical history, chronology, and geography of the Middle East with the intent that students would grasp how individual incidents fit into the larger biblical narrative. He included both boys and girls and even mixed English and Indian students together. He integrated music into the curriculum for two reasons. First, he believed music engaged learners in the harmony and beauty of truth. Second, he perceived that music had the power "to change the taste of the Indians . . . off from their barbarism and brutality." This harsh language reflected common English notions of the Indians at the time.[55] Although Edwards saw great capacity for Indians to learn and complemented them as "discerning people," he was somewhat pessimistic about their culture overall. Unlike **John Eliot**, who had learned Indian languages and translated English works into native languages, Edwards worked through translators and required Indians to learn English because he judged their own languages as "ill-fitted for communicating things moral and divine, or even things speculative and abstract."[56] To immerse them into English culture, he encouraged Indian families to allow their children to live with an English family for a year. His own family hosted at least one Indian boy.[57]

Because of the significance of relationships in his philosophy of education, personal mentoring was a key aspect of Edwards' teaching. Through the years, he had mentored a number of future ministers as they lived with him and his family in what came to be known as a parsonage school. Joseph Bellamy and Samuel Hopkins are just two of those he mentored. Edwards began a tradition of parsonage-school mentoring that continued for generations and that led many in the **New Divinity** movement to be involved in higher education. A few of these protégés include his own son Jonathan Edwards, Jr., (Union); Timothy Dwight (Yale); Edward Dorr Griffin (Williams); Samuel Austin (Union of Vermont); Moses Stuart and Edwards Amasa Park (Andover); Nathaniel William Taylor (Yale); and Mary Lyons (Mt. Holyoke).[58] A great number of universities were impacted by men and women who were mentored by Jonathan Edwards.

© Everett Historical/Shutterstock.com

When asked to name an individual who impacted the development of education in America, people most readily name Horace Mann or John Dewey. These names are certainly afforded more ink in books on the history of education. It may well be argued, however, that Jonathan Edwards' philosophy of education was much more influential than Mann's or Dewey's. His synthesis of Enlightenment ideas with Calvinist theology provided a *via media* that served as a framework for curriculum in New England and early American schools. It may also be argued that the lifting up of common laypeople in the Great Awakening served as an impetus that eventually led to the nineteenth-century common school movement.

John Eliot (1604-1690), English Puritan missionary, known as the Apostle to the Indians

 Go to www.khlearn.com to watch a video about colonial North America.

Reflection

For personal reflection, content review, and further research:

1. In what way did philosophical ideas from Europe influence educational developments in the colonies?

2. What types of events dissuaded early attempts to develop schools in the colonies, and what do these examples convey about early colonial society's priorities?

3. Explore how the doctrine of the priesthood of all believers influenced New England ideas of mass education.

4. What philosophical beliefs of John Amos Comenius might have drawn John Winthrop, Jr., to consider him for the appointment to the presidency of Harvard College?

5. In what ways was the *New England Primer* instrumental in grounding colonial society in the Calvinist ethic?

6. Analyze revisions made to the *New England Primer* over time and how these revisions reflected changes within society.

7. Though he opposed some Enlightenment ideas, Jonathan Edwards rejected others. Which Enlightenment ideas did he reject, and which did he embrace?

8. Similar to how Augustine and Aquinas synthesized Christian thought with idealism and realism respectively, how did Jonathan Edwards synthesize Christianity with Enlightenment ideas?

9. Describe Edwards' main tenets in his philosophy of education. What implications might these beliefs hold for current-day education?

10. How did Isaac Newton and John Locke influence Jonathan Edwards?

11. In what ways did Indian culture inform Edwards' philosophy and practice regarding teaching and learning?

12. In Edwards' day, there was not so much a divide between upper story and lower story knowledge as Francis Schaeffer, Nancy Pearcey, and other Christian philosophers have noted. Edwards and others, like Isaac Newton, were comfortable pursuing both scientific and theological truths with no concern about a conflict between the two. Why do you think this difference exists between the Enlightenment era and current Western culture? Analyze what you perceive to be the shift that has caused the current divide.

13. Why did the Presbyterians found the College of New Jersey, which later became Princeton University? How were they hoping that it would be different from Harvard and Yale? What trends brought the changes in these universities and what lessons might current Christian universities learn from these changes?

14. Conflicts between Unitarianism and Calvinism were present both in Jonathan Edwards' lifetime and also during the common school movement of Horace Mann's day. Compare these two eras of conflict and the implications these conflicts had on education.

15. Compare the ideas of Plato, Augustine, Calvin, and Edwards. How did Edwards synthesize the ideas of the first three?

16. What key ideas of John Locke did Edwards embrace?

17. Discuss the concept *summum bonum*. What role did it play in Edwards' ethics and what implications does it have for character education in today's schools?

18. Compare your own philosophy of education to that of Jonathan Edwards. In what ways are your philosophies similar and different?

19. Compare the epistemological beliefs of Jonathan Edwards with those of Thomas Hobbes. Why did Edwards take such an opposing view?

20. Considering Edwards' epistemology, what are your own thoughts on the ultimate source of valid knowledge and truth? What roles do sensory experience, reason, authority, intuition, and revelation play?

21. A great deal of research has been done on emotional intelligence. How does this notion compare with concerns during the Great Awakening that Christian revivalism was becoming too emotionally driven? To what degree was the Great Awakening driven by emotion and by intellectual pursuits?

22. What was the difference between the Old Lights and the New Lights during the Great Awakening?

23. How was the notion of the importance of the common person during the Great Awakening incorporated into a philosophy of education that later influenced the common school movement?

24. To what degree is it important for educators to strike a balance between the dichotomies, such as Edwards' notions of head-heart, reason-emotion, thinking-feeling, sensual-spiritual, science-revelation, notional-sensible, and understanding-affections? Is there a need to be concerned when educators heavily emphasize one over the other? See Francis Schaeffer and Nancy Pearcey's explanation of lower story and upper story for thoughts to consider on this topic.

25. In what ways were some of Edwards' ideas similar to those of Romantic European thinkers, such as Jean-Jacque Rousseau, Johann Pestalozzi, and Friedrich Froebel?

26. Both Augustine and Edwards are known as masters of mentoring others. Compare how they mentored and what current educational leaders might gain by studying the mentoring practices of each.

27. What was Edwards' *via media* and what role did it play in his philosophy of education?

ENDNOTES

1. Lawrence A. Cremin, *American Education: The Colonial Experience* 1607-1783 (New York: Harper & Row, 1970), 176-80.
2. Ibid., 196-224
3. From *Encyclopedia of Educational Reform and Dissent* by Thomas C. Hunt. Copyright © 2010 by Sage Publications, Inc. Reprinted by permission.
4. Paul Leicester Ford, ed., *The New England Primer: A History of Its Origin and Development* (New York: Dodd, Mead and Co., 1897). Public Domain.
5. See Daniel A. Cohen, "The Origin and Development of the New England Primer," *Children's Literature* 5 (1976): 52-57; Patricia Crain, *The Story of A: The Alphabetization of America from the* New England Primer to The Scarlet Letter (Stanford, CA: Stanford University Press, 2000); Ford, ed., *The New England Primer: A History*; David H. Watters, "'I Spake as a Child': Authority, Metaphor and the New-England Primer," *Early American Literature* 20, no. 3 (1985): 193-213.
6. Benson John Lossing, *Jonathan Edwards*, print, New York Public Library Digital Collections, accessed December 20, 2019, http://digitalcollections.nypl.org/items/510d47db-11c9-a3d9-e040-e00a18064a99. Public Domain.
7. George M. Marsden, *Jonathan Edwards: A Life* (New Haven: Yale University Press, 2003), 2, 7-9.
8. William Edgar and K. Scott Oliphint, eds., *Christian Apologetics: Past & Present*, vol. 2. (Wheaton, IL: Crossway, 2009), 219.
9. Marsden, *Jonathan Edwards*, 19.
10. Ibid., 14-25.
11. Michael A. G. Haykin and Dustin Bruce, "Jonathan Edwards: Influencing and Shaping the Heart," in *A Legacy of Religious Educators: Historical and Theological Introductions*, ed. Elmer L. Towns and Benjamin K. Forrest (Lynchburg, VA: Liberty University Press, 2017), 18, 254.
12. Lockerbie, *A Passion for Learning*, 223.
13. Marsden, *Jonathan Edwards*, 37-9.
14. Ibid., 45, 51-3.
15. Haykin and Bruce, "Jonathan Edwards," 254-5.
16. Ibid., 256.
17. Lockerbie, *A Passion for Learning*, 223.
18. Marsden, Jonathan Edwards, 321-3.
19. See Edgar and Oliphint, *Christian Apologetics*, 219; Marsden, Jonathan Edwards, 323, 386-7.
20. Edgar and Oliphint, *Christian Apologetics*, 219.
21. Haykin and Bruce, "Jonathan Edwards," 256.
22. Edgar and Oliphint, *Christian Apologetics*, 220.
23. Marsden, *Jonathan Edwards*, 59-71.
24. Jonathan Edwards, "The 'Miscellanies': Number 1340," in *Christian Apologetics: Past & Present*, vol. 1, ed. William Edgar and K. Scott Oliphint (Wheaton, IL: Crossway, 2009), 225-38.
25. Marsden, *Jonathan Edwards*, 59-61.
26. Alan Heimert, *Religion and the American Mind: From the Great Awakening to the Revolution* (Cambridge: Harvard University Press, 1966), 184.
27. Lockerbie, *A Passion for Learning*, 225.
28. Heimert, *Religion*, 190.
29. Edgar and Oliphint, *Christian Apologetics*, 220.
30. Marsden, *Jonathan Edwards*, 63-4.
31. George P. Fisher, "The Philosophy of Jonathan Edwards," *The North American Review* 128, no. 268 (1879): 285-6.
32. Ibid., 288-90.
33. Tim Keller, *The Reason for God: Belief in an Age of Skepticism* (New York: Riverhead Books, 2008), 174-5.
34. Marsden, *Jonathan Edwards*, 464.
35. Ibid., 497, 503.
36. Ibid., 76-81.
37. Ibid.
38. Jonathan Edwards, "Jonathan Edwards Describes the Awakening in His Congregation in Northampton, Massachusetts, 1737," in *Major Problems in American Colonial History*, 3rd ed., ed. Karen Ordahl Kupperman (Boston: Wadsworth, 2013), 272.
39. Sarah Pierrepont Edwards, "Sarah Pierrepont Edwards Recounts Her Religious Experience, 1742," in *Major Problems in American Colonial History*, 3rd ed., ed. Karen Ordahl Kupperman (Boston: Wadsworth, 2013), 273.
40. Vishal Mangalwadi, *The Book That Made Your World: How the Bible Created the Soul of Western Civilization* (Nashville: Thomas Nelson, 2011), 88-9.

41. Alan Taylor, *American Colonies: The Settling of North America*, ed. Eric Foner (New York: Penguin Books, 2001), 352.
42. See Cremin, *American Education*, 318; Pearcey, Total Truth, 269.
43. Taylor, *American Colonies*, 351.
44. Pearcey, *Total Truth*, 269.
45. Lockerbie, *A Passion for Learning*, 224.
46. Haykin and Bruce, "Jonathan Edwards," 262-4.
47. Jonathan Edwards, *Religious Affections* (Mineola, NY: Dover Publications, 2013), 49-50.
48. Thomas W. Hagedorn, *Founding Zealots: How Evangelicals Created America's First Public Schools, 1783-1865* (Maitland, FL: Xulon Press, 2013), 85-71.
49. Mark A. Noll, *A History of Christianity in the United States and Canada* (Grand Rapids: William B. Eerdmans Publishing Company, 1992), 103.
50. Jonathan Edwards, *Thoughts on the Revival of Religion in New England, 1740; To Which Is Prefixed, A Narrative of the Surprising Work of God in Northampton, Mass., 1735* (New York: American Tract Society, 1800), 225-6.
51. Kenneth P. Minkema, "Jonathan Edwards on Education and His Educational Legacy," Oxford Scholarship Online (2017): 32, doi:10.1093/acprof:oso/9780199756292.003.0003.
52. Ibid., 33.
53. Marsden, *Jonathan Edwards*, 390.
54. Haykin and Bruce, "Jonathan Edwards," 267, 271-2.
55. Minkema, "Jonathan Edwards," 34.
56. See Haykin and Bruce, "Jonathan Edwards," 268-9; Marsden, Jonathan Edwards, 390.
57. Marsden, *Jonathan Edwards*, 390.
58. Minkema, "Jonathan Edwards," 39-40, 49-50.

CHAPTER 9

REVOLUTIONARY IDEAS

Benjamin Franklin's warning to the British colonies in America (ca. 1754)

© Everett Historical/Shutterstock.com

FOCUS: KEY TOPICS AND TERMS

Adams, John
College of William and Mary
Declaration of
    Independence
Deist
Dickinson College
Èmile
Enlightenment
Franklin, Benjamin

Jefferson, Thomas
Locke, John
Madison, James
Meritocracy
Murray, Judith Sargent
Paine, Thomas
Pestalozzi, Johann Heinrich
Praxis
Republicanism

Rush, Benjamin
Scottish Common Sense
    Realism
Second Great Awakening
Sensory experience
Tabula Rasa
Universalist Church
University of Virginia
Wollstonecraft, Mary

In order for thirteen diverse colonies to unite in the effort for independence from Britain, there must have been forces for unity present among them. Such a force might have been their sense of oppression from taxes, from dissolution of their legislative bodies, and from the British standing army. As common an enemy as the perceived tyranny might have been, without an ideology that could coexist among a variety of colonial influences, the unity needed to achieve independence might not have been realized. In "The Bible and the Political Culture of the American Founding," historian Daniel L. Dreisbach argues that what united the colonists did not emerge primarily from Enlightenment thought. Yes, Locke and others made a great impact, but there was something much more pervasive and unifying. That something was a biblical influence throughout the colonies.

Though Dreisbach has been disappointed in past historians' neglect to write about the Bible's influence on America's founders, he is encouraged that researchers are increasingly giving the topic more serious consideration. After presenting ample evidence of a number of founders whose writings, speeches, and actions reflect strong biblical influence, Dreisbach concedes that the sparse attention historians have given the Bible's influence may be because of its ubiquity; the biblical metanarrative was pervasive during the era of the American Revolution. Yet, as Dreisbach indicates, philosophical thought among colonists in America was far from monolithic: "Biblical influences coexisted with other—even seemingly competing—influences, such as Enlightenment, republican, and English constitutional and common law sources."[1] This coexistence reflects the universality and the cohesion of God's Truth and how relevant it is to the human experience.

An illustration of this coexistence may be witnessed in the Great Awakening preacher Jonathan Edwards. Though a student of John Locke's work and greatly influenced by Enlightenment thought and by the Scientific Revolution, Edwards held firmly to his biblical convictions without compromise. For example, when he joined forces with Gilbert Tennent and others to found the College of New Jersey, Edwards made clear his strong support of the science curriculum while simultaneously insisting that theology be preeminent.[2] Its original purpose being primarily to prepare ministers, the college was later named Princeton and educated more leaders of early America than any other university. Its graduates included signers of the Declaration of Independence, such as Richard Stockton and Benjamin Rush, and its sixth president from 1768 to 1794 was John Witherspoon, who also signed the Declaration.[3]

In addition to the Enlightenment and Scientific Revolution, other coexisting influences were republicanism and **Scottish Common Sense Realism**. It was republicanism that united Enlightenment thinkers, deists, and liberal theologians with orthodox Christians for a common cause. Examples of this may be found in Thomas Paine's biblical imagery and Calvinist preachers' republican-sounding sermons. The influence of Scottish Common Sense Realism is evidenced by the statement "We hold these truths to be self-evident" in the Declaration of Independence and in the title of Paine's *Common Sense*. Scottish Common Sense Realism has been called the Evangelical Enlightenment and was most prominent among Presbyterian and Congregational ministers who were leaders in the nation's first colleges.[4]

Unity was important not only for achieving independence but also for sustaining the new nation. To this end, common education was called for by Thomas Jefferson, Benjamin Franklin, and others. If the masses were educated, **Benjamin Rush** asserted, citizens would be "turned into republican machines," which would ensure sustenance and prosperity.[5] In a letter to Boston's Reverend Jeremy Belknap, Rush revealed that, along with propagating republicanism, he was also concerned with cultivating the Gospel in America's schools. With the following five propositions, he defended the use of the Bible as a textbook: (1) people will be happier and wiser the more they adopt Christian principles; (2) acquisition of these principles is best accomplished by reading the Bible; (3) more than any other book, the Bible contains necessary information for humanity; (4) if learned early in life, such knowledge is more likely to be applied throughout the span of one's life; and (5) if children do not study the Bible in school, they will not likely read it thereafter.[6]

The rhetoric and actions of Benjamin Rush exemplify how biblical influences coexisted with so many diverse influences. Rush was a respected renaissance man who served as an officer of the Bible Society of Philadelphia, a medical doctor who wrote theological discourses, and an Enlightenment thinker who fought to ensure the Bible was maintained as a school textbook. Rush was not alone, other founders also illustrate the coexisting influences of the Founding era: Thomas Jefferson's admiration of the morality of Christ, Benjamin Franklin's relationship with George Whitfield, and Thomas Paine's biblical imagery— all of these and more support Dreisbach's argument that the Bible was extremely influential in the thoughts and actions of America's founders.

Source: Library of Congress

Benjamin Rush (1746-1813)[7]

 ## Benjamin Rush and His Revolutionary Proposal

Benjamin Rush was a signer of the Declaration of Independence, surgeon general of the Continental Army, social activist, and an educational theorist. Like Thomas Jefferson, he proposed a plan for free public education that was rejected at the time, but his ideas were foundational to American educational theory. Rush's philosophy of education was influenced by republican political theory, Scottish Common Sense Realism, the Enlightenment, and Christianity. Though some have criticized him for pointing America's schools toward secularization and for presenting inconsistencies in his thoughts, Rush was revolutionary in his proposal to educate African Americans and women and in the groundwork he laid for developments in American schools.

As a physician, Benjamin Rush was criticized for stubbornly upholding the questionable practice of bleeding his patients. As an educational theorist, he has been criticized for leading American education toward secularism and for presenting inconsistent, erratic thoughts. Though certainly not as prominent in the history of education as are **Thomas Jefferson** and **Benjamin Franklin**, Rush is worthy of study, especially for those interested in understanding more about the early synthesis of ideas that merged eventually to form a uniquely American philosophy of education. Though some inconsistencies indeed exist in his ideas, Benjamin Rush's educational theory and practice contributed to a foundation on which later educational leaders built as they developed the mid-nineteenth century common school movement.

PHILOSOPHICAL INFLUENCES

The dialectic of thesis, antithesis, and synthesis can be a messy process—as is epitomized by the American Revolution. The synthesis of philosophical ideas can also be messy but can result in revolutionary applications of theory. Such is the case in the philosophies that converged to influence Benjamin Rush's philosophy of education.

Statue of Founder of University of Pennsylvania, Benjamin Franklin, at College Hall

REPUBLICANISM. The war may have ended, but for Rush the revolution had only just begun. His was a revolution of developing people and reforming American culture to reflect the republicanism that the founders had envisioned. As a signer of the Declaration of Independence and as surgeon general of the Continental Army, Rush had legitimately played a meaningful role in the revolutionary effort. With America's form of government changed, the "first act of the great drama"—as Rush put it—was over. What remained to be fought was a "revolution in principles, opinions, and manners."[8] In this second act, Rush was determined to play a role in propagating republican ideology through education.

After independence, schools in various states continued on as they had beforehand, but Rush had two concerns about them: (1) they were structurally weak, and (2) they were unprepared to cultivate republican principles. If the new republic was to be sustained, an infrastructure of schools was needed. According to Rush and other educational theorists—such as Thomas Jefferson, Benjamin Franklin, Robert Coram, and Samuel Harrison Smith—the educational system should reflect the scientific emphasis of the **Enlightenment**, instill civic knowledge for participation in government, and assist in building a unique culture.[9] During the Revolutionary era, **republicanism** had united Enlightenment thinkers (e.g., Jefferson and Franklin) with orthodox Christians (e.g., John Witherspoon and Patrick Henry). Both groups could rally behind the classical notion that citizens of a republic should be educated to be virtuous, so—just as it had united Christians and deists during the Revolution—republicanism would now unite them in developing an educational system.[10] Rush believed that education, if properly designed and implemented, would "convert men into republican machines" that would sustain the nation and result in great prosperity.[11]

His proposed curriculum that would create these "republican machines" would include the study of eloquence, history, chronology, chemistry, commerce, and the "nature and principles of money." Rush considered the study of commerce and money usage to be a guard against entails and aristocracy.[12] The practice of entails, which Jefferson successfully fought to end in Virginia with his 1776 *Bill for the Abolition of Entails*, involved policies passed down from English common law. Entails, also known as fee tails, ensured land would be held within the same family in perpetuity. For Rush, it was important that school curriculum teach how such policies built aristocracies, which would threaten a republican government.

Fittingly called "the conscience of the American Revolution," Rush maintained that an imperative of a republic is to educate its citizenry in a manner consistent with its form of government. Doing so creates a reciprocal relationship between individuals and society. As individuals are educated to be virtuous and industrious, they interact with society in ways that strengthen virtue in the political sphere. In turn, the government promotes goodness in its citizenry. To illustrate this principle, Rush described his observations of local Indian tribes. Before they were educated, Rush observed, individual Indians were unhappy and immoral. Their actions, therefore, contributed negatively to their tribal community. This was due to "the want of action in their brains from a deficiency of ideas." Once tribal members began a program of educational study, both their individual and collective virtue increased and contributed one to the other.[13]

Rush saw a strong correlation between education and liberty. In his essay "Education Agreeable to a Republican Form of Government," he wrote, "[Learning] is favourable to liberty. Freedom can exist only in the society of knowledge. Without learning, men are incapable of knowing their rights, and where learning is confined to a few people, liberty can be neither equal nor universal."[14] Education was more than just an important facet of a republican government. It was foundational, especially considering that the nation was founded upon ideas and principles that would not be propagated unless they were systematically taught to future generations. In his essay entitled "Of the Mode of Education Proper in a Republic," Rush wrote, "Our schools of learning, by producing one general and uniform system of education, will render the mass of people more homogeneous, and thereby fit them more easily for uniform and peaceable government."[15] Such an education would cultivate patriotism and nationalism.

Regarding property and economics, Rush wanted children to be taught that they had an obligation to their country above their personal interests of self and family and that they themselves were "public property." They were to avoid both extreme wealth and poverty. Wealth, however, would be appropriate only if it were used to advance a public cause.[16] He wrote in his proposal for Pennsylvania schools,

> Next to the duty which young men owe to their Creator, I wish to see a supreme regard to their country, inculcated upon them. . . . Let our pupil be taught that he does not belong to himself, but that he is public property. Let him be taught to love his family, but let him be taught, at the same time, that he must forsake and even forget them, when the welfare of his country requires it. . . . While we inculcate these republican duties upon our pupil, we must not neglect, at the same time, to inspire him with republican principles.[17]

Though this may seem like political indoctrination, Rush believed it was necessary for the good of the country.

Philosophically, Rush's proposed education would merge Enlightenment thought with republicanism, which he envisioned would encourage a scientific, progressive approach to society. Not unique to Rush, the intent of using education for the purpose of building the new nation and of promoting progress was shared by other educational theorists at the time—most notably Thomas Jefferson. They, along with Franklin, Coram, and Smith, sought to make education a tool of republicanism for political purposes. For this reason, some historians charge these republican theorists with leading American education toward secularization. Though none of their proposals were adopted directly as law, they provided the theoretical framework for what would eventually develop into an American approach to common education.[18]

SCOTTISH COMMON SENSE REALISM. Epistemologically, Rush aligned himself with **John Locke's** theory that knowledge is acquired primarily through **sensory experience**—a notion that ran contrary to typical classroom instruction of the time. Knowledge had been passed down from an authority who required students to display their learning through rote memory, drill, catechisms, and recitations. Rush believed these practices failed to reflect the spirit of republicanism, of the Enlightenment, and also of Scottish Common Sense Realism. It was the influence of Scottish Realism that led Rush to believe that, just as people were endowed with certain unalienable rights, they were likewise endowed with certain faculties of the mind. These faculties provided a framework for learners to reflect and to act upon the environment, while at the same time, the environment may act upon the faculties of the mind to change them. The Scottish element of Rush's epistemology tempered Locke's *tabula rasa*, which had given greater sway for the environment to etch on the learner's "blank slate." In the Scottish model, learners did the etching on the environment to create a transformed future for themselves.[19]

The influence of Scottish Common Sense Realism is illustrated by the statement in the Declaration of Independence "We hold these truths to be self-evident" and by the title of **Thomas Paine**'s pamphlet *Common Sense*, which would have been *Plain Truth* had Rush not convinced Paine to change the name.[20] Expressions of Scottish Realism may also be seen in revivalist camp meetings, voluntary associations, and college curriculum. Its impact was most influential in Presbyterian and Congregational Churches.[21]

Often called the "Father of American Psychiatry," Rush addressed both the moral faculty and the faculty of intelligence. He believed that the moral faculty was a natural part of the mind and that it was capable of intuitively knowing good from evil. Faculties could develop separately from each other, so it would be possible for someone with a highly developed intelligence to be morally corrupt and for a morally upright person to be a "benevolent idiot." Because the various faculties could develop independently one from the other, Rush encouraged a curriculum that intentionally targeted the faculty of intelligence through strong academics and the faculty of morality through religious doctrine and instruction in virtue.[22]

Thomas Paine (1737-1809) on U.S. Stamp (ca. 1969)

© Olga Popova/Shutterstock.com

ENLIGHTENMENT THOUGHT. The interplay of Scottish Common Sense Realism, republicanism, and Enlightenment thought was evident in the proposals for American education by Rush, Jefferson, and others. Their plans were practical blueprints with details on organization, funding, and curriculum; yet, the intentional connection was evident between theory and practice. While Rush proposed an unapologetic indoctrination of republican principles, he balanced this with an open-mindedness to encourage experimental progress. Thought was not to be disconnected from action in Rush's educational proposals.[23] After all, it was under such a prevailing attitude that the Revolution was birthed.

Today, the term ***praxis*** is used in educational literature to express this theory-to-practice principle. The theme of praxis has been explored by ancient philosophers Plato and Aristotle, by Christian theologians Augustine and Kierkegaard, and by educational theorist Paulo Freire and other proponents of critical pedagogy. Since the mid-twentieth century, the concept has often been associated with Marxist theory. Though praxis rejects notions of indoctrination, its proponents struggle with accusations that they indeed are indoctrinating principles that are foundational to their cause. In Rush's case, he acknowledged the need to indoctrinate republican principles. This type of acknowledgment is not as common among recent proponents of praxis, who generally deny that they are indoctrinating any ideology other than open-mindedness and free thinking.

Was Rush's Enlightenment approach moving American education toward secularization? Not all agree. Christian historian Thomas W. Hagedorn, for example, rejects the notion that it was the ideas of early founders that eventually brought about secularized education in the United States. Hagedorn also rejects Horace Mann as the assumed "Father of American Public Education," and—in his book *Founding Zealots: How Evangelicals Created America's First Public Schools, 1783-1865*—he argues that the development of public school systems was influenced more by reform movements motivated by a revival of Christian thought. He lists a number of "founding zealots." Among them, however, was not Benjamin Rush. Rather than accuse Rush of promoting secularization in education, Hagedorn simply dismisses Rush's influence. Rush, Jefferson, and Franklin—according to Hagedorn—followed an educational philosophy grounded in the Enlightenment; they "rejected society's traditional reliance on Faith in favor of a progressive trust in Reason." In turn, society rejected their "unorthodox concepts," replacing them eventually with the more biblical philosophy stimulated by the **Second Great Awakening**. Hagedorn considers Jefferson and Franklin's secularism to be outside the mainstream of the Revolutionary era and claimed that "the erratic turns of Rush's thinking made him impossible to follow."[24] Hagedorn is ambiguous as to what Rush's "erratic turns" might have been. Were they contradictions in Rush's claims to open-minded enlightenment while unapologetically indoctrinating republican principles? Was it erratic for Rush to claim the Bible as the most important textbook while seeming to welcome any religious teaching as long as it taught the character of God and an eternity of rewards and punishments? Or was he erratic for changing his mind about the value of mass higher education? Might Hagedorn be troubled by Rush's proposal for a single federal university through which every holder of national office would be required to attend? Hagedorn might also be concerned about how Rush proposed that education be funded—partially by the church and partially by the government. Whatever may have caused Hagedorn to identify Rush's thinking as "erratic," his conclusion is clear that Rush was not among those he considers to be "founding zealots."

Another Christian author to consider is David Barton. Though not an academician or an established historical researcher, Barton founded Wallbuilders, which is "an organization dedicated to presenting America's forgotten history and heroes." Barton's books, videos, television appearances, and social activism have influenced the historical perspectives of many evangelicals. Though Barton's work clearly attacks the secularization of American schools, Rush is not one of his suspects for bringing this about. Barton does not critically evaluate Rush, nor does he address any inconsistencies or "erratic turns" in Rush's thinking. To the contrary, Barton celebrates Rush as "The Father of Public Schools under the Constitution" and applauds him as one who staunchly upheld a biblical philosophy of education that progressives later corrupted.[25] The contrast between the views of Hagedorn and Barton is worthy of consideration, especially in light of Rush's emphasis on the Bible as a textbook and on the role of the church in his proposal for universal education.

CHRISTIAN THOUGHT. After observing schools in a Pennsylvania German community, Rush expressed his admiration of their commitment to teaching Christian principles. He wrote,

> All the different sects among them are particularly attentive to the religious education of their children. . . . They settle as much as possible together and make the erection of a school house

and a place of worship the first objective of their care. They commit the education and instruction of their children in a peculiar manner to the ministers and officers of their churches: hence they grow up with biases in favor of public worship and the obligation of Christianity.[26]

In *A Plan for the Establishment of Public Schools and the Diffusion of Knowledge in Pennsylvania* (1786), Rush declared virtue as a necessary condition for liberty. There could, however, be no virtue without an education built on the foundation of religion.

> Such is my veneration for every religion that reveals the attributes of the Deity or a future state of rewards and punishments, that I had rather see the opinions of Confucius or Mahomed inculcated upon our youth, than see them grow up wholly devoid of a system of religious principles.[27]

These sentiments might have concerned some evangelicals and might also illustrate the "erratic turn" that troubled Hagedorn. Rush, however, followed with this clarification: "But the religion I mean to recommend in this place, is the religion of Jesus Christ."[28]

He then went on to suggest a fundamental relationship between Christianity and republicanism. While it may be possible to be a republican and not a Christian, Rush reiterated his conviction that it may be impossible to be a Christian and not a republican: "A Christian cannot fail of being a republican."[29] He expounded on this by explaining how the Bible refutes the concept of the divine right of kings and supports the notion that all mankind are created equal. Although Rush refused to recommend one Christian denomination over another, he did embrace sectarian education according to the preference of the parents, and he argued for the Bible to continue to be used as a textbook. No other book in the world, Rush claimed, came close to the Bible in the amount of practical knowledge for individuals and for governments. Though his Enlightenment sensibilities valued other sources of knowledge, Rush cautioned against preferring other textbooks over the Bible.

Addressed in a letter to Reverend Jeremy Belknap, Rush's "A Defence of the Use of the Bible as a School Book" presents a variety of reasons why the Bible should serve at the core of the American school curriculum. The letter reads very much like an educational policy paper, opening with proposals arguing that, as the only true religion, the more Christianity is adopted in its principles, the happier and wiser people will be. Because reading the Bible is the best way to acquire its principles, it should be studied in schools. If it is not read in schools, the Bible will less likely be read by students once they become adults. Rush concluded the letter with a strong admonition of what the result might be if the Bible were ever removed from the curriculum. For instance, more effort would be required to enforce and punish crimes. He reiterated that, more so than any other book, the Bible upholds the key principle of the **Declaration of Independence**—that all men are created equal. Rush makes the bold claim that the "only means" of ensuring the propagation of republicanism in the fledgling nation is "universal education of our youth in the principles of christianity, by means of the bible."[30] Some of Rush's arguments, particularly those related to crime and punishment, foreshadow the rationale for common schools as presented later by Horace Mann.

Contrary to the disdain Hagedorn conveys for Rush, historian Daniel L. Dreisbach holds Rush in high regard. Dreisbach describes him as a "respected polymath," reflecting what other authors have observed as Rush's wide variety of interests in a number of intellectual topics and social issues. He also notes that Rush served as the first vice president of the Bible Society of Philadelphia, which was the first society of its kind in America. Dreisbach also lists Rush among those founders who were known for their writings in Christian theology and doctrine. To illustrate how Rush incorporated such topics in personal correspondence, Dreisbach cites a letter from **John Adams** to Rush in which Adams described the Bible as "the most republican book in the world."[31] So while some historians label Rush as one who led American education away from its Christian philosophy of education, Dreisbach and Barton hold him up as an example of a defender of biblical principles being taught in the school curriculum.

BENJAMIN RUSH AND THOMAS JEFFERSON COMPARED

Since it is often noted that Jefferson was a **deist** and founder of the University of Virginia, the first secular university in America, it may be helpful to compare the educational proposals of Jefferson with those of Rush. Doing so may bring clarity and context regarding the criticisms of Rush.

There are indeed commonalities between the two men. As noted above, both held Enlightenment sensibilities, valuing scientific progress as a vital element in the new republic. They agreed that educational reform was needed to develop a system more conducive to post-Revolutionary America. Both Rush and Jefferson promoted government-supported public education, and both developed detailed plans for educational systems in their respective states of Pennsylvania and Virginia. Although neither of their proposals for public elementary and secondary schools were adopted or directly implemented, both men influenced a vision for an American philosophy of education.[32] Still standing today are tributes to the contribution both men made to higher education—Jefferson's **University of Virginia** and Rush's **Dickinson College** in Carlisle, Pennsylvania.

There were also noteworthy differences between the two. Though both men embraced republicanism, they disagreed on the role politics should play in the public classroom. While Rush proposed to indoctrinate students unapologetically with republican principles, Jefferson believed that schools should focus more on providing citizens with basic literacy so that they would then be empowered to reason through their own political beliefs. For Jefferson, the reading of newspapers was one of the most important means of developing political reasoning.[33]

Regarding the role of religion in public schools, Rush proposed a partnership between church denominations and the government. Because schools would be free to teach sectarian doctrines, they would in actuality be religious schools partially supported by the state government. Parents would enroll their children in denominational schools of their choice. Rush saw no harm in the government promoting sectarian schools. Any disadvantage of promoting sectarian beliefs would be outweighed by the benefit of teaching children values that religious groups held in common. Jefferson, on the other hand, believed that government-sponsored schools should be nonsectarian and should be disassociated from church denominations.[34]

Obviously, because of the partnership he encouraged between religious denominations and the state government, Rush's plan for funding schools was in contradiction with Jefferson's. Combining private and public interests, Rush proposed that private groups of citizens would initially raise funds to establish a school. In essence, these private groups would be local churches or denominations. Once sufficient private funds were solicited and an acceptable plan was drawn for the school, the group would be eligible to apply for a state charter to receive public funds to subsidize the school budget. Rush did not perceive this as an establishment of religion because of the freedom of any group to apply for a charter and because of the ability of parents to enroll their children in the school of their choice.[35]

Rush departed from Jefferson in the question of who should be served by public education. Though Jefferson penned the phrase "all men are created equal" and though he proposed ending the slave trade and gradually emancipating slaves, he owned slaves, believed—once emancipated—they could not peaceably live in an integrated society with Whites, and did not propose that slaves or freed Black people be served in his educational plan for public schools in Virginia. Rush, being an outspoken abolitionist, strongly believed in the need for African Americans to be educated. He wrote, "Let the young negroes be educated in the principles of virtue and religion—let them be taught to read and write—and afterwards instructed in some business whereby they may be able to maintain themselves."[36]

The extent to which females should be educated was quite limited under Jefferson. He believed that women should be capable of providing basic education to their daughters, and—in the case of an absent father—they should also be prepared to teach their sons. Rush, however, was more far-reaching than Jefferson when it came to the education of females.

FEMALE EDUCATION

"Thoughts upon Female Education" was initially presented as a speech in July 1787 to the Board of Visitors of the Young Ladies' Academy at Pennsylvania. In addition to addressing specific issues of female education, Rush revealed aspects of his overall philosophy of education for all students. He believed that women would play a more crucial role in this new nation than they had in any other nation throughout history. Though his statements may not seem groundbreaking by today's standards, they were very progressive at the time he voiced them. Early in his address, Rush proclaimed that the education of women in the United States should be starkly different from what it had been in Great Britain. He went on to outline unique circumstances in the new nation that made the education of women a practical necessity. One factor was the early marriage of women, which shortened the window of opportunity for education at an early age. Other factors dealt with how women were more involved with property in America than in Europe and how—because servants in America were less skilled in private family affairs than those in Europe—American women needed to be educated in family business matters. In describing the curriculum most appropriate for a female education, Rush outlined the importance of literature, grammar, penmanship, and—in order "to be an agreeable companion for a sensible man"—geography, history, biography, and travels. Also, to prevent superstition, women should study natural philosophy.[37]

Rush was in tune to the prejudices some men held that caused them to oppose the education of females, but he rejected those positions and presented two arguments against them. First, he called their opposition "the prejudice of little minds" and said that it was rooted in "the same spirit which opposes the general diffusion of knowledge among the citizens of our republics."[38] His second argument was that strong, educated women would be easier to govern than weak, ignorant ones. Though certainly ahead of his time in promoting education for women, Rush's second argument exposed his own acceptance of some prevailing views of women at the time.

It was revolutionary to propose education for African Americans and females as Rush did in the late eighteenth century. It was also revolutionary to propose free schools funded by the government. To arrive at these and other transformational ideas required the synthesis of philosophical influences into a newly articulated theory. Rush accomplished this by integrating republicanism, Scottish Common Sense Realism, Enlightenment thought, and Christianity. Were some of his ideas inconsistent? And might he have pointed American education to some degree in the direction of secularism? Possibly so, but Benjamin Rush's influence helped to put American education on a trajectory that led to the common school movement of the mid-nineteenth century.

Thomas Jefferson: Educational Reformer

Thomas Jefferson's philosophy of education held something in common with the philosophies of Confucius and Plato. They all three believed that it should be the intelligentsia that leads the government. Plato wrote of philosopher kings, and Confucius taught of the wise sage who should be trained in morality. Jefferson agreed with these concepts but added the notion of **meritocracy**, the idea that anyone from any station in life should be able to rise to leadership through hard work and study. In order to ac-

Thomas Jefferson, third President of the United States

© Everett Historical/Shutterstock.com

complish this, Jefferson realized the need for free education available to the citizenry. It is important to note here that he neglected to include a large portion of the population, particularly those in slavery.

On his tombstone, Jefferson indicated prior to his death that he wanted to be acknowledged for three specific accomplishments. Thus, his relatively modest-sized, obelisk-shaped tombstone in the small cemetery of his plantation home in Monticello, Virginia, simply reads,

Here was Buried
Thomas Jefferson
Author of the
Declaration
of
American Independence
of the
Statute of Virginia
for
Religious Freedom
and Father of the
University of Virginia

There is no mention of his having served as the second governor of the Commonwealth of Virginia, the United States Minister to France, Secretary of State, Vice President under John Adams, or the nation's third President.

© Daniel M. Silva/Shutterstock.com

An accomplishment of interest to historians of education was Jefferson's Bill for the More General Diffusion of Knowledge, which he presented to the Virginia House of Delegates. The bill proposed for the Commonwealth to be divided into wards and that each ward would be provided an elementary school. All children of citizens, which excluded African Americans, would be permitted to attend elementary school at no cost for the first three years. This included both boys and girls, which was a radical proposal for that time. After the first three years, girls would no longer be permitted to attend, but boys could continue if parents paid the required tuition. The proposed curriculum would cover basic reading, writing, arithmetic, and history. The purpose of schools would be to prepare informed citizens to vote for government leaders who would effectively represent their interests, beliefs, and values.

The elementary schools proposed in Jefferson's bill would feed into a limited number of secondary grammar schools located throughout the Commonwealth. One boy would be selected from each elementary school to attend on scholarship. This would provide three additional years of education to these select students. Other qualified students would be welcome to attend on a tuition basis. The secondary curriculum would comprise Latin, Greek, English, geography, and higher mathematics. Upon graduation, half of the scholarship students would return to the elementary schools as teachers and the others would advance to the College of William and Mary where their scholarship status would continue.

Not having been passed when he initially presented it in 1778, the bill was presented again in 1780 and was once more rejected. Later, while Jefferson was residing in Paris as Minister to France, **James Madison** presented the bill multiple times to the House where it was rejected each time. Finally, in 1796, a much weaker version of the bill was passed that did not accomplish the centralized educational system with strong state government oversight that Jefferson envisioned. Prior to the common school movement of the mid-nineteenth century, most Americans perceived education to be in the purview of families, churches, and local communities. They supported the expansion of private education, but suspicion of a centralized political power was still strong as wounds from the Revolution remained fresh in the collective American mind. They were not yet ready for an educational system whereby state or federal government would control the curriculum and instruction offered to their children.

Although Jefferson believed in limited government, he felt so strongly about the role of government in free education that he wrote to James Madison, "[Providing free education] is the most certain, and the most legitimate engine of government." Expressing his disappointment in the bill's rejection, Jefferson wrote to John Adams, "Had [the bill] been adopted by the legislature, our work would have been complete." He had been attempting educational reform from the bottom up, beginning with elementary school reforms and then on to secondary and higher education. Since that had failed, he redirected his efforts to the reform of higher education and to work from the top down.

Jefferson proposed that his *alma mater*, the **College of William and Mary**, a private school, be placed under the auspices of Virginia's General Assembly. He also suggested that the academic structure be reorganized. Traditionally, the faculty had been organized into two major fields. Professors were categorized as belonging either to the faculty of grammar or to the faculty of divinity. Jefferson's restructuring would eliminate these two categories and would create department chairs of medicine, law, and modern languages. Traditionalists rejected the proposal.

It would not be until more than three decades later—after Jefferson had served as Secretary of State, Vice President, and President—that he would return to his passion for reforming higher education. He researched Oxford and Cambridge, observing that their curriculum was more focused on the preservation and transmission of knowledge and on the teaching of ancient language and literature. He imagined a different kind of university for America, one that would underscore science. His image of a university was that of an engine, fueled by academic freedom, to generate a progression of knowledge.

Jefferson also researched New England universities, concluding that his planned institution would not be rooted in denominationalism as were Harvard and Yale, founded by Congregationalists and Presbyterians respectively. Instead, he strove for a university that would be state established, publicly supported, and publicly controlled. This time, Jefferson's proposal was met with better success. In 1816, the Virginia legislature approved Central College and in 1818 a commission selected Charlottesville as its location. Later renamed the University of Virginia, the school is known for initiating a new model for higher education that encouraged academic freedom without any denominational affiliation and without a department of theology. "This institution," Jefferson wrote in 1820, "will be based on the illimitable freedom of the human mind. For here we are not afraid to follow truth wherever it may lead, nor to tolerate any error so long as reason is left free to combat it."

A group of thirty students enrolled at the University of Virginia in 1825. Just over a year later, on July 4, 1826—the fiftieth anniversary of the Declaration of Independence—Jefferson died. As he had requested, the third accomplishment noted on his tombstone was that he was Father of the University of Virginia. Having declared as one of his life's goals to lay "the axe to the root of Pseudo-aristocracy," Jefferson succeeded in large part through his political and educational reforms, and even though his proposals for elementary and secondary schools were not approved, his ideas helped to lay the groundwork for the forthcoming common school movement.[39]

Judith Sargent Murray: A Revolutionary Woman

Judith Sargent Murray (1751-1820) was an influential woman of the Revolutionary era. Her name may not be as recognizable as is Betsy Ross or Abigail Adams, but since the discovery of her personal papers in 1984 and their publication in 1996, researchers continue to learn more about this prominent woman. Judith helped change what it meant to be a "learned lady." In her day, the term held somewhat of a negative connotation, but she helped change that perception.

Judith Sargent was born in Gloucester, Massachusetts, where her family was involved in trade with England and the West Indies. As a child, she observed her brother being tutored in preparation for Harvard College. She would listen in on his lessons, but she was mostly self-educated by reading books in her family library.

Judith Sargent Murray: educator, author, playwright, and political activist[40]

© The Picture Art Collection/Alamy Stock Photo

At the age of eighteen, Judith married a ship captain by the name of John Stevens. He had been reading the works of James Relly and shared these ideas with Judith and her family. Relly's ideas, especially from his 1759 book entitled *Union*, became foundational for what would become the Universalist Church. As Judith's family became increasingly involved in the movement, they became familiar with a Universalist lecturer named John Murray. They invited Murray, who lived in Boston, to their home in Gloucester where he spoke throughout the community and visited with the Sargent and Stevens families. Judith and John Murray became close friends and began writing frequently after Murray's return to Boston. Though it was unusual for a married woman to write a single man who was not a family member, their relationship was platonic with topics of their correspondence being limited to philosophy, theology, politics, and current events.

In 1774, as tensions between the colonies and England escalated, the ports were closed, and there was a great deal of turmoil in Boston. In the tumult, revolutionaries accused John Murray of spying for the British. To show his devotion to the cause of independence, Murray joined the revolutionary army as a chaplain. However, when he was invited to become the pastor of a new church in Gloucester, he accepted. This became the first **Universalist Church** in the United States. The starting of this church led to a Supreme Court case in Massachusetts because the Universalists wanted to support their own church financially rather than the established Congregational Church. The Universalists won the legal battle.

As an educator in the Universalist Church, Judith wrote a curriculum to teach children doctrines of the new church. She began classes with her adopted children and with children from the community. Later, she helped establish a female academy in Dorchester, Massachusetts.

Her husband, John Stevens, found himself in a financial crisis and fled to the West Indies to avoid debtor's prison. A year after receiving word of Stevens' death in the West Indies, Judith married John Murray. She gave birth to their stillborn son, and—as she was grieving his death—her writing increased. In addition to the catechisms she had written for children, she began writing more poetry, articles, short stories, and plays. When she published her works, she did so under a number of pen names, one of which was Constantia. To increase readership among men, she used the pen name of Mr. Gleaner. One of Judith's major works was *On the Equality of the Sexes*, which was written in 1790—two years prior to Mary Wollstonecraft's *A Vindication of the Rights of Woman*. Also in 1790, Judith wrote *On the Domestic Education of Children*.

Judith had many supporters among the nation's founders. Among those who endorsed her work were Benjamin Franklin, Nathanael and Catharine Green, George and Martha Washington, and John and Abigail Adams. Judith and Abigail Adams were involved together with the Republican Motherhood movement. This movement encouraged the education of women and their daughters in the ideals of republicanism.

Judith also faced opposition among the founders. When she moved to Boston, Thomas Paine, who was a publisher there, invited her to write a series of five articles that would be called "The Reaper." The theme was to be the virtues she had reaped through her life experiences. In his editing of her first article, Paine scrutinized and revised her sentences so much that she decided not to write the remaining four columns of the series. Paine sought revenge by ruthlessly critiquing her plays that were performed in Boston. He accused her of having her husband John Murray write the plays under her name. The contention between the two was intense and very public.

Because of Judith, what it meant to be a "learned lady" was no longer as disparaging a term as it had once been. She argued that women typically did not achieve as much as men because they were not educated to the extent that men were. She insisted that women had the same, if not more, potential as men. She illustrated this in her interpretation of the biblical account of Adam and Eve. Judith claimed that Eve was motivated by rational thought. Eve's yearning for knowledge was the root of her temptation to eat the forbidden fruit. Adam's motivation, however, was simply in his passionate desire to be with a woman.

In the final years of her marriage with John Murray, he became incapacitated from chronic illness and could not function without her help. Upon his death, Judith moved to live with their daughter in Mississippi, where she died in 1820. It was not until 1984 that some of her letters and papers were discovered. Most historians believed that these artifacts had been destroyed, but their discovery renewed interest in her work and influence. In 1996, historian Bonnie Hurd Smith began to transcribe Judith's works for publication, and now more people are becoming aware of the impact Judith made in the nation's founding era.[41]

Papa Pestalozzi playfully interacting with orphan children[42]

© Art Collection 3/Alamy Stock Photo

Johann Heinrich Pestalozzi: Meanwhile, Back in Europe[43]

While revolutionary ideas were making political and educational inroads in the New World, back in Europe, educational developments were occurring that would later impact the United States during and after the common school movement of the mid-nineteenth century. One significant shift was in what was perceived as the key source of knowledge. Prior to the Enlightenment, authority was seen as the main source of knowledge. The authority for truth was found predominantly in the Roman Catholic Church, but also in classical literature, Scripture, family tradition, and the government. John Locke's concept of *tabula rasa* (i.e., blank slate) brought a drastic change in this perception. Knowledge and truth came to be found in personal experience. Contrary to the Calvinist notion that human nature was basically sinful and in need of accountability and of teaching through catechisms and direct instruction, Jean-Jacque Rousseau propagated the idea that human nature was basically good—that generally left to their own devices, without outside interference, children would naturally grow and develop into good adults. Rousseau introduced the concept of natural stages of childhood development, upon which psychologists Jean Piaget, Lawrence Kohlberg, and Erik Erikson later built their own stage theories of cognitive, moral, and psychosocial development.

Two contemporaries of Rousseau were **Mary Wollstonecraft** (1759-1797), a harsh critique of Rousseau, and **Johann Heinrich Pestalozzi** (1746-1827), an ardent proponent. Wollstonecraft opposed Rousseau's view of how women should be educated. In his novel *Èmile*, Rousseau had described what he held to be the ideal education of a boy named Èmile. He traced Èmile's stages of development and described the boy's process of education, which included natural experiences with as minimal imposition as possible from societal institutions, such as the family, church, and government. "Man is born free," Rousseau claimed, "but he is everywhere in chains." These chains inhibited freedom in personal development and were to be regulated by social contract. Therefore, education should be as natural a process as possible with teachers as facilitators and mentors. Wollstonecraft's criticism of Rousseau was not so much with what he proposed for Èmile but with his description of Sophie's education. Sophie was the girl who would become Èmile's wife, and Rousseau proposed that her education be much different from that of Èmile. She was to be educated to please and serve Èmile. Not so, argued Wollstonecraft in *A Vindication of the Rights of Woman*. She proposed that women, equally as rational as men, should be educated in the same way and to the same ends.

Pestalozzi, on the other hand, was so inspired by Rousseau's *Èmile* that he wrote his own similarly styled novel *How Gertrude Teaches Her Children*—a treatise expanding on Rousseau's theories and also conveying Pestalozzi's nuances to this Romantic view of education. Pestalozzi's approach to learning gained international attention and eventually would impact education throughout the Western world.

The Pestalozzian movement of the nineteenth century was based on the premise that learning occurs best in an emotionally secure environment where knowledge is acquired by sense perception. He introduced psychology into education and was the first to systematize the science of teaching. Though known for the object lesson, he also influenced the transformation of elementary schools and planted seeds for teacher licensure.

After the death of his father when Pestalozzi was only five years old, his mother brought him up in a loving but sheltered environment where outdoor excursions and interactions with other children were limited. His grandfather, a pastor, cultivated in him a concern for social justice, which was developed further in 1762 when he joined the Helvetic Society, a group of social activists. These early influences later impacted Pestalozzi's educational theory and practice.

Pestalozzi married a wealthy lady from Zurich in 1769. He considered following his grandfather into the ministry but chose to study law, only to decide later to toil the land as a farmer. He bought Neuhof, a large farmhouse in Zurich, where he opened the first industrial school, which became home for more than fifty underprivileged boys. They were an undisciplined lot, many of whom took advantage of his generosity by running off after receiving food and clothing. The first in a series of administrative bungles, Neuhof went bankrupt. Although reduced to poverty, he did not consider the six-year experiment a complete failure. Leaving the Neuhof experience with a stronger conviction than ever, he began writing.

From 1780 to 1798, he gained prominence as a novelist, positioning himself for future success to promulgate his educational agenda. A novel about the original goodness of human nature, his 1781 *Leonard and Gertrude* earned him the most notoriety. Emphasizing the role of mothers in education, this novel served a double purpose for Pestalozzi. It propagated his concept of the ideal educational system and also pointed out the need for social reforms.

Although drawing heavily from Rousseauan principles regarding the inherent goodness of children and their need to develop freely, Pestalozzi's writings displayed three noteworthy differences. First, he did not support the glorification of nature as a utopia. He observed that nature can often be brutish, necessitating that teachers be assertively intentional, especially in the moral instruction of children. Second, he was concerned about the education of the poor while Rousseau did not see such a need. Third, he applied theory to practice whereas Rousseau's ideology remained chiefly abstract. Unlike Rousseau, who relinquished his children to an orphanage, Pestalozzi educated his own son, implementing principles from *Èmile*. Through application, he tempered Rousseau's ideas while refining his own praxis.

As he gained recognition for his writings, Pestalozzi also became identified as a sympathizer of the French Revolution. He became convinced that the French regime could bring about moral regeneration and social reform. Funded by the new government, an orphan asylum was opened in Stans, Switzerland, with Pestalozzi as headmaster and sole teacher. Locals, who were predominantly Catholic, expressed hostility to the Protestant Pestalozzi and were resentful of his ties to the French government. Despite its difficulties, however, the school at Stans earned a reputation as "The Cradle of the Modern Elementary School."

At Stans, the theories in Pestalozzi's writings were first implemented systematically. Even with eighty students and only one assistant, an atmosphere of familial love was cultivated. No books were used, as instruction was based on sense impression. Rather than traditional recitation of meaningless words, his goal was to develop the students' powers of attentiveness, carefulness, and reliability. He viewed the strengthening of these skills at a young age as much more significant for later learning than what typically occurred in traditional classrooms. He refused to operate Stans on the broadly held assumptions that the purpose of school was to teach the written word, that children were innately bad and should be punished for not meeting academic expectations, and that education was inessential for the poor. After only five months, this successful experiment ended abruptly when French soldiers retreating from Austria sequestered the facility to establish a hospital.

Shortly thereafter, Pestalozzi moved to the Burgdorf castle, also in Switzerland, where he began to fuse psychology and education and where he developed the first teachers' college. Using the German word *anschauung* to refer to the acquisition of knowledge, he taught that no words should be used for instruction until after students had engaged in a process of sense impression. Inadequately translated as intuition, observation, sense experience, perception, or contemplation, *anschauung* was defined by Pestalozzi as "things before words, concrete before abstract." This concept served as the framework for what popularly became known as the object lesson.

Students at Burgdorf engaged in field trips to the countryside, woods, or seashore where they collected specimens for object lessons. They closely examined the items, drawing and talking about their observations. They were then instructed to write about their objects and to read to others what they had written. Only after a process involving such concrete observations were teachers permitted to introduce vocabulary or concepts previously unfamiliar to the students. In addition to advancing the object lesson at Burgdorf, Pestalozzi refined and promoted such methods as movable letters, tactual arithmetic aids, slates, oral group answers, increased student–teacher interaction, and physical education.

Another psychological principle Pestalozzi advocated at Burgdorf was the need for balanced instruction in intellectual, moral, and physical development. Harmony among these powers was essential for proper growth and led him to include innovative activities such as drawing, singing, and physical exercise. Also radical for his time was the notion of the affective pedagogical element, that teachers should love their students. He identified the following dispositions as essential for effective teachers: fatherliness, cheerfulness, affection, and kindness.

Burgdorf closed due to a lack of funds in 1801. Though his ineptitude as an administrator led to several school failings, Pestalozzi continued to gain prominence as an innovative educator, especially during his twenty-year tenure at Yverdon, another castle in Switzerland where he established a boys' school. Among international visitors to Yverdon were Friedrich Froebel, Johann Herbart, and William Maclure. Through these and many other visitors, Pestalozzianism spread to Germany, the United States, and other countries, impacting the following developments: kindergarten, scientific pedagogy, New Harmony experiment, common school movement, Oswego movement, and normal school training.

Critics indicate the enigmatic nature of Pestalozzi's method, arguing that it fragmented the sciences and neglected history and literature. Unfortunately, the object lesson was later so formalized that it became widely misunderstood, no longer representing the theoretical framework of its originator. Nevertheless, his influence wrought considerable change in the emphasis given to student interest, the respect of the child's natural development, and the overall tone of the modern elementary school.[44]

 Go to www.khlearn.com to watch a video about revolutionary ideas.

Reflection

For personal reflection, content review, and further research:

1. To what degree has Benjamin Rush's philosophy of education been implemented in the United States? Are there remnants of his ideas remaining today? If so, what are they? If not, why might they have been rejected?
2. Critique Benjamin Rush's philosophy of education. What aspects appeal to you, and which ideas do you oppose?
3. Paraphrase the main tenets of Scottish Common Sense Realism, and explain their contribution to American politics, religion, and education.
4. Compare the perspectives of Thomas W. Hagedorn, David Barton, and Daniel L. Dreisbach regarding Benjamin Rush's influence on American education. With which author do you most agree, and why?
5. Analyze the similarities and differences between Benjamin Rush's and Thomas Jefferson's philosophy of education. To what degree were they similar? Which of the two philosophies appeals most to you and why?
6. Critique Benjamin Rush's beliefs regarding female education. How do his ideas compare with feminist views before and after his time?
7. In what ways does Judith Sargent Murray serve as a model for current day educators to emulate?
8. Compare Rousseau's and Pestalozzi's theories and practices regarding the nature of children and of the learning process.

ENDNOTES

1. Daniel L. Dreisbach, "The Bible and the Political Culture of the American Founding," in *Faith and the Founders of the American Republic*, ed. Mark David Hall and Daniel L. Dreisbach (Oxford: Oxford University Press, 2014), 169.
2. Heimert, *Religion*, 184-190.
3. David Barton, *Four Centuries of American Education* (Aledo, TX: Wallbuilder Press, 2004), 10.
4. Hagedorn, *Founding Zealots*, 66-67.
5. Ibid., 58.
6. Benjamin Rush, "A Defence of the Use of the Bible as a School Book. Addressed to the Rev. Jeremy Belknap, of Boston, March 10, 1791," letter, from *Evans Early American Imprint Collection*, accessed July 15, 2018, 94-95.
7. Public Domain.
8. Wayne J. Urban and Jennings L. Wagoner, Jr., *American Education: A History* (Boston: McGraw Hill, 2004), 74.
9. Gutek, *Historical and Philosophical Foundations*, 180.
10. Thomas W. Hagedorn, *Founding Zealots: How Evangelicals Created America's First Public Schools, 1783-1865* (Maitland, FL: Xulon Press, 2013), 58.
11. Benjamin Rush, "A Plan for the Establishment of Public Schools and the Diffusion of Knowledge in Pennsylvania; to which are Added Thoughts upon the Mode of Education, Proper in a Republic: Addressed to the Legislature and Citizens of the State, 1786," 27.
12. Ibid., 27-30.
13. John. J. Holder, Jr., "The Political and Educational Philosophy of Benjamin Rush," *Transactions of the Charles S. Peirce Society* 24, no. 3 (1988): 409-15.

14. Benjamin Rush, "On the Mode of Education Proper in a Republic," in *The Selected Writings of Benjamin Rush*, ed. Dagobert D. Runes (New York: Philosophical Library, 1947), 97.

15. Ibid., 88.

16. Hyman Kuritz, "Benjamin Rush: His Theory of Republican Education," *History of Education Quarterly* 7, no. 4 (1967): 437-8.

17. Rush, "A Plan," 20-2.

18. Gutek, *A History*, 162-82.

19. Kuritz, "Benjamin Rush," 433-4.

20. Donald J. D'Elia, "Philosopher of the American Revolution," *Transactions of the American Philosophical Society* 64, no. 5 (1974): 52.

21. Hagedorn, *Founding Zealots*, 66-7.

22. Joel Spring, *The American School: A Global Context from the Puritans to the Obama Era* (New York: McGraw Hill, 2011), 59.

23. Holder, "The Political and Educational Philosophy," 409-10

24. Hagedorn, *Founding Zealots*, 57.

25. Barton, *Four Centuries*, 23-24.

26. Paul A. Kienel, *A History of Christian School Education* (Colorado Springs, CO: Purposeful Design Publications, 2005), 103.

27. Rush, "A Plan," 15.

28. Ibid.

29. Ibid.

30. Rush, "A Defence," 93-4.

31. Dreisbach, "The Bible," 144-73.

32. James W. Fraser, ed., *The School in the United States: A Documentary History* (New York: Routledge, 2010), 18.

33. Spring, *The American School*, 55.

34. Urban and Wagoner, American Education, 77.

35. Ornstein, Levine, Gutek, and Vocke, *Foundations of Education*, 130.

36. Abraham Blinderman, "Three Early Champions of Education: Benjamin Franklin, Benjamin Rush, and Noah Webster," *Phi Delta Kappa* (April 7, 1976): 21.

37. Benjamin Rush, "Thoughts upon Female Education, Accommodated to the Present State of Society, Manners, and Government, in the United States of America," *Evans Early American Imprint Collection* (1787), 6-10.

38. Ibid., 25.

39. See Gutek, *A History*; Gutek, *Historical and Philosophical Foundations*; Thomas Jefferson, "A Bill of the More General Diffusion of Knowledge," in *The Papers of Thomas Jefferson*, ed. Julian P. Boyd (Princeton: Princeton University Press, 1950) 526-533; Urban and Wagoner, *American Education*.

40. John Singleton Copley, *Portrait de Madame Judith Sargent Murray*, 1770-1772, oil on canvas.

41. See Elizabeth Galewski, "The Strange Case for Women's Capacity to Reason: Judith Sargent Murray's Use of Irony in 'On the Equality of the Sexes' (1790)," *Quarterly Journal of Speech* 93, no. 1 (2007): 84-108; Karen L. Schiff, "Objects of Speculation: Early Manuscripts on Women and Education by Judith Sargent (Stevens) Murray," *Legacy: A Journal of American Women Writers* 17, no. 2 (2000): 213-28; Bonnie Hurd Smith, "Judith Sargent Murray Biography," *Judith Sargent Murray Society* (2018).

42. Konrad Grob, *Pestalozzi with the Orphans in Stans*, 1879, oil on canvas.

43. From *Encyclopedia of Educational Reform and Dissent* by Thomas C. Hunt. Copyright © 2010 by Sage Publications, Inc. Reprinted by permission.

44. See Lewis Flint Anderson, *Pestalozzi* (New York: AMS Press, 1931); Gerald. L. Gutek, *Pestalozzi and Education* (New York: Random House, 1968); Johann Heinrich Pestalozzi, *How Gertrude Teaches Her Children*, trans. Lucy E. Holland and Francis C. Turner (Syracuse, NY: C. W. Bardeen, 1898); Kate Silber, *Pestalozzi: The Man and His Work* (London: Routledge and Kegan Paul, 1960).

CHAPTER 10

EARLY NATIONAL ERA AND THE COMMON SCHOOL MOVEMENT

Horace Mann[1]

From The New York Public Library, https://digitalcollections.
nypl.org/items/510d47d9-b768-a3d9-e040-e00a18064a99

FOCUS: KEY TOPICS AND TERMS

Balance-wheel
Beecher, Catharine
Bushnell, Horace
Calvinism
Christian nurture
Common school movement
Hall, G. Stanley
Hodge, Charles
Immigrants

Lancaster model
Mann, Horace
McGuffey Eclectic Readers
McGuffey, William
Monitorial schools
Northwest Ordinances
Progressive Orthodoxy
Raikes, Robert
Religious education movement

Revivalism
Romanticism
Scottish Common Sense
  Realism
Stowe, Calvin
Sunday school movement
Unitarianism
Webster's *Blue-Backed
  Speller*

Dressed in commencement regalia, the 1859 graduates of Antioch College heard **Horace Mann** challenge them with what has often since been quoted by other inspirational speakers: "Be ashamed to die until you have won some victory for humanity." This statement has challenged many to take on a cause and to see it through. Horace Mann's cause was the common school movement. Many claim that, were it not for Mann's skillful politicking and persuasive arguments, there would be no free public schooling in the United States today. Movements, however—though often led by an individual—rarely occur simply because an individual person wished them to be so, and this was also true with the common school movement. Although there is no denying that Mann played an extremely significant role as Secretary to the Board of Education in Massachusetts, state legislator, U.S. Congressman, and editor of *The Common School Journal*—there were plenty of other people and factors fueling the momentum that spawned the common school movement.

 ## Background and Historical Context

Three centuries before Horace Mann, the Protestant Reformer Martin Luther proposed a free educational system for all. Driven by a doctrine called "the priesthood of all believers" or "the universal priesthood," Luther believed that it was wrong for clergy to be educated while the masses were so illiterate that they could not read the Bible for themselves. Had they been able to read Scripture, Luther argued, abuses of the church—such as the sale of indulgences and the call to fight in crusades—would have ended by revolt of those who knew the truth for themselves. Thus, Luther strove for universal literacy through mass education.

This same doctrine of the universal priesthood was espoused by John Calvin, whose influence was strong on the Puritans who founded Massachusetts Bay Colony. This influence led them to pass the first compulsory education law in 1647 called the Old Deluder Satan Act. It required towns of fifty or more families to hire a teacher. Towns of one hundred families were to start a school that would prepare students for the university. The Old Deluder Satan Act established a tradition of education and literacy in the northern colonies that carried into the National Period.

Another advocate for free public education was Thomas Jefferson. As Representative to the Virginia House of Delegates and later as Governor of Virginia, Jefferson proposed a Bill for the More General Diffusion of Knowledge. Unfortunately, the bill was repeatedly rejected by the Virginia legislature. While Luther and the Puritans were driven by doctrinal convictions, Jefferson was motivated by his philosophical belief in meritocracy over aristocracy. He envisioned a nation ruled by those who had the opportunity to advance through hard work and education rather than by those who had been born into an aristocratic ruling class.

It was into this fledgling nation that Horace Mann was born in 1796. He grew up watching the nation grapple with its identity, not merely as a political entity but also as a moral, ethical, and religious entity. In addition to building a distinct government structure, the United States was distinguishing itself from Great Britain with Noah Webster's lexicon and with Benjamin Franklin's practical philosophy. Jonathan Edwards' preaching had sparked the First Great Awakening in colonial Massachusetts, laying a foundation of Puritan and Calvinist principles for the imminent nation, and currents of the Second Great Awakening were well underway. Stoked by increasing spiritual sensibilities, reform movements were set aflame and burning brighter: abolition, women's rights, temperance, treatment of the mentally ill, and education.

NORTHWEST ORDINANCES

Although the Constitution did not make any provision for education, a series of **Northwest Ordinances** made it clear that education was important to this early nation. For example, the 1785 Ordinance required land in the Northwest Territory to be divided systematically into townships of thirty-six square miles each. Townships were then further subdivided into rectangular square miles, one of which—Section 16—being set aside for the purpose of public schools. The 1787 Ordinance not only prohibited slavery but also stated, "Religion, morality, and knowledge, being necessary to good government and the happiness of mankind, schools and the means of education shall forever be encouraged." The federal government was paving the way for the common school movement that would occur decades later and would eventually be embraced state by state.

OTHER MASS EDUCATION MOVEMENTS

Before the common school movement, there were other efforts toward mass education. One such effort was the **Sunday school movement**, which journalist **Robert Raikes** began in England in the mid-eighteenth century as a proactive measure against childhood crime and poverty in urban centers. Raikes believed that education could help prevent crime and poverty, but because so many children worked in factories for long days Monday through Saturday, the only practical time to teach them basic literacy would be on Sundays. He recruited church volunteers to serve as teachers and scheduled the class sessions before or after worship services. The concept quickly spread to the United States, providing basic literacy and education in morality and Christian doctrine.

Statue of Robert Raikes, Victoria Embankment Gardens, London, England

© Peter Moulton/Shutterstock.com

Another effort at mass education that began in England and quickly spread to the United States was the monitorial system, which was also known as mutual instruction or the **Lancaster model**. In **monitorial schools**, one teacher introduced a particular skill to older or more advanced students who in turn taught the skill to a group of younger or less skilled students. The model caught on quickly because it was an extremely inexpensive method to teach a large number of students. In the words of New York Governor DeWitt Clinton in 1809,

> When I perceive one great assembly of a thousand children, under the eye of a single teacher, marching, with unexampled rapidity and with perfect discipline, to the goal of knowledge, I confess that I recognize in [Joseph] Lancaster the benefactor of the human race. I consider his system as creating a new era in education, as a blessing sent down from heaven to redeem the poor and distressed of this world from the power and dominion of ignorance.[2]

Monitorial schools were eventually displaced in the United States by the Common School Movement.

Horace Mann

Horace Mann's metaphor for education was that of a balance wheel. He said, "Education, then, beyond all other devices of human origin, is the great equalizer of the conditions of men—the **balance-wheel** of the social machinery."[3] He spoke of a utopian society in which the more schools there were, the fewer prisons we would need. Common schools would not only reduce crime and eliminate poverty, they would distinguish this new nation from its mother country by providing opportunity for social mobility from one class to another.

One of the challenges that Mann faced was that—in order for his proposal to work—citizens would be required to pay for the education of other people's children. His role was to persuade them that it would be to their benefit and to the benefit of the social order as a whole to provide free education for all. As an articulate, eloquent, and popular speaker, Horace Mann was able to appeal to a common desire to reduce crime and poverty and also to assimilate immigrants, Native Americans, and freed African Americans into a common national identity. The metaphor that was often used for this idea was that of the melting pot.

The melting pot metaphor has been problematic in many ways over time, but it was immediately problematic for the new wave of Catholic **immigrants**. Their perception was that American schools were so steeped in Protestantism that their Catholic heritage would melt away if they enrolled their children into these new public schools. A system of Catholic private schools soon was established.

One of Mann's great compromises was over the role of religion in public schools. Though nurtured in strict Orthodox **Calvinism**, Mann had converted to **Unitarianism** and was caught up in an internal as well as a societal conflict between the two. His answer was that a nonsectarian form of biblical teaching would be presented in the schools as a means to teach morality. This compromise satisfied most people, except for those who wanted no religion at all or those who believed that doctrinal catechisms were necessary for any meaningful teaching of religion.

William McGuffey, Textbook Author[5]

Because the common school movement was a state-by-state issue rather than a federal concern, it was important that others in addition to Horace Mann take up the baton for the cause to spread nationally. **William McGuffey** was one of these. A Presbyterian minister and college professor, McGuffey lobbied Ohio and Virginia legislatures to adopt Mann's model for common schools. He also authored a series of readers that sold over one hundred twenty-two million copies over

William McGuffey, Presbyterian minister, professor, and textbook author[4]

Source: Public Domain

a span of seventy years. No other textbook series before or after has held such prominence in the public schools. The **McGuffey Eclectic Readers**, **Webster's Blue-Backed Speller**, and the Bible were the most prominent textbooks in early common schools, reflecting the moral tone of the time while also weaving it further into the fabric of American posterity.

The *McGuffey Eclectic Readers* taught more Americans to read than any other textbook. Initial publication coincided with a unique period in United States history as the West was settled, newly arrived immigrants assimilated, and the common school movement gained momentum. At this time, the nation was at a critical point of forming a distinct identity. These phenomena created a demand for textbooks that would not only meet the practical need for curriculum in developing schools but would also extend prevailing American values both to children new to the frontier and to those new to the nation. In the emerging textbook industry, the *McGuffey Readers* reformed the content of America's textbooks and how that content was presented to students.

 Go to www.khlearn.com to watch a video showing images of McGuffey's *First Eclectic Reader* and discussing schools in the 1950s.

The success of the *Readers* might be credited as much to the astute business tactics of Cincinnati publisher Winthrop B. Smith as to the authors and compilers themselves. Smith observed the dominance New England publishers held over the growing textbook industry and determined the need for a graded series of readers marketed to the burgeoning West and to the South. He first sought the assistance of Harriet Beecher Stowe, who declined his offer but recommended her friend William Holmes McGuffey. A professor and Presbyterian preacher, McGuffey had already begun work on such a project. Smith contracted him to compile a primer, four readers, and a speller. His compensation would be ten percent of the profits not to exceed $1,000. Though a great sum at the time, it was not representative of the vast profits publishers earned and hardly compensated McGuffey for the impact his work had on the nation.

The first and second readers were published in 1836 with the third and fourth following within the year. McGuffey had compiled and written the material to be age appropriate. To establish which material best suited particular ages, he experimented with his own children and those in the community, teaching them in his home as well as outdoors on logs. Incorporating the element of competition, he reserved the largest end of the log for students who recited their lessons most accurately. He documented the effect of the content on various age groups and made necessary adjustments before submitting the final work. Typical in many ways to other graded readers of the time, the primer began with the alphabet and phonetically taught single-syllable words. Not as successful as the series that followed it, the primer was pulled from publication shortly after its introduction. The content of the first reader moved on to more difficult words and introduced simple sentences. The second reader progressed to multi-syllabic words, and the stories grew more complex as the book progressed. Comparable to the level of junior high school material, the third and fourth readers taught thinking skills and included selections from authors such as Washington Irving, Lord George Gordon Byron, Thomas Jefferson, and William Shakespeare. Two particular characteristics made McGuffey's work distinct from other readers of the day. First, it included more illustrations than was common for school books at the time. Second, it was a complete language arts curriculum integrating spelling, speech, comprehension, and word studies.

Though it was common for readers to include selections from various authors, McGuffey's readers initially drew criticism from Samuel Worcester, a Boston author, for "over-imitation" of material. Citing ten identical pieces in both his and McGuffey's readers, Worcester filed suit against McGuffey and his publishers for violation of copyright laws. Whether it was a legitimate case or not, the conflict reflected the intense rivalry between New England and Cincinnati publishers over the growing market for schoolbooks. Nevertheless, after only two years in print, the *McGuffey Readers* underwent a redaction, ridding them of any selection that could be considered an infringement of copyright. The plaintiffs agreed to settle out of court for $2,000. The looming lawsuit brought about the first and most sweeping of many revisions to come.

In the 1840s, William H. McGuffey's younger brother Alexander added a *Rhetorical Guide*, which was later developed into the fifth and sixth readers. Literary selections in these volumes comprised portions of the Bible and the works of Henry Wadsworth Longfellow, Charles Dickens, Joseph Addison, and many others. In addition to the variety of literature, these higher-level readers incorporated elocutionary exercises and lessons on such broad topics as farming, science, history, and biography. The instruction in elocution was deemed necessary because of the increasing number of immigrants learning the English language. These final books of the series have been credited for determining America's taste for literature and for exemplifying themes foundational to the American experience.

Although a forerunner to the twentieth-century basal readers, such as the *Dick and Jane* series, the *McGuffey Readers* were distinctly different. Their selections were much shorter, were intended for oral rather than silent reading, and were more culturally and morally monolithic. Unlike modern basals conceived and produced by publishers, nineteenth-century readers like McGuffey's were largely written and compiled by a single author—normally a clergyman or schoolmaster. While they were not as stern in moralizing as the *New England Primer* had been, the *McGuffey Readers* clearly taught a Calvinistic ethic that both reflected the moral tone of the time and proliferated it into the fabric of American society. The *New England Primer* included a greater degree of religious content and emphasized eternal damnation in hell as punishment for wrongdoing, whereas McGuffey's readers focused on practical consequences children might experience here on earth for lacking in kindness or productivity. Like the modern basals, McGuffey's stories resonated with what children found interesting, such as fables about animals and play.

William H. McGuffey was born in Pennsylvania in 1800 before his family moved to Ohio during his infancy. A prodigious child, he was issued a teaching certificate at fourteen years of age and served as an itinerant teacher, traveling to various communities to teach children, much as itinerant preachers traveled to share the gospel. He graduated from Washington College with a degree in ancient languages in 1826, was ordained as a Presbyterian minister three years later, and wrote his readers while teaching at Miami University in Oxford, Ohio. He continued to contribute to revisions of the readers while he was president of Cincinnati College and later when he returned to Miami University as president. However, in 1845 when he left Ohio to serve as professor of philosophy at the University of Virginia, his input into further editions ceased. The most popular edition was published in 1879, six years after his death. Although remembered primarily for his series of readers, McGuffey was a popular professor and an outspoken advocate for the common school movement in both Ohio and Virginia.

Other than the first revision in 1838, which was conducted to avoid copyright infringement, all other revisions of *McGuffey's Eclectic Readers* were completed to make the books more visually and conceptually appealing to a changing society. The flourishing magazine industry of the 1870s, with its improvements in pictorial images, influenced an overhaul in the quality of the readers' illustrations. Religious content was gradually diminished over time, but the high moral tone was retained.

Among critics of the *McGuffey Readers* was Horace Mann. While he agreed with McGuffey in promoting the spread of free public schools throughout the nation, Mann vociferously argued that much of the content in the readers was inappropriate for children's textbooks. Other critics have pointed out omissions. For instance, though moralistic about many issues, including cruelty to animals, they did not address the injustice of slavery as the textbooks of New England had. Also absent are mentions of Abraham Lincoln, Mark Twain, and such events as the California Gold Rush and the Oregon Trail. Only cursory mention is made of the Civil War. Political critics indicate that these oversights reflect the pro-Whig Party leaning of the compilers and an effort not to offend consumers in the South. Other concerns have existed over anti-Semitic references, identification of Native Americans as "savages," and the limitation of women to domestic roles.

© Historic Images/Alamy Stock Photo

Cover of 1841 Eclectic First Reader[7]

Three books ubiquitous in nineteenth and early twentieth-century schools and homes, particularly in the West and South, were the Bible, Webster's dictionary, and the *McGuffey Readers*. Along with Webster's *Blueback Speller*, the *McGuffey Readers* helped to standardize English vocabulary and language usage in the United States. They not only reflected the moral values of the nineteenth century but also shaped them. Since the first publication in 1836, they continue to be in print and to sell tens of thousands of copies each year. They are mainly popular in the home-school movement but are also implemented in a few school systems.[6]

Beecher Family: Preachers and Social Reformers

Though Horace Mann is widely known as Father of the Common School Movement, some have called this status into question.[8] Instead of an individual reformer, the leading role of the common school movement might better be attributed to philosophical thought, political trends, religious revivals, and doctrinal developments. Undeniably, individual reformers such as Horace Mann, Samuel Lewis, Calvin Stowe, Lyman Beecher, William McGuffey, and many others led the way. However, it may have been the confluence of a variety of social movements and philosophical trends that actually played the most important role. The family of Lyman Beecher illustrates how a number of individuals driven by their doctrinal beliefs helped to bring about the common school movement. The Beecher family was extremely active in a variety of social reforms, education being just one of many.[9]

"This country is inhabited by saints, sinners and Beechers,"[10] said a close friend of the Beecher family. The quote reflects the major theme of Lyman Beecher Stowe's 1834 book. As a descendent of the Beecher family, Stowe explained that the Beechers were more complex than most people realize. The Beecher family could not easily be categorized as either saints or sinners, so Stowe granted them their own category.

LYMAN BEECHER: FATHER, THEOLOGIAN, AND SOCIAL REFORMER

Lyman Beecher (1775-1863)

Lyman Beecher epitomized social reformers of the antebellum era.[11] Like many other common school proponents, Beecher was a Yankee, descended from Puritans, and strongly influenced by Calvinistic doctrine. He enrolled in Yale where Reverend Timothy Dwight's preaching brought revival to the campus and led Beecher to a spiritual transformation in 1796. Nathaniel William Taylor also directly influenced him to follow New Haven Theology and to become involved in revivals and missions. In 1826, the conservative Hanover Street Congregational Church in Boston called him to join them in their fight against the Unitarians, who rejected orthodox Calvinist doctrines of the original sin, salvation, hell, and the Trinity. In 1830, he accepted an offer to become the first president of Lane Seminary in Cincinnati. He felt called to go west to Ohio for two reasons: (1) the growth of Catholicism in that area concerned him, and (2) he believed that the West was ripe for revival before the imminent return of Christ.

Lyman Beecher was a social activist who directed the energy of the Second Great Awakening revivalism into reform movements. At least in part, those like Beecher may have wanted to "control an American society that was escaping their grip."[12] Evidence of this may be seen in Beecher's strongly worded tract entitled *Plea*, in which he warned of the looming danger to democratic freedoms and to Christianity itself if Roman Catholicism were to spread unchecked on the Western Frontier. Beecher was also active in the temperance movement, abolition, and in publications that called for a Christian moral purpose in the United States.

CALLS FROM THE PULPIT FOR SOCIAL REFORM. The Reverend Beecher's concern for social reform was apparent in his sermons. He preached messages entitled "The Remedy for Dueling" and "The Nature, Occasions, Signs, Evils, and Remedy of Intemperance." He also preached sermons that provided specific insight into his views on education. One such sermon was preached in New London in 1804 and was entitled "The Practicality of Suppressing Vice by Means of Societies Instituted for that Purpose." His message opened with a reference to Ecclesiastes 4:9-12 regarding a cord of three strands not being easily broken. The message continued on to discuss how family, church, and society must collaborate to defeat vice. In 1812, he preached a sermon in New Haven entitled, "A Reformation of Morals Practicable and Indispensable." The text for this sermon was Ezekiel 33:10, "Therefore, O thou son of man, speak unto the house of Israel; Thus ye speak, saying, If our transgressions and our sins be upon us, and we pine away in them, how should we then live?" (King James Version). This message discussed the decline of individual and societal morality, mentioned the need for religious education, and acknowledged that a reformation had already begun. The conclusion was a clear call for repentance. Throughout both sermons was a clear call for universal mass education so that morality could be instilled systematically.[13]

© Morphart Creation/Shutterstock.com

In an 1828 sermon entitled "Resources of the Adversary, and Means of their Destruction," Beecher addressed the need for the church to display more faith, intense love, and decided action. It was his emphasis on the sermon's final point of "decided action" that demonstrated his activist spirit. The message cast a vision of an imminent army with plentiful munitions being implemented for Kingdom work. Beecher lamented, however, that the nation was at that time "panic-struck," skirmishing around before the battle. He called his listeners to action, indicating that "nothing great on earth, good or bad, was ever accomplished without decisive action." He also called for more courage and more evangelistic efforts to bring about church growth. Specifically regarding education, he stated, "Special effort is required, to secure to the rising generation an Education free from the influence of bad example, and more decidedly Evangelical." He expounded on this by discussing the environment children experience and the great need for common schools to be part of that experience. He decried the effort in colleges to "separate religion from science" but expressed his belief in the right of parents to send their children to colleges that do so. [14]

ACTIVISM BEYOND THE PULPIT. Beecher's activist sensibilities were present from the very beginning of his ministry. In addition to drawing individuals to a conversion experience, he saw his role as a pastor to reform and transform the nation. His activist efforts were carried out in missions, Sunday schools, and literature distribution. Even the revival itself was an instrument that would lead to parachurch organizations for the purpose of reforming the ills of society. Although he valued theology and was consistent with his daily study routine, he approached his role of theologian as that of "physician, who would go to the store of the apothecary to be applied." His daughter Harriet wrote that her father considered "a sermon that did not induce any body to do any thing . . . a sermon thrown away." [15]

A criticism of Beecher may be the irony of his efforts to limit the role of Catholicism in the United States. "Because Catholics are propagating their anti-democratic beliefs through immigration and education," he argued, "Protestants must defend democracy by controlling immigration, protecting their children from Catholic influence, and supporting Protestant education." [16] He was a prominent but controversial pastor, who—although not directly involved in politics himself—was accused of inciting violence against Catholics through his preaching and publications. His views have been described as "authoritarian, bigoted, and hence profoundly dangerous." [17] Ironically, he was an abolitionist, but because of what his students and faculty perceived was not a direct enough stand on the issue, many withdrew from Lane Theological Seminary to transfer to Oberlin College. His brand of activism was questioned as possibly being more regressive than progressive, and one historian described him as one who "lived in the present, but his heart was often in bondage to the past." [18] Could it be that he desired to take society back to what he perceived as a better time and place, reminiscent of how it was in Jonathan Edwards' New England?

Beecher not only stood in opposition to Catholics but also led a campaign against Unitarianism. One point of conflict was their different views on **revivalism**. Beecher supported the revivalist movement, but Unitarians did not value the movement as contributing positively to society. Between 1820 and 1840, the Boston population doubled, which brought with it many problems—moral decline being one of the primary issues. To Beecher, it was useless to rely on any other means of social reform than conversion to Christ. Therefore, he rejected the Unitarian proposals for solutions that were based in "science, legislation, philosophy, eloquence and argument." [19] Unitarians criticized the Beecherites, as his followers were called, for their harsh tone in the argument. One of Beecher's concerns was the "perverted literature" in the curriculum of the common schools that was written by liberal Unitarians. The Unitarians sought to provide all children, especially the poor, a practical and moral education. Without the teaching of Bible doctrine, this was insufficient for the Beecherites.

Although Beecher was an influential voice in the common school movement in Ohio, it was his son-in-law **Calvin Stowe** who has often been called the "Father of Common Schools in Ohio."[20] Calvin was married to Lyman's daughter, Harriet, who wrote *Uncle Tom's Cabin*. Calvin was commissioned by the Ohio legislature to visit Prussia in order to study its educational system. Upon his return, he voiced admiration for the Prussian system, especially its educational philosophy that was influenced by Reformation thought and its commitment to compulsory education.[21]

CATHARINE BEECHER, PROPONENT OF FEMALE TEACHERS

While Mann fought politically for financing and for infrastructure of the common school and while McGuffey provided a practical curriculum tool for the classroom, **Catharine Beecher** advocated for the teaching positions in these new common schools to be filled by women. Like McGuffey, Catharine's father Lyman Beecher was a Presbyterian minister. Their families were friends and fellow proponents of moral education being taught in the common schools. Like Mann, Beecher family members were abolitionists who joined forces with him in the belief that education would serve as a tool eventually to bring about the abolition of slavery.

Catharine Beecher, textbook author, advocate for common schools and for women's education[22]

Source: Public Domain

Until the common school movement, most teachers had been men. The feminization of teaching could be credited to or blamed on Catharine Beecher, depending on one's view. She could by no means be confused with a feminist according to today's standards. She was against women's suffrage, thinking that involvement in politics would corrupt women. Women, she believed, were moral compasses for society and were uniquely suited as teachers and mothers. Their education, then, should prepare them to be moral leaders of children in the home and in the school. She promoted normal schools and encouraged graduates to consider acquiring teaching jobs in the developing Western Frontier where they could bring a mediating influence morally.

The titles of some of her written works give insight into her views about the role of women in society:
- *A Treatise on Domestic Economy for the Use of Young Ladies at Home and at School* (1841)
- *Woman's Profession as Mother and Educator, with Views in Opposition to Woman Suffrage* (1871)
- *Housekeeper and Healthkeeper* (1873)

Though certainly not a groundbreaking feminist, Beecher's impact on the common school movement was palpable.

WOMEN'S ROLE IN SOCIETY. In 1874, Catharine wrote *Educational Reminiscences and Suggestions*, which she dedicated to the "American women, who, as housekeepers, mothers, and school teachers, are to decide the safety and prosperity of our country."[23] This dedication alone was significant in that it conveyed the role she believed women should play in society, specifically in domestic and nurturing roles. In this work, she addressed topics regarding her philosophy pertaining to the intellectual connection to domestic work and pedagogical training required for women desiring to become teachers. She reminisced on topics related to her own education and on the impact her family had on her development. Acknowledging the controversy of women who sought to enter men's colleges, Beecher presented the benefits for women to attend institutions of higher learning that specifically address a curriculum more appropriate to female endeavors. The faculties of reason and common sense were presented as valuable commodities for a woman to develop. She pictured women as empowered to impact society by the decisions they made in governing their homes. Such decisions, she argued, were subject to the husband's veto, "which in most sensible families is seldom used."[24] Throughout her reminiscences, she portrayed women in traditional roles while always attributing great honor and dignity to these roles.

Today's feminists are reluctant to embrace Catharine as a role model. They have criticized her philosophical and ethical perspectives regarding the role of women in society and have vacillated over whether or not to declare her a true feminist in the sense of current views. Two reasons supporting the consideration of her as a feminist include observations that (1) Catharine perceived herself as working toward the empowerment of women, and (2) she was the only female voice in **Scottish Common Sense Realism** and in Calvinist theology.[25] However, she did not push the boundaries of the role of women in her times and is, therefore, not embraced by most recent feminists. Though advocating for women's education and promoting them as the ideal moral educators for children, she did not envision a transformation in their social order in relation to men. She saw the social order of her time as being divinely ordained and as God's plan for the happiness of humanity. Women's power over men was to be found in their role as the moral education of children. Though the virtues she held as most important for women to display were submission and self-denial, it was through these virtues that women gained influence in society. Yet, she opposed women's suffrage, believing it inappropriate for women to enter the traditional arenas of men.

CHILDREN'S EDUCATION. At the time that Catharine wrote *Religious Training of Children in the School, the Family, and the Church* (1864), she had been involved in educating more than a thousand women over a span of nearly four decades. This work presented her philosophy of education and addressed a process of religious training for children and also the rationale for doing so. She clearly delineated roles for both the family and the church, highlighting specifically the woman's role. Her understanding of childhood development was conveyed from infancy through adulthood, and—although there seemed to be allusions to Rousseau's principles of early childhood—the nature of the learner was more Calvinistic. In her discussion of religious and moral development of the child, she often quoted Scripture. For instance, she noted that children learn from natural consequences by "tasting the tree of knowledge of good and evil" and that from the very beginning of their lives they needed to learn to "walk by faith and not by sight."[26] She stressed the direct teaching of good and evil and the importance of obedience.

HISTORIOGRAPHY OF BEECHER IN TEACHER PREPARATION LITERATURE. Since Catharine was such a proponent for teacher training, it is interesting to see how she is portrayed in the literature commonly used in current teacher preparation programs. For example, in Gerald Gutek's *Historical and Philosophical Foundations of Education: A Biographical Introduction*, he highlights Catharine in a discussion on John Calvin's influence on American education. He describes her as "a persuasive advocate of women's education and common schools."[27] He explains how, as a daughter and sister of ministers, Catharine shared her family's Calvinist sensibilities and integrated these doctrinal principles into her writings and actions. Gutek discusses Catharine's 1829 book *Suggestions Respecting Improvements in Education* in which she presented the teacher's role primarily as being that of a moral agent to develop students' values. Gutek calls her an "early advocate of character education" as she called for the church, family, and school to collaborate toward common moral principles.[28] Beecher and other common school proponents pushed for two Calvinist elements to be pervasive in American schools: (1) an individual work ethic and (2) an emphasis on commonly shared societal values. To this end, Beecher advocated for a public school curriculum that would reflect values shared by the majority, which was predominantly Protestant. By so doing, her belief was that this would help strengthen, especially in the growing Western Frontier, the values that had made New England strong: capitalism, diligence, hard work, order, industriousness, and other traits that were passed down from the Puritan heritage.

In his *Philosophical, Ideological, and Theoretical Perspectives on Education*, Gutek discusses Catharine Beecher in a section entitled "Neo-Conservative Interpretation of the American Past." Gutek presents here as a "pioneer teacher educator" who "held ideas that contemporary Conservatives would endorse."[29] Beecher perceived Evangelical Christianity as a vital part of normal schools where female teacher candidates were prepared to be missionaries not just of the Gospel of Christ but also of Western culture and of common civic virtues. She believed that women inherently would make better teachers in the growing common school movement because they were naturally more nurturing and would therefore serve as better moral examples to tame the Western Frontier. She promoted a common curriculum for all students that would promote a common language for all, including the increasingly diverse immigrant population.

More so than other such textbooks, *Foundations of Education*—by Allan C. Ornstein, Daniel U. Levine, Gerald L. Gutek, and David E. Vocke—dedicate a relatively large amount of attention to Catharine Beecher. Interestingly, though, the section opens with a statement that leads the reader into thinking that Catharine was a prominent leader among such suffragettes as Elizabeth Cady Stanton, Emma Willard, and Susan B. Anthony. To the contrary, she was opposed to women's suffrage, believing that women should leave the world of politics to men. She is credited with having established the Harford Female Seminary and the Western Female Institute, a normal school to prepare teacher candidates to serve in Frontier schools. There are three reasons given for Beecher's move to promote women as teachers: (1) teaching was one of the few socially acceptable careers for women at the time: (2) it provided a means of financial independence for unmarried women; and (3) it allowed women a degree of empowerment as they influenced the moral tone of the nation. Her goal was to recruit ninety thousand teachers who would be willing to move to the Western Frontier with a missional mindset of taming this crude region.[30]

In Janice B. Tehie's textbook for teacher candidates, she chose to discuss Catharine Beecher in the context of a section on "Teacher Unions: Protection for Teachers," which seems a bit misplaced chronologically, especially since this chapter is entitled "Urbanization and Expansion of the Public Schools (1890-1930)"[31] and since Catharine had died by 1878. Nevertheless, the point Tehie makes in the section is understood and appreciated. Women, because of their nurturing sensibilities, are generally perceived by society as being more fit than are men to teach young students, especially in the elementary grades. The feminization of the teaching force increased after 1870, especially in the Northeast where the common school movement was initiated. Proponents, such as Emma Willard and Catharine Beecher, encouraged the feminization of the field, arguing that women naturally made better teachers because that is how God designed them—with more patience and a maternal instinct to understand young minds. In 1870, sixty percent of the nation's teachers were women. By 1920, it was eighty-six percent and continues to be a similar figure today.

Most people are familiar with the *McGuffey Readers* and their impact on American education; however, many are unaware that they could have very easily been called the "*Beecher Readers.*" A Cincinnati publisher approached Catharine Beecher to write a series of readers that he could market to the expanding school market in the South and the West. However, as one historian noted, "Because she was then heavily involved in her campaign for women's education, she declined, recommending one of the people she and her father had met . . . William Holmes McGuffey."[32]

 ## Unitarianism and a Tale of Two Horaces

Part of the social tension of the late colonial and early national period included conflict between Calvinists and Unitarians. Allusions to this tension may be found in the historiography of religion, politics, and education of this era and can be illustrated by two Horaces. One Horace was a Unitarian and, although the other was not, the second Horace tried to bridge the tension between the two religious groups. The first was Horace Mann, the father of the common school movement, a Unitarian who worked with both Calvinists and Unitarians to establish public schools in Massachusetts. The second was **Horace Bushnell**, a theologian who lived at the same time as Mann. Bushnell was not a Unitarian, but he worked to bridge the divide between the Orthodox Calvinists and Unitarians. His efforts did not seem to work well for him at the time because the Calvinists tried him for heresy, and Bushnell himself rejected the Unitarians. Bushnell is considered the father of liberal theology and of Christian nurture in religious education. The more people learn about these two Horaces, the more questions they seem to have about Unitarianism.

UNITARIANISM

In 1808, the Andover Theological Seminary was founded as a reaction to Harvard College's drift away from its Calvinist Puritan roots toward Unitarianism. In 1870, there were thirty thousand Unitarians in the United States, and though that may seem like a large number, in perspective, the population of the nation at the time was forty million. There were over three million Catholics and two million Baptists. In that context, the population of Unitarians was marginal, but their societal impact was tremendous because of their tradition to value higher education and to involve themselves in politics and social activism. Some of their key social causes in the nineteenth century included education, abolition, and women's rights.

William Ellery Channing was instrumental in the founding of the Unitarian Church and in promoting its beliefs in Boston. He became pastor of a Congregationalist Church in 1803 and remained there until he died nearly forty years later. He preached a groundbreaking sermon in 1819 that outlined some of the fundamental beliefs of Unitarianism. Even though Unitarians claimed not to embrace a specific creed, what Channing preached represented the core beliefs of the movement. He preached against the Trinity, which is the central doctrine representing the movement's name—the term "Unitarian" representing the belief that God is one person rather than three. Channing also preached against the deity of Christ, the total depravity of man, and the substitutionary atonement of Christ for man's sins. After making his opposition clear to these traditional Christian doctrines, Channing outlined beliefs that he supported. He favored utopianism, which is the belief that the human race is perfectible. He preached on the fatherhood of God, the moral perfection of Christ, and the reality of the resurrection and of other New Testament miracles. When it came to the authority of the Bible, Channing claimed that the Bible recorded inspiration but that the Bible itself was not an inspired book.

Although Channing distanced himself from traditional Christianity, he later criticized the Transcendentalists for moving too far away from orthodoxy. Critics observed that Channing may not have been sufficiently self-aware to sense just how far he had stepped outside the bounds of the gospel. In addition to Channing, Ralph Waldo Emerson and other Transcendentalists influenced Unitarianism. Speaking to Harvard graduates, Emerson encouraged them to turn away from historical Christianity and to acquaint themselves with the deity through firsthand experience rather than through the authority of the Bible or the church.

In 1961, the Universalist Church merged with the Unitarian Church and became known as the Universalist Unitarian (UU) Church. Since then, especially through the decade of the 1970s, the UU Church has embraced abortion, gay marriage, women in the ministry, and gay clergy. UU Church membership experienced a decline in the 1970s related to scandals within the church, but in recent years, their membership has increased. Their doctrine aligns closely with that of liberation theology. More can be learned about the impact of liberation theology on the philosophy of education by studying Brazilian educator Paulo Freire and the literature on critical pedagogy.[33]

HORACE BUSHNELL: PROGRESSIVE ORTHODOXY AND CHRISTIAN NURTURE IN THE CHURCH[34]

Horace Bushnell was born into a fledgling nation that had been grappling with its identity, not merely as a political entity but also as a moral, ethical, and religious people. In addition to building a distinct government structure, the United States was distinguishing itself from Great Britain with Noah Webster's lexicon, with Benjamin Franklin's practical philosophy, and later with Horace Mann's common school approach to education. Jonathan Edwards' preaching had sparked the First Great Awakening in colonial Massachusetts, laying a foundation of Puritan and Calvinist principles for the imminent nation, and currents of the Second Great Awakening were well underway. In this New England religious milieu Bushnell was born and reared; it was an era in which clear divisions had emerged among Orthodox Calvinists, Unitarians, and Revivalists.[35]

© Morphart Creation/Shutterstock.com

Horace Bushnell (1802-1876)

MEDIATING BRIDGE BETWEEN CALVINISM AND UNITARIANISM. Bushnell became a mediator between the dividing factions and taught a theology that might best be represented by the term **Progressive Orthodoxy**. Always proud of his Puritan heritage, Bushnell often traced the positive influence Puritans had on early American culture, defending them against what he perceived as unwarranted criticism.[36] As a mediating force, though, he was critical both of Calvinist Orthodoxy and of Unitarian Liberalism. He soundly condemned closed-minded attitudes toward doctrine wherever they were found, whether in orthodox or progressive camps. He challenged both Orthodox Calvinists and Unitarians for holding their theological views as ends in themselves rather than critically evaluating them in a meaningful way.[37] While presenting a blend of orthodox Christianity along with liberal notions of the nineteenth century—he always preached that Jesus Christ was the Son of God. This was a clear departure from Ralph Waldo Emerson, whom he admired but whose denial of Christ's divinity was a bridge too far for Bushnell.[38]

By holding to the core tenets of the gospel, Bushnell may be considered orthodox; however, it was his adherence to notions of **Romanticism** that earned his thinking the label of Progressive Orthodoxy.

Where, then, is Bushnell best situated in his thinking? He would not be aligned with his contemporaries Lyman Beecher and Nathaniel Taylor, both orthodox protestant theologians who viewed God as "a distant being who oversaw a sin-prone humanity that needed guidance from churches in order to attain salvation."[39] Neither would he be categorized among the Unitarians, whom he criticized for their deism, self-perfectionism, and denial of Christ's divinity.[40] Though influenced by Romantic ideas, he preached doctrines such as the efficacious death and resurrection of Christ for the forgiveness of the sins of all humanity, which clearly were contradictory to the religious views of the likes of Emerson. Though difficult to categorize because of his tendency to bridge divides, Bushnell may be situated between the Orthodox Calvinists, who at one point tried him for heresy, and the Unitarians, whom he rejected.[41]

CHRISTIAN NURTURE. Bushnell held a unique doctrine of the family. He considered it a unity, a body, and that "a power over character is inserted therein, which cannot properly be called influence."[42] This power is exerted by parents over children "not only when they teach, encourage, persuade, and govern, but without any purposed control whatever."[43] Bushnell wrote further that the child "sees the world through his parents' eyes. Their objects become his. Their life and spirit mold him. If they are carnal, coarse, passionate, profane, sensual, devilish, his little plastic nature takes the poison of course. . . . He lives and moves and has his being in them."[44] The parents' power is absolute before the child learns to reason, and it affects the child throughout his life. Bushnell felt that a long line of godly fathers and mothers might induce a religious temperament in the child, producing a godly consciousness and stemming his tendency to compromise his integrity. Character development begins even in early infancy, for it is never too early for good to be communicated. Infancy and childhood are the ages in which children are most malleable to good. Bushnell baptized infants primarily because of his belief in the unity of the family—illustrated in the New Testament by the baptism of entire families—and he accepted them into church membership:

> The propriety of this membership does not lie in what those infants can or cannot believe, or do or do not believe, at some given time, as, for example, on the day of their baptism; but it lies in the covenant of promise, which makes their parents, parents in the Lord; their nurture, a nurture of the Lord; and so constitutes a force of futurition by which they are to grow up, imperceptibly, into "faithfuls among faithfuls," in Christ Jesus.[45]

This led to Bushnell's view that the child born in a Christian home is to be nurtured, not converted. Bushnell explained his oft-repeated axiom that

> The child is to grow up a Christian and never know himself as being otherwise. In other words, the aim, effort, and expectation should be, not, as is commonly assumed, that the child is to grow up in sin, to be converted after he comes to a mature age; but that he is to open on the world as one that is spiritually renewed, not remembering the time when he went through a technical experience, but seeming rather to have loved what is good from his earliest years. I do not affirm that every child may, in fact and without exception, be so trained that he certainly will grow up a Christian.[46]

Bushnell anticipated orthodox reaction to his view of Christian nurture in a sermon on regeneration. Crucial to his defense was his definition of a Christian:

But my child is a sinner, you will say; and how can I expect him to begin a right life, until God gives him a new heart? This is the common way of speaking, and I state the objection in its own phraseology, that it may recognize itself. Who then has told you that a child cannot have the new heart of which you speak? Whence do you learn that if you live the life of Christ, before him and with him, the law of the Spirit of Life may not be such as to include and quicken him also? And why should it be thought incredible that there should be some really good principle awakened in the mind of a child? For this is all that is implied in a Christian state. The Christian is one who has simply begun to love what is good for its own sake, and why should it be thought impossible for a child to have this love begotten in him?[47]

Bushnell implied that the child achieves right standing before God by living the "good life." But how can the young child do good when he has no will of his own, or believe when he has no power to comprehend or make rational choices? Bushnell believed that the parents' faith includes faith on the part of the child, and that the righteous nature of the parents is transmitted to the child. He argued that if evil can be imputed to children, as the Calvinists believed, righteousness can also be imputed to them. He discerned a natural flow of Christian life from the parent to the child, a flow that continues as the child grows and that finally diminishes as he matures.

This is the very idea of Christian education, that it begins with nurture or cultivation. And the intention is that the Christian life and spirit of the parents, which are in and by the Spirit of God, shall flow into the mind of the child, to blend with his incipient and half-formed exercises; that they shall thus beget their own good within him—their thoughts, opinions, faith, and love, which are to become a little more, and yet a little his own separate exercise, but still the same in character.[48]

Bushnell also anticipated two more possible objections to his views. He did not hold to a liberal, humanistic concept of human nature, nor did he replace the work of the Holy Spirit in the regeneration of children with the work of parents: "The strong language I have used concerning the organic connection of character between the parents and the child . . . is not designed to assert [that there is] a power in the parent to re-new the child, or that the child can be renewed by any agency of the Spirit less immediate than that which renews the parent himself."[49] Bushnell distinguished between children of Christian parents and those of unbelievers; the former are to be nurtured, the latter converted.

Bushnell's view of Christian nurture was by no means rejected in all orthodox circles. **Charles Hodge** a Princetonian Calvinist who was one of the best-known theologians of the day summarized the central truth of *Christian Nurture*: "There is an intimate and divinely established connexion between the faith of parents and the salvation of their children; such a connexion as authorizes them to plead God's promises, and to expect with confidence, that through his blessing on their faithful efforts, their children will grow up the children of God."[50] Hodge considered this "the great truth . . . that gives [Bushnell's] book its chief value," although he thought the form in which this truth appeared in *Christian Nurture* to be "strange" and "distort-ed."[51] Arthur Cushman McGiffert credited Bushnell's *Christian Nurture* with doing "more than any other single factor to break down the extreme individualism of the old Puritanism."[52] Yet others acknowledge this work as the pilot light that later ignited the twentieth-century religious education movement.

CHRISTIAN EDUCATION. Bushnell's concept of Christian nurture found a voice at a unique time in the nation; individual states were beginning to adopt educational reforms as churches began rethinking how they propagated religious education. As the Second Great Awakening began to subside in the late

1830s, the common school movement was gaining momentum under the leadership of Horace Mann. In his own effort to bridge the divide between Calvinists and Unitarians while also safeguarding the future of tax-supported schools, Mann—a Unitarian himself—proposed that public schools should not teach sectarian religion. Teachers could present Bible readings without doctrinal commentary and could pray generic Christian prayers, but overall, particular denominational doctrines would not be taught.

The Sunday school movement, which was already well underway, stepped up at this point to carry the torch of teaching biblical doctrine. From the 1790s until the common school movement, Sunday schools had primarily offered basic academic skills for children and even some adults who were too busy working in industrial manufacturing plants during the week to attend school and who were too poor to pay for education otherwise. Influenced by revivalism, however, the purpose and curriculum of the Sunday school evolved. As common schools became more prevalent, Sunday schools surrendered to them the task of teaching basic literacy and ciphering skills and shifted their emphasis to preparing children for the future moment in which they would be converted to the Christian faith.[53] This was antithetical to Bushnell's nurturing model, which called Christian educators to bring up children in the faith and not for some dubious future conversion.

Nature of the Learner. Models of education flow from the basic question of the nature of the learner: Are children inherently good or sinful? Innocent or depraved? Romantic notions of the natural goodness of children were spreading in nineteenth-century America from Europeans such as Rousseau, Pestalozzi, Herbart, and Froebel. This impact was seen in the Unitarian definition of sin as "a neutral state of incompleteness."[54] Bushnell rejected this definition of sin. Having himself been influenced by the Romantics through the writings of Coleridge and Emerson, Bushnell also refused to embrace fully the Calvinist doctrine that children are totally depraved. From the Calvinist perspective, children should be educated to develop a sense of their own sinfulness, which was a prerequisite for them to come one day to salvation.[55] Bushnell, holding to a more moderate concept of limited depravity, argued that "a self-accusing spirit of sin" hinders redemption rather than advancing it."[56]

Bushnell has been credited with reversing the then traditional practice of regarding a child's nature "in precisely the same manner as adults, with no recognition of any differences in their religious characteristics or in their normal religious experiences."[57] He alleged that learners are living organisms developing through stages—yet another Romantic notion espoused specifically by Rousseau.[58] The most critical stage in the nurturing process, Bushnell noted, is what he termed the "age of impressions." This stage occurs even before the child learns to speak and is when parents can have the greatest impact on the child's character development.[59]

Role of Teachers and Parents. By its very emphasis on organicism, *Christian Nurture* clearly was addressed to an audience of parents who would instruct in the home rather than to teachers in a classroom environment. On the question of the role of churches and schools, Bushnell remained vague. Nevertheless, the principles of which he wrote for parents may be applied by any adult in a nurturing role to children. As Lockerbie commented, "No person presuming to love God and love children can be free from this responsibility [of providing children a Christian upbringing]—just as no Christian educator can afford to ignore the influence of Horace Bushnell's *Christian Nurture*."[60]

Bushnell's model of nurture was not strictly a maternal one. He called for both father-centered and mother-centered nurture, and although vague about the specific role of churches and schools, he certainly included them in his concept of "organic unity," which represented naturally occurring, close relationships. These relationships would involve the family, church, and nation—the family being a microcosm of the church, the church being an enlarged family, and the nation being born out of the church and mirroring its structure. Organic unity was in opposition to the individualism Bushnell found in revivalism. No soul, he felt, acts as an independent entity, but all entities within an organic unity are interdependent. Therefore, the roles of the family, church, and nation are naturally woven together. It would not be the individualism of personal conversion that would spread Christianity through the nation, but it would be the organic unity of family, church, and nation. [61]

Instructional Methods. Bushnell's approach to education—exhibiting a greater interest in experiences and imitation than in the transmission of content or in indoctrination—was a forerunner of educational practices a century later. He "put himself, perhaps unconsciously, into the central current of the great educational reform of the nineteenth century."[62] By directing parents to teach in a manner appropriate to the age of the child, by valuing play, and by addressing the problems of language, Bushnell touched on many issues that developmental psychologists, such as Piaget and Vygotsky, would not introduce into the common pedagogical narrative until the twentieth century.[63]

Religious Education Movement. It was fifty-six years after the first edition of Bushnell's *Christian Nurture* before William Rainey Harper founded the Religious Education Association in 1903. How, then, may it be argued that Bushnell's teachings served as the pilot light to ignite the religious education movement? Harper was exposed to Bushnell's ideas by Henry Clay Trumbull, a pioneer in the U.S. Sunday school movement. Trumbull often echoed Bushnell's sermons refuting the common notion that children were incapable of having a relationship with God through Christ in their childhood years. According to Trumbull, Bushnell's impression of the Sunday school improved over time. [64] In Bushnell's eyes, the Sunday school deserved much higher regard than did revivals and other attempts to spread Christianity in America.

Delayed acceptance of the Christian nurture model may be attributed to a variety of factors: (1) the prevailing religious traditionalism hindered the acceptance of new ideas; (2) common schools in their infancy were themselves narrow, traditional, and repressive; (3) the notion of developmental stages of learning was absent from the dominant discourse on childhood; and (4) radical conversion was valued over an organic spiritual growth model of salvation.[65] Well into the late nineteenth century, with distinguished preaching from Charles G. Finney and Dwight L. Moody, revivalism continued to be the preferred avenue for church growth. Additionally, with the final edition of *Christian Nurture* released in 1861, the Civil War and Reconstruction may have postponed people from considering new ideas.

By the twentieth century, however, religious teaching had been drastically minimized in the public schools, compelling the church to become more open to new ideas of how to cultivate Christianity among children. Psychologist **G. Stanley Hall**'s work in childhood development was gaining a great deal of attention among educators both in the public schools and in the Christian arena, and—despite the prominence of Billy Sunday and other evangelists—revivals did not intrigue twentieth-century religious seekers as they previously had done. Eventually, these and many other cultural changes paved the way for Bushnell's ideas to hold great sway over the methods used to educate children within the church.[66] So much so that George A. Coe, widely considered to be the father of the religious education movement, held Bushnell up as one of the most important figures in the history of religious education in America: "If it were necessary to give a date to mark the transition to the modern conception of Christian training, we could not do better than to name the year 1847, which saw the first issue of Horace Bushnell's *Christian Nurture*."[67] Of Bushnell's dictum that "the child is to grow up a Christian and never know himself as being otherwise," Paul H. Vieth wrote that it "is now widely known and accepted."[68]

Horace Bushnell's optimistic view of human nature burst like a rocket into the black night of what many historians, psychologists, and theologians have referred to as the "pessimism of Calvinism" in New England. He reflected the growing American middle-class confidence in the reforming powers of good men—with the help of natural science and the Industrial Revolution—and its shift away from the dogmatic, creedal approach to Christianity to a more scientific one. Bushnell was a member of the growing American cult of education, believing that education can solve any problem, even the religious ones.

 Go to www.khlearn.com to watch a video about the early national era and the common school movement.

 ## Reflection

For personal reflection, content review, and further research:

1. How was the doctrine of the priesthood of all believers influential in the eventual development of free mass education for all?
2. Explain the metaphors of the balance wheel and the melting pot and their significance in the argument for common schools.
3. Describe the societal conflict between Unitarians and Calvinists and how this conflict was related to the common school movement.
4. Compare the *McGuffey Readers* with the earlier *New England Primer* and the basal readers of the twentieth century.
5. Compare Horace Mann and William McGuffey. In what ways did they agree and disagree regarding the common school movement and the curriculum to be taught. Analyze their worldviews and how their life experiences influenced their philosophy of education.
6. Analyze the influence of the Second Great Awakening on social reform movements, including educational reform.
7. Compare Lyman Beecher's social concerns with those that Americans may have today.
8. Why was the revivalist movement so controversial?
9. Describe the conflict between Calvinism and Unitarianism and the implications of this for social reforms such as the common school movement.
10. Compare the educational influences of Horace Mann with the common school movement and of Horace Bushnell with the Christian nurture movement in the church.
11. How do your own ideas regarding the spiritual education of children compare with those of Horace Bushnell?
12. What did Bushnell mean by "Christian Nurture"?
13. Discuss Bushnell's statement: "The child is to grow up a Christian and never know himself as being otherwise." To what extent do you agree with Bushnell?
14. Compare Bushnell's notion of the nature of the learner with those of other educational thinkers. Consider how Jean-Jacque Rousseau, John Calvin, and others perceived the nature of the learner.

ENDNOTES

1. Horace Mann, New York Public Library Digital Collections, accessed December 23, 2019, http://digitalcollections.nypl.org/items/510d47d9-b768-a3d9-e040-e00a18064a99. Public Domain.

2. Kenneth T. Jackson, and David S. Dunbar, eds., *Empire City: New York Through the Centuries* (New York: Columbia University Press, 2002), 129.

3. Massachusetts Board of Education, *Twelfth Annual Report of the Board of Education, together with the Twelfth Annual Report of the Secretary of the Board (1848)*, Boston: Commonwealth of Massachusetts, Board of Education, 1849.

4. *McGuffey*, oil painting, Ohio University, Athens. Public Domain.

5. From *Encyclopedia of Educational Reform and Dissent* by Thomas C. Hunt. Copyright © 2010 by Sage Publications, Inc. Reprinted by permission.

6. See Stanley W. Lindberg, *The Annotated McGuffey: Selections from the McGuffey Eclectic Readers 1836-1920* (New York: Van Nostrand Reinhold, 1976); Dolores P. Sullivan, *William Holmes McGuffey: Schoolmaster to the Nation.* (Rutherford, NJ: Fairleigh Dickinson University Press, 1994); R. L. Venezky, "The American Reading Script and Its Nineteenth-Century Origins," *Book Research Quarterly* 6, no. 2 (1990): 16-29; John H. Westerhoff, III. *McGuffey and His Readers: Piety, Morality and Education in Nineteenth Century America* (Nashville, TN: Abingdon, 1978).

7. Cover of *McGuffey's First Eclectic Reader* by William Holmes McGuffey, Truman and Smith Publishing, 1841.

8. Hagedorn, *Founding Zealots*, 256.

9. James W. Fraser, "Abolitionism, Activism, and New Models for Ministry," *American Presbyterians* 66, no. 2 (Summer 1988): 89-103.

10. Lyman Beecher Stowe, *Saints, Sinners, and Beechers* (Indianapolis: The Bobbs-Merril Company, 1934), 7.

11. Hagedorn, *Founding Zealots*, 177-181.

12. Noll, *A History of Christianity*, 189.

13. Lyman Beecher, *Lyman Beecher and the Reform of Society: Four Sermons, 1804-1828* (New York: Arno Press, 1972).

14. Lyman Beecher, "Resources of the Adversary, and Means of their Destruction," *The Wesleyan-Methodist Magazine* 7 (August 1828): 516-24.

15. Fraser, "Abolitionism," 91.

16. Michael Schnell, "Lyman Beecher's Nativist History," *Nineteenth-Century Prose* 27, no. 1 (Spring 2000): 29.

17. Ibid., 28.

18. Ibid., 32.

19. David Turley, "Religion and Approaches to Reform: Boston Unitarians Versus Evangelicals in the Context of the 1820s and 1830s," *American Nineteenth Century History* 10, no. 2 (June 2009): 191.

20. James W. Fraser, *Pedagogue for God's Kingdom: Lyman Beecher and the Second Great Awakening* (Lanham, MD: University Press of America, 1985), 182.

21. Hagedorn, *Founding Zealots*, 197.

22. *Catharine Esther Beecher*, Public Domain.

23. Catharine E. Beecher, *Educational Reminiscences and Suggestions* (New York: J. B. Ford and Company, 1874), iv.

24. Ibid., 8.

25. Catherine Villanueva Gardner, "Heaven-Appointed Educators of Mind: Catharine Beecher and the Moral Power of Women," *Hypatia* 19, no. 2 (Spring 2004): 3.

26. Catharine E. Beecher, *Religious Training of Children in the School, the Family, and the Church* (Ann Arbor, MI: University of Michigan Library, 1864), 12.

27. Gutek, *Historical and Philosophical Foundations*, 123.

28. Ibid.

29. Gutek, *Philosophical*, 260.

30. Ornstein, Levine, Gutek, and Vocke, *Foundations of Education*, 136-9.

31. Tehie, *Historical Foundations of Education*, 204.

32. Fraser, *Pedagogue for God's Kingdom*, 138-139.

33. See Hagedorn, *Founding Zealots*; Daniel McKanan, "Unitarianism, Universalism, and Unitarian Universalism," *Religion Compass* 7, no. 1 (2013): 15-24; Noll, *A History of Christianity*; Samuel James Smith and Elmer L. Towns, "Horace Bushnell: Advocate of Progressive

Orthodoxy and Christian Nurture," in *A Legacy of Religious Educators: Historical and Theological Introductions*, ed. Elmer L. Towns and Benjamin K. Forrest (Lynchburg, VA: Liberty University Press, 2017).

34. From *A Legacy of Religious Educators: Historical and Theological Introductions* by Elmer L. Towns and Benjamin K. Forrest. Copyright © 2016 by Elmer L. Towns and Benjamin K. Forrest. Reprinted by permission.

35. Robert Bruce Mullin, *The Puritan as Yankee: A Life of Horace Bushnell* (Grand Rapids, MI: William B. Eerdmans), 33.

36. Mullin, *The Puritan and the Yankee*, 15.

37. Lee J. Makowski, *Horace Bushnell on Christian Character Development* (Lanham, MD: University Press of America), 37.

38. Lockerbie, *Passion for Learning*, 296-297.

39. Michael Ryan, "'The Puritans of Today': The Anti-Whig Argument of *The Scarlet Letter*," *Canadian Review of American Studies* 38, no. 2 (2008): 203.

40. Makowski, *Bushnell on Christian Character*, 13, 135.

41. Gary Dorrien, *The Making of American Liberal Theology: Imagining Progressive Religion 1805-1900* (Louisville, KY: Westminster John Knox Press, 2001), 150.

42. Horace Bushnell, *Christian Nurture* (New York: Scribner, 1861), 93.

43. Ibid., 94.

44. Ibid., 106-107.

45. Ibid., 166-167.

46. Horace Bushnell, *Sermons for the New Life* (New York: Scribner, 1867), 4.

47. Ibid., 9.

48. Ibid., 21.

49. Ibid., 22.

50. Charles Hodge, "Bushnell on Christian Nurture," *Biblical Repertory and Princeton Review* 19 (1847): 502.

51. Ibid.

52. Arthur Cushman McGiffert, *The Rise of Modern Religious Ideals* (New York: Macmillan, 1915), 277.

53. Broadman W. Kathan, "Horace Bushnell and the Religious Education Movement," *Religious Education* 108, no. 1 (2013): 45.

54. Makowski, *Bushnell on Christian Character*, 48.

55. Ryan, "The Puritans of Today'," 217.

56. Bushnell, *Christian Nurture*, 212-213

57. Sandford Fleming, *Children and Puritanism* (New Haven, CT: Yale University), 185.

58. Kathan, "Horace Bushnell," 42.

59. Mark H. Senter, "Horace Bushnell, Theodore Cuyler, and Francis Clark: A Study of How Youth Ministry Began," *Journal of Youth Ministry* 2, no. 2 (2004): 40.

60. Lockerbie, *A Passion for Learning*, 296.

61. Michiyo Morita, *Horace Bushnell on Women in Nineteenth-Century America* (Lanham, MD: University Press of America, 2004), 6, 89-92.

62. George A. Coe, *The Religion of the Mature Mind* (Chicago: Revell, 1962), 305.

63. Kathan, "Horace Bushnell," 44.

64. Ibid., 41-46.

65. Ibid., 50-51.

66. Kathan, "Horace Bushnell," 52.

67. Coe, *Mature Mind*, 305.

68. Paul H. Vieth, *The Church and Christian Education* (St. Louis: Bethany), 20.

CHAPTER 11

EDUCATION IN THE ANTEBELLUM, CIVIL WAR, AND RECONSTRUCTION ERAS

Phillis Wheatley, poet[1]

FOCUS: KEY TOPICS AND TERMS

Anti-Literacy Law
Armstrong, Samuel
  Chapman
Douglass, Margaret
Du Bois, W. E. B.
Freedmen's Bureau

Hampton Institute
Historiography
Horizontal Relational
  Framework
Howard University
Howard, Oliver Otis

Nat Turner Rebellion
New South
Old South
Vertical Chronological
  Framework
Washington, Booker T.

# Except in the South: Historiography of Education in the American South

Attempting to explain the ways of the South is often a challenge. John Hardin Best, in his historiographic essay "Education in the Forming of the American South," illustrates this phenomenon by discussing a phrase commonly interjected into conversations: "except in the South." Best's thesis is that—while some specific generalization might seem true in the history of American education—the case may be that education in the South more accurately represents the American educational experience than do the prevailing narratives.

HISTORIOGRAPHIC NARRATIVES OF AMERICAN EDUCATION

According to Best, the original tale of the American South was told by "a relentless breed" of White male historians. This is the traditional narrative dichotomized into stories, whether fact or fiction, of hero and villain, Black and White, rich and poor, male and female, oppression, and pride. These accounts serve as the "background for considering the education of the South" and were conveyed both formally and informally through history, literature, religion, and the arts.[2]

Best discusses two other narratives, the progressive and revisionist perspectives, neither of which addressed to Best's satisfaction the phenomenon of Southern education in relation to the development of American education in general. The progressive narrative is represented by the works of Paul Monroe and Ellwood P. Cubberley, who wrote in the early twentieth century and whose views were couched in a context of societal transformation. They credited the public school system as the impetus behind advancements in industry, technology, and the economy, believing that the school created the ground on which the nation's progress was built. Later progressive historians, such as Lawrence Cremin and Bernard Bailyn, did not ascribe to public schools such a prominent role. They recognized contributions of other societal elements for contributing as significantly, if not more so, to the rapid development of the nation.

Emerging in the 1960s was a group of revisionist historians who began to reject the benevolent portrayal of schools. The likes of Clarence Karier and Michael Katz presented quite a different history in which schools systemically propagated "social control, bureaucracy, and oppression."[3] In their eyes, schools had failed—but not for the same reasons that Arthur Bestor and Admiral Hyman Rickover, critics of progressive education, believed schools had failed. For revisionists, the inadequacy of schools was not in their inability to help the nation win the Space Race. The shortfall of schools was in their becoming the antithesis of the social balance wheel that Horace Mann had envisioned. The very instrument that was to empty the prisons, eliminate poverty, and eradicate social injustice had become oppressive to the disenfranchised, specifically to the poor, to disempowered ethnic groups, and to women.

After tracing the traditional, progressive, and revisionist narratives, Best claims, "The history of education in recent years has done its job remarkably well, with one striking exception: it does not explain the South." Although he acknowledges writers, such as W. E. B. Du Bois, Horace Mann Bond, Edgar Knight, and others who gave attention to Southern education in their works, Best concurs with Thomas Dyer that "there seems to be no proper frame for looking at the history of southern education."[4]

HISTORIOGRAPHIC FRAMEWORKS FOR THE SOUTH

Best then suggests two dimensions, or historiographic frameworks, that may support an understanding of Southern education—a **horizontal relational framework** and a **vertical chronological framework**. The horizontal frame takes into account the interaction of three elements that sculpted Southern culture: (1) land and climate; (2) people; and (3) traditions. Best expounded on each of these elements, explaining the agrarian society, family structures, caste divisions, and codes of behavior—all of which interacted to "create a base for southern education history."[5]

The vertical chronological frame includes three historical eras: (1) the **Old South**, from colonial settlement through the Civil War; (2) the **New South**, through the Civil Rights Act of 1964; (3) and the **American South**, which represents the late twentieth-century rise of the Sun Belt. Best concluded with a series of questions regarding the horizontal dimensions that are applicable to each vertical dimension. As these questions are examined more fully, Best proposes that historians may concur with C. Vann Woodward's claim that "The South was American a long time before it was Southern in any self-conscious or distinctive way. It remains more American by far than anything else, and has all along."[6]

Margaret Douglass: Prosecuted for Teaching Freed Black Children[8]

In the nineteenth century, voices for social reform reached a high pitch—both figuratively and literally. Recognizable women's voices were heard in various reform movements: Susan B. Anthony, Jane Addams, Dorothea Dix, Harriet Tubman, Catharine Beecher, and her sister Harriet Beecher-Stowe. These women were active in bringing about change in the societal roles and treatment of women, children, slaves, freedmen, and persons who were illiterate, disabled, poor, or incarcerated. A name not as recognizable, yet often held as an example of activism for educational rights of emancipated Blacks, is that of **Margaret Douglass**—a White Virginian woman who was jailed for a month for violating an 1849 law prohibiting the teaching of reading and writing to freedmen. Although Douglass' actions and the consequences faced for them have earned

Margaret Crittendon Douglass[7]

Source: *Educational Laws of Virginia*, 1854

her a modicum of notoriety, further consideration may affirm that the limited status she holds as a social activist is warranted.

By no means does exploring such a thesis intend to discredit the commendable actions of Douglass or in any way question her motives. It is a significant pursuit, however, to understand how benevolence toward a marginalized group or how provision of a valuable service to them may not equate to social activism that intentionally pushes boundaries to transform society. Questions to be considered include the following: (1)

To what degree did Douglass' resistance result in societal reform? (2) Was reform actually her intent, and—if so—what was her role and how sustained were her efforts? (3) What methods did she implement in her civil disobedience?

BACKGROUND AND HISTORICAL CONTEXT

From the Colonial era through the Early Republic, there was little perceived threat to White society by teaching slaves or freed Blacks to read or write. Prominent among the various religious groups who committed themselves to this work were the Quakers, who began Black schools in Norfolk in the late eighteenth century, and when the Sunday school movement spread to Virginia, churches commonly taught literacy both to White and Black children in separate classes. After the 1831 **Nat Turner Rebellion**, however, these literacy efforts were viewed with increased suspicion for fear that literate Blacks might embolden slaves to rebel.[9] In 1849, the General Assembly of the Commonwealth of Virginia passed a series of anti-literacy laws. Of which, Chapter 198, Section 32, stated, "If a white person assemble with negroes for the purpose of instructing them to read or write, . . . he shall be confined in jail not exceeding six months, and fined not exceeding one hundred dollars . . ."[10]

After the law's enactment, Sunday schools were expected to present orally their biblical and moral lessons to Black children, but many churches continued to do so in written format. There is no record, however, of any church-related instance in which an individual was charged with violating the law. Though there were many violations, rarely were Whites brought to trial. There was a great deal of "winking at the violation," and most infractions were handled extra-judicially by intimidation and social pressure.[11] Only one known prosecution of the law exists, and that is of Margaret Douglass.[12]

TRIAL OF MARGARET DOUGLASS

Much of Margaret Douglass' life is a mystery. After the death of her son in 1845, she moved to Norfolk from South Carolina with her teenaged daughter Rosa. Though she identified herself as "Mrs. Douglass," it is unknown whether she was widowed or divorced. Whatever the circumstances of her son's death and the absence of her husband, Douglass led a seemingly paradoxical life of isolation from her community while also being recognized, even by Norfolk's Mayor Stubbs, as a humanitarian who cared for sick children and women victims of domestic violence. She was a well-spoken, confident woman, who described herself as an "independent spirit" and a "superior work woman," earning a modest income, with Rosa's help, sewing and embroidering vests for wealthy men.[13]

In 1852, Douglass learned from a freed Black barber that he and his five children were illiterate. Thinking that the **anti-literacy law** applied only to slaves, she offered to have Rosa tutor his children at no cost. He took her up on the offer, and—after teaching for a short while—Rosa expressed that she enjoyed it so much that she would rather teach than to sew vests. With the help of the barber's family, the Douglasses announced that they were opening a school for freed Black children in their home. It would begin June 1, 1852, and would cost three dollars tuition per quarter, per child. On the first day of class, Rosa opened school with twenty-five boys and girls in a second-floor room of their home. Rosa taught basic reading and writing while her mother assisted in biblical and moral instruction. They were committed to students and their families beyond academic instruction. They often visited the children, taking food to them when they were sick, and cared for one ill child until her death.[14]

Eleven months after school opened, class was unexpectedly disrupted on May 9, 1853, when a law-enforcement officer knocked on the door and insisted to access the upstairs classroom. Douglass described Rosa as being "paralyzed" and the children as "clinging in terror" as they all were led like a "flock of little lambs going to the slaughter" on their way to meet Mayor Stubbs. Douglass explained that she was unaware that the law applied to freed Black children and that she would close the school immediately. Seeming satisfied, the mayor dismissed her without bond, and—although the case would be presented to the grand jury for review—she assumed the matter was resolved.[15]

Two months later, however, she received a summons to appear for trial in November. Since Rosa was a minor, the charges were directed only at Margaret. As she waited for her trial date, she refused to discuss the matter with anyone or to seek counsel. She would represent herself.[16]

In her boldly written memoir, Douglass meticulously described the morning of November 15. She deliberately dressed to appear authoritative and carried a small red pocket Bible. In her preparations, she seemed aware of the elements of class, gender, religion, and race that were very much a part of her situation—all of which she would reference that day in her defending arguments. Upon arriving at the courthouse, Douglass informed the government-appointed defense attorney that she would serve as her own counsel. The *Baltimore Sun* described the sensation that was created when the "intrepid female" sat at the bar—a place reserved for those in "coats and pantaloons."[17] She called three men as her witnesses—all of whom were prominent wealthy men in the community and who were members of Christ Church where she and most of her students worshipped. Her line of questioning was to indicate that the church's Sunday school program had taught literacy to the same children for some time, that the books the children used in her school were provided to them by the church, and that, if she were guilty of violating the crime, so were many of the Sunday school teachers at the church. Court documents reveal Douglass' words to her witnesses and also to the jury as being confident, bold, articulate, logical, and pointed. Though the men denied the teaching of literacy within the church, they were far from convincing. One claimed ignorance because the "ladies had all to do with that." Another admitted to knowing the children were literate because he had heard them read the Bible aloud, but he feigned ignorance as to how they got to be so. He stated, "When they came to the hard words, I allowed them to skip over them."[18]

In her closing arguments, Douglass told the jury that she was not an abolitionist, was not acting on behalf of Northern instigators as accused by the press, had been a slaveholder herself, and "would be again if so disposed." Although she did speak of the "misery and distress" of Blacks, she affirmed her loyalty to the South and to its traditions, including that of slavery. She claimed complete ignorance of the law, stating, "Had I known . . . I would not have set myself in opposition to the law."[19] She then went on to address a socially taboo topic and, by doing so, may arguably have brought on her guilty verdict by the jury and the judge's sentence. The topic of miscegenation.

After describing her own humanitarian actions to visit and care for Black families, she stated, "It is not expected that gentlemen will take the trouble to seek out a negro hut for the purpose of alleviating the wretchedness he may find within it."[20] Her subsequent statements clarified that her insinuation was that men indeed seek out negro huts—but for another cause altogether:

> In my opinion, we have nothing to fear from the true blooded negro. It is the half-breed, or those with more or less white blood in their veins, whom I have always found presumptive,

treacherous and revengeful. And do you blame them for this? How can you? Ask yourselves the cause. Ask how that white blood got beneath those tawny skins, and let nature herself account for the exhibition of these instincts. Blame the authors of this devilish mischief, but not the innocent victims of it.[21]

She later wrote in her memoir even more boldly about miscegenation: "Sable scholars . . . did I say? No, not all; for in many cases the difference could scarcely be perceived between them and white children. Yes, Mrs. D 'condescended' to teach free black men's children, and free white men's children—some of the latter being, very probably, among her real persecutors." For Douglass, it was miscegenation, not slavery, that was "the one great evil hanging over the South," and it was White women who were the greatest victims as they had to tolerate silently the smell of Black women on their husbands. Regarding the anti-literacy laws, she wrote, "How important, then, for these Southern sultans, that the objects of their criminal passions should be kept in utter ignorance and degradation. They must not read the Bible because that teaches them the sin of their masters."[22]

The jury deliberated for two days before rendering a verdict of guilty with a one dollar fine. The long deliberation indicated that the decision may have been problematic, but the minimal fine—considering that the maximum allowable fine was one hundred dollars—conveyed that the jury may have sympathized with her argument, her cause, or her condition as a woman of modest means. The judge set the sentencing date for January and was not as sympathetic in his sentence or in his statement as he delivered it.[23]

In his lengthy statement, Judge Richard Baker addressed many issues that were unrelated directly to Douglass' crime. For instance, Baker defended the institution of slavery and railed against "Northern incendiaries" even though Douglass never taught slaves and had no connection to the North. "If you were of a different sex," he told her, "I should regard the full punishment of six months imprisonment." He went on to rationalize that a minimal sentence of less than a week would be inappropriate because this had been "a case in which the question of guilt is free from doubt, and there are many facts and circumstances of aggravation." He did not, however, expound on what the aggravation had been, especially considering that she closed the school immediately upon learning that her actions were illegal. Her sentence was one month in the city jail.[24]

During her sentence, the jailor and his wife showed Douglass special care. After her release, they hosted her in their home for several days before she and Rosa moved to Philadelphia. In her memoir, she described her new home as a place "where we are now quietly residing, happy in the consciousness that it is here no crime to teach a poor child, of any color, to read the Word of God."[25]

PERSPECTIVES ON DOUGLASS

The newspapers were not kind to Douglass. They described her as a "dangerous white woman" and an "intrepid female." The *Norfolk Argus* bid her good riddance by writing, "Let her depart hence with only one wish, that her presence will never be intruded upon us again."[26] The *Baltimore Sun* compared her to "Lucy Stone, or any other member of the 'strong-minded' sisterhood."[27] Yet, how has she been perceived over time?

A. Leon Higginbotham repeatedly recognized Douglass as an example of a White woman deserving of heroine status in the struggle for fair and just treatment of African Americans.[28] A number of others have also portrayed her as a heroine and as one who boldly defied the law as a social activist.[29] Some, such as Mary Cathryn Cain, have criticized her harshly. Cain cited Douglass as an example of a White woman motivated more by the negative impact of slavery on Whites rather than the actual oppression of Blacks. Cain used Douglass' own words to illustrate her White supremacy, disdain for Black women, and support for slavery.[30]

Evidence indicates that Margaret Douglass was a true benefactor to poor, ill, and disenfranchised people—both White and Black. She was a bold, outspoken woman at a time when such a quality in females was not appreciated as much as it might be in more recent times. There is no reason to doubt the sincerity of her intentions regarding the teaching of the Bible and morality to freed Black children. However, none of the evidence leads to the conclusion that she was a social reformer who intentionally acted to transform society. To the contrary, her own words—both in court and in her memoir—support the notion that she never deliberately violated the law. She unapologetically admitted to having owned a slave, claimed that she would have no issue with doing so again, denied being an abolitionist, and spoke openly of the superiority of the Caucasian race. Furthermore, her decision to open a school for freed Black children seemed more pragmatic than altruistic. It was a mutually beneficial arrangement. Her teenaged daughter, who enjoyed teaching more than helping her mother sew vests, was able to contribute to the modest family income while also contributing to the academic, religious, and moral instruction of the disenfranchised. Douglass' story is interesting, a bit mysterious, and dramatic enough to merit a stage play or film. It does not, however, warrant her the status of social reformer.

General Oliver Otis Howard: Educational Reformer and Christian Soldier

Contemporaries of **Oliver Otis Howard** and historians alike have disagreed on the degree of his success as a Civil War general and as commissioner of the **Freedmen's Bureau**. Some describe his performance as inept and others as skillful. Some laud his Christian example while others believe that he allowed his religious and political beliefs to diminish his efforts. Whatever one's perspective, evidence indicates that Howard's political and religious beliefs influenced his actions as Civil War general and as Freedmen's Bureau commissioner, and—although he experienced some failure in both arenas—his leadership is exemplified by what may be remembered as his finest hours in the battle of Gettysburg and in the development of African-American education.

General Oliver Otis Howard[31]

CHRISTIAN SOLDIER OF THE CIVIL WAR

Howard grew up in Maine on a family farm, working beside his brother and a Black servant, but not until Howard was enrolled as a cadet at West Point did religion begin to play a prominent role in his life. While a student there, he joined a Bible class and lived an openly pious life. After graduating, he served in various posts in the army, eventually being stationed in Florida where, in 1857, he attended a meeting of a Methodist church. There he prayed with the preacher at the altar, experiencing a spiritual conversion that markedly changed his life. Shortly after his conversion, he read a book about British Army Captain Hedley Vicars who fought during the Crimean War. Captain Vicars was known for being a strong evangelical Christian and an exemplary soldier. Howard determined that he would follow the model set by Vicars.[32]

From Florida, Howard returned to West Point as a professor of mathematics. In addition to his teaching role, he led prayer meetings, served in the chaplain's office, and volunteered in a local church as a Bible teacher and Sunday school superintendent. In a dedication service for troops departing to Utah, Howard preached a sermon inspired by Vicars entitled "The Christian Soldier." This became the moniker by which Howard became known in the Union Army.[33]

Howard's spiritual fervor was such that he considered leaving the army to enter the full-time ministry. At the outbreak of the Civil War, however, Howard was convinced that his primary duty was to fight for his country. During the war, Howard's religious convictions were expressed in a number of ways, many of which irritated other soldiers. For example, he was reluctant to engage troops in fighting on Sundays, did not condone the drinking of alcohol, and often led his men in prayer and Bible study.[34] His prayer meetings welcomed as equals Black men who served the troops as teamsters and cooks.[35] Howard perceived his ministry to people and service to God as inclusive of his work in the army and in social causes. Some of his volunteer work involved helping to establish the First Congregational Church in Washington, D.C., providing relief efforts to the Chinese in Portland, Oregon, and serving as president of two YMCA affiliates.[36]

CIVIL WAR SERVICE

Howard entered the Civil War as a brigade commander. Marching his troops across the Potomac River into Virginia, he observed conduct among them, such as profanity and drinking, that did not sit well with his evangelical sensibilities. After the first battle of Bull Run—in which he led his brigade commendably despite their loss—Howard became more intentional about cultivating a Christian environment among his men by implementing regular prayer meetings and Bible studies.[37]

In the Virginia Peninsula Campaign at the battle of Fair Oaks, Howard lost his right arm and thirty-one years later would receive the Congressional Medal of Honor for his service that day. Even during his three-month recovery in his home state of Maine, he served the army as a recruiter. He then returned, having earned a reputation for bravery, ready to participate in the second battle at Bull Run, Antietam, and Fredericksburg.[38]

Just prior to the battle of Chancellorsville, Gen. Hooker appointed Howard to command the 11th Corps, which found itself on the defense against Confederate Gen. Stonewall Jackson. The 11th Corps was made up primarily of German-speaking troops and, due in part to the blunders of its previous commander, had a bad reputation of not fighting heartily enough. The reputation of the 11th Corps and the mistakes of Gen. Hooker may have saved Howard from harsher criticisms for his own failures at Chancellorsville, which were the inadequate protection of his left flank and lack of preparedness for Jackson's attack.[39]

Perhaps Howard's finest display of generalship and also his most controversial actions were on July 1, 1863, at the first day of the battle of Gettysburg. The night before, Howard had stayed up late chatting with his old friend from West Point, commander of the 1st Corps, Gen. John Reynolds. They discussed Meade's most recent orders directing Reynolds to fall back to Emmitsburg if he encountered a Confederate force, but they were expecting more current orders that night to prepare for the morning. When no orders came, they parted and retired for the evening.[40]

The next morning, Howard received an order from Reynolds directing him to move his 11th Corps to Gettysburg. Upon arriving, Howard found himself in a battle already underway in which Reynolds was killed. This placed Howard in the position of command over Reynolds' 1st Corps and his own 11th Corps. In the chaos of the moment, Howard had to decide whether to follow Meade's earlier orders to fall back or Reynolds' most recent plans. He chose to follow Reynolds' plan, dispatching his 11th Corps to position itself on Cemetery Hill. Anticipating that he might become outnumbered by the Confederates while waiting for reinforcements, Howard separated out a third of his corps as backup, positioning them a mile away—close enough to arrive quickly when needed. He found that his hunch was correct when two additional Confederate divisions arrived. It was this quick strategic thinking for which Howard was later praised.[41]

Critics, however, focus on what happened next. Outnumbered and with no additional reinforcements beyond the third of his corps that he had set aside for backup, Howard called for a withdrawal to a designated position on Cemetery Hill. The timing and orderliness of the withdrawal were questionable. Howard definitely made mistakes; he waited too long to call for the withdrawal and no specific directions were given for moving artillery. Considering the conditions and how events played out, however, his key decisions ultimately proved advantageous.[42]

A further incident that provided fodder for critics resulted from the cavalry commander's written plea to his superior: "General Reynolds was killed early this morning. In my opinion, there seems to be no directing person. . . . P.S. We need help now."[43] Gen. Winfield Scott Hancock, 2nd Corps commander, then arrived on the scene with orders from Gen. Meade to take command. Howard refused. He was four steps above Hancock in seniority. Also, by the time Hancock had arrived, most of the day's decisions had already been made. They agreed at the time to work together so that Howard would give the orders and Hancock would second them. Later, however, each would claim to have had full command without the assistance of the other until Slocum arrived, who outranked them both and took over command.[44]

In January 1864, Congress passed a resolution to extend gratitude not just to Gen. Meade but also to two other officers, Howard and Hooker. This action set off a firestorm of controversy, especially between Howard and Hancock, that would continue through the remainder of their lives. Howard was recognized as "the man who selected the position where the battle of Gettysburg was fought."[45]

Politically, Howard was a Radical Republican and an abolitionist, which was rare in the Army of the Potomac, especially among officers. While his religious views resulted in his being periodically mocked and ostracized, his political views resulted in more serious conflicts. For instance, Gen. Meade, a Democrat, could not hide his disdain for Howard, so much so that he transferred him to the western frontier to serve with Gen. Tecumseh Sherman soon after Gettysburg. Sherman, also a Republican but not as religious as Howard, spoke commendably of Howard, and the two worked well together.[46] "When exposed to the fire," Sherman spoke of Howard, "there is no braver man living than he." Regarding Howard's religion, Sherman said, "I believe Howard is a real Christian. . . . he has something about him, which I haven't, but which I wish I had."[47]

Reviews of Howard's generalship have been mixed—from commendations to accusations of being incapable of controlling the conduct of his troops. For example, in the occupation of Columbia, South Carolina, his troops looted during a fire. He directed his officers to ensure the looting ceased, but then he proceeded to take a nap as the looting continued.[48] Overall, however, Howard proved, especially in difficult circumstances, to provide effective leadership. This was true in the Civil War and also in his subsequent service with the Freedmen's Bureau.

Candidates in Howard's teacher preparation program[49]

Elementary students of the practice school in the foreground with Howard teacher education candidates in the background[50]

FREEDMEN'S BUREAU AND HOWARD UNIVERSITY

Volunteer freedman's aid societies in the North had joined together to lobby Congress for a government agency to assist in the transition of emancipated people into their roles as citizens.[51] One such organization was the New England Freedman's Aid Society that lobbied especially for the establishment of free schools in the South.[52] Their efforts were rewarded when on March 3, 1865, Congress passed a bill approving the Bureau of Refugees, Freedmen, and Abandoned Lands, known more commonly as the Freedmen's Bureau. It was to last until one year after the war but was later extended until 1872.[53] Before his assassination, Lincoln had selected Gen. Howard as the bureau's Commissioner, and later President Johnson officially appointed him to the position. The nation overwhelmingly supported Howard's appointment as have historians over time—despite criticisms of poor judgment, fiscal mismanagement, conflicts of interest, and politicization of the bureau.[54] Howard was only thirty-four years old as the war came to a close and had been considering what he would do afterward. He accepted the commission as God's providential will and would go on to lead the agency to provide medical and hunger relief, negotiate work contracts, distribute abandoned lands, and educate millions of children and adults. Of these efforts, education was by far the most successful initiative of the bureau.[55]

Considering anti-literacy laws in the South that had severely limited the education of slaves and even freed Blacks, the bureau's educational efforts would be transformational for the Black population and highly controversial among White Southerners. African Americans had displayed a strong desire for schooling and—even before the creation of the bureau—had already been involved in self-education and cooperative efforts with Northern aid societies. By 1869, bureau schools had enrolled 114,000 students.[56]

Go to www.khlearn.com to watch a video about the education of African Americans after the Civil War.

The bureau's role was primarily in renting or constructing school buildings and in the administration of the schools. Howard appointed J. W. Alvord as superintendent of schools for this purpose. The bureau was limited in that it could not fund teacher salaries or curriculum materials, so it relied on the aid societies for teachers and textbooks.[57] Some schoolbooks were customized for freed students. One such textbook with content for both children and adults was L. Maria Child's *The Freedman's Book*. Published in 1865, it contained a collection of writings by Frederick Douglass, William Lloyd Garrison, Frances E. W. Harper, Harriet Beecher Stowe, and many other authors both White and Black. Like other readers of its day, it included selections from the Bible, poems, short stories, and biographies of Benjamin Banneker, John Brown, and Phillis Wheatley.[58] Other curriculum materials were the same as those used in New England schools, following the idea that a traditional education would better prepare freedmen to assimilate into society. These New England textbooks taught traditional subjects of reading, writing, grammar, history, geography, and mathematics.[59]

Bureau teachers were made up of Blacks and Whites both from the North and the South. To prepare future teachers and to promote higher education among the Black population, universities were established with the bureau's assistance, including Fisk, Atlanta, and Hampton. Named in honor of Gen. Howard was **Howard University** in the nation's capital city. Gen. Howard would serve as the university's president from 1869 to 1874.[60]

Go to www.khlearn.com to watch a video about notable African Americans from historically black universities.

Much of the college-level curriculum focused on industrial education. For example, **Hampton Institute**, founded by Col. **Samuel Chapman Armstrong** with the help of the Freedmen's Bureau, followed a philosophy of industrial education. The premise was that Black students needed practical vocational training and moral instruction more so than a traditional university curriculum. This experience offered male students training in such trades as brickmaking, bricklaying, shoemaking, carpentry, and blacksmithing. Female students learned domestic skills.[61] Many freedmen welcomed practical education as a means of gaining a livelihood and sought basic skills to help them ensure fairness in dealing with contracts, weights, and measures. However, this narrow curriculum in higher education came to be criticized as a means of keeping freed people at the bottom levels of society.[62]

Howard's detractors claimed that he refused to eliminate corruption.[63] Some individual agents were accused of acting more in the best interest of Whites than of freedmen, of mistreating clients, and of imbibing excessively in liquor. Howard was therefore portrayed by critics as a weak and ineffective leader, yet the record indicates that he went to great lengths to monitor and to take action against incompetent and corrupt agents in the field. Perhaps the agents that were monitored least were those who served in the Washington, D.C., headquarters—especially in the disbursement of funds. When it came to financial issues, there were complaints that the bureau simply was too costly; an article in the *The Baltimore Sun*, for example, complained that a sub-agency of the bureau cost more than the entire U.S. President's salary.[64] There were, however, more legitimate financial concerns; Howard himself was guilty of stretching the parameters. For instance, in his zeal to promote education, he manipulated funds to arrange payment for teachers, which was prohibited by bureau regulations. One of the most publicized financial controversies was related to the use of funds for manufacturing bricks for the construction of Howard University. As the practice was intended to create brickmaking jobs for university students, it was so questionable that it came under Congressional investigation. Though Howard was exonerated, the incident tainted his leadership and the bureau's reputation.[65]

Another criticism of Howard was that, as a Republican, he was politically motivated, used the bureau as a tool for the Republican Party, and sought to indoctrinate freedmen to become Republican voters. While Howard clearly preferred Republican ideology, his official stance with bureau agents was that they were to remain politically neutral in their conversations and actions. This, however, was difficult to monitor, and questionable incidents indeed occurred.[66]

The early historiography of the bureau included a single national survey and a few state studies written from the South's perspective.[67] Later **W. E. B. Du**

Booker T. Washington (1856-1915), speaking on a raised platform in Mound Bayou, Mississippi

© Everett Historical/Shutterstock.com

Bois concluded that both Howard and the bureau had been a failure by allowing outside forces to limit its efforts and by missing a historic opportunity to bring about monumental change for African Americans. In the twentieth century, Paul Skeels Peirce depicted the bureau as an arm of the Republican Party[68] while George R. Bentley acknowledged the bureau's relief efforts and educational accomplishments but claimed that it was detrimental to race relations and to equality for African Americans.[69] A shift began, however, especially with the biography of Howard written by John A. Carpenter at the end of the twentieth century. Carpenter conveyed great respect for Howard as both Civil War general and Freedmen's Bureau commissioner. Any failings of the Bureau, Carpenter claimed, would have been much worse without the leadership of Howard.[70] In the twenty-first century, Robert Harris—acknowledging the complicated context in which Gen. Howard and the bureau functioned—wrote, "Within the parameters set by the unforgiving dynamics of Reconstruction, Freedmen's Bureau agents, most of them at least, struggled manfully to negotiate terms of freedom for African Americans."[71]

Considering the challenges faced by the bureau, Gen. Howard provided commendable leadership. He managed a vast operation in the face of harsh opposition by White Southerners, constant turnover of personnel, and a relatively short window of time for the bureau to achieve such massive goals. As a result of the bureau's work, in the early 1870s, a higher percentage of Black children than White children were enrolled in Southern schools.[72] By 1870, there were 4,329 new schools created with approximately 9,500 teachers working with over 247,000 students.[73] Disappointing as it was that neither land nor sufficient civil rights were obtained by freedmen, the bureau's legacy of education was built in large part by Oliver Otis Howard's determination to carry out what he perceived was a calling of God.[74]

On November 8, 1900, a gathering of over two hundred friends met in New York to celebrate Howard's seventieth birthday. He was honored by organizations such as the American Tract Society and the YMCA and by a variety of individuals. "His life in peace," stated former Speaker of the House Thomas B. Reed, "has been as great as his life in war." Naval officer Captain Alfred Mahan said, "In him we see the combination of the Christian and the soldier." **Booker T. Washington** said, "The name of Howard is in the hearts of the negro race beside the names of Garrison, Grant, and Lincoln. . . . We went into slavery a piece of property; we came out American citizens. Thanks to such men as Gen. Howard, we came out with the spelling book in one hand and the Bible in the other." In response, Howard told of the last time he met with Lincoln. The president had pointed to a map of the Cumberland Gap, asking, "Can't we go through and free those people?" In his birthday celebration closing remarks, Howard said, "And now as the last act of my life, I am anxious to bring about the education of

General Oliver O. Howard, head of the Bureau, mediating between belligerent groups of Whites and Blacks

© Everett Historical/Shutterstock.com

the boys and girls of Lincoln's beloved mountains."[75] Consistent with the pattern of his life, Howard indeed spent his last years following what he sensed as his calling, his mission, and his purpose.

 Go to www.khlearn.com to watch a video about education in the Antebellum, Civil War, and Reconstruction eras.

 Reflection

For personal reflection, content review, and further research:

1. In what way does the phrase "except in the South" apply to the development of education in America?
2. Explain John Hardin Best's horizontal relational framework and vertical chronological framework to understand the history of education in the South.
3. How did the elements of (a) land and climate, (b) people, and (c) traditions sculpt education in the South?
4. Why were anti-literacy laws passed in the South?
5. Margaret Douglass may have had a number of motivations to teach freed Black children. What might have been those motives?
6. Consider issues of race, gender, class, and religion in the narrative of Margaret Douglass. To what degree did she display resistance to discrimination in each of these areas?
7. What motivation drove Gen. Howard in his educational reform efforts?
8. Trace the development of Historically Black Colleges and their role in the advancement of African Americans.

ENDNOTES

1. Scipio Moorhead, *Phillis Wheatley: Negro servant to Mr. John Wheatley*, of Boston, 1773, engraving, Library of Congress Rare Book and Special Collections Division Washington, DC, accessed December 29, 2019, http://loc.gov/pictures/resource/cph.3a40394/. Public Domain.

2. John Hardin Best, "Education in the Forming of the American South," *History of Education Quarterly* 36, no. 1 (1996): 39-51.

3. Ibid.

4. Ibid., 44-5.

5. Ibid.

6. Ibid., 44.

7. Margaret Douglass, *Educational Laws of Virginia: The Personal Narrative of Mrs. Margaret Douglass, a Southern Woman Who was Imprisoned for One Month in the Common Jail of Norfolk, Under the Laws of Virginia for the Crime of Teaching Free Colored Children to Read* (Boston: J. P. Jewitt & Co., 1854). Public Domain.

8. From Liberty University, *Bound Away: The Liberty Journal of History*, Volume 2, Issue 2, Article 4 by Samuel J. Smith. Copyright © by Scholars Crossing. Reprinted by permission.

9. See Janet Duitsman Cornelius, *'When I Can Read My Title Clear': Literacy, Slavery, and Religion in the Antebellum South* (Columbia, SC: University of South Carolina Press, 1991), 11-32; Philip S. Foner and Josephine F. Pacheco, *Three Who Dared: Prudence Crandall, Margaret Douglass, Myrtilla Miner—Champions of Antebellum Black Education* (Westport, CT: Greenwood Press, 1984), xv; A. Leon Higginbotham and Anne F. Jacobs, "The 'Law Only as an Enemy': The Legitimization of Racial Powerlessness through the Colonial and Antebellum Criminal Laws of Virginia," *North Carolina Law Review* 70, no. 4 (1992): 1020.

10. Virginia. *The Code of Virginia: With the Declaration of Independence and Constitution of the United States; and the Declaration of Rights and Constitution of Virginia* (Richmond: William F. Ritchie, 1849).

11. Carter Godwin Woodson, *The Education of the Negro Prior to 1861: A History of the Education of the Colored People of the United States from the Beginning of Slavery to the Civil War* (New York: Putnam, 1915), 79-81.

12. See I. Bennett Capers, "Reading Back, Reading Black," *Hofstra Law Review* 35, no. 1 (2006): 19; E. Jennifer Monaghan, "Reading for the Enslaved, Writing for the Free: Reflections on Liberty and Literacy," *American Antiquarian Society* 108, no. 2 (January 1998): 337.

13. See Douglass, *Educational Laws of Virginia*, 16; Foner and Pacheco, *Three Who Dared*, x.

14. Foner and Pacheco, *Three Who Dared*, 58-60.

15. Douglass, *Educational Laws of Virginia*, 14-21.

16. Foner and Pacheco, *Three Who Dared*, 63.

17. "Trial of a Female at Norfolk," *The Baltimore Sun* (November 28, 1853): 1.

18. Albert P. Blaustien and Robert L. Zangrando, ed. *Civil Rights and the American Negro: A Documentary History* (New York: Trident Press, 1968), 134-138.

19. Ibid., 135.

20. Ibid.

21. Ibid., 136.

22. Douglass, *Educational Laws of Virginia*, 14, 64-65.

23. Blaustien and Zangrando, *Civil Rights*, 136.

24. See Richard Baker, "The Crime of Mrs. Douglass in Teaching Colored Children to Read," January 10, 1854, in *The Annals of America*, vol. 4, 1850-1857, *A House Dividing* (Chicago: Encyclopedia Britannica, 1968), 224-226; Blaustien and Zangrando, *Civil Rights*, 138.

25. Douglass, *Educational Laws of Virginia*, 50.

26. See Douglass, *Educational Laws of Virginia*, 42-43; "Trial of a Female at Norfolk," 1; Woodson, *The Education of the Negro*, 34.

27. "Trial," *Baltimore Sun*, 2.

28. See A. Leon Higginbotham, "Rosa Parks: Foremother and Heroine Teaching Civility and Offering a Vision for a Better Tomorrow," *Florida State University Law Review* 22, no. 4 (1995). 899-911. Higginbotham and Jacobs, "The 'Law Only,'" 969-1070. A. Leon Higginbotham and Greer C. Bosworth, "'Rather Than the Free': Free Blacks in Colonial and Antebellum Virginia," *Harvard Civil Rights—Civil Liberties Law Review* 26, no. 1 (1991): 17-66.

29. See "Antiliteracy Laws," in *The American Mosaic: The African American Experience*, ABC-CLIO, 2017; Stephen T. Butterfield, "The Use of Language

in the Slave Narratives," *Negro American Literature Forum* 6, no. 3 (Autumn 1972): 74-75; James Freeman Clarke, "Nullifying the Fugitive Slave Law," *The Liberator* (March 25, 1859) Accessible Archives; Elizabeth R. Varon, *We Mean to Be Counted: White Women & Politics in Antebellum Virginia* (Chapel Hill: University of North Carolina Press, 1998), 29.

30. Mary Cathryn Cain, "Rhetorics of Race and Freedom: The Expression of Women's Whiteness in Anti-Slavery Activism," *Studies in Popular Culture* 29, no. 2 (October 2006): 10.

31. Mathew Brady or Levin C. Handy, *Gen. O. O. Howard*, 1855-1865, photo, Library of Congress, Washington, DC. Public Domain.

32. David Thomson, "Oliver Otis Howard: Reassessing the Legacy of the 'Christian General,'" *American Nineteenth Century History* 10, no. 3 (2009): 276-82.

33. Ibid., 282.

34. John H. Giltner, "Oliver Otis Howard: Dimensions of a Christian Soldier," *The Journal of Religious Thought* 24, no. 1 (1967): 6-10.

35. Allen C. Guelzo, *Gettysburg: The Last Invasion* (New York: Alfred A. Knopf, 2013), 125.

36. Giltner, "Oliver Otis Howard," 9-10.

37. Thomson, "Oliver Otis Howard," 283-4.

38. John A. Carpenter, "General O. O. Howard at Gettysburg," *Civil War History* 9, no. 3 (1963): 262.

39. John C. Fredriksen, "Oliver O. Howard," in *The American Mosaic: The African American Experience*, *ABC-CLIO*, 2019.

40. Carpenter, "General O. O. Howard," 262-3.

41. Ibid., 263-5.

42. Ibid., 265.

43. Ibid.

44. Guelzo, *Gettysburg*, 157-65, 210.

45. Ibid., 451.

46. Ibid., 119-25, 450.

47. Thomson, "Oliver Otis Howard," 285-9.

48. Ibid., 290-1.

49. *Practice School Teachers, Howard University*, c. 1900, photo, Library of Congress, Washington, DC. Public Domain.

50. *Practice School, Howard University*, c. 1900, photo, Library of Congress, Washington, DC. Public Domain.

51. Michelle L. Jay and Lisa Wills, "Freedmen's Bureau," in *Encyclopedia of Educational Reform and Dissent*, ed. Thomas C. Hunt, James C. Carper, Thomas J. Lasley, and C. Daniel Raisch (Los Angeles: Sage, 2010), 388.

52. "New England Freedmen's Aid Society—Official Records, 1862-1872," in *The School in the United States: A Documentary History*, ed. James W. Fraser (New York: Routledge, 2010), 109-10.

53. "Freedmen's Bureau Act," in *Reconstruction Era Reference Library*, vol. 3, Primary Sources, *U.S. History in Context*, ed. Lawrence W. Baker, Bridget Hall Grumet, Kelly King Howes, and Roger Matuz (Detroit, MI: UXL, 2005), 34-45.

54. William S. McFeely, *Yankee Stepfather: General O. O. Howard and the Freedmen* (New York: W. W. Norton & Company, 1968), 8.

55. Daniel J. Sharfstein, *Thunder in the Mountains: Chief Joseph, Oliver Otis Howard, and the Nez Pierce War* (New York: W. W. Norton & Company, 2017), 33.

56. Ornstein, Levine, Gutek, and Vocke, *Foundations of Education*, 146.

57. Jay and Wills, "Freedmen's Bureau," 387-9.

58. L. Maria Child, ed. *The Freedmen's Book* (Boston: Ticknor and Fields, 1865).

59. Jay and Wills, "Freedmen's Bureau," 389.

60. Ibid.

61. Gutek, *Historical and Philosophical Foundations*, 430.

62. Spring, *The American School*, 186.

63. Fredriksen, "Oliver O. Howard."

64. "Freedmen's Bureau," *The Sun (1837-1993)*, May 22, 1866, 1.

65. Sharfstein, *Thunder in the Mountains*, 27-8.

66. John A. Carpenter, *Sword and Olive Branch: Oliver Otis Howard* (New York: Fordham University Press, 1999), 139-46.

67. Robert Harrison, "New Representations of a 'Misrepresented Bureau': Reflections of Recent Scholarship on the Freedmen's Bureau," *American Nineteenth Century History* 8, no. 2 (2007): 205.

68. McFeely, *Yankee Stepfather*, 2-7.

69. George R. Bentley, *A History of the Freedmen's Bureau* (New York: Octagon Books, 1970).

70. McFeely, *Yankee Stepfather*, 5-7.

71. Harrison, "New Representations," 219.

72. Spring, *The American School*, 186.

73. Murphy, *The History and Philosophy*, 286.

74. Carpenter, *Sword and Olive Branch*, 156.

75. "Dinner in Honor of Gen. O. O. Howard," *New York Times (1857-1922)*, November 9, 1900, 2.

132 | Windows into the History and Philosophy of Education

CHAPTER 12

NATIVE AMERICAN EDUCATION: JOURNEY TO AUTONOMY AND RECIPROCITY

Source: David Brainerd, the Apostle to the North American Indians, 1891[1]

FOCUS: KEY TOPICS AND TERMS

Armstrong, Samuel
Brainerd, David
Carlisle School
Cherokee
Cultural learning
Edwards, Jonathan
Hampton Institute
Incas
Indian Removal Act
Iroquois Confederacy

Jesuits
Landscape learning
de Las Casas, Bartolomé
Learning from mistakes
Loyola, Ignatius
Mayans
Meriam Report
Mesoamerica
Mohicans
de Montaigne, Michel

Northwest Ordinance
Pratt, Richard
Red Jacket, Chief
Seneca Nation
Sequoyah
Society of Jesus
Wheelock, Eleazar
Whitefield, George

As the five hundredth anniversary approached of Christopher Columbus's arrival to the New World, hundreds of Native Americans, representing 120 Indian nations, gathered in Quito, Ecuador, to write a joint declaration entitled "500 Years of Indian Resistance." Reflecting on their struggles and identity as a people, they rejected the planned celebrations for 1992. They reaffirmed their commitment to self-determination, demanded respect for their culture, and defended their ability to educate autonomously.[2] Since the arrival of Europeans in the New World, Native Americans have indeed struggled to educate future generations autonomously. At times, indigenous peoples have willingly embraced the ways of settlers, but more often, Europeans coerced them into doing so. Native philosophy of education was so drastically different from the European framework that it took centuries of conflict before policies and practices moved toward cultural autonomy rather than external control, and—although Europeans had some sense that the educational exchange was reciprocal—it took reflective analysis of historians, philosophers, social activists, and policy makers to heighten appreciation for the contributions natives have made to Western thought.

 ## American Indian Perspectives on Education

Just as there are various perspectives on education within other cultures, Native Americans have held diverse educational views. In fact, it is important to keep in mind when studying any aspect of native life that Indian culture currently and historically has been extremely diverse. Overgeneralizations are common, not always out of disrespect but often from a desire to simplify the complexities of a multitude of Amerindian nations. This chapter, for example, may at times include such simplifications and may require readers to remind themselves that there are always exceptions to general statements. Regarding the problem of overgeneralization, Bryan Brayboy, an anthropologist of the Lumbee tribe, acknowledges that even his own efforts are limited in scope when he attempts to convey native perspectives on the philosophy of education.[3]

The problem for an Amerindian to define a Native American philosophy of education, Brayboy explains, is that the concept is intimately familiar to him while at the same time so intensely complex that it is challenging to convey to others. Education serves to transfer knowledge but also is an empowering agent. As K. Tsianina Lomawaima of the Creek nation says, "The history of American Indian Education can be boiled down to three simple words: Battle for power." For Seneca tribe member Arthur C. Parker, education must relate to the learner's intentional actions and spontaneous experiences. Another problem is the pervasive nature of education in Indian thought; it is everywhere and considers everyone as a potential teacher or learner. As one Apache retorts, "Wisdom sits in places" and comprises smoothness, resiliency, and steadiness. Education instills these qualities and does so from "particular places where stories and wisdom reside."[4]

Milton Gaither outlines three forms of indigenous education: (a) **landscape learning**, (b) **cultural learning**, and (c) **learning from mistakes**. First, landscape learning is the acquisition of knowledge about the environment—especially about plants and animals and through observation and experimentation. Natives were so extraordinarily knowledgeable of their landscape that scientists have been unable to find an American plant with medicinal qualities of which natives were not already aware. Second, cultural learning draws from human technologies and beliefs. Such technologies involve the use of fire to burn undergrowth so that herbivores and their predators are drawn to the edge of forests; this makes hunting much easier. Beliefs are taught through stories, ceremonies, and indoctrination. Finally, when failures occur in interactions with the landscape or culture, natural consequences teach natives to learn from their mistakes.[5]

Pre-Columbian Education

A challenge for researchers of Native American education prior to the arrival of Europeans is that neither written records nor firsthand accounts are available. Sources are limited to surviving oral traditions, early European chronicles, and archaeological artifacts. In addition to these sources are a number of relatively new scientific techniques from fields such as genetics, climatology, linguistics, and epidemiology. There are problems, however, with each of these sources. Oral accounts are usually slanted and rarely tell the whole story. Early European chronicles reveal more about biases and interests of the Europeans than about the natives, and archeological and scientific evidence tends to result in speculation.[6] Nevertheless, from a variety of sources, historians have gained valuable knowledge about pre-Columbian education of Native Americans.

Literacy in the European sense was limited in pre-Columbian America, yet languages were rich and complex. Over 1,200 dialects had developed from 300 diverse language groups. The **Mayans** of **Mesoamerica** developed pictographs, ideographs, hieroglyphics, and a limited phonetic system; all of which required formalized study to read and create.[7] Mayans also made great strides in astronomy, arithmetic, architecture, medicine, and art—teaching these skills in schools attended only by the sons of chiefs and priests. The **Incas**, of what is now present-day Peru, were not as advanced as the Mayans in their writing, but they did develop a system of communicating numbers by strategically knotting strings. In Cusco, the sons of Incan noblemen attended a school where they studied warfare, history, religion, and language; while at another school, select girls trained to serve in the emperor's palace.[8]

Being so isolated from the rest of the world, pre-Columbian America was limited in its development of formal reading and writing. The lack of beasts of burden—such as horses and oxen—required such intense human labor that there was little time remaining for intellectual development. They did not develop wheeled vehicles or other inventions that could have saved on human labor. The absence of domesticated animals limited their immune system because—unlike Eurasians—people in America were not exposed to diseases carried by the animals, which would have helped build their immunities. Their isolation, intense labor, and health factors contributed to the delay in developing literacy.[9]

Spiritual and moral instruction was integrated into daily life. The **Cherokee**, of the Tennessee River valley of Appalachia, were known for high ethical standards, teaching values through storytelling, rituals, and prayers. They taught children the importance of living in harmony with nature, and—when youth reached puberty—they held coming-of-age rituals to signify the separation between childhood and adulthood. These rituals sometimes involved solitude, fasting, and physical tests of endurance. Youths might experience a vision of an encounter with a spiritual guide. The ritual culminated in renaming the youth to represent either the presence of the guiding spirit or the youth's new status within the tribe.[10]

Moral correction rarely involved corporal punishment, but embarrassment and shame were often employed. In the Blackfeet tribe, for example, they publicly announced a youth's poor conduct. At night, one person started by shouting out what the youth had done wrong. A person in a nearby tepee in turn shouted it again until it had spread throughout the tribe. Praise, rewards, and warnings were used as incentives for good conduct. If they did not behave, children were sometimes told, a large bird would fly down and grab them up.[11]

Bartolome de las Casas (1474-1566)

 European Contact and Exchange of Knowledge

Many Europeans who made early contact with the New World perceived the natives as wild savages incapable of learning. Later observers, however, like Dominican Friar **Bartolomé de Las Casas**, saw something different. Las Casas viewed the Caribbean Taíno as wise people who—rather than being innately inferior—were simply delayed culturally because they had not yet developed writing skills nor had they been exposed to scientific and religious knowledge outside their limited experience. Both the natives and the Europeans, however, were ignorant of each other's world, but it was the European's very survival that depended upon knowledge from the natives.[12] Long before ships from the Old World arrived, natives had sophisticated skills in seed germination, soil rotation, forest management, city planning, and the creation and preservation of art.[13]

Engagement with the New World benefited European intellectual growth. It provided opportunities for the application of knowledge from the scientific revolution. For example, the friars who traveled to Mexico were not only skilled in evangelism but many of them were also accomplished as researchers, linguists, and anthropologists. Their zeal for evangelism helped to feed the scientific revolution. Furthermore, as Europeans found themselves revolted by what they considered barbaric practices, their introspection may have had a taming effect on their own barbarism. Las Casas was one who challenged the notion that Indians—even with their cannibalism, idol worship, and nudity—were any more barbaric than Europeans who stretched people on racks and burned them at the stake. Las Casas argued that the Indians were humane, rational beings. Ethnographic studies by Bernardino de Sahagún may have prepared Europeans to be much more tolerant as a society. Sahagún challenged European superior attitudes, comparing ancient Indian cultures to those of classical Europe. Pedro Cieza de León reported how surprised the Incas were to see Pizarro stoop to pillaging villages to provide food for his army, comparing Pizarro's actions to the much more civilized process the Incas used of preparing freeze-dried food for their soldiers.[14] Could it be that Europeans were somewhat humbled, surprised, and even ashamed?

French philosopher **Michel de Montaigne** was another who may have shamed Europeans into being less barbaric and more tolerant. In his essay *Of Cannibals*, Montaigne, like Las Casas and others, described ritual cannibalism practiced by some Indians as being much less tortuous than to draw and quarter a body as the French did. The critical look inward that these writers provided to Europeans served useful in the long run and may have cultivated the very ideas that later sparked the Age of Revolution. As historian Thomas Benjamin noted, "Montaigne, John Locke, David Hume, Thomas Paine, Jean-Jacque Rousseau and others drew upon New World ethnography as well as other sources to invent such ideas as the noble savage, the social contract, individual autonomy, religious liberty and natural rights."[15] Some cultural analysts, such as Neil Postman, more specifically claim that the most enlightened parts of the United States Constitution are based, at least in part, on political principles drawn from the Iroquois.[16]

 ## Catholic and Protestant Missionaries

Early motives for educating the Indians were to teach them religion and to civilize them. This is exemplified by both Catholic and Protestant educational efforts. Being Catholic nations, the Spanish, Portuguese, and French sent a number of religious orders to evangelize the New World, but the **Jesuits** became the most influential. In Lima, Peru, the Spanish Jesuits founded the University of San Marcos in 1551 and established a printing press in 1584. By 1630, Lima established religious schools for Indians and welcomed wealthy Indians to enroll their sons into the same Jesuit boarding schools as did the colonists.[17] Education, however, became a blatant weapon by the Spanish government as exemplified in its response to the rebellion led by Peruvian Túpac Amaru in the early 1780s. In a public statement condemning Amaru at his execution, the government declared, "We shall introduce more vigorously than we have done up to now the use of school, imposing the most rigorous and fair penalties on those who do not attend." The declaration required Peruvian natives to speak Castilian and prohibited them from wearing "heathen" clothes.[18]

When Portugal's colonization of Brazil began in 1531, the king stated his main purpose for colonization as being "to settle the land of Brazil . . . in order that the people of that land might be converted to our Holy Catholic Faith." To that end, he sent six Jesuits in 1549 and increased that number within a few decades to 125. Their work, however, was more as conquistadores than as missionaries. Jesuits created mission villages, known as *aldeias*, to house natives who allied themselves with the Portuguese against hostile Indians. At the villages, natives were required to assimilate to Spanish religion and customs and to grow food for the *aldeias*.[19]

As discussed in Chapter 6 regarding Jesuit missionaries in the Atlantic World, both Portuguese slave raiders and Jesuits ventured into the interior of Brazil. At first, the two groups kept to their own devices—one group capturing Indians for enslavement while the other converting them to Christianity. Eventually, their aims collided. In an effort to appease slave raiders while also protecting Indians from enslavement, Jesuits agreed to lease out the labor of Indians living with them. This unfortunate arrangement weakened the long-range impact of the missions, and when the Portuguese forced the Jesuits out, the Indians returned to their traditional religion.[20]

In seventeenth-century New France, the French required their native partners to accept evangelization as part of the trade agreement. Therefore, along the St. Lawrence River, Jesuits created mission settlements where the Algonquians, Montagnais, Huron, and Iroquois were baptized and lived. Natives—having been weakened by disease—willingly agreed to these arrangements. For those natives who refused to move into the mission settlements, the Jesuits began to conduct "flying missions," which were evangelistic expeditions into the Indian towns. The Jesuits learned the native languages and religions so they could better teach the Indians. Some Jesuits were martyred. Eventually, the Jesuits in New France abandoned their cause, concluding that the natives were savages so corrupt that they could not be redeemed. They were also discouraged by their observation that Indians who did convert to Christianity were more likely to die of disease than those who did not convert.[21]

In British North America, Protestants educated natives through their evangelistic efforts. In 1636, the Virginia Council of London informed colonial Governor Thomas Gates that he was responsible for educating natives in Christianity. While the council's directions conveyed a sincere intent to uplift native children, it also revealed a pessimism about the native culture. It directed Gates to "procure from them some convenient number of children . . . by a surprise of them all and detain them prisoners." The justification for this was that natives were "wrapped up in the fog and misery of their iniquity" and that without such measures there would be

no eventual peace between the English and the natives.[22] Two decades later, the Virginia colonial legislature outlined its own terms for the education of natives. Instead of encouraging the kidnapping of native children, it offered education as a voluntary option and provided parents a choice of instructors. "If the Indians shall bring in any children as gauges of their good and quiet intentions to us," the law stated, ". . . then the parents of such children shall choose the persons to whom the care of such children shall be entrusted." It went on to promise to teach Christian civility, to prepare them for trades, and not to enslave them.[23]

Two examples of individual Protestant missionaries in the early eighteenth century were **David Brainerd** and **Jonathan Edwards**. During Brainerd's second year as a student at Yale, a revival occurred, influenced by the work of **George Whitefield**. Joining the Great Awakening movement, Brainerd began a preaching tour

© Morphart Creation/Shutterstock.com

George Whitefield (1714-1770), English Revival Preacher of the Great Awakening

through his home state of Connecticut. While preaching about life after death, he noticed that "some Indians cried out in great distress, and all appeared greatly concerned." This incident contributed to Brainerd's decision to partner with the Society in Scotland for Propagating Christian Knowledge. The Society assigned Brainerd to Kaunaumeek, New York, where he started a school for native children and began translating the Bible into the language of the Housatonic tribe. He later served native communities in Pennsylvania and New Jersey.[24]

Jonathan Edwards was a student of Brainerd's ministry and wrote a biography of Brainerd's life just two years before becoming a missionary to natives himself. Brainerd's death left a vacancy in the mission to the **Mohicans** at Stockbridge, Massachusetts. Edwards accepted the open position, serving there from 1751 to 1758. The Massachusetts Commissioners for the Propagation of the Gospel among the Indians in New England had established the mission just a year before Edwards' arrival. He continued good relations with the Mohicans and observed that parents were eager for their children to learn. The curriculum focused on agriculture, and—because the Mohicans traditionally relegated agricultural duties to women—the English perceived Mohican men as lacking discipline. Edwards, though seeing great potential in the natives' capacity to learn, was himself pessimistic about their culture. For example, while Brainerd valued the Housatonic language so as to translate biblical passages into it, Edwards was convinced that the Mohican language was insufficient for conveying Christian doctrines. He wrote, "Indian languages are extremely barbarous and barren, and very ill-fitted for communicating things moral and divine, or even things speculative and abstract." For this reason, Edwards required Mohicans to become proficient in English.[25]

 ## Education of Natives by the United States Government

The conflict in philosophies of education between Anglo-Americans and Native Americans was illustrated when—a year after the United States won its independence—Commissioners from Virginia offered scholarships for the youth of the Six Nations of the **Iroquois Confederacy** to attend the College of William and Mary. Benjamin Franklin recorded the official response from the Six Nations:

Native American students at Carlisle School in Pennsylvania

> We are convinced therefore that you mean to do us Good by your Proposal, and we thank you heartily. But you who are wise must know, that different Nations have different Conceptions of things; and you will therefore not take it amiss, if our Ideas of this Kind of Education happen not to be the same with yours. We have had some Experience of it: Several of our Young People were formerly brought up at the Colleges of the

Northern Provinces; they were instructed in all your Sciences; but when they came back to us they were bad Runners, ignorant of every means of living in the Woods, unable to bear either Cold or Hunger, knew neither how to build a Cabin, take a Deer, or kill an Enemy, spoke our Language imperfectly; were therefore neither fit for Hunters, Warriors, or Counsellors; they were totally good for nothing. We are however not the less obliged by your kind Offer, tho' we decline accepting it; and to show our grateful Sense of it, if the Gentlemen of Virginia will send us a dozen of their Sons, we will take great Care of their Education, instruct them in all we know, and make Men of them.[26]

The spokesmen for the Iroquois Confederacy had clearly differentiated between the two distinct philosophies of education.

Within four years of winning independence from Britain, the United States Congress passed legislation including its first philosophy statement of education with a specific reference to the Indian population. The 1787 **Northwest Ordinance** primarily served to set up the five states that would eventually become Ohio, Indiana, Illinois, Michigan, and Wisconsin, but—as part of this plan—it conveyed the significance of education within the territory:

> Religion, morality, and knowledge being necessary to good government and the happiness of mankind, schools and the means of education shall forever be encouraged. The utmost good faith shall always be observed toward the Indians . . .[27]

From the nation's very beginning, the United States struggled with developing and practicing a philosophy of education that properly addressed the needs and culture of natives. Should they be "civilized" gradually and eventually granted citizenship? If so, what would be the best method? Since the sixteenth century, missionaries had been evangelizing and educating natives, and that effort gained momentum in the early national period. With the Civilization Act of 1819, education was stated as carrying out the following purpose:

> . . . for the purpose of providing against the further decline of final extinction of the Indian tribes . . ., and that the means of instruction can be introduced with their own consent, . . . to instruct them in the mode of agriculture suited to their situation; and for teaching their children in reading, writing, and arithmetic.[28]

The act began to finance some missionary efforts with federal grants, distributing funds to "capable persons of good moral character," which, in practice, was for Protestant missionaries. Although the annual amount was only $10,000 for the entire program in 1819, today it would amount to nearly a quarter of a million dollars each year. A noticeable shift in these govern-

Sequoyah (ca. 1770-1843), Inventor of Cherokee Syllabary

© Morphart Creation/Shutterstock.com

ment-funded programs was that many schools began using native languages as a medium for instruction, which contributed to the retention and growth of native languages. Shortly after the passing of the Act, **Sequoyah** created a written syllabary for the Cherokee that drastically increased literacy rates for the tribe.[29]

Some of these government-funded missionaries worked among the Iroquois of upstate New York and were disappointed to face resistance from some of the natives who were not as enthusiastic to receive their teachings as they had hoped. **Chief Red Jacket** of the **Seneca nation** was one of them. Known as an orator of great eloquence, Red Jacket voiced his resistance to the teachings of the missionaries in a famous speech: "Brother, you say that you have not come to get our land or our money, but to enlighten our minds," Red Jacket said respectfully, and—in defense of the Seneca tribal religion—he continued,

> Brother, if your white men murdered the son of the Great Spirit, we Indians had nothing to do with it, and it is none of our affair. If he had come among us, we would not have killed him; we would have treated him well, you must make amends for that crime yourselves.[30]

Red Jacket's speech is just one of many examples of resistance. Another form of resistance was the use of knowledge gained from government education to inform the natives' fight against cultural extinction. While some of the educated Indians assimilated into the dominant culture, others would return home to lead resistance efforts. Armed with a critical understanding of the motives behind their own schooling, graduates often returned to warn their tribes of the dangers of such education.[31]

After the **Indian Removal Act** of 1830 and after the Civil War, off-reservation boarding schools became a prominent means of educating natives. Boarding schools were nothing new and had been a method of educating natives from as early as **Eleazar Wheelock**'s colonial Indian charity school during the Great Awakening. Wheelock had also founded Dartmouth College to teach Indian men, especially to prepare them for ministry. The late-nineteenth-century movement was different in that it was sponsored by the federal government and focused on mass cultural assimilation. The movement's first adult boarding school program began at Virginia's **Hampton Normal and Agricultural Institute**, initially begun for African American students. In 1878, **Captain Richard Pratt** requested General **Samuel Armstrong**, Hampton's founder, to enroll fifteen male hostages from the Indian Wars. The following year, Pratt began the **Carlisle Indian Industrial School** in Pennsylvania, which became a model for eventually 106 similar boarding schools. Like Carlisle, many of these schools were held in abandoned military barracks.[32]

Native children were frequently enrolled in boarding schools as young as six years of age and did not return home until after graduation over a decade later. While some graduates entered mainstream American society or stayed to work in the employment of the school, the majority returned home to the reservation. Having been disconnected from their families and cultures for so long, they struggled to adjust. Also, having been assimilated to White American ways, they seemed as strangers to their own people and had to regain the trust of the tribe before being fully accepted back into the community.[33]

For fifty years, the boarding school system continued in the same manner until the release of the 1928 **Meriam Report**, which brought about a turning point in government education of natives. Lewis Meriam investigated Indian education and wrote the report for the U.S. Department of the Interior. He described conditions as "grossly inadequate" in a number of areas. Food was insufficient and lacking in proper nutritional value. Dormitories were overcrowded and poorly stocked with supplies for personal hygiene. Meager teacher pay and low standards resulted in weak classroom instruction, and the curriculum was excessively regimented. Beginning in the upper elementary grades, students worked half days performing duties that Meriam considered violations of child labor laws, and disciplinary procedures were developmentally inappropriate. Meriam recommended a practical curriculum more representative of the progressive educational philosophy of John Dewey—adapting learning experiences to the interests, needs, and culture of the students.[34]

A series of influences in the early twentieth century began to bring improvements to Native American education. In addition to the Meriam Report, the psychological research of

Statue in Pulaski, Tennessee, Commemorating the Trail of Tears

G. Stanley Hall, founder of the child-study movement, and Dewey's progressive education movement ushered in a more culturally sensitive curriculum in local schools within the native communities.[35] Though the 1960s and 1970s were times of great tension between American Indians and the U.S. government, legislative action brought about significant reforms. Indian communities gained more control over government schools, and the curriculum included a stronger bilingual and bicultural approach.[36]

 Go to www.khlearn.com to watch a video about education of the Pueblo people in New Mexico.

Even now, just decades after the quincentennial anniversary of European contact with American natives, educational policies and practices continue to be debated. A difference, however, in the twenty-first century from half a millennium ago is that critical theorists now remind Western culture of its injustices from the not too distant past. Also, the movement among educators to promote cultural intelligence and to practice cultural proficiency has made great strides in the collective sensibilities of both educators and policy makers. Native autonomy and self-determination have been at least partially realized as the conversation continues as to how to move forward.

A Historically Black College, Hampton Institute (now University), also accepted Native Americans (ca. 1899)

Go to www.khlearn.com to watch a video about Native American education.

 Reflection

For personal reflection, content review, and further research:

1. How does Native American philosophy of education differ from traditional European perspectives on learning?
2. Expound on the Apache concept that "Wisdom sits in places."
3. What factors contributed to the delay in literacy among most Amerindian cultures?
4. Describe values taught in the pre-Columbian era and the methods used to teach these values?
5. In what ways did European exposure to Amerindians heighten awareness of their own barbaric behavior?
6. Trace the impact of Thomas Aquinas on Amerindian education.
7. To what degree were Indians sincere about conversions to Christianity?
8. Compare and critique the missionary efforts of David Brainerd and Jonathan Edwards.
9. Why did Jonathan Edwards require Mohicans to become literate in the English language? How does this expectation compare to research and best practices regarding Teaching English as a Second Language?
10. What was the main point in the speech by the Iroquois regarding the offer of scholarships to the College of William and Mary?
11. Summarize the philosophy of education conveyed by the 1787 Northwest Ordinance.
12. What was the main point of Chief Red Jacket of the Seneca tribe in his famous speech to the missionaries?
13. Compare the founding of Hampton Institute with the founding of Howard and Dartmouth.
14. Describe the impact of the 1928 Miriam Report.
15. How did the progressive instructional methods of John Dewey impact schools for Native Americans?

ENDNOTES

1. Jesse Page, *David Brainerd: The Apostle to the North American Indians*, 3rd ed. (London: S. W. Partridge, 1891), http://www.sermonindex.net/modules/myalbum/photo.php?lid=600. Public Domain.

2. "American Indians Respond to the Columbian Quincentennial, 1990," in *Major Problems in Atlantic History*, ed. Alison F. Games and Adam Rothman (Boston: Houghton Mifflin Company, 2008), 456-7.

3. Bryan McKinley Jones Brayboy, "Culture, Place, and Power: Engaging the Histories and Possibilities of American Indian Education," *History of Education Quarterly* 54, no. 3 (2014): 395-401.

4. Ibid., 396-401.

5. Milton Gaither, "The History of North American Education, 15,000 BCE to 1491," *History of Education Quarterly* 54, no. 3 (2014): 326-43.

6. See Gaither, "The History," 323-6; Donald Warren, "American Indian Histories as Education History," *History of Education Quarterly* 54, no. 3 (2014): 256.

7. Christopher J. Frey, "Native American Education," in *Encyclopedia of Educational Reform and Dissent*, vol. 2, ed. Thomas C. Hunt, James C. Carper, Thomas J. Lasley, and C. Daniel Raisch (Los Angeles: Sage, 2010), 653.

8. Murphy, *The History*, 211-2.

9. Benjamin, *Atlantic World*, 22-24; Yeboah, "Education Among Native Americans," 3.

10. Urban and Wagoner, *American Education*, 4-5.

11. Ibid.

12. Benjamin, *Atlantic World*, 275-83, 324.

13. Warren, "American Indian Histories," 258.

14. Ibid., 280-284.

15. Ibid., 289-93.

16. Neil Postman, *The End of Education: Redefining the Value of School* (New York: Vintage Books, 1995), 55.

17. Benjamin, *Atlantic World*, 178-9.

18. "Execution of Túpac Amaru in Cuzco, 1781," in *Major Problems in Atlantic History*, ed. Alison F. Games and Adam Rothman, (Boston: Houghton Mifflin Company, 2008), 306-7.

19. Benjamin, *Atlantic World*, 153, 155-6.

20. Ibid., 199, 203-4, 308-10.

21. Ibid., 309-10.

22. "Virginia Council [London], Instructions to Sir Thomas Gates, Knight, Governor of Virginia, 1636," in *The School in the United States: A Documentary History*, ed. James W. Fraser (New York: Routledge, 2010), 4.

23. "Virginia Statutes on the Education of Indian Children Held Hostage, from the Virginia Statutes at Large, 1656," in *The School in the United States: A Documentary History*, ed. James W. Fraser (New York: Routledge, 2010), 4-5.

24. "David Brainerd: Missionary to the Indians," *The Sunday at Home: A Family Magazine for Sabbath Reading* (May 9, 1861): 289-92.

25. Marsden, *Jonathan Edwards*, 320-3, 375-89.

26. Benjamin Franklin, "Remarks Concerning the Savages of North America, 1784," *Founders Online*, National Archives, accessed August 9, 2019, https://founders.archives.gov/documents/Franklin/01-41-02-0280.

27. "United States Congress, The Northwest Ordinance, July 13, 1787," in *The School in the United States: A Documentary History*, ed. James W. Fraser (New York: Routledge, 2010), 41-2.

28. "United States Congress, Civilization Fund Act, March 3, 1819," in *The School in the United States: A Documentary History*, ed. James W. Fraser (New York: Routledge, 2010), 42-3.

29. Frey, "Native American Education," 653; "United States Congress, Civilization Fund Act, March 3, 1819," 42.

30. "Speech of Red Jacket, Seneca Chief, to a Missionary, circa 1830," in *The School in the United States: A Documentary History*, ed. James W. Fraser (New York: Routledge, 2010), 101.

31. Deirdre A. Almeida, "The Hidden Half: A History of Native American Women's Education," *Harvard Educational Review* 67, no. 4 (1997): 757-71.

32. Ibid., 762-4.

33. Ibid., 764-6.

34. Lewis Meriam, "The Problem of Indian Administration, 1928," in *The School in the United States: A Documentary History*, ed. James W. Fraser (New York: Routledge, 2010), 190-5.

35. Urban and Wagoner, *American Education*, 214-5.

36. Frey, "Native American Education," 654.

CHAPTER 13

PROGRESSIVE TRAILBLAZER: SUSAN MILLER DORSEY[1]

Source: *Educational Review, 1921*

Susan Miller Dorsey, Progressive Era Superintendent of Schools, Los Angeles California[2]

FOCUS: KEY TOPICS AND TERMS

Bobbitt, Franklin
Democratic Education
Dewey, John
Dorsey, Susan Miller
National Education Association
Progressive Education Association

Progressivism
Sinclair, Upton Beall
Sloyd Schools
Vocational training
Young, Ella Flagg

Though women have been increasingly breaking the glass ceiling into the position of school superintendent, the profession has predominately been occupied by men. This chapter examines the impact of a progressive-era trailblazer for women in educational leadership, Susan Miller Dorsey, superintendent of Los Angeles City Schools from 1920 to 1929. Two questions are addressed: (a) What factors influenced Dorsey? (b) Can her experiences in administration reveal any critical influences for present-day female teachers who pursue administrative positions?

Susan Miller Dorsey (1857-1946) practiced her craft as an educator from 1890 until her death in 1946. The distinctive era in which Dorsey served was at the height of the progressive era. Resolute, fair-minded, and concerned about education are attributes that could fairly be attributed to Dorsey. Though history has left her relatively unknown, as is the case with many female historical figures, her successes and accolades deserve recognition. Dorsey triumphed in an era in which men had dominated. She encountered obstacles and tragedies in her life, but she succeeded beyond all expectations in her time period. Dorsey is a historic personage and a testament to female tenacity and diligence.

Educational historian Lawrence A. Cremin suggested that there has been no concise definition of progressive education, no defined progressive model, and no particular progressive leadership style. **Progressivism** meant different things to different people at different times. Cremin found that diversification and individualism made American education unique and flexible to the needs of the multicultural demographic taking shape in America at the time. He argued that many educators adopted a more practical curriculum and methodology for teaching and learning but in many cases tweaked the methodology to fit their personal needs and concerns. Because of these nuances, progressive education took on a specific philosophy mirrored by the region or state enacting it.[3] For instance, Dorsey utilized a personal version of a socially minded curriculum but maintained local control of her vision for the Los Angeles schools, which departed from the practical nationalist approach encouraged by **John Dewey** adherent **Ella Flagg Young** in Chicago.

 ## Development of Progressive Education

From early on, the United States developed a unique educational philosophy. Thomas Jefferson had believed that education of the nation's youth should be under the control of local government, free from religious influences, and available to all citizens. In the 1840s, common-school reformers argued that common schooling for all children would result in citizens who could make informed choices that would support the republic, unite society, and prevent crime and poverty. Free public education at the elementary level became available for all children by the end of the nineteenth century. Massachusetts implemented the first compulsory school attendance laws in 1852. By 1918, all states had laws requiring children to attend elementary school through the sixth grade.[4]

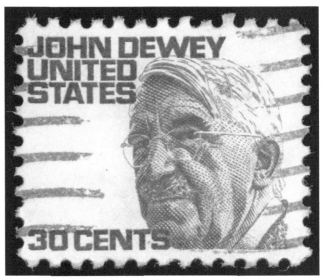

© artnana/Shutterstock.com

John Dewey (1859-1952)

Before the progressive movement, education was characterized by a classical platonic philosophy. Knowledge, disseminated with a passive, rote methodology discouraged active student participation. These educational practices, however well-intended, became an outdated system as the nation matured. The prevailing model was not responsive to the largest number of potential consumers of education, especially to America's poor and immigrant children. The needs of children in general were not addressed, regardless of socioeconomic status. Ellwood P. Cubberley and Elaine Key found that learning was mostly rote memorization and teacher centered, which lacked the ability to inspire children. Key further reminded readers that children, girls and boys alike, were treated as little adults. Key asserted that children needed to be the center of the educative or learning process if they were to achieve a sense of worth and gain the most benefit.[5]

Cubberley agreed that children were not receiving the greatest benefit from education and the prevailing curriculum methodology. He contended that the schooling of children, because of a forced curriculum designed by well-intended men who misinterpreted the "social connections [and] social efficiency" of schools and their new role in society, lagged behind with regard to the modern expectations and needs of an industrial society. Cubberley sought to revise the educative process to reflect a **democratic education** befitting the intellectual needs and expectations of the students. To accomplish this task, he insisted that it should begin with teachers. The new educator was to "embrace knowledge of democracy's needs and problems."[6]

Cubberley blamed the educational malaise in America on the superfluity of women teachers. Ironically, when advocating a conditional democracy, Cubberley accused females of being uninterested in learning the needs of a democracy and in leading students in social activism. Cubberley contended women too often studied for examinations for qualification rather than to encourage or inspire intellectual inquiry, and they resorted to the anachronistic models of a rote methodology. Women were too sheltered from the realities of the world and therefore failed to grasp the real need for a democratic study and practical solutions to a changing world. Susan E. Chase suggested this cultural perception of frailty juxtaposed alongside assumed gender inequality evolved into institutional obstacles concerning female educational leadership and has persisted throughout American history.[7]

Cubberley inferred that, as soon as practicable, education should eliminate the examination process and instill a more rigorous method of qualification for new teachers. It appeared that Cubberley desired to replace female teachers with more politically aware and assertive men. In spite of Cubberley's apparent misogynistic attitude toward female teachers, many progressive reformers agreed such a methodology would be a travesty of social justice and would impede American culture. Female reformers ignored Cubberley and continued to agitate for reform.[8] Regardless of Cubberley's pronouncements, females were well entrenched in the educative process and the social reform movements. Women—no longer inexperienced with political and reform initiatives because of their involvement in the temperance and suffrage movements—took on a larger role concerning education and social reform.

Women were at the forefront of many progressive initiatives such as social welfare reform, child labor laws, suffrage, and most importantly education. The collective power of activist women reached its height during this era of social and gender consciousness. Progressive women were typically "solid middleclass who voted Republican . . ., and the heroines were the new college educated women."[9] Women established a political and social voice, believing themselves to be equal to men. The traditional male reaction was to ignore or relegate women to the domestic sphere, claiming that in everything but politics, business, and school leadership roles, the majority of women were to retain domestic roles. The women-driven quasi-liberation movement

Suffragettes participating in a New York City parade (ca. 1910-1915)

opened doors previously barred to women. Male academic administrators closely mirrored the gender politics of society, as it was the rare occasion when women were exalted to administrative positions. There were some notable exceptions, but conventional perceptions concerning women and administration barred them from such positions. Regardless of obstacles, opportunities in education began to expand to include female administrators entering at the local and state levels.

By the 1920s, American attitudes increasingly embraced various reforms. Women not only had gained the vote but also appeared more frequently as leaders of school facilities, school districts, and school boards. The newly formed **Progressive Education Association** envisioned schools to be the vehicle to move America forward and influenced the **National Education Association** to develop a creed committed to propagating the principles of American democracy and patriotism. To ensure credibility, reform needed to be extended to all citizens, regardless of gender. Though women had made up the largest share of educators since 1850, their leadership opportunities were nominal at best. It seemed they could teach America but not lead America.

It would be in education that many progressives pinned their hopes of culturally and socially transforming America. Conceivably, if the masses were educated in practical vocations, many societal ills could be resolved. Much of societal decadence, in progressive minds, could be associated with unemployment and inability to assimilate wholly into modern American society. Lack of adequate education and job training were deemed culpable.[10]

© Everett Historical/Shutterstock.com

Progressivism spanned some sixty years before its waning in the 1950s. During the progressive era, the United States faced the challenges of massive democratization, immigration fluxes, and technological expansion. Educational leaders had little choice but to rethink learning models. During this time—one of the longest periods of expansion in the country's history— the Los Angeles County student population rose ten-fold from just over 40,000 students to over 400,000 students. During this explosion of enrollment, **Susan Miller Dorsey**, a rare female administrator, managed an efficient administration of schools and community colleges in Los Angeles County. She oversaw the expansion of campus construction, implemented practical curriculum changes, and fostered **vocational training**.[11]

 ## Susan Miller Dorsey's Legacy

Susan Miller Dorsey was born in 1859 in Penn Yan County, New York, in the upstate Finger Lakes resort area. Her father and mother incorporated education prominently in their children's upbringing. Susan was an energetic child, resourceful, and detail oriented. She excelled at school, in particular the classical languages of Greek and Latin. Upon turning sixteen, she applied and entered Vassar College where she earned a bachelor of arts degree in the classics. After working for a short time as a professor of languages at Vassar, she met and married Rev. Patrick Dorsey. They immediately made the transcontinental trip to settle in Los Angeles, California. At an unidentified time within the next nine years, Patrick took the couple's nine year-old son Paul and deserted Susan in Los Angeles, never to make personal contact again.

Without any prospects, Susan applied to a Los Angeles high school and received a teaching position. Within a few years, she became head of the classics department and held that position until 1913, at which time she accepted a position as assistant superintendent within the Los Angeles County School District (LACSD). Dorsey remained at this post until unanimously appointed by the all-male school board to become the Superintendent of LACSD in 1920. Dorsey reluctantly accepted the duties, but once in office, she immediately began stamping her legacy on the school district.

Dorsey, a prominent progressive educator during the 1920s, has been largely unrecognized by historians for her contributions to education. She was a self-proclaimed conservative Republican, believing in a pragmatic philosophy immersed in progressivism. A conservative fundamentalist Christian and skeptical of government regulation, she ironically embraced philosopher John Dewey's pragmatic education principles and **Franklin Bobbitt's** progressive and social curriculum models, suggesting that successful curriculum measures must be "social in nature." To Dorsey, academic standards were commendable, but students needed socialization and integration into society.[12]

Dorsey managed her education responsibilities according to the circumstances and needs of her particular environment. This theme dominated Dorsey's superintendence of LACSD. Her worldview matured based upon intrinsic demographics particular to her region of influence, her educational philosophy, and her middle class and religious background. She was not known to compromise her principles, but she willingly admitted when she was wrong and moved forward. She possessed integrity and was known to be extremely ethical in her practices, leading by example and modeling the leadership she expected of others.

Dorsey hired her own assistant superintendents. She reevaluated school administrators and immediately became a strong advocate for increased teacher benefits. She called for paid maternity and sick leave and promoted a plan to secure health and retirement insurance for all teachers in LACSD. She improved the school system with modern available technology. She figured prominently in a relationship with the Los Angeles Police Department to have security available for in-school and after-school events. She pushed through several bond referendums of some $130 million dollars to build new schools. Dorsey advocated and—with community backing—implemented night schools and vocational schools. She also started community colleges and **Sloyd Schools** to assist the needs of an expanding economic and multicultural community.[13]

Sloyd School began in Finland in the 1860s and spread handicraft education, especially in woodwork, to the US

However, Dorsey could be strict and regimented with her teachers. She reevaluated many of the teachers and made it mandatory that all teachers in the district achieve teaching certification. None were grandfathered in. Each teacher was allotted a reasonable amount of time to gain certification, or they faced termination. Dorsey believed in quality education and that it could only be accomplished by quality teachers controlling the education process.

Though she implemented many benefits for the teachers, Dorsey refused to allow them to organize, igniting controversy of the right to bargain collectively. Her angst was that unions would undermine the integrity of the educative process. Dorsey refused to allow political corruption to taint education, yet she was not averse to using her office to influence the political process to secure materials and new initiatives for the school system. She demanded much from her teachers and from herself as well. Integrity and accountability were standards of her administrative philosophy. All were to abide within the established educative parameters—no exceptions.

Similarly, Dorsey would go to great lengths to shield her teachers from the press when confronted with sensitive issues until her office had exhausted a thorough investigation. One such incident arose over the abduction and brutal murder of 12-year-old Marion Parker. The school had released Marion, the daughter of a wealthy banker, to a man claiming to be an employee of her father. The man told school personnel that Marion's father had been seriously injured and had requested him to bring his daughter to him immediately. Dorsey retrospectively would never have allowed the incident to play out as it did. According to her niece Susie Miller, who recounted the incident years later, Dorsey staunchly defended her teacher. In Dorsey's mind, the teacher in question had suffered enough having to live with the unfortunate incident for her remaining days. Constant public condemnation in the media seemed beyond reason.[14]

Dorsey's leadership style was student-centered and humanitarian but always within the framework of established rules and regulations. She exuded enormous business acumen and a firm grasp of management principles. For instance, Dorsey asked the following of any problem put to her: What is it? Why is it? Moreover, what of it? To avoid a waste of time and talents, it was important to scrutinize any issue vigorously before deeming it worthy of action. Dorsey possessed a simple ethic: "Do each day's work each day."[15]

Dorsey managed controversy and adversaries with skill and respect. She refused to engage in petty verbal jousting with adversaries such as muckraker **Upton Beall Sinclair**. Sinclair had taken personal issue with Dorsey and her style of education management. Dorsey spoke her piece and communicated frequently and skillfully with the political apparatus and the community to achieve her initiatives. She left the political bantering to the media, politicians, and muckrakers, focusing her efforts on student learning and community access to education. Dorsey was politically shrewd, winning her converts and community support for many initiatives despite some controversy. She was confident enough to know what to do, how to do it, and when to do it. She displayed discernment with personal and professional issues, knowing when to ask or how to ask but never in a commanding or coercing manner. Simply put, Dorsey led with unwavering principle.

During the Progressive era, the feminization of education that had begun during the nineteenth-century common school movement exploded on a grand scale. Women made up the lion's share of teachers; however, in the administrative sector they remained underrepresented. Women quickly began filling administrative jobs in education, which prompted Chicago City Schools superintendent Ella Flagg Young to suggest that "women would soon dominate school leadership in the same way they

Poster advertising Upton Sinclair's novel attacking political corruption and unsanitary conditions of the meat industry in Chicago (1906)

© Everett Historical/Shutterstock.com

did teaching."[16] By 1930, women claimed eleven percent of the overall superintendent positions in America. Unfortunately, Young's bold prediction never came to fruition. Nearly a hundred years later, women remain underrepresented. Though there is a dearth of extant information, recently there has been a revival of searching as to why this phenomenon persists. The reason most prominently put forth is typically sexist and prejudicial in nature. Because of these barriers, the biggest issue is that presently, women have fewer role models or experienced mentors, compared to their male peers. This admission is itself a pertinent reason to study Susan Miller Dorsey. Her story needs telling if for no other reason than to help fill a void much needed in American education history.

Go to www.khlearn.com to watch a video about Susan Miller Dorsey.

Reflection

For personal reflection, content review, and further research:

1. Describe the general trends of progressive education and the factors that led to the progressive model in American schools.

2. Prior to the common school movement, the vast majority of teachers were male. Catharine Beecher had encouraged women to enter the profession, but—according to the progressive E. P. Cubberley—the feminization of teaching was problematic for the progressive agenda. How so?

3. Many are surprised that a progressive educator such as Susan Miller Dorsey might also be politically conservative. Analyze this seeming contradiction both in its historical context of the progressive era and in current times.

4. Compare Dorsey's perceptions of teacher unions with those more recently held. Consider views such as those from the documentary *Waiting for Superman*.

ENDNOTES

1. Taken from J. Steve Strickland and Samuel James Smith, "Susan Miller Dorsey (1857-1946): Trailblazer for Women School Superintendents," (paper presented at the Conference of the National Council for Professors of Educational Administration, Portland, OR, August, 2011).

2. *Susan Miller Dorsey*, ca. 1921, portrait, Educational Review Archive, accessed December 27, 2019, https://archive.org/stream/education-alrevie62newyuoft#page/n295/mode/2up. Public Domain.

3. Lawrence A. Cremin, *The Transformation of the Schools: Progressivism in American Education, 1876-1957* (New York: Random House, 1961).

4. Robert Freeman Butts, *Public Education in the United States: From Revolution to Reform (1776-1976)* (New York: Holt, Rhinehart and Winston, 1978).

5. See Ellwood Patterson Cubberley, *Changing Conceptions of Education* (Boston: Houghton Mifflin, 1908); E. Key, *The Education of the Child* (New York: Knickerbocker Press, 1908).

6. Cubberley, *Changing Conceptions*, 203-6.

7. Susan E. Chase, *Ambiguous Empowerment: The Work Narrative of Women School Superintendents* (Amherst, MD: University of Massachusetts Press, 1995).

8. Janet Zollinger Giele, ed., *Two Paths to Women's Equality: Temperance, Suffrage, and the Origins of Modern Feminism* (New York: Twayne Publishers, 1995).

9. Ibid., 146.

10. J. B. Bury, *The History of Freedom of Thought* (New York: Henry Holt & Company, 1913).

11. See Samantha B. Maddox, "Margaret Willis: Leading Explorers of the Past, Pioneers of the Future," doctoral dissertation (University of South Carolina, Columbia, 2001); Georgette F. McGregor, "The Educational Career of Susan Miller Dorsey," doctoral dissertation (University of California, Los Angeles, 1949).

12. McGregor, "The Educational Career," 82.

13. Ibid.

14. Ibid.

15. Ibid., 51.

16. See Jackie M. Blount, *Destined to Rule the Schools : Women and the Superintendency, 1873-1995* (New York: State University of New York Press, 1998), 4; Cryss C. Brunner and Margaret Grogan, *Women Leading School Systems: Uncommon Roads to Fulfillment* (Lanham, MD: Rowman & Littlefield Education, 2007), 4.

CHAPTER 14

WORLD WAR II: IMPACT ON EDUCATIONAL POLICY AND PRACTICE

Stamp printed in USA shows GI bill student 1944 (ca. 1999)

© catwalker/Shutterstock.com

FOCUS: KEY TOPICS AND TERMS

Air-Raid Shelter
American Red Cross
Birmingham Blitz
Counts, George S.
Defense Regulation 58A
Dewey, John
Finnebørn
GI Bill

Herbart-Zillerism
Hitler, Adolf
National Education
   Association
Nazis
Operation Barbarossa
Phony War

Progressive Education
   Movement
Rugg, Harold
Servicemen's
   Readjustment Act
Soviet Union
Walker, Dorothy

A cost rarely considered in the study of war is its impact on education. Government budgets shift funding from schools to armies. Parents and teachers go off to war or modify their own activities to support the cause. Older students prepare to fight while younger ones are evacuated or kept safe at home. Educational experiences are certainly different for students in war-torn countries than for those in countries far from battle. Nevertheless, war impacts education in a number of ways, and there are many examples of how World War II certainly did this.

European War and Non-War Countries: Individual Income Potential

The disruption of children's education during World War II held long-lasting implications for their future economic well-being. This phenomenon is illustrated in a longitudinal study comparing children in the war countries of Austria and Germany to children in non-war countries of Sweden and Switzerland. The disruption of education in war countries delayed academic progress of school-aged children, primarily because of inconsistent attendance. On approximately twenty percent of school days, children in war countries could not physically access their schools because of transportation problems or battle activity, and in many cases, schools were taken over as facilities for the military. Even when they could attend classes, children were distracted from their studies by concerns about fathers or other family who were fighting in the war.[1]

Both during the war and also in subsequent years, Austrian and German children attended school for a significantly shorter period than did Swedish and Swiss children whose school attendance and academic progress generally went unhindered. Once they were adults, those who had been educated in the war countries were less likely to pursue a college degree and were more likely to get lower-paying jobs than those who spent their childhoods in non-war countries. Even into the 1980s, the average individual earnings were much less for those who had spent their school-age years in war countries. The study found a strong positive correlation between low income levels and low school attendance during the war. No such phenomenon was found in non-war countries.[2]

Poland: Cultural Adjustment and Readjustment

In addition to the economic repercussions of a disrupted education, there is the issue of sudden relocations—whether temporary or permanent—and the related cultural adjustments for students. This is illustrated by the experiences of Polish and Finnish children. After the Soviets invaded eastern Poland on September 17, 1939, they sought to Sovietize the Poles. One method of accomplishing this was through a system of schools in the interior of the **Soviet Union**, to which approximately 320,000 Poles were deported. However, when **Adolf Hitler** launched **Operation Barbarossa** in June 1941, Stalin reluctantly agreed to permit the Poles to return to the homeland with the expectation that they would eventually support the Soviets against the **Nazis**. Back in their homeland, children were educated with the goal of being de-Sovietized and re-Polonized. Further complicating the children's experience was that many of them had become orphaned, abandoned, or lost from their families. Up to 50,000 of these children were aided by the **American Red**

Cross and by the governments of Canada and Britain. Another 15,000 were evacuated to refugee camps in Iran, Palestine, New Zealand, Mexico, and other countries. Those who did not make it out of the Soviet Union were the responsibility of the Polish embassy, which set up a network of schools for Polish children throughout the Soviet Union. These schools emphasized Polish culture, history, language, and the Catholic religion in an effort to help the children maintain a measure of stability among all the other adjustments they had endured.[3]

Finland: Teacher Education and the Finnebørn

Beyond its impact on elementary and secondary education, the war also influenced colleges and universities. For example, teacher training colleges in Finland were temporarily closed from 1939 to 1945 while several of the campuses functioned as hospitals. Male teacher candidates were drafted for service in the military, while females returned home or stayed on campus to help with the hospitals. Finland defended itself twice against the Soviet Union during World War II

Little Insurrectionist, a statue in memory of the child soldiers who fought and died during the Warsaw Uprising of 1944

© Georgios Tsichlis/Shutterstock.com

and proudly retained its status as a democracy. Its teacher colleges retained and even considerably strengthened the philosophical framework they held prior to the war—**Herbart-Zillerism**.[4]

In the mid-nineteenth century, Finnish educators had adopted the Herbart-Zillerism model of education from the Germans. Finland embraced this framework because it supported the value they placed on ethics, morality, character development, and Christianity. The school curriculum, therefore, encouraged students to develop hobbies that would instill perseverance. Through literature and history, schools sought to instill a sense of nationalism. Because school teachers were expected to cultivate a unified nation, colleges of teacher education were especially strong in building a Christian-nationalist spirit.[5]

During the war years, Finnish schools changed emphasis in both curricular and extra-curricular activities. The three most prominent themes in writing lessons dealt with nationalism, Christianity, and decency. Physical education increased concentration on gymnastics, folk dancing, and self-defense. Skiing lessons were combined with orienteering, which is the sport of navigating an unfamiliar area with map-reading skills and a practical skill to be developed in future soldiers. Art classes were limited because of the lack of raw materials to create projects. Instead of producing paintings or sculptures, students were required to complete more practical tasks, such as darning socks. Lunchtime meals were meager, so students were frequently hungry while trying to focus on their studies.[6] The thought of death was never far from their minds as several thousands of Finnish children died of hunger and disease during the war; 340 children were killed by bombing; and 50,000 were orphaned.[7]

Like the relocated Polish children, the Finnebørn faced their own challenges of cultural adjustment and readjustment. The **Finnebørn** was a group of approximately 4,000 children who were evacuated without their parents to Denmark and who later returned to Finland. It was anticipated that the Finnebørn would be in Denmark for no more than six months, but the war lasted much longer than expected and returning home became more of a risk after the German occupation of Denmark. Approximately 2,600 children stayed with Danish host families for over a year and 451 never returned home. Their Danish teachers had helped them to assimilate into their temporary culture and to learn a new language; upon their return to Finland, however, they were met by schools and teachers ill-prepared to reintegrate them back into Finnish society. Many of the Finnebørn were so young at the time of their evacuation that they forgot the Finnish language and over time felt a stronger connection to their Danish families than to their Finnish families. This severely complicated their return home.[8]

Because of these complications, some historians contend that the evacuated children's experiences, particularly for those aged two to nine years old, were more traumatic than for children who remained in Finland during the war—especially considering the psychological effects on their sense of self. Schools, however, served to provide a meaningful structure and continuity to their lives, despite all the other challenges the Finnebørn faced. School routines were familiar enough from one country to the next that it added a measure of stability to their lives, and—even with the language barrier—at school they felt a sense of community and normality. Reflecting on their transition from Denmark back to Finland, adult Finnebørn recalled more difficulties with language returning to their homeland than they did in adjusting to Denmark. As a refugee in Denmark, they had been granted special attention by schools and teachers to assist in their assimilation. For instance, their host families were provided with booklets including information to help them guide the children through their adjustment. The booklets included common Finnish words and phrases they could use in communicating with the children. Support was intentional from the Danish government, school, and host families. Back home, the Finnebørn held a different status; instead of vulnerable refugees, they were considered the fortunate ones who were saved from enduring the terrible war. Accommodations provided to them in Denmark were not offered by the Finnish schools and teachers. Additionally, the children were returning to a poor, war-torn country with many families that were rendered homeless and fathers suffering post-traumatic stress disorder from war activity.[9]

 England: Schools and Air Raids

In England, schools that experienced air raids struggled to provide consistent education because of the shortage of buildings, equipment, and staff. To minimize such interruptions, the Ministry of Education tried to prevent schools from being used for military purposes and teachers' homes from serving as quarters for soldiers. In London alone, 651 schools suffered some kind of structural damage from the raids, 35 of which were seriously damaged. With constant reorganization of buildings and personnel, it was difficult to maintain compulsory attendance. Most children who were evacuated to the countryside were away for only a few months; some, however, were evacuated for up to three years.[10]

Monument to Finnish soldiers fallen during World War II

In addition to children, a number of teachers were evacuated to ensure education continued for the evacuated children in their new setting. Many teachers refused to evacuate because the payment for doing so did not sufficiently cover evacuation expenses, and they were concerned that their homes may be used for military quarters while they were away. Because there were not enough teachers willing to evacuate, the London Minister of Education, under **Defense Regulation 58A**, required them to do so.[11]

Dorothy Walker was a school administrator in Birmingham, England, and if her job was complicated by government policies and local concerns under normal circumstances, it was intensified even more under conditions of war. Walker's assignment was to administrate a primary school during the **Birmingham Blitz**. In extensive letters, she chronicled her experiences and feelings regarding the challenges of trying to maintain a semblance of normality both at home and at work. She wrote of how the rationing of resources along with additional burdens, both personally and professionally, weighed upon her. Walker's biographer, Kate Rousamier, compared the stresses experienced by Walker to those of current urban school administrators who serve in underfunded, high-crime settings. While Rousamier's comparison may be far-reaching, it serves to illustrate how schools during the Blitz were operating with limited resources and serving students who were emotionally unsettled and physically deprived.[12]

Walker dealt with the same circumstances, such as evacuations and air-raid drills, as other Birmingham school administrators faced as a result of German bombings. She had twice accompanied students in evacuations, first to Worchester during the **Phony War**—a period of months in 1939 and 1940 during which Britain anticipated a blitzkrieg that did not occur until later—and second, to southern Wales. In Wales, she complained about the disruption the experience was causing the children, and she was also concerned about the negative influence of the "wild Welsh" on her students. Despite the risks, she preferred to hold school in her familiar setting. Back in Birmingham, Walker was reaffirmed rather than deterred in her progressive approach to education by holding class sessions in an **air-raid shelter**. Her commitment to innovative instruction with a focus on student–teacher relationships was renewed by the experience of providing lunches and emotional support for her students. Although she was proud of having trained 250 children to reach

the air-raid shelter in just a little over two minutes, the multiple drills each day wore on the students and faculty. Many became ill from so much time in the cold wet shelters and from sleep deprivation. Student absences, especially on the morning after a blitz, were as high as sixty percent, and many days, those in attendance spent all but an hour or two in the shelter. While students could nap in the shelter to catch up on lost sleep, faculty were prohibited from doing so. Ultimately, the Birmingham Blitz killed over 2,000 civilians and injured over 6,000 others.[13]

Battle of Britain Monument, London

 United States: Wartime Educational Reforms

In the United States, there were no evacuations or air raids as in Europe, but the war did serve to bring about many educational reforms. The teaching force was drained as male teachers left to join the military and as women opted for higher-paying factory jobs. This resulted in a teacher shortage, with classrooms often being taught by unqualified instructors. Licensed teachers who did stay in the classroom noticed how much more women were being paid in the factories and began to demand—with support from the **National Education Association**—more equitable wages. Teachers also successfully fought to end the differing pay scales for elementary and secondary teachers that had been used to justify paying a higher income to male teachers, who more frequently taught in secondary schools, than to elementary teachers, who were predominantly female.[14]

The nation began to see teachers as crucial to influencing young people regarding the war effort; teachers were encouraged to build morale and an expectation of victory while they helped students understand the war itself. From 1930 to 1940, there was an increase in the high school graduation rate from thirty to fifty percent. This growth—and the fact that a third of the nation's population was under sixteen years of age—caught the attention of policymakers. A national Educational Policies Commission was formed that issued a 1941 report entitled *Education and the Morale of a Free People*. In this report, education was declared as the primary means of building the nation's morale. The American Federation of Teachers agreed by publishing a statement regarding the importance of schools in the development of a "unified will-to-win."[15]

Intentional efforts were made to revise the curriculum—especially science, math, and history. In higher education, the land-grant universities were asked to conduct scientific research to discover improved methods for federal defense,[16] and in the science literacy movement, Gordon Mork led the way to show the public how the same scientific method used to develop tools for war could also be used to solve everyday problems. Mork argued that the same discovery processes that resulted in the atomic bomb, radar, codes, and computers could be "utilized for better living and greater happiness for the individual among all men."[17] Critics of **John Dewey's progressive education movement** were concerned that enrollment in rigorous science and math courses had declined as students opted for more practical topics, such as "family living." One of those critics was Army General Brehon B. Somervell, who—at the 1942 conference of the National Institute on Education—referred to classrooms as "citadels" and charged teachers with considering their responsibility that "no American soldier is ever killed or injured because you failed to do your part to provide adequate training."[18]

History and social studies textbooks that did not instill a sense of uncritical nationalism were considered controversial and subversive. **Harold Rugg** and **George S. Counts** authored many materials that fell under such criticism in the interwar through the postwar eras. Critics labeled their works as treasonous, and the United States Office of Censorship, which was active from 1941 to 1945, encouraged states and communities to self-censor such textbooks that would undermine the war effort. Some localities went beyond self-censorship, passing mandatory ordinances like the one in St. Cloud, Minnesota, that banned any material that "advocates un-American or subversive activities."[19]

Immediately after World War II, American textbooks focused almost exclusively on the causes, events, and political results of battles with hardly any mention of opposition to the war. Over time, however, in an effort to avoid the glorification of war, textbook publishers increasingly attended to the experiences of soldiers and the atrocities brought about by the war. Much of this transition in the interpretation of World War II has occurred following the Vietnam War. As textbooks began to cover the antiwar movement of the 1960s, they also began to intensify the harsh realities of all previous wars and to eliminate what might be perceived as unquestioned patriotism. To this end, more attention has been given in recent decades to the suffering of other nations caused by the United States. Also, more has been made of the hardships of the military and of civilians during wartime. Even with this increased negative portrayal of war, many curriculum theorists have become concerned that recent textbooks include few open criticisms of actions by the United States in World War II and that Americans increasingly have been shown more as victims than as perpetrators.[20]

In addition to the changes over time in textbook narrative content, the visual imagery of World War II in textbooks began to shift. For example, earlier textbook photographs typically depicted generals, battleships, aircraft, and the raising of the American flag in Iwo Jima. Images related to death were commonly represented by cemetery crosses. More recently, however, publishers have not shied away from picturing dead or wounded soldiers with captions descriptive of what led to the casualty.[21]

Perhaps the most significant educational reform occurred as a result of the 1944 **Servicemen's Readjustment Act**. Commonly known as the **GI Bill**, the law provided tuition benefits for veterans to attend college and vocational schools. This drastically changed the landscape of higher education, leading to more diverse student bodies, burgeoning enrollments in existing colleges, and an increase in the number of newly established colleges.[22]

Go to www.khlearn.com to watch a video discussing the return of soldiers from WWII.

Momentum was slow at first, but as veterans began to understand the implications of the tuition benefit, over twice as many participated than expected. Over half of all who served during World War II attended college or a vocational school on the GI Bill. Because these benefits extended to all veterans—despite ethnicity, race, religion, or socioeconomic status—opportunities were opened for many who, otherwise, would never have considered further education a possibility. As one soldier expressed, the GI Bill provided "a way out, a route to go, an opportunity. I think anybody that didn't take advantage of it missed on an opportunity, because it was rather magnanimous."[23]

Recipients of the GI Bill were fortunate to be positively impacted. Many who could never have envisioned a college education for themselves or for their children found their postwar livelihood to be very different from what they had anticipated. Others, however, such as Austrian and German children whose education was chronically disrupted, were doomed to a much gloomier economic future. Whether related to socioeconomics, cultural adjustments, or curriculum reform, the educational impact of World War II is still being felt in schools, families, and individuals.

National D-Day Memorial in Bedford, Virginia, the U.S. town that suffered proportionally the greatest loss of the campaign.

© Stirling Martin/Shutterstock.com

Go to www.khlearn.com to watch a video about the impact of World War II on educational policy and practice.

 Reflection

For personal reflection, content review, and further research:

1. Compare the effects World War II had on children of various European countries. What types of adjustments did schools, teachers, and students make?
2. How did the circumstances of the war lead to both positive and negative results in American schools?
3. What roles did John Dewey, Harold Rugg, and George S. Counts play in controversies related to public school curriculum and instructional methods?
4. After the Vietnam War, how has American curriculum changed in its portrayal of World War II?
5. Explain the relationship between the GI Bill and the expanding educational opportunities and burgeoning growth of higher education in the United States.

ENDNOTES

1. Andrea Ichino and Rudolf Winter-Ebmer, "The Long-Run Educational Cost of World War II," *Journal of Labor Economics* 22, no. 1 (2004): 57-8.
2. Ibid., 81.
3. Magdalena Gross, "Reclaiming the Nation: Polish Schooling in Exile during the Second World War," *History of Education Quarterly* 53, no. 3 (2013): 233-5.
4. Merja Paksuniemi, Uusiautti, Satu, and Määttä, Kaarina, "Teacher Education in Finland during the War Years, 1939-45," *War & Society* 33, no. 1 (2014): 12-4.
5. Ibid.
6. Ibid., 21-22.
7. Pia Pannula Toft, Merja Paksuniemi, and Johannes Westberg, "The Challenge of Returning Home: The Role of School Teachers in the Well-being of Finnish War Children, 'Finnebørn,' during and after World War II," *Paedagogica Historica* 54, no. 6 (2018): 737.
8. Ibid., 736.
9. Toft, Paksuniemi, and Westberg, "The Challenge," 738-47.
10. P. H. J. H. Gosden, *Education in the Second World War: A Study in Policy and Administration* (New York: Routledge, 1976), 52-5.
11. Ibid., 56-57.
12. Kate Rousmaniere, "Dorothy's Wars: School Leadership during the Birmingham Blitz," *Journal of Educational Administration and History* 48, no. 3 (2016): 211-3.
13. Ibid., 214-5
14. Urban and Wagoner, *American Education*, 279-80.
15. Ronald D. Cohen, "Schooling Uncle Sam's Children: Education in the USA, 1941-1945," in *Education and the Second World War: Studies in Schooling and Social Change,* ed. Roy Lowe (New York: Routledge, 2012), 46-47.
16. Murphy, *The History and Philosophy*, 324.
17. Tehie, *Historical Foundations of Education*, 225.
18. Ibid., 226.

19. Gerard Giordano, *Twentieth-Century Textbook Wars: A History of Advocacy and Opposition* (New York: Peter Lang, 2005), 35-53.

20. Richard Lachmann and Lacy Mitchell, "The Changing Face War in Textbooks: Depictions of World War II and Vietnam," *Sociology of Education* 87, no. 3 (2014): 188-201.

21. Ibid., 199.

22. Urban and Wagoner, *American Education*, 281.

23. Suzanne Mettler, *Soldiers to Citizens: The G.I. Bill and the Making of the Greatest Generation* (New York: Oxford University Press, 2005), 41-58.

CHAPTER 15

POLITICS AND EDUCATIONAL POLICY

From left to right: © mark reinstein/Shutterstock.com, © Joseph Sohm/Shutterstock.com, © Jason and Bonnie Grower/Shutterstock.com, © Drop of Light/Shutterstock.com, © Drop of Light/Shutterstock.com

Presidents G. H. W. Bush, Clinton, G. W. Bush, Obama, and Trump

FOCUS: KEY TOPICS AND TERMS

A Nation at Risk
Accountability Movement
America 2000
American Federation of
    Teachers
Bennett, William
*Brown vs. Board of
    Education of Topeka*
Bush, George H. W.
Bush, George W.
Carter, Jimmy
Civil Rights Act
Clinton, Bill
Clinton, Hillary
Debs, Eugene V.
Eisenhower, Dwight D.

Elementary and Secondary
    Education Act
English Language Learners
Equal Educational
    Opportunities Act
Goals 2000
Great Society
Head Start
Johnson, Lyndon Baines
Kennedy, John F.
Moral Majority
Morrill Land Grant Act
National Commission on
    Excellence in Education
National Defense
    Education Act

National Education
    Association
New Deal
No Child Left Behind
Obama, Barack
Race to the Top
Reagan, Ronald
Roosevelt, Franklin D.
Sputnik
Students with Disabilities
Tenth Amendment
Trump, Donald
Vouchers
War on Poverty

Official White House Photo by Amanda Lucidon

In some presidential elections, more so than others, education has been a political pawn. When not focused on foreign policy or the economy, politicians may give lip service to the topic of education more so than they normally would. In the second half of the twentieth century, however, education became an increasingly critical issue in national politics. Tracing its role, especially from Lyndon B. Johnson to Donald Trump, reveals some unexpected paradoxical moments. An exploration of party platforms, speeches, and legislative proposals reveals how education has been used for purposes such as national defense, economic competition, and civil rights.

Race to the Top: Clinton, Bush, Obama, and Trump

Just days before the election that would decide his successor, President **Barack Obama** visited Benjamin Banneker High School in Washington, D.C. He spoke to an assembly of high school students and their teachers about recent accomplishments in education. His audience, of course, was also television viewers, as he hoped to boost his former Secretary of State **Hillary Clinton** in a victory over **Donald Trump**. "By 2020," he declared, "I want us to be number one again," a statement reminiscent of **Goals 2000**, the education plan of **Bill Clinton**'s administration. Obama went on to celebrate accomplishments during his two-term administration: the spread of state-funded preschool, increased Head Start enrollment, and the highest ever graduation rates, especially for African-American and Latino students. He referred to the U.S. Department of Education's **Race to the Top** program—which provided billions of federal dollars to states for school improvements—and to Congress's "fix" made to **No Child Left Behind**, allowing teachers more flexibility so that they would no longer just be "teaching to a test."[1]

In the 2016 presidential election, neither Hillary Clinton nor Donald Trump had made education a major issue in their campaigns, but their parties' platforms included obligatory education planks. The Democratic Party stood for universal preschool and quality schools for all students. Opposing for-profit charter schools and not mentioning private schools at all, it stated, "A strong public education system is an anchor for our democracy." It emphasized the importance of schools to address specific needs of "low-income students, students of color, **English Language Learners**, and **students with disabilities**" and to close gaps in opportunity, curriculum, and achievement.[2] The Republican Party made no mention of preschool but supported a broad range of schooling choices including public, private, charter, magnet, parochial, and on-line options. It reminded the nation that the U.S. Constitution included no mention of education, so it was therefore a community concern with parents as the child's first and most important teacher. "Centralizing forces" outside the community and family were blamed as having wrought "immense damage." It opposed national standards and in a statement with the heading "Academic Excellence for All" decried the $2 trillion spent since 1965 on scores of programs that had produced minimal results. "If money were the solution," it concluded, "our schools would be problem free." Reminiscent of **Ronald Reagan** and the **Moral Majority**, the Republican platform supported the teaching of the Bible and prayer at public school events. The theme of opportunity was present throughout the platform, evident in sections entitled "A Chance for Every Child," "Academic Excellence for All," and "Choice in Education." Access to educational options was identified as a civil right that should not be based on "address, ZIP code, or economic status."[3]

"I honestly don't think we need a Department of Education," said Senator Marco Rubio, a Republican from Florida, during the 2016 Republican primaries. He was not alone. Ted Cruz, Rand Paul, Rick Perry, and Donald Trump joined him in this sentiment. Ever since President **Jimmy Carter** reluctantly opened the Department of Education as a campaign promise to the **National Education Association**, Republicans beginning with Ronald Reagan had threatened to shut it down, but—based on the Trump administration's 132-page proposal to merge the Education and Labor Departments—carrying out the threat would not be the easy task that Republicans had made it appear. If it were easy, the succinct House Bill proposed by Kentucky's Thomas Massie simply stating, "The Department shall terminate December 31, 2018," might have gained more support from his fellow Republicans than it did.[4]

During his 2016 campaign, Trump made school vouchers his main civil rights argument. Urban public schools, he argued, were such a "disaster" that vouchers were needed as a path of opportunity for African-American children to improve their educational options. Hillary Clinton agreed that education was a path for creating opportunity, but her solution followed the long-held Democratic Party approach that increasing federal funds was the main answer. In both cases, while the candidates' messages seemed to be directed at African Americans, their campaign strategists had ensured that these messages reflected what White voters expected of each party based on their attitudes toward education and race. This connection between race and education had been strong, though sometimes subtle, since the 1960s.[5] However, before exploring more recent education reforms, this chapter will provide an overview of key initiatives from the nation's founding up to President Johnson's signing of the 1965 Elementary and Secondary Education Act.

Developments Prior to the Space Race

With its focus on community and family control of education, the 2016 Republican Party platform was referring to the **Tenth Amendment** to the Constitution, which reserves powers not delegated to the federal government for state control. Education then, since it is not addressed in the Constitution, is one of those state powers. Therefore, earlier presidents and presidential candidates spoke more in terms of educational principles and philosophy rather than policies and practices. The Enlightenment presidents, George Washington through James Madison, held up education as a purveyor of virtues necessary for good citizens of a republic. Thomas Jefferson did attempt, however, to gain a role for federal government in education by advocating for a Constitutional amendment to permit this, and James Madison advocated for a national university. Other than these failed attempts, early presidents mostly gave lip service to issues of education. Later, Abraham Lincoln supported the **Morrill Land Grant Act** of 1862, creating a number of agricultural colleges. James A. Garfield, as a congressman, worked to open the first U.S. Office of Education, which Herbert Hoover unsuccessfully attempted to make a cabinet-level post.[6]

In the early twentieth century and with the rise of the progressive movement, education proposals gained more traction in presidential politics. In 1908, Socialist Party candidate **Eugene V. Debs** promised to create a federal department of education. In 1920, his party responded to African-American migration to northern urban centers by advocating for their "civil, political, industrial, and education rights." In the same election, the Democratic Party platform proposed that states cooperate with the federal government in educational endeavors.[7] It seemed by 1932—especially with the **New Deal** momentum involving a multitude of new government programs—that federal involvement in education might soon become a reality. After all, **Franklin D. Roosevelt** had named education among a long list of new rights. Although the Supreme Court later rejected the concept of education as a "right"—identifying it instead as a "privilege"—the push for increased federal support for education would continue. Indeed, in 1944, Roosevelt signed the most significant education act to be passed to that point, the G.I. Bill. This bill provided university and vocational training opportunities to over two million World War II veterans, transforming family trajectories for people of all ethnicities and socioeconomic backgrounds.[8]

Though Lincoln and Roosevelt signed bills into law that resulted in substantial changes to higher education, the nation still seemed ill prepared for federal involvement in elementary and secondary education. Congress rejected Harry Truman's attempts in 1947 and 1949 to provide federal funds to public schools, both times calling it an "intrusion" into state affairs. The nation's fear of government intrusion, however, was suddenly replaced in 1957 by another fear—the potential loss of the Cold War to the Soviets. This fear was initiated by a metallic sphere less than two feet in diameter, a Soviet satellite called *Sputnik*.[9] Fear quickly turned to blame. Why did it appear the United States might be losing the space race and possibly even the Cold War? Was America not producing engineers and scientists capable of developing comparable technologies?

Elementary and secondary education became an issue of national security and defense, leading to the first major initiative that would influence pre-collegiate education, the **National Defense Education Act** (NDEA). The 1958 NDEA stated,

> ...the security of the Nation requires the fullest development of the mental resources and technical skills of its young men and women.... [NDEA] will correct as rapidly as possible the existing

imbalances in our educational programs which have led to an insufficient proportion of our population educated in science, mathematics, and foreign languages, and trained in technology.

The Congress reaffirms the principle and declares that the State and local community have and must retain control over and primary responsibility for public education.[10]

The act that President **Dwight D. Eisenhower** signed into law provided $70 million annually for four years to support the instruction of science, mathematics, and modern foreign languages—thus beginning a trend of federal government reach into the education arena. Unlike future reforms, however, NDEA did not impose systematic accountability measures.

A Lever Long Enough: LBJ and the War against Poverty

Education reforms of the 1960s were influenced by a social consciousness of poverty represented by the ideas of three individuals. First, Swedish economist Gunner Myrdal wrote a 1940 study entitled *An American Dilemma: The Negro Problem and Modern Democracy* that explored the circle of poverty and its causes within African-American communities. An individual's poor education, he explained, would lead to limited employment opportunities, resulting in a low standard of living and inadequate nutrition, housing, and education for children in the family. Myrdal's study influenced the 1954 U.S. Supreme Court decision in ***Brown vs. Board of Education of Topeka***, and his concept of the circle of poverty impacted the social agenda of **John F. Kennedy** in the early 1960s.[12] The second individual was Michael Harrington who authored a 1962 book of which Kennedy requested copies to share with members of his administration. Harrington's book, *The Other America: Poverty in the United States*, painted a picture of two Amer-

Johnson signs ESEA in front of his childhood schoolhouse seated beside his first teacher[11]

icas—one that was made up primarily of affluent Whites and another consisting of poor non-Whites. The latter group, the new "invisible poor," had silently grown in the 1950s and, unlike the poor of previous generations, were trapped in a "culture of poverty." Education had been a way of escaping poverty in the past, but the new poor perceived it as an institution that made them feel inferior to the rest of society. Kennedy's economic advisor Walter Heller was a third individual key to the 1960s educational reforms. In his Congressional report, Heller, borrowing language from Myrdal and Harrington, described "the vicious circle" in which "poverty breeds poverty." His solution was to use education as a weapon to fight a **War on Poverty**. In a 1963 radio interview with Senate majority whip Hubert Humphrey, Heller explained that—even with proposed tax cuts—the education programs would easily be covered by projected increases in the

LBJ Library photo by Frank Wolfe

gross national product of $30 to $40 billion.[13] Kennedy—armed with the research, theoretical framework, and economic plan to carry out his vision—was prepared to launch a War on Poverty.

Kennedy's assassination in November of 1963 did not squelch enthusiasm for his agenda. If anything, it may have actually fed his successor's determination to carry it out all the more. Only two months after the tragic incident, **Lyndon B. Johnson** stood before the joint houses of Congress to declare the nation's War on Poverty, describing how it would be fought with better schools, health, homes, training, and employment opportunities.[14] The following year, as Congressional hearings opened for the **Elementary and Secondary Education Act** (ESEA) of 1965, Anthony J. Celebrezze, Secretary of Health, Education, and Welfare, quoted Johnson: "Just as ignorance breeds poverty, poverty all too often breeds ignorance in the next generation . . . . [This program] is designed to break this cycle which has been running on from generation to generation in this most affluent period of our history." At the same hearing, Education Commissioner Francis Keppel, supported the bill with the following dramatic statement: "Archimedes . . . told us many centuries ago, 'Give me a lever long enough and a fulcrum strong enough and I can move the world.' Today, at last, we have a prospect of a lever long enough and supported strongly enough to do something for our children of poverty."[15]

Education was only one of three pillars in Johnson's **Great Society**. The other two were social welfare and civil rights, with all three being closely intertwined.[16] In 1964, Johnson had signed the **Civil Rights Act** and the Economic Opportunity Act. Part of the first act served to codify into law what the Supreme Court had already declared in the 1954 *Brown* decision, that schools may not be segregated by race. Part of the second act created an enduring, popular program called **Head Start**. From its inception, Head Start was intentionally planned as an independent agency so as not to fall under the auspices of the federal education bureaucracy. This arrangement would avoid criticism that the federal government was intruding into the state's domain of public schools and would also simplify the provision of funds. The justification for this was that Head Start, as a social welfare initiative for preschoolers in poverty, was much more than an educational program. It involved parents and focused on the holistic development of the child—socially, physically, and cognitively.[17]

It may be considered a reasonable comparison to parallel Johnson with Horace Mann, who was considered the father of the nineteenth-century common school movement. Both acted on the assumption that education had the potential to end poverty, injustice, and crime. Certainly, Johnson was aware of the magnanimity of the bill he was about to sign, staging the signing ceremony in such a way as to reflect its historical importance. On Palm Sunday, Johnson sat behind a bench at the Texas one-room schoolhouse where he had begun his own education. Seated on the bench beside him was his first teacher, flown in from California where she had retired. He spoke of the "sense of urgency" behind the ESEA, stating,

> Over a century and a quarter ago, the president of the Republic of Texas, Mirabeau B. Lamar . . . made the mistaken prophecy that education would be an issue 'in which no jarring interests are involved and no acrimonious political feelings excited.' For too long, political acrimony held up our progress. For too long, children suffered while jarring interests caused stalemate in the efforts to improve our schools.[18]

The document Johnson signed that day stated as its purpose "to strengthen and improve educational quality and educational opportunities in the Nation's elementary and secondary schools." Title I provided funds to local education agencies for the education of children in low-income families. Title II, a provision that appealed especially to private schools, supported the purchase of library resources, textbooks, and other instructional materials for both public and private schools. Other title programs supported supplementary educational centers, research, and teacher training.[19]

Go to www.khlearn.com to watch a video showing Lyndon B. Johnson talking about his administration and education.

Controversy amid Increasing Reforms

Concerned about federal intrusion into state responsibilities, eighty percent of Republicans in the House had voted against ESEA. However, by the time of its renewal in 1974, little opposition remained. Part of the reason for such a shift in Republican support was that ESEA required only limited accountability from the states. States were permitted a great degree of latitude in spending the funds and suffered no penalties for failing to fulfill ESEA's purpose. Since no evidence was required from states proving increased academic achievement for students in poverty, funds continued to flow to the states whether student achievement improved or not. Republican fears subsided when they realized that federal control was minimal. Besides, states were still providing approximately ninety-two percent of their own education budgets, so the federal contribution—though valued by the states—was still a relatively small portion.[20]

While the ESEA required little academic accountability, there was another type of accountability that proved significant for African Americans, especially for those in the South. Until ESEA delivered federal funds directly into the public schools' budgets, there was little teeth behind the 1954 *Brown* decision or the school desegregation requirement of the 1964 Civil Rights Act. Southern states in particular could often get by with maintaining segregated schools without any repercussions. Because of Title VI of the Civil Rights Act, however, this could no longer be the case:

> No person in the United States shall, on the ground of race, color, or national origin, be excluded from participation in, be denied the benefits of, or be subjected to discrimination *under any program or activity receiving Federal financial assistance* [emphasis added].[21]

Now that states were receiving eight percent of their education budgets from the federal government, they were bound to comply with desegregation; otherwise, they would lose those funds. The controversy would be about what method to use to bring about compliance.

Though most voters claimed to be in agreement with the concept of desegregation of schools, the vast majority were not quite as agreeable to the most prominent solution offered—busing. Politicians therefore found navigating the issue problematic. Hubert Humphrey's 1968 campaign strategists advised him to avoid using the term "integration" of schools because it was too closely tied with the controversial concept of busing. The same voters who rejected busing, however, were likely to embrace the language of "equal opportunity." In George McGovern's 1972 campaign, strategists found that White voters responded well to the idea of taking funds currently being used for busing and applying them instead to inner-city school facilities, instructional materials, and teacher salaries. Richard M. Nixon's and Gerald Ford's advisors cautioned them that—although White voters may not be supportive of busing—they generally were supportive of equal educational opportunities for African Americans and were troubled by political language that seemed insensitive to the educational needs of African-American children.[22]

The 1972 Republican Party platform did not shy away from the issue of busing. The Republican platform reminded its constituency,

> Months ago President Nixon sent Congress a two-part comprehensive proposal on school busing. The first is the Student Transportation Moratorium Act of 1972—legislation to halt immediately all further court-ordered busing and give Congress time to devise permanent new arrangements for assuring desegregated, quality education. [23]

The platform went on to describe Nixon's companion legislation, the **Equal Educational Opportunities Act** that would provide $2.5 billion to help urban schools and to broaden assistance to Latinos, American Indians, and English language learners. While reaffirming a commitment to equality of education opportunity, the platform declared that busing brought "division within communities and hostility between classes and races" and that it was "unnecessary, counter-productive and wrong." [24]

The 1972 Democratic Party platform avoided the negative connotation held by the word "busing" by replacing it with "transportation" and by mentioning student transportation only once among other possible strategies to accomplish desegregation. They had to tread carefully because overt statements on busing might alienate White voters. Instead, they focused heavily on support of desegregation by way of a number of options:

> School attendance lines may be redrawn; schools may be paired; larger physical facilities may be built to serve larger, more diverse enrollments; magnet schools or educational parks may be used. Transportation of students is another tool to accomplish desegregation. It must continue to be available according to Supreme Court decisions to eliminate legally imposed segregation and improve the quality of education for all children.[25]

Nixon, having run both in 1968 and in 1972 as the "law and order" candidate, saw busing as undermining his efforts because it contributed to racial tension and school violence. Eliminating busing might reduce turmoil in the schools, but there had to be a plan to replace it with something else. Sidney Marland, Nixon's Commissioner of Education, believed that student delinquency could be eased in part by a strong career education program that aligned closely to the needs of the labor market. Using discretionary funds, Marland ignited a reform movement that by 1973 had involved 750,000 students in a career education program. Such an alignment of public school curriculum with the needs of business, Marland thought, would make learning more relevant and would thus help to resolve "high unemployment and the attendant problems of disaffection and drug excess among the young."[26]

After Nixon's resignation, Gerald Ford was neutral toward initiatives birthed from Johnson's Great Society. He took no measures to expand them but neither did he try to limit them. Regarding education, Ford maintained the traditional approach that control of public schools should remain under the auspices of state and local governments.[27] This approach would begin to shift after Ford lost the 1976 election to Jimmy Carter when, for the first time in history, the National Education Association (NEA) endorsed a presidential candidate. The NEA had contributed a great deal of both money and volunteers to see Carter elected. In competition with them, the **American Federation of Teachers** (AFT) had supported Ted Kennedy in the primaries. Carter's win meant a victory also for the NEA. They gained prestige for their association but wanted more; they wanted sustained influence on education through the federal government. The NEA called for Carter to fulfill his campaign promise to create a cabinet-level Department of Education. He would eventually, but reluctantly, do so.[28]

Carter took two full years to fulfill his promise to the NEA. As a Georgian, he had to be cautious not to offend the states-rights sensibilities of his Southern supporters. Elevating the Office of Education to a department would revive the notion that the federal government was intruding into powers that constitutionally belonged to the states. Additionally, he had campaigned on being a uniter and one who would reduce the power of interest groups in politics. This move would contradict much of what he had represented during the election. Nevertheless, he pushed for the new department on the grounds that it would increase efficiency.[29]

Presidents Johnson, Nixon, Ford, Carter, and Reagan

From left to right: LBJ Library photo by Yoichi Okamoto, Source: National Archives, Courtesy Gerald R. Ford Library, © Joseph Sohm/Shutterstock.com, © Joseph Sohm/Shutterstock.com

 ## Accountability Movement

It did not take long after the creation of the Department of Education for critics to call for shutting it down. One of its most vocal detractors was Republican presidential candidate Ronald Reagan. Referring to it as Carter's "new bureaucratic boondoggle," Reagan reiterated his belief that functions such as welfare and education are handled best when they are in the control of state and local governments. Upon taking office in 1981, Reagan appointed Terrel H. Bell as Secretary of Education with the task of dismantling the department. Bell, however, grew to believe that the department was helpful and should remain in place. In **William Bennett**, Reagan found someone willing to carry out the task and replaced Bell with Bennett starting with Reagan's second term. Though Reagan and Bennett were somewhat successful in temporarily weakening the department and cutting its budget, the U.S. Department of Education did survive.[30]

Perhaps Reagan's influence on education could be summarized by one of his radio addresses. Just weeks before the 1986 midterm election, Reagan used his weekly radio airtime to chat about his accomplishments in education—most likely in hopes of encouraging voters to send Republican legislators to Washington to continue his conservative agenda. "The schools are the best they've been in years," he said, "markedly better and still improving." In his folksy way, Reagan reminisced back to 1981 when "there was a widespread feeling in our country that our schools were not doing their job." He explained that it was the people's concern that motivated him to establish the **National Commission on Excellence in Education** for the purpose of evaluating the status of America's schools. In a much more informal manner than *A Nation at Risk* report had originally stated it, Reagan paraphrased, "If a foreign nation had done to our schools what we'd stood by and let happen, we would have considered it an act of war." In addition to the reforms resulting from the commission's report, Reagan went on to discuss increased test scores, the First Lady's *Just Say No* campaign to "rid schools of drugs," and the recent governor's conference where school choice was encouraged.[31]

School choice by way of vouchers had become a controversial proposal from the Reagan administration. Secretary Bennett had pitched vouchers as a means for disadvantaged children to attend either a private or a different public school outside of their own district. **Vouchers** would create a rivalry among schools, Bennett argued, that would result in an improved educational experience for all children. In response to a question about potential entanglements between church and state, Bennett explained that the aid would go directly to parents who would then redeem the voucher at the school of their choice.[32] Republican support for vouchers in one sense was logical because the idea aligned with principles of competition in the marketplace. In another sense, the idea conflicted with the party's stand during the 1970s' battles over desegregation in which Republicans had supported neighborhood-based schools. Nevertheless, beginning with Reagan and continuing through Donald Trump, vouchers were used as a key civil rights plank for the Republican Party.[33]

An interesting paradox about Reagan is that—while he was for limited government—his administration by way of *A Nation at Risk* was credited with birthing the accountability movement. The man who wanted to shut down the Department of Education introduced such a paradigm shift in the relationship between the federal government and public schools that the intrusion that was fought against for so long flowed into the states with increasing force.[34] Under Reagan, states were required to increase standards, improve instruction, and make curriculum reforms—all without any real increases in federal funding.

Credited with having sparked the accountability movement was Leon Lessinger's 1970 book *Every Kid a Winner: Accountability in Education*. Harkening back to the early twentieth century progressive movement's demand that experts fill government-appointed jobs rather than political cronies, Lessinger's theme was that schools should be centrally controlled by experts who reported their progress to the public. Locally controlled schools, he believed, bred mediocrity; shining light on measures of success would encourage progress. The best way to do this was through standardized achievement tests, the results of which would identify the degree to which a school had succeeded or failed.[35] Lessinger's ideas gained attention under the Reagan administration and increasingly were applied with each education reform thereafter.

 Go to www.khlearn.com to watch a video showing Ronald Reagan talking about religion and education.

In the 1988 election, **George H. W. Bush** benefited from Reagan's popularity, but he still needed to find his own niche as a candidate. He did so by promising to be an 'education president.' Oddly, his supposed niche was just more of the same from Reagan's agenda: school prayer, tuition tax credits, choice, and vouchers for private schools—none of which were high priorities for most voters.[36] Bush seemed surprised after winning the election that Americans were generally pleased with their schools, although they did perceive that inner city schools had been in decline. With the nation's concern for urban schools and with the Los Angeles police brutality incident against Rodney King in March of 1991, the time was ripe to propose a program to help the nation's inner cities. Bush's advisors believed that education reform with an emphasis on vouchers was the answer. The concept of vouchers was appealing for a number of reasons. It was consistent with conservative principles, would cost the federal government nothing, expanded educational options to low-income families, and gained favor with socially minded voters.[37]

In April of 1991, with the following year's election in sight, Bush rolled out his plan: **America 2000**, which was developed in cooperation with the National Governor's Association (NGA), of which Bill Clinton was head. With criticisms that he had focused on foreign policy to the neglect of domestic issues, Bush needed a domestic accomplishment under his belt, and this education plan would serve that purpose well. In addition to proposing vouchers, America 2000 continued Reagan's theme of excellence, and—to stiffen accountability—it called for national standards and standardized achievement tests. To this end, Bush's administration collaborated with Congress and the NGA to create the National Council on Education Standards and Testing.[38]

Congress never passed America 2000, but after defeating Bush, Clinton made minimal revisions to the bill and changed its name to Goals 2000, which he signed into law in March 1994. Internal polling data during the 1992 election had informed Clinton that school choice was popular among voters of all races, so he left that provision in the act. Additionally, because offering school choice did not require federal funding, it was compatible with his campaign promise to deliver a "leaner not meaner" government. A major difference between Goals 2000 and Bush's plan was that Clinton limited school choice only to public schools. Vouchers for private school enrollment would not be an option.[39]

Clinton's greatest contribution to public education may have been that he helped to tone down the criticism. Otherwise, he basically continued the accountability trend started under Reagan but supported it with minimal financial commitment. In Clinton's first term, such reservations may have been as a result of his "leaner not meaner" government promise. In his second term, however, his hands were tied from the 1994 midterm Republican Revolution and the Republican Party's Contract with America. The conservative wing of the Republican Party controlled both houses of Congress, which caused Clinton to declare, "The era of big government is over." The impact of this on education would be that, by the end of his second term in 2001, Clinton—despite all the rhetoric—had left the status of public schools generally as he had found them in 1993.[40]

Ironically, it was a Democratic president who announced that "the era of big government is over," and it was a Republican president who extended the government's reach into education farther than it had ever been. **George W. Bush**, as governor of Texas, had earned a reputation of being strong on education reform. During the 2000 presidential campaign, this image was enhanced by his wife Laura, who had been a teacher and librarian, and also by his talk of "compassionate conservatism," which sounded similar to his father's "kinder, gentler" rhetoric. Bush's verbal commitment to work toward academic achievement for minority students was buttressed when, after the election, he appointed Roderick Paige to be Secretary of Education. Paige was an African American who, as superintendent of Houston Independent School District, had modeled increased academic achievement for students in high-poverty schools. Bush sought to replicate this type of achievement in the nation's schools. As governor of Texas, Bush had implemented an accountability system that increased certification requirements for teachers, imposed rigorous curriculum standards, and assessed students on proficiency of those standards via standardized achievement tests. Though many of his initiatives had been unpopular with Texas educators, the data reports on achievement gave him credibility to run on education as one of his major campaign issues.[41]

With the ESEA up for renewal, the timing was right for Bush to infuse his educational agenda into the new act. He called it No Child Left Behind (NCLB). Although he had bipartisan support in the likes of Senator

Ted Kennedy, many Democrats and the NEA were leery, especially with verbiage referencing vouchers, merit pay, and state flexibility in spending federal funds. They, nevertheless, saw NCLB as an opportunity to strengthen funding for education, and—especially after the September 11, 2001, terrorist attacks—were ready to unite the nation through something positive. NCLB overwhelmingly passed in both Houses.[42]

Title I continued to be for the improvement of academic achievement of disadvantaged students. Title II increased qualifications for educators, and Title III required special language instruction for English language learners. Subsequent titles outlined a number of programs, but one that received a great deal of criticism related to the conditions for schools not meeting Adequate Yearly Progress.[43] Over time, educators and communities increasingly perceived that the measures for "failing" schools were too punitive and harmed the schools and students most in need of assistance. This criticism was one of the factors leading to measures taken during Barack Obama's administration in 2012 to allow states more flexibility in how they met the standards. The criticism also led to revisions when the act was renewed in 2015 as Every Student Succeeds Act (ESSA). ESSA included slight modifications to what was in NCLB, one of which was to give back to the states more authority in how they hold schools and districts accountable.

A look at the background of school reform since the 1960s reveals three stages that provided conditions leading to the accountability era. Johnson's Great Society agenda and ESEA represented the first stage, as the federal government began to expand in sustained and unprecedented ways into public school funding. The second stage involved enforcement of students' civil rights during the Nixon and Ford years, and the third stage followed the 1983 *A Nation at Risk* report and was sparked by discussions of excellence in education.[44] After these stages progressively strengthened the accountability movement, it would seem improbable that federal control would diminish any time soon. Yet, as recently as the 2012 presidential primary, a teacher from the debate audience in Orlando asked Republican presidential contenders, "What as president would you seriously do about what I consider a massive overreach of big government into the classroom?" Michelle Bachmann's response was the most direct: "I would go over to the Department of Education. I'd turn off the lights. I would lock the door. And I would send all the money back to the states and localities." Several of the other candidates on the panel expressed similar sentiments.[45]

The rhetoric, party platforms, and legislation have served many purposes. At times, that purpose has been as a frivolous prop to create a certain image of a political party or candidate. There have been opportunities, however, and there will continue to be further opportunities to place education reform in the context of other current circumstances—of larger societal problems—and to accomplish something meaningful for students and society. Just as education reform has played a role in issues of national defense, economic competition, and civil rights, it may in the future serve a role in an unexpected issue that may contribute further to the vision of a Great Society.

 Go to www.khlearn.com to watch a video about politics and educational policy.

Reflection

For personal reflection, content review, and further research:

1. In recent years, how have Democratic Party and Republican Party platforms typically differed in their approaches to educational proposals?
2. Because the U.S. Constitution makes no provision for education, the controversy between local and centralized control has prevailed. At what points has this controversy been at its peak, and at what critical junctions have there been significant shifts toward centralization? What events brought about these shifts?
3. What reforms did the 1958 National Defense Education Act initiate?
4. The "lever long enough" referred to what and was intended to accomplish what outcome in societal reforms?
5. The Elementary and Secondary Education Act (ESEA) of 1965 has been renewed throughout the years and known as No Child Left Behind (NCLB), as Every Student Succeeds Act (ESSA), and by other names. Trace its development and how it has been revised over time.
6. What were the three pillars of Johnson's Great Society, and how was each pillar to support the other two?
7. Discuss the implications for schools from the U.S. Supreme Court's 1954 decision in *Brown versus Topeka Board of Education*.
8. Compare Horace Mann and Lyndon B. Johnson regarding their beliefs about the societal impact of education.
9. Explain the connection between the 1965 ESEA and the desegregation of public schools.
10. Who was the first presidential candidate endorsed by the National Education Association (NEA)? What was the NEA's motive for doing so?
11. For what reason have there been calls to close the U.S. Department of Education?
12. What impact did Ronald Reagan's National Commission on Excellence in Education and its *A Nation at Risk* report have on education policy?
13. What arguments have politicians used for or against vouchers and school choice?
14. Analyze the impact of Leon Lessinger's 1970 book *Every Kid a Winner*. What are the advantages and disadvantages of its impact on public schools?
15. Trace the accountability movement in education from its inception to relevant current events occurring most recently.
16. Explain the irony behind Ronald Reagans' and Bill Clinton's educational initiatives related to typical stands by their corresponding political parties.
17. Outline the three stages of the accountability movement and describe what you anticipate will be the next stage.

ENDNOTES

1. Barack Obama, *Remarks by the President on Education* (Washington, DC: Benjamin Banneker Academic High School, 2016).
2. Democratic Party Platform 2016, The American Presidency Project, accessed May 25, 2019, https://www.presidency.ucsb.edu/node/273239.
3. Republican Party Platform, 2016, The American Presidency Project, accessed May 25, 2019, https://www.presidency.ucsb.edu/node/273433.
4. Dan Bauman, and Brock Read, "A Brief History of GOP Attempts to Kill the Education Dept," *The Chronicle of Higher Education* (June 21, 2018): 3.

5. DeeAnn Grove, "White Voters, a Key Piece of the Puzzle: Education, Race, and Electoral Politics," *Political Science & Politics* 51, no. 3 (2018): 520.

6. Thomas C. Hunt, James C. Carper, Thomas J. Lasley, and C. Daniel Raisch, eds. *Encyclopedia of Educational Reform and Dissent*, vol 2. (Los Angeles: Sage, 2010), 710-20.

7. Gil Troy, Arthur M. Schlesinger, Jr., and Fred Israel, eds., *History of American Presidential Elections, 1789-2008*, vol. 2, 4th ed. (New York: Facts on File, Inc., 2011), 860-953.

8. Hunt et al., *Encyclopedia of Educational Reform*, 720.

9. Ibid.

10. "National Defense Education Act of 1958," in *The School in the United States: A Documentary History*, ed. James W. Fraser (New York: Routledge, 2010), 258. Public Domain.

11. Frank Wolfe, *Johnson Signs ESEA*, 1965, photo, The Lyndon Baines Johnson Library, Austin, Texas.

12. Spring, *The American School*, 371.

13. Walter Heller and Hubert H. Humphrey, *Report on the Economy*, January 27, 1963, Minnesota Historical Society, accessed May 25, 2019, http://www2.mnhs.org/library/findaids/00442/pdfa/00442-01157.pdf.

14. Lyndon B. Johnson, "The State of the Union Message to Congress, 8 January 1964," in *A Time for Action: A Selection from the Speeches and Writings of Lyndon B. Johnson*, (New York: Antheneum, 1964), 164-179.

15. U.S. Congress, House Committee on Education and Labor, *Aid to Elementary and Secondary Education: Hearings before the General Subcommittee of the Committee on Education and Labor*, 89th Cong., 1st sess., 1965, U.S. Government Printing Office, pp. 63-82.

16. Hunt et al., *Encyclopedia of Educational Reform*, 721.

17. Urban and Wagoner, *American Education*, 328.

18. Lyndon B. Johnson, "Johnson's Remarks on Signing the Elementary and Secondary Education Act," Johnson City, TX, April 11, 1965, http://www.lbjlibrary.org/lyndon-baines-johnson/timeline/johnsons-remarks-on-signing-the-elementary-and-secondary-education-act, accessed May 25, 2019.

19. Elementary and Secondary Education Act of 1965, Public Law 89-10, Government Publishing Office, 27-47, accessed May 25, 2019, https://www.govinfo.gov/content/pkg/STATUTE-79/pdf/STATUTE-79-Pg27.pdf.

20. Gareth Davies, *See Government Grow: Education Politics from Johnson to Reagan* (Lawrence, KS: University Press of Kansas, 2007), 1-2.

21. *Title VI of the Civil Rights Act of 1964*, The United Stated Department of Justice, accessed June 27, 2019, https://www.justice.gov/crt/fcs/TitleVI.

22. Grove, "White Voters," 518.

23. Republican Party Platform, 1972.

24. Ibid.

25. Democratic Party Platform 1972.

26. Spring, *The American School*, 429-31.

27. Hunt et al., *Encyclopedia of Educational Reform*, 721.

28. Urban and Wagoner, *American Education*, 331-2.

29. Ibid.

30. Bauman and Read, "A Brief History of GOP," 1-2.

31. Ronald Reagan, "Radio Address to the Nation on Education and Drug Abuse," Santa Barbara County, CA, September 6, 1986, accessed May 25, 2019, https://www.reaganlibrary.gov/research/speeches/090686a.

32. Robert Pear, "Reagan Proposes Vouchers to Give Poor a Choice of Schools," *The New York Times*, November 14, 1985, accessed June 27, 2019, https://www.nytimes.com/1985/11/14/us/reagan-proposes-vouchers-to-give-poor-a-choice-of-schools.html.

33. Grove, "White Voters," 517-8.

34. Jal Mehta, "How Paradigms Create Politics: The Transformation of American Educational Policy, 1980-2001," *American Educational Research Journal* 50, no. 2 (2013): 285.

35. Leon Lessinger, *Every Kid a Winner: Accountability in Education* (New York: Simon & Schuster, 1970).

36. Urban and Wagoner, *American Education*, 361.

37. Grove, "White Voters," 519.

38. Spring, *The American School*, 435.

39. Grove, "White Voters," 520.

40. Urban and Wagoner, *American Education*, 364-5.

41. Ibid., 365-7.

42. Davies, *See Government Grow*, 286.

43. No Child Left Behind Act of 2001, Public Law 107-110, Government Publishing Office, accessed May 25, 2019, https://www.govinfo.gov/content/pkg/PLAW-107publ110/pdf/PLAW-107publ110.pdf.

44. Davies, *See Government Grow*, 282-3.

45. Bauman and Read, "A Brief History of GOP," 3.

CHAPTER 16

EXISTENTIALISM AND KIERKEGAARD: STUDENT CHOICE AND AUTHENTIC RELATIONSHIP

Søren Kierkegaard, "Father of Eistentialism"[1]

FOCUS: KEY TOPICS AND TERMS

Critical Pedagogy	Kierkegaard, Søren	Piaget, Jean
Despair	Kohlberg, Lawrence	Rationalism
Dewey, John	Kohn, Alfie	Sartre, Jean-Paul
Disequilibrium	Leap of Faith	Subjective Knowledge
Double Contingency	Maslow, Abraham	Summerhill School
Erikson, Erik	Naturalism	Theistic Existentialism
Existentialism	Neil, A. S.	Vicarious Experiences
Freire, Paulo	Nietzsche, Friedrich	
Hegel, Georg W. F.	Objective Knowledge	

Chronologically, this chapter should appear much earlier in the book, perhaps in conjunction with individuals and events that occurred in the early nineteenth century. Topically, this chapter might better be placed in a context including philosophers and theologians—such as Augustine, Thomas Aquinas, Martin Luther, and John Calvin—whose ideas impacted the history and philosophy of education. As out of place as it may seem, addressing Søren Kierkegaard's influence on education might best be reserved for the end of the book. In recent decades, existentialism has found proponents among educational philosophers and is often synthesized with Marxism and multiculturalism to form a postmodern approach to education. Existential sensibilities are included in current research on emotional intelligence, intrapersonal intelligence, individualized instruction, and personalized learning. Therefore, Kierkegaard and the ideas he developed in Denmark nearly two centuries ago are appropriate to consider in the context of current educational trends.

Kierkegaard on a Danish stamp (ca. 1955)

© tristan tan/Shutterstock.com

Though known primarily as a Christian theologian, philosopher, and apologist, **Søren Kierkegaard** (1813-1855) has also greatly influenced the field of education through his existential notions of subjective knowledge, student choice, and an emphasis on the individual as thinker and believer. At first, educators may find it a challenge to understand the complexities of his writings, but once they take the "leap"—to use a term central to Kierkegaard's philosophy—they may discover that his approach to learning serves to inspire their practice. They may not be familiar with his name, but educators will recognize Kierkegaard's ideas as having influenced educational theory and practice throughout the past century. A fresh examination of his theories may bring new life into a dead classroom just as he sought to bring new life into the nineteenth-century church.

Søren Kierkegaard: Background and Historical Context

Like Hamlet, Søren Kierkegaard has been referred to as a "melancholy Dane." This moniker may be justified by the focus in his writings on the topics of despair, dread, and doubt. It may also have roots in his early life experiences. His mother and five of his six siblings died before he was twenty-one years old, but there seemed to be hope for a brighter future as he finished his studies to become a Lutheran minister and as he anticipated marriage to the daughter of a prominent government official. Neither of these opportunities would come to fruition as he rejected the ministry and broke off his engagement. Though he sincerely loved his fiancée, he was convinced that marriage to her would not satisfy the void for meaning that Kierkegaard so longed to fill. He was convinced that conformity to societal definitions of success was not the path for him.[2]

Kierkegaard was concerned with the lack of spiritual vibrancy in the established Lutheran Church. Except for those born into Jewish families, all Danish children were considered members of the church at birth. Kierkegaard was convinced that this practice was dangerously leading people to believe that they were Christians when they were not. Exacerbating this was the idea that a rational belief in right doctrine would lead to one's salvation.[3] The church had been corrupted by the ills of modernity and so had other social institutions, such as businesses and schools. These institutions were sacrificing individual choice on the altar of conformity, uniformity, and systematization.[4] He conveyed these convictions in his many works—some of his most prominent being *Either/Or* (1843), *Fear and Trembling* (1843), *Philosophical Fragments* (1844), *Stages on Life's Way* (1845), and *Sickness Unto Death* (1849). Having a rebellious spirit, Kierkegaard disregarded the harsh responses to his writings as the press caricaturized his appearance and attacked his ideas as the "ludicrous ravings of a madman."[5]

His countercultural ideas were not only critical of the church and other social institutions, but he also attacked the prominence of reason in modern philosophy. **Rationalism**—both in the religious realms of theology and apologetics and in the secular realms of science and philosophy—was an illegitimate means to prove anything of value.[6] For example, though common for apologists to use miracles as evidence for God's existence, Kierkegaard believed this type of argument was pointless, for "whoever does not believe does not see the miracle."[7] In the philosophical realm, a primary target of his criticism was the dialectical idealism of **Georg W. F. Hegel**, who emphasized objective rationality to the neglect of the individual persons doing the reasoning.[8] His reaction to Hegel has led Kierkegaard to be known as the "father of existentialism."

 # Existentialism

During his lifetime, Kierkegaard received little recognition for his ideas, but after a global economic depression, rapid industrialization, and two devastating wars in the twentieth century, disillusioned people were seeking answers to the dehumanization they observed.[9] How could one live with meaning and purpose in a world of such massive death and destruction? Many found answers in Kierkegaard's **existentialism,** especially with its emphasis on the value of the individual, freedom of choice, and authentic relationships.[10]

Ironically, though outspoken against rational theology and apologetics, Kierkegaard is known as both a Christian theologian and an apologist. However, the universality of his philosophy is such that there also developed an atheistic form of existentialism. While **theistic existentialism** developed as a response to lifeless orthodox religion, atheistic existentialism reacted to the nihilistic pessimism of **naturalism**.[11] If naturalism held no inherent meaning in the universe, what hope was there for the atheist? Friedrich Nietzsche, Fyodor Dostoevsky, Jean-Paul Sartre, and Albert Camus offered their answers in secular versions of existentialism. **Friedrich Nietzsche**, for example, declared that God was dead and that individuals should strive to become *Übermensch*, or supermen.[12] **Jean-Paul Sartre** later suggested that—though humans are indeed insignificant in a universe without ultimate meaning—they should live their lives *as if* it held intrinsic meaning[13]—which seems quite inauthentic for a philosophy that claims to encourage authenticity!

Kierkegaard's theistic existentialism, on the other hand, advocated an authentic relationship with God and the universe as a result of a "**leap of faith**." Rather than being born or baptized as an infant into an institutionalized church, individuals enter into relationship with God by choosing to convert and to live as a disciple of Christ, though it may be at a great personal cost. This holistic experience of spiritual development involves individuals acting upon their beliefs, thoughts, emotions, and hopes, even when those actions may not appear to be rationally logical.[14] The leap of faith is a movement by choice from despair to the authentic self—**despair** being Kierkegaard's definition of sin. Individuals in the condition of despair are in sin because they have resigned themselves to be inauthentic before God.[15]

Kierkegaard's influence has been incorporated by subsequent theologians, such as Karl Barth, Dietrich Bonhoeffer, Emil Brunner, and Rudolf Bultmann. Barth, for example, embraced the concepts that religious truth is subjective, that paradoxes must be acknowledged in order to discuss God, and that an "infinite qualitative distinction" separates God from His creation so that God is the "wholly other."[16] Considering Kierkegaard's antipathy to apologetics, it is ironic that Brunner wrote, "Kierkegaard is incomparably the greatest Apologist or 'eristic' thinker of the Christian faith within the sphere of Protestantism."[17]

 ## Epistemology

Though Kierkegaard's philosophical ideas may seem esoteric to educators of children, his epistemic concepts hold a great deal of relevance for the learning process and have been incorporated by a number of educational theorists. His concept of despair functions similarly to **Jean Piaget**'s theory of **disequilibrium**, and his teachings on doubt sound strikingly like descriptions of critical thinking.

DOUBT, REFLECTION, AND HUMILITY

True to his theory of learning, Kierkegaard's writings are not didactic; they do not directly teach the reader. They engage readers, forcing them to assign meaning on their own. His themes are presented indirectly as he often wrote using a pseudonym representing a narrator of a fictional story. Therefore, to claim Kierkegaard teaches

Leap of faith

© Gwoeii/Shutterstock.com

this or that specific principle can be problematic. In *Philosophical Fragments*, for instance, Johannes Climacus is the pseudonymous narrator and central character of the story. Though Climacus is much like Kierkegaard, he is more skeptical and less willing to take the leap of faith. One of the themes explored in *Fragments* is the role of doubt in the learning process, and—true to his notion regarding the value of doubt—Kierkegaard leaves readers doubting if they fully comprehend what he intended about the role of doubt. Like despair, doubt can drain both learners and their teachers, and as despair may lead to resolution through a leap of faith, doubt may lead to resolution through choices. As negative as despair and doubt may appear, if properly resolved, they serve to motivate learners to develop themselves. Doubt, however, cannot simply be shut off like a switch, even by making choices, because doubt is embedded into the human condition.[18]

Kierkegaard illustrated the insufficiency of rational arguments by portraying Climacus as one who seems to be a good listener but who does so only to strategize an argument to tear down the speaker's logic. When Climacus observes his father doing the same thing, he is uncomfortable with the realization that he has learned from his father a form of ruthless debate. In his contemplation, he eventually concludes that the Greeks were wrong; philosophy does not begin with wonder, because wonder does not induce reflection. Instead, philosophy begins with doubt. Therefore, everything must be doubted. In his earnest attempt to doubt every thought, Climacus is overwhelmed to the point of losing consciousness. Although doubting wears upon the body and mind, taking away one's youthful innocence, it is a meaningful reflective exercise—unlike the wonder of the Greeks.[19]

For Climacus, then, learning involved listening/observing, doubting/reflecting, and choosing/acting. Yet, recalling how uncomfortable he was observing his father tear down another's arguments, he resolved to begin listening and observing with humility, not to win a debate, but to learn. Even in the context of humility, however, doubting has its risks. It may lead to a pervasive sense that nothing is resolved. Everything is contaminated. Something is always wrong. On the other hand, there are also risks with choosing not to doubt. Those who choose not to doubt risk apathy and deterioration of the mind.[20]

FAITH AND REASON: SUBJECTIVE AND OBJECTIVE KNOWLEDGE

In *Fragments*, Kierkegaard distinguishes between two types of knowledge. The first is objective or declarative knowledge, that which is stated as fact. **Objective knowledge** comes from outside the self and, as such, is doubted by the self. Kierkegaard believed that there could be no certainty in objective knowledge. The nearest one could arrive at certainty would only be found in approximation. In other words, one can never know for sure that an objective or declarative claim is true. The second type is subjective or procedural knowledge—the process of how something is experienced by the learner. **Subjective knowledge**, according to Kierkegaard, is the only meaningful knowledge and cannot be transmitted directly from the teacher to the learner. Subjective knowledge, by its very nature, must be experienced and has the potential of transforming the learner.[21]

Climacus illustrates the difference between objective and subjective knowledge by discussing how one perceives a star. Upon initially seeing a star, the learner experiences meaningful interaction with it visually and emotionally. The star exists, and the learner has meaningful knowledge of that existence.[22] However, when presented with scientific objective facts about the star's origin and its characteristics, the learner doubts these facts. There is no intimate relationship or context to this objective knowledge, and—according to Kierkegaard via Climacus—these facts are only approximations. All approximate knowledge requires faith or belief to be acquired meaningfully. This again is a leap of faith, but it is not the same religious faith involved in spiritual conversion. It is a faith that acknowledges that the one observing the star and also the star itself are in flux. The learner is in the process of becoming and is therefore a contingent being. The star itself and the objective knowledge about the star are also contingent. Kierkegaard refers to this as "**double contingency**." Consequently, objective knowledge about the star is only approximate knowledge and requires more faith than reason for this knowledge to be meaningful. It did not take faith to believe the star's existence upon seeing it, because—according to Hebrews 11:1—faith is in what is *not* seen. The observer cannot see the origin or scientific characteristics of the star, so those approximations must be taken on faith. This in part explains why Kierkegaard was known by some as the "epistemologist of belief" and why others accused him of being an anti-rationalist.[23]

Are the critics correct in their accusations that Kierkegaard was an irrational skeptic? He was certainly skeptical about any knowledge outside of the knower's experience. This would include historical or empirical claims, which he described as contingent or approximate. Such objective knowledge would be unfinished until its uncertainty was removed by faith or belief.[24] In Kierkegaard's mind, faith indeed was irrational, but it served as the fulfillment of reason. Though clearly a paradox, passionate faith achieves what reason strives to do but cannot accomplish. Faith, for Kierkegaard, is clearly preeminent over reason in gaining a meaningful understanding of either religious or secular knowledge.[25]

 ## Nature of the Learner and Stages of Development

If "I think; therefore, I am" represents Descartes's ontology, "I choose; therefore, I am" is central to Kierkegaard's notion of what it means to exist. According to Kierkegaard, individuals rise out of despair by choosing—by exercising agency in a decision-making process. The learner's identity emerges through this series of choices. To choose is to learn and to exist as a person. That is the nature of the learner.[26]

The importance of choosing is more fully understood in the context of Kierkegaard's leap of faith and also in his theory of three stages. Unlike Jean Piaget's cognitive stages, **Lawrence Kohlberg**'s moral stages, or **Erik Erikson**'s psychosocial stages, Kierkegaard's three stages are not cumulative. Higher stages do not incorporate lower ones as do Piaget's and Kohlberg's theories; neither are they dialectic, bringing about a synthesis from conflict as do Erikson's stages of identity. They are simply "stages on life's way" and are identified as aesthetic, moral/intellectual, and religious. In the first stage, the individual is motivated by aesthetic pleasure of the senses and of the mind—essentially, by entertainment. There is no "oughtness" in this stage because choices are made primarily based upon the degree of pleasure each experience will bring. To illustrate the aesthetic stage, Kierkegaard points to the character of Don Juan—a womanizer who lives in the here and now with little concern for the consequences of his actions. Socrates is the model for the moral/intellectual stage; he has an orientation to the past, present, and the future—regretting immoral acts of the past and committing to make moral decisions in the present and the future, whatever the cost may be. Abraham serves as the example of the religious stage—a life lived by faith and not by reason. Had Abraham relied on intellectual or moral reasoning, he would not have climbed Mount Moriah with the intent of sacrificing his son Isaac. Instead, he took a leap of faith to obey God's command. It is in such a leap of faith that one becomes an authentic person.[27]

 ## Implications for Curriculum and Instruction

Because it is in the nature of the learner to choose and to become an authentic self, the content and methods of education—from an existentialist perspective—should maximize opportunities for students to make decisions. The more these decisions are free of teacher direction, the more authentic the learning experience becomes. The instructor surrenders responsibility of learning to the students, focusing on their self-regulation of metacognitive abilities. Consequently, education is less about what content students study and more about the actions they take in the process. Ideally, students should be exposed to as many first-hand experiences as possible. **Vicarious experiences**, however, may also be valuable. For this reason the humanities play an important role in the curriculum. The stories of historical and fictional characters may resonate with students as they examine the characters' choices in their own journeys to become an authentic self. Also, the fine arts and performing arts are important avenues for students to express themselves. The social environment of the classroom and school should be democratic, allowing for student self-government and participation in cultivating the environment.[28]

While a student at the University of Copenhagen, Kierkegaard wrote a letter contemplating what his life's work might be. He wrote,

> What I really need is to become clear in my own mind what I must do, not what I must know—except in so far as a knowing must precede every action. The important thing is to understand what I am destined for, to perceive what the Deity wants me to do; the point is to find the truth for me, to find that idea for which I am ready to live and die. What good would it do me to discover a so-called objective truth, though I were to work my way through the systems of the philosophers and were able, if need be, to pass them in review?[29]

For Kierkegaard, an education that focuses on the transmission of objective knowledge is meaningless and absurd. It causes students to become static and inauthentic rather than to move them to personal growth and authentic development.[30]

Since paradox is pervasive in life experience and spiritual understanding, it is expected that paradox would also be present in Kierkegaard's theory of learning, and it most certainly is. For example, while opposed to coercion in instruction, Kierkegaard supports the use of what he calls "seduction." Before one explores the notion of seduction in an instructional setting, it is helpful to understand how he believed seduction could be a tool either for harm or for good. Kierkegaard believed that—in the established Lutheran Church of Denmark—people were seduced into believing that they were Christians when they were not. They were born into the church but had not experienced a leap-of-faith conversion into a relationship with God through His Son Jesus Christ. This, along with dry orthodox theology, was to blame for the dead religion prevalent among the Danish people. Kierkegaard perceived it as part of his life's purpose to awaken the church from its slumber, but how would he approach this? In part, through seduction—by writing engaging stories that resonate with readers, by provoking readers to assign meaning to the text, and by introducing pseudonymous narrators whose thoughts may or may not represent his own. In this way, instead of didactically coercing ideas upon his readers, he would seduce them into reflectively thinking and choosing for themselves.[31]

In *Fear and Trembling* and in *Either/Or*, Kierkegaard addressed the role of seduction in education. He did not use the term in its common erotic sense but in a spiritual and intellectual sense. Educationally, seduction may be used to help students "catch up" with themselves. He posed, "What then is education? . . . . It is the course the individual goes through in order to catch up with himself."[32] From a somewhat Rousseauian notion, Kierkegaard believed individuals had been corrupted by society and needed to return to their condition prior to being conformed to culture. The teacher can enable students to "catch up" with themselves by cultivating their individuality—those unique qualities that make them different from society as a whole. This process of individualization is the opposite and the undoing of socialization.[33]

Teachers may also use seduction in stories that keep students in suspense "by means of minor actions of an episodic nature to ascertain how they want it to turn out, and then in the course of the telling to fool them."[34] Deception in this case is an innocent tool to engage students' attention and to build anticipation. The deception may be an instructional risk, but it is intended to build student confidence in their own reflective thinking. Seduction is not the same as indoctrination. Contrary to indoctrination, proper intellectual seduction invites students to experiment in making decisions with minimal teacher intervention. Rather than to limit students' options, seduction opens up space for possibilities—space for students to choose their own paths.[35]

Kierkegaard's ideas about truth, knowledge acquisition, and the nature of the learner are not so foreign to educators after all. Teacher preparation programs include his ideas—though adapted, assimilated, and often distorted—in prevailing theories about childhood stages, personality development, and **Abraham Maslow's** hierarchy of needs. Hints of Kierkegaard can be seen in **John Dewey's** progressive classroom, **A. S. Neil's Summerhill School**, **Paulo Freire's critical pedagogy**, and **Alfie Kohn's** movement against grades, homework, and teacher coercion. As public policy increasingly promotes objective knowledge measured by standardized achievement tests, it will be interesting to observe how existentialist voices respond.

 Go to www.khlearn.com to watch a video about existentialism and Kierkegaard.

 Reflection

For personal reflection, content review, and further research:
1. How did Kierkegaard's theological beliefs influence his beliefs about education?
2. If rationalism is illegitimate to prove anything to be of value, how did Kierkegaard propose the teaching of values apart from reason?
3. Compare the philosophies of Hegel and Kierkegaard. What was it about Hegel's philosophy that Kierkegaard rejected and why?
4. Kierkegaard died in 1855, but his ideas gained more attention in the twentieth century than during his lifetime. Why is this so? What drove philosophers to reconsider his theories?
5. What causes so many evangelical Christians to reject existentialism?
6. What is the difference between theistic existentialism and atheistic existentialism?
7. How is the existentialism of Kierkegaard different from that of Friedrich Nietzsche and Jean-Paul Sartre?
8. What was the essence of Kierkegaard's "leap," and what was the role of the leap in religion and in education?
9. Why was Kierkegaard opposed to the field of apologetics, defending the faith, and how was this stance ironic?
10. How have other educational theorists incorporated concepts from Kierkegaard? Consider how Jean Piaget, Howard Hardner, Alfie Kohn, and others may have done so.
11. Compare Kierkegaard's writing style, especially as it relates to seducing the reader, to the concept of indirect instruction.

12. Explain the prominent role of choice in Kierkegaard's theory.

13. Thomas Aquinas and the scholastics of the Middle Ages valued debate as an instructional method. Compare Kierkegaard's view of debate with that of the scholastics.

14. Compare Kierkegaard's notion of doubt in the learning process with the Calvinistic approaches to learning, such as the catechism, rote learning, recitations, and memorization.

15. The question of whether faith or reason is more important in the learning process has been argued throughout the history of philosophy. Compare Kierkegaard's thoughts with those of Augustine, Aquinas, Luther, Calvin, and others. What are your conclusions on the matter?

16. Kierkegaard uses the example of a star to illustrate his theory of the learning process. Choose an example of your own and trace the learning process according to Kierkegaard.

17. What significance does Hebrews 11:1 hold in existentialism?

18. Compare Kierkegaard's perspective of the nature of the learner with other philosophers and theologians. What are the implications for learning based on whether an educational approach assumes the learner is basically good, neutral, or sinful?

19. Kierkegaard presents Don Juan, Socrates, and Abraham respectively as illustrations for his three life stages: aesthetic, moral/intellectual, and religious. Present your own illustrations for each stage and justify your selections. Your illustrations may be from historical or current popularly known individuals.

20. Compare and contrast the role of freedom in the theories of Jean-Jacques Rousseau and of Kierkegaard.

21. The humanities are important in the curriculum of both educational philosophies of traditional perennialism and of existentialism. In what ways do these two philosophies value the humanities differently? How are the humanities used in the two philosophies for different learning outcomes?

22. Kierkegaard believed that seduction could be used in learning both for good or bad purposes. Provide an example of how, according to Kierkegaard, seduction may be used in learning for positive outcomes.

ENDNOTES

1. *Søren Kierkegaard*, ca. 1840, photograph, The Royal Library, National Collections Department, Denmark. Public Domain.

2. Gutek, *Philosophical*, 108-9; Woodbridge and James, *Church History*, vol. 2, 634.

3. Gutek, *Philosophical*, 109-10; Gene Edward Veith, Jr., *Reading Between the Lines: A Christian Guide to Literature* (Wheaton, IL: Crossway Books, 1990), 201.

4. Edgar and Oliphint, *Christian Apologetics*, 314.

5. Gutek, *Philosophical*, 109-10.

6. Dulles, *A History of Apologetics*, 218-19; Edgar and Oliphint, *Christian Apologetics*, 313.

7. Søren Kierkegaard, *Philosophical Fragments*, trans. Edna H. Hong and Howard V. Hong (Princeton, NJ: Princeton University Press, 1985), 77.

8. Dunn, *Philosophical Foundations of Education*, 195.

9. Ibid.

10. Shalika Sharma, "The Educational Philosophy of Søren Kierkegaard: The Origin of Existentialism." *Indian Journal of Research* 5, no. 5 (2016): 368.

11. James W. Sires, *The Universe Next Door* (Downers Grove, IL: InterVarsity Press, 2009), 118, 143.

12. George R. Knight, *Philosophy & Education: An Introduction in Christian Perspective* (Berrien Springs, MI: Andrews University Press, 2006), 76.

13. Jack Layman, "Modern Educational Philosophies," in *Philosophy of Christian School Education*, ed. Paul A. Kienel, Ollie E. Gibbs, and Sharron R. Berry (Colorado Springs: Association of Christian Schools International, 1995), 85.

14. Gutek, *Philosophical*, 109-11.

15. Søren Kierkegaard, *The Sickness Unto Death. A Christian Psychological Exposition for Edification and Awakening*, trans. Alastair Hannay (London: Penguin Books, 1989), 111, 113.

16. Dietrich Bonhoeffer, *The Cost of Discipleship* (New York: Simon & Schuster, 1959), 51; Woodbridge and James, *Church History*, 634, 712-15.

17. Dulles, *A History of Apologetics*, 218.

18. Peter Roberts, "Learning to Live with Doubt: Kierkegaard, Freire, and Critical Pedagogy," *Policy Futures in Education* 15, no. 7-8 (2017): 835-6.

19. Kierkegaard, *Philosophical Fragments*, 119-64.

20. Ibid.

21. Ibid., 206-22. Risa Della Rocca, Michael Foley, and Colin Kenny, "The Educational Theory of Søren. Kierkegaard," *New Foundations* (2011): 1-4.

22. Kierkegaard, *Philosophical Fragments*, 81.

23. Nathan P. Carson, "Passionate Epistemology: Kierkegaard on Skepticism, Approximate Knowledge, and Higher Existential Truth," *Journal of Chinese Philosophy* 40, no. 1 (2013): 34-37.

24. Ibid., 29.

25. Dulles, *A History of Apologetics*, 207-8, 221, 337.

26. Maxine Greene, "Wide-Awakeness and the Moral Life," in *Foundations of Education: The Essential Texts*, ed. Susan F. Semel, (New York: Routledge, 2010), 197; Rocca, Foley, and Kenny, "The Educational Theory," 2-3.

27. Dulles, *A History of Apologetics*, 219-21; Gutek, *Philosophical, Ideological, and Theoretical Perspectives*, 110-11; Sharma, "The Educational Philosophy of Søren Kierkegaard," 368.

28. Rocca, Foley, and Kenny, "The Educational Theory," 1-2; Sharma, "The Educational Philosophy of Søren Kierkegaard," 369.

29. Sires, *The Universe Next Door*, 136.

30. Rocca, Foley, and Kenny, "The Educational Theory," 4.

31. Herner Sæverot, "Kierkegaard, Seduction, and Existential Education," *Studies in Philosophy and Education* 30, no. 6 (2011): 558-71.

32. Søren Kierkegaard, *Fear and Trembling*, trans. Edna H. Hong and Howard V. Hong (Princeton, NJ: Princeton University Press, 1983), 46.

33. Sæverot, "Kierkegaard," 559.

34. Søren Kierkegaard, *Either/Or*, trans. Edna H. Hong and Howard V. Hong (Princeton, NJ: Princeton University Press, 1987), 370.

35. Sæverot, "Kierkegaard," 559.

CHAPTER 17

PAULO FREIRE, LIBERATION THEOLOGY, AND CRITICAL PEDAGOGY

FOCUS: KEY TOPICS AND TERMS

Banking Pedagogy
Banking System
Behaviorism
Conscientization
Critical Pedagogy
Culture of Silence
Dewey, John
Freire, Paulo
Giroux, Henry

Gutiérrez, Gustavo
hooks, bell (Gloria
   Watkins)
Imagery
Liberation Theology
Marxist Ideology
McLaren, Peter
No Child Left Behind
Operant Conditioning

Orthodoxy
Orthopraxy
Praxis
Reflexive Teaching
Social Gospel
Transformational
   Education

Since the 1970s, principles of liberation theology have been increasingly influential in American religion and education. The Universalist Unitarian Church has largely embraced the doctrine of liberation theology, but many other Christian denominations in the United States have also been impacted to varying degrees by these Marxist-infused doctrines. Both liberation theology and critical pedagogy were birthed in Latin America and were developed by a merging of Catholic doctrine and Marxist tenets. Currently, Paulo Freire's critical pedagogy is a leading educational theory espoused by prominent authors and educational theorists. One proponent is critical feminist theorist Gloria Watkins, whose pen name is "bell hooks." Others include Henry Giroux and Peter McLaren.

 Gustavo Gutiérrez and Liberation Theology

In 1968, a group of Roman Catholic clergy in Latin America met for a conference to discuss the plight of the poor. The church had a long history of ministering to those in poverty, but these priests believed that it should take a different approach in its outreach to the poor. Following the conference, **Gustavo Gutiérrez**, a Dominican priest, wrote a book called *Theology of Liberation* (1971), which helped to secure his status as one of the founders of liberation theology.

TWO INTUITIONS AND TWO VIOLENCES

In his revolutionary book, Father Gutiérrez discussed two intuitions. The first is the theoretical intuition, referred to as **orthodoxy**. It deals with beliefs that individuals hold about God, other people, the supernatural realm, and the natural world. The first intuition is practiced through reflection, prayer, and reading. Reading the world is an analogy for understanding the world and how it works.

The second and much more important intuition is **orthopraxy**, or **praxis**. It deals with actions individuals take as they put their theory into practice. Writing and talking serve as analogies for engaging the world and transforming it when necessary. Writing the world is the creation of culture rather than the passive reading of it to understand the status quo in society.

Gutiérrez's main concern was that of oppression. He defined theological terms differently than either traditional Catholicism or Protestant Evangelicalism had defined them in the past. He identified sin as social injustice and class oppression. The poor are not necessarily individuals in need of food, shelter, and clothing, but they are the working class—a group of people exploited by the capitalist system.

According to Gutiérrez, **conscientization** is the main priority of the gospel, to bring about awareness of and action against oppression. Liberation theology discusses two types of violence. The first violence is that of institutionalized oppression or injustice. The second violence is the act against injustice. As a form of self-defense, the second violence is justified because it fights against the first violence, which is oppressive.

IMAGERY IN LIBERATION THEOLOGY

Powerful **imagery** has served to propagate liberation theology throughout Brazil, South America, and many other parts of the world. One such image is a sketch of poor people ostensibly standing in line for food; in the middle of the line, a silhouette of a man with a halo around his head appears to be Jesus. The image reminds people, "Inasmuch as ye have done it unto one of the least of these my brethren, ye have done it unto me" (Matthew 25:40, King James Version). It also conveys a Marxist principle that fighting oppression means standing in solidarity with the oppressed themselves and that neutrality is not an option. Those who do not stand in solidarity with the poor are, in actuality, standing with the oppressors.

Many paintings and other prominent images promoting liberation theology portray Jesus as militant. For example, when Jesus overturned the tables in the temple courts and drove out the money changers,[1] he was not simply teaching that his father's house was to be a house of prayer, but he was committing the second violence against injustice. Traditionally, the event has been described as Jesus, in righteous indignation, driving animals and people out of the temple without harming anyone:

> So he made a whip out of cords, and drove all from the temple courts, both sheep and cattle; he scattered the coins of the money changers and overturned their tables. To those who sold doves he said, 'Get these out of here! Stop turning my Father's house into a market!'[2]

Liberation theologians, however, claim that Jesus may very well have inflicted human pain with the whip of cords, and if so, he was justified in doing so.

One painting shows Jesus hanging on the cross with blood flowing from the crown of thorns and double bandoliers hanging over his shoulders and across his chest. A bandolier is a leather belt stocked with rows of bullets and, particularly in South America, is symbolic of revolutionary movements. Another image depicts Jesus hanging not on a cross but instead on a giant hammer encircled by a sickle, evoking the emblem of international communism and solidarity with the working class. "Che Jesus" is an image that was to promote church attendance for Easter in 1999. Jesus is presented in the likeness of Che Guevara with a crown of thorns on his head. Under the image are the words "Meek. Mild. As if. Discover the real Jesus. Church. April 4." A multitude of other images picture Jesus with rifles, pistols, and communist symbolism. The imagery of liberation theology clearly promotes the militant aspect and the Marxist social activism of the movement.

CRITICISMS OF LIBERATION THEOLOGY

Opponents of liberation theology point to three main criticisms. The first is that the gospel of individual salvation in Jesus Christ is overshadowed by **Marxist ideology** and the concept of **social gospel** through societal reform. Even Fidel Castro commented on this issue by stating, "The theologians are becoming Communists and the Communists are becoming theologians." A second criticism is that the human physical

Che Guevara (1928-1967), Argentinian Marxist influential in the Cuban Revolution

© baldyrgan/Shutterstock.com

condition is given priority over spiritual eternity. This emphasis is a result of the universalism that liberation theologians espouse—a belief that all people will eventually experience salvation and will spend eternity in Heaven. Therefore, they focus their efforts on meeting current physical needs. The third criticism relates to the option of violence to end oppression. Unlike the Rev. Dr. Martin Luther King, Jr., and Mahatma Gandhi, who stood for peaceful resistance, liberation theology supports violence when it is used to fight against social injustice.

Paulo Freire and Critical Pedagogy[3]

Brazilian educator **Paulo Freire** applied the tenets of liberation theology to the field of education. In 1976, he wrote a seminal work entitled *Pedagogy of the Oppressed*, which has become one of the most cited works by researchers writing about foundations of education. Freire's **critical pedagogy** is a form of **transformational education**. Reminiscent of **John Dewey**, critical pedagogy promotes problem posing and projects revolving around issues drawn from learners' real-life experiences. The central precept is that education has value only insofar as it helps students liberate themselves from the social conditions that oppress them.

Freire denounced traditional education as an imposition of one man's choice upon another. His work criticizes education for having as its primary aim to reproduce the dominant ideology rather than to generate a critical consciousness. Freire points out the inadequacy of traditional education in that it does not permit an open exchange of ideas, debate, or discussion of themes; rather, it dictates and lectures to students, and—instead of working with them—it works on them. Freire repudiates Skinnerian **behaviorism**, also known as **operant conditioning**, as the dominant model for traditional teaching. Behaviorism, according to Freire, dismisses humans as machines, fails to acknowledge the dialectic relationship between individuals and the world, and values the act of memorizing over that of knowing, which results in a sterile, bureaucratic approach to learning.[4]

A prevailing theme in the literature of critical pedagogy is the denigration of behaviorism and other forms of traditional education. Proponents of critical pedagogy assert that behaviorism causes the student–teacher relationship to become manipulative. It "attempts to instill in the young an attitude of passivity and unthinking docility."[5] Democracy relies upon the engagement of citizens as they act upon their opinions. Yet, our educational system denies students opportunities to express their opinions or to act on them. Proponents illustrate this by research indicating that barely five percent of instructional time in most schools was designed to create students' anticipation of needing to respond; not even one percent required some kind of open response involving reasoning or even an opinion from students. If this is the case, they ask, then whose opinions occupy the remaining ninety-nine percent of school time, and what does this communicate to students about the importance of their own ideas?[6]

Freire introduced the metaphor of the "**banking system** of education." The banking approach to learning is rooted in the notion that students consume information as it is fed to them by the instructor. Students are then expected to memorize and store what was fed to them. The student's role in the banking system is that of a passive consumer rather than an active participant. There is little or no responsibility on the student's part to contribute to learning in the classroom. Furthermore, the banking system assumes a dichotomy between individuals and the world. It separates them from interacting with the world or with others. As an alternative to "**banking pedagogy**," Freire presented a "problem-posing" curriculum whereby students become aware of problems they encounter and how they might respond to these problems. Community, reflection, and conscientization are vital elements in Freire's teaching methodology.[7] Disciples of Freire describe how he built a sense of community among his students by creating an atmosphere of shared commitment and by valuing each individual voice. This process produced a climate of openness and intellectual rigor.[8]

Reflection is another critical component of Freire's pedagogy. He encouraged students to unite theory with practice to create a new social order, stressing that true reflection always leads to action. He used the term "praxis" to denote a type of thinking that requires both reflection and action on the part of the learner. Referred to as "**reflexive teaching**," the practice involved teachers re-presenting (i.e., presenting once again) to the class what the students themselves had already conveyed so that students could then reflect further and more deeply on their own thoughts.

In addition to community and reflection, Freire valued conscientization. **Conscientization** is a "process in which people acting as knowing subjects—not as recipients—achieve a deepening awareness of their socio-cultural reality, how it shapes their lives, and how they can transform that reality."[9] In order for conscientization to exist, dehumanizing structures in society must be denounced. Otherwise, these oppressive structures will continue to act upon individuals as objects, rendering them powerless. Conscientization is an awareness that people themselves can be knowers and actors as they solve their own problems. Reliance on others to solve these problems is seen as dehumanizing and oppressive.

Some educational environments may claim to offer students choice and voice, but in reality, according to Freire, it is an illusion. Somehow students are fooled to believe that they are deciding and being heard when they are actually being manipulated; others are doing the thinking and deciding for them. Freire equates this manipulative illusion to an act of violence. He refers to this type of an environment as a "**culture of silence**," where individuals are prohibited from creatively participating in societal transformation. He parallels the position of students in this type of environment with the condition of colonies under European imperialism. Colonization instituted a "culture of silence" whereby colonies were mere objects not to be heard but to be used. However, "every human being, no matter how 'ignorant' or submerged in the 'culture of silence' he may be, is capable of looking critically at his world in a dialogical encounter with others."[10]

 Protégés of Freire

A number of Freire's disciples carry on his work. One of his protégés is Canadian **Peter McLaren**, author of *Life in Schools* (1994), one of the highest selling textbooks in the field of education. McLaren also wrote *Che Guevara, Paulo Freire, and the Pedagogy of Revolution* (2000) and describes himself as follows:

> I am a transdisciplinary scholar who works in the area of critical pedagogy, critical social theory, Marxist humanist philosophy, and ethnographic research. My activist work involves engaging educational workers worldwide, and developing a philosophy of praxis directed at creating a post-capitalist, socialist future.[11]

Others carrying Freire's torch include bell hooks and **Henry Giroux**. Author and social activist **Gloria Jean Watkins** is better known by her pen name, **bell hooks**, which is a name that she derived from her great-grandmother and that she chooses not to capitalize. Using popular media in her curriculum as a means to illustrate how society oppresses marginalized groups, bell hooks addresses issues of race, class, and gender. In her 1994 book *Teaching to Transgress: Education as the Practice of Freedom*, hooks dedicated a chapter to Paulo Freire and reflected his pedagogical principles throughout. Henry Giroux, an outspoken critic of **No Child Left Behind**, authored a prominent book entitled *Theory and Resistance in Education: Towards a Pedagogy for the Opposition* (2001).

Liberation theology and critical pedagogy have influenced religion and education in the United States and throughout the world. Proponents of Marxism have become increasingly vocal in academia and in various Christian denominations, particularly in the Universalist Unitarian Church. There are no signs that critical pedagogy, sometimes known as education for liberation, will be waning any time soon as a prominent educational philosophy.[12]

Go to www.khlearn.com to watch a video about Paulo Freire, liberation theology, and critical pedagogy.

Reflection

For personal reflection, content review, and further research:

1. Evaluate the impact of liberation theology on American religion and education. Identify both positive and negative developments and explain why you perceive them as such.
2. Comment on aspects of American society you believe to have led to the broad acceptance of critical pedagogy among educational theorists.
3. Many educators relate the word *praxis* to a series of teacher licensure exams. The term, however, has a distinct meaning in the philosophy of education. Explain how the term is used in liberation theology and in critical pedagogy.
4. According to Paulo Freire, conscientization is the main purpose of education. Explain what he meant by this and evaluate the degree to which you believe conscientization should be the primary outcome of learning.
5. Compare how Paulo Freire perceived the role of violence in the fight against oppression with how the Rev. Dr. Martin Luther King, Jr., spoke of violence.
6. Compare critical pedagogy with B. F. Skinner's behavioral theory of operant conditioning. Which theory is most present in American schools?
7. Many educational theorists use metaphors to convey their philosophies of education. Some metaphors include Plato's cave, Horace Mann's balance wheel of society, and Booker T. Washington's head-hands-and-heart. Paulo Freire's metaphor, however, illustrated what he perceived to be the status quo of education that should be transformed into something else. Describe Freire's metaphor of the "banking system" and how he proposed this approach should be changed.
8. Explain what Freire meant by the "culture of silence." What are the implications of this culture for schools, students, and society?

ENDNOTES

1. See Matthew 21; Mark 11; John 2.
2. John 2:15-16, New International Version.
3. Parts taken from Samuel James Smith, "The Role of Controversial Issues in Moral Education: Approaches and Attitudes of Christian School Educators" (doctoral dissertation, Oklahoma State University, 2000).
4. See Paulo Freire, *Pedagogy of the Oppressed* (New York: Herder and Herder, 1970); Paulo Freire, *Education for Critical Consciousness* (New York: The Seabury Press, 1973); Paulo Freire and Donaldo Mecado, Literacy: *Reading the Word and the World* (South Hadley, MA: Bergin & Garvey, 1987).
5. See David E. Purple and Svi Shapiro, *Beyond Liberation and Excellence: Reconstructing the Public Discourse on Education* (Westport, CT: Bergin & Garvey, 1995), 102.
6. Ira Shor, *Empowering Education: Critical Teaching for Social Change* (Chicago: University of Chicago Press, 1992).
7. Freire, *Pedagogy of the Oppressed*.
8. bell hooks, *Teaching to Transgress: Education as the Practice of Freedom* (New York: Routledge, 1994).
9. Freire, *Pedagogy of the Oppressed*, 27.
10. Freire, *Pedagogy of the Oppressed*, 13.
11. Peter McLaren, Academia, accessed January 4, 2020, https://chapman.academia.edu/Peter-McLaren.
12. See Javier Alanis, "Peace and Liberation Theology," *Global Virtue Ethics Review* 7, no. 3 (2016): 34-43; bell hooks, *Teaching to Transgress: Education as the Practice of Freedom* (New York: Routledge, 1994); Garth Kasimu Baker-Fletcher, "Liberation Theologies in the United States: An Introduction," *Religious Studies Review* 37, no. 4 (2011): 297-8; Dorothy Folliard, "Sparks from the South: The Growing Impact of Liberation Theology on the United States Hispanic Church," *International Review of Mission* 78, no. 310 (1989): 150-4; Henry A. Giroux, "Curriculum, Multiculturalism, and the Politics of Identity," *NASSP Bulletin* 6 (1992): 1-11; James D. Kirylo, "Hate Won, but Love Will Have the Final Word: Critical Pedagogy, Liberation Theology, and the Moral Imperative of Resistance," *Policy Futures in Education* 15, no. 5 (2017): 590-601; Eddy Muskus, "Liberation Theology: Its Origins and Early Development," *Foundations* 29 (1992): 31-41; Judith Soares, "A Future for Liberation Theology?" *Peace Review* 20, no. 4 (2008): 480-6; Shari J. Stenberg, "Liberation Theology and Liberatory Pedagogies: Renewing the Dialogue," *College English* 68, no. 3 (2006): 271-90.

EDUCATIONAL THINKERS FOR FURTHER STUDY

The educational thinkers listed below have all influenced the history and philosophy of education in a meaningful and significant way. Many others could be added to the list, but these are the ones most prominently featured in the literature of the foundations of education. Most of them fall into the category of philosophers while others, especially those beginning in the twentieth century, could be classified more as developmental or behavioral psychologists or as sociologists. Nevertheless, their theories and actions influenced how people answered questions related to the purpose of education or process of learning. They are provided as suggestions for further study and are categorized roughly into general historical eras simply for ease of categorization.

Educational Thinker	Birth Year	Death Year
Ancient Era		
Confucius	551 BC	479 BC
Socrates	470 BC	399 BC
Plato	428 BC	348 BC
Aristotle	384 BC	322 BC
Quintilian	35 AD	100 AD
Augustine	358 AD	430 AD
Medieval Era		
Aquinas, Thomas	1225	1274
de Pizan, Christine	1364	1430
Erasmus, Desiderius	1466	1536
Luther, Martin	1483	1546
Calvin, John	1509	1564
Comenius, Johann Amos	1592	1670
Enlightenment Era		
Milton, John	1608	1674
Locke, John	1632	1704
Franklin, Benjamin	1706	1790
Rousseau, Jean-Jacques	1712	1778
Kant, Immanuel	1724	1804
Jefferson, Thomas	1743	1826
Pestalozzi, Johann Heinrich	1746	1827
Webster, Noah	1758	1843
Wollstonecraft, Mary	1759	1797
Hegel, Georg Wilhelm Friedrich	1770	1831
Modern Era		
Owen, Robert	1771	1858
Seton, Elizabeth	1774	1821
Herbart, Johann Friedrich	1776	1841
Froebel, Friedrich	1782	1852
Gallaudet, Thomas	1787	1851
Willard, Emma	1787	1870
Mann, Horace	1796	1859
Beecher, Catharine	1800	1878

McGuffey, William	1800	1873
Mill, John Stuart	1806	1873
Spencer, Herbert	1820	1903
Progressive Era		
Eliot, Charles W. (Committee of Ten)	1834	1926
Parker, Colonel Francis Wayland	1837	1902
Washington, Booker T.	1856	1915
Binet, Alfred	1857	1911
Eastman, Charles & Elaine	1858	1939
Dewey, John	1859	1952
Addams, Jane	1860	1935
Whitehead, Alfred North	1861	1947
Du Bois, W. E. B.	1868	1963
Gandhi, Mohandas	1869	1948
Montessori, Maria	1870	1952
Kilpatrick, William Heard	1871	1965
Bagley, William Chandler	1874	1946
Thorndike, Edward L.	1874	1949
Bethune, Mary McLeod	1875	1955
Neill, A. S.	1883	1973
Rugg, Harold	1886	1960
Counts, George S.	1889	1974
Piaget, Jean	1896	1980
Vygotsky, Lev	1896	1934
Hutchins, Robert M.	1899	1977
Rickover, Admiral Hyman	1900	1986
Adler, Mortimer	1902	2001
Erikson, Erik	1902	1994
Rogers, Carl R.	1902	1987
Tyler, Ralph	1902	1994
Skinner, B. F.	1904	1990
Bestor, Arthur	1908	1994
Postmodern Era		
Maslow, Abraham	1908	1970
Bruner, Jerome	1915	2016

Gagne, Robert	1916	2002
Greene, Maxine	1917	2014
Ausubel, David	1918	2008
Freire, Paulo	1921	1997
Holt, John	1923	1985
Bandura, Albert	1925	
Illich, Ivan	1926	2002
Kohlberg, Lawrence	1927	1987
Hirsch, E. D., Jr.	1928	
Noddings, Nel	1929	
Bloom, Allan	1930	1992
Elkind, David	1931	
Rorty, Richard	1931	2007
Kozol, Jonathan	1936	
Kolb, David	1939	
Banks, James A.	1941	
Gardner, Howard	1943	
Giroux, Henry	1943	
McLaren, Peter	1948	
Hammond, Linda Darling	1951	
Kohn, Alfie	1957	

 Go to www.khlearn.com to watch a video about educational thinkers for further study.

OVERVIEW OF SELECT PHILOSOPHIES OF EDUCATION

This appendix outlines selected philosophical approaches to education as applied in schools in the United States. This is not to claim that these philosophies are not implemented elsewhere; they most certainly are. The purpose of the outline is to provide a brief overview for those interested in researching specific theories more thoroughly.

Transmission and Transformation of Culture

Admittedly, the categories of transmission and transformation as presented below are overly simplistic. Nevertheless, they are provided as a structure to help those new to the foundations of education grasp how philosophers of education tend to lean more toward the transmission of knowledge, skills, and dispositions as they have been valued in the past and how others tend to lean more toward the transformation of society for a potential utopia in the future.

THEORIES FOR TRANSMISSION: PASSING THE BATON

The select theories for transmission are based on the notion that there are ideas from the past that should be embraced and passed down to future generations. A metaphor to illustrate this philosophy is a runner with a baton who passes it on to another runner, who then passes it to another, and so on. Educators who lean more toward transmission might see themselves as runners in a relay race. They have appreciated being recipients of the wisdom of the ages, and they are now prepared to pass on these values to the next generation.

Transmission theorists see their responsibility as teaching students what society has been like in the past and what it is currently like in the present. They strive to do so as accurately as possible and to encourage students to apply skills they learn in school to change society in the future. While transmission theorists most certainly want to see society improve, they perceive their role as preparing students to change the world in the future rather than to lead students in social activism in the present.

Transmission theorists may use technology and other innovative instructional strategies, but they tend to be cautious about trendy fads. Their teaching methods, whether traditional or not, serve to pass on the baton—the tried and true wisdom of the ages to their students.

1. **Perennialism**
   a. Based on platonic idealism, valuing abstract concepts and virtues, such as beauty and integrity.
   b. Assumes that there is universal, absolute knowledge valuable to all people and for all time.
   c. Illustrated by the inscription under the *Heritage* sculpture at the U.S. National Archive building in Washington, D.C.—"The heritage of the past is the seed that brings forth the harvest of the future." The sculpture is of a mother holding her baby on her lap. The mother represents the past, while the baby represents the future. This symbolizes the idea that society should embrace the past so that the future can be secure.
   d. Perennialism was found in . . .
      1) Colonial and early American schools.
      2) Great Books Society, which promotes the study of classic literature.
      3) Classical Christian school movement.
   e. Perennial curriculum emphasizes . . .
      1) Classical literature, the knowledge that has been proven tried and true by prevailing through time.
      2) Classical languages: Greek, Hebrew, and Latin.
      3) Traditional teaching methods: Socratic questioning, lecture, story-telling, books, discussion, reasoning, logic. The teacher writes objectives and selects most of the learning activities and topics of study.
   f. The roots of perennialism are found in the teachings of the theologian Thomas Aquinas but have been secularized over the past century. The current implementation of perennial education encourages teaching about religion but not necessarily teaching doctrinal truths for spiritual salvation.
   g. Moral development of the individual and instruction in the virtues are highly valued.
2. **Essentialism**
   a. Back-to-the basics education; the idea that there is core knowledge that makes people culturally literate so they can be successful in their vocations and as contributing citizens.
   b. E. D. Hirsch's book illustrates the importance of essential knowledge and skills in the curriculum: *Cultural Literacy: What Every American Needs to Know* (1988).

    c. Encouraged and promoted by . . .
        1) Back-to-the-basics movement, which was a reaction to . . .
           a) Soviet success in the launching of *Sputnik* (1957). An essentialist philosophy in U.S. schools was considered a strategy for winning the Space Race with the Soviets. The United States had become fearful that they would be surpassed and possibly overtaken by the Soviets, so they increased funding for and efforts in the teaching of science and math.
           b) Reagan administration's *A Nation at Risk* report (1983), which claimed that America was at risk of being surpassed economically by Japan and other countries because of America's poor educational system. Returning to the basics and holding educators accountable was the approach to solving this problem.
        2) Homeschool movement: E. D. Hirsch's *Cultural Literacy: What Every American Needs to Know* (1988).

3. Behaviorism
    a. While essentialism is a theory focusing on the content or curriculum (i.e., the knowledge and skills) to be taught in schools, behaviorism is a theory that addresses teaching methodology and philosophy of learning. It stresses more of *how* the baton is passed to students. Behaviorism is more psychological as it is based on assumptions about human nature.
    b. The nature of the learner is perceived by behaviorists as neutral; it is neither sinful, like the Bible teaches, nor is it good, like Rousseau, progressives, or constructivist educators claim. Because students are neutral, they can be programmed through stimulus and response.
    c. A naturalistic idea that . . .
        1) All learning is displayed through behaviors that can be measured. Therefore, we have the high-stakes achievement testing environment.
        2) Learning occurs through stimulus–response and reinforcement
        3) Choice is an illusion. Learners have no free will or spiritual nature but are simply machines that can be programmed or conditioned.
    d. Behaviorism and its major proponent B. F. Skinner believed that education could be a tool to bring about a utopian society. A utopian perspective is contrary to a biblical worldview that sees the world as broken and in need of redemption. Only in Heaven, according to the Bible, will perfection be realized.

THEORIES FOR TRANSFORMATION: CHANGING THE CULTURE

The select theories for transformation are based on the notion that individuals and society need to progress beyond the status quo. Therefore, the purpose of education is to lead students in the change process both individually and culturally. Theorists in this camp are generally leery of the baton. Because the baton represents society's errors of the past—a compilation of oppression and injustice—passing the baton on to students is not the top priority for transformation theorists. A more acceptable metaphor to illustrate the transformation philosophies is the hammer. Hammers can destroy, and they can also build new structures. Educators who lean more toward transformation might see themselves as handing a hammer to students and encouraging them to eliminate societal errors of the past and to build a new utopia, or at least to get as close as possible. Transformationists see themselves as progressive and are willing to take risks to bring about change. Rather than to instill certain values in their students, they may prefer students choose their own.

Transformation theorists see their responsibility as teaching students what society could possibly be like in the future. They encourage students to apply skills they learn in school immediately rather than to wait until later. While more traditional teachers might see themselves as preparing students to be good citizens in the future, transmission theorists are likely to encourage students to change society now.

Transformation theorists are likely to use technology and other innovative instructional strategies, and they tend to use them to help students solve problems rather than to convey information.

1. **Progressivism**
   a. Affiliated with John Dewey, Jane Addams, and William Heard Kilpatrick.
   b. Is a belief that . . .
      1) Learners are social animals, so they learn best in social environments.
      2) Learning occurs best when situated in real-life problems that are age appropriate.
   c. John Dewey was the most outspoken proponent of progressive education, which peaked in the 1930s and has experienced a resurgence as a reaction to policies of No Child Left Behind.
   d. Progressivism was influenced by European educators who believed that the nature of the learner was basically good, not neutral as behaviorists claimed or sinful as the Bible teaches.
   e. Student centered: Because students are basically good and society is what corrupts them, classrooms should be student centered, a place where students make curriculum decisions based on interest and experience. There should be plenty of student choice.

2. **Social Reconstructionism**
   a. The Social Reconstructionist approach is rooted in the ideas of George S. Counts, who at first supported the Progressive Education movement but later became one of its most vocal critics. His concern was that the progressive movement was not accomplishing what John Dewey and the Progressive Education Association had set initially as its goal: "an improved social order." Progressive educators were not aggressive enough in changing society; progressivism had become too child-centered and project-oriented rather than focusing on the problems of society and on changing them. Progressive education was not reconstructing society as it had initially planned to do and was not solving the ills of society.
   b. Counts authored *Dare the Schools Build a New Social Order* in 1932, which challenged teachers and schools to be change agents and to recruit students to be active in approved social causes. This led him to be considered the "Father of Reconstructionism."
   c. Like Skinner's Behaviorism, Reconstructionism is a utopian theory, believing that—through the efforts of man—the world can become a utopia.
   d. Critics of Reconstructionism ask if children are developmentally prepared to be social activists. Are students developmentally ready to decide what is wrong with society and to take action?

3. **Critical Pedagogy or Liberation Education**
   a. Similar to Reconstructionism but a bit more radical in that it embraces principles of Marxism and social justice and was influenced by the teachings of liberation theology.
   b. The main purpose of critical pedagogy is to increase awareness of oppression—both for the oppressed and the oppressors.
   c. The content of the curriculum is viewed through the lens of politics and power. Language and teaching itself are considered oppressive acts.
   d. *Pedagogy of the Oppressed* (1976), a book written by Brazilian author Paulo Freire, is one of the most widely used books in colleges of teacher education today, and—while it is extremely inspiring and thought provoking—its Marxist element has gone largely unrecognized by future teachers who are either unable to identify the presence of this worldview in critical pedagogy or who simply embrace

those principles as being a primary purpose of education. It is also interesting to note that another prominent book read in schools of education is authored by William Ayers, who was a member of the self-described Communist group that bombed federal buildings in the 1960s and 1970s.

BIBLICAL LENS

Educators with a Christian background often ask, "Which purpose for education has more biblical support, theories for transmission or theories for transformation?" My response is that there is biblical support for both:

1. **Transmission:** In Deuteronomy 6 and Hebrews 12 we see strong support for passing down a heritage to children so that they will always remember what God has done in the past. This is to be taught to them . . .
   a. Formally and informally
   b. Verbally through stories
   c. Tangibly through symbols and ceremonies
   Hebrews 12 refers to a great cloud of witnesses that is made up of people who have gone before; the implication is that those left behind need to pass the baton to future generations.
2. **Transformation**
   a. Romans 12:2
      1) Do not conform to the pattern of this world
      2) Be transformed by the renewing of your mind
   b. 2 Corinthians 5:17: "If anyone is in Christ, he is a . . .
      1) New creation
      2) The old has gone, the new has come
   c. God speaks to Isaiah saying, "See, I am doing a new thing! Now it springs up; do you not perceive it? I am making a way in the desert and streams in the wasteland" (Isaiah 43:19).

As established earlier, the separation of theories into categories of transmission and transformation is simplistic. Educators, of course, carry out both purposes. Transformation of individuals and of society is an ultimate goal, but there must be some aspect of truth transmitted before transformation can occur. If education is to develop critical thinkers, learners must have content to evaluate. The content is what we pass down in the baton.

Consider the purposes of transmission and transformation as a cross. The vertical aspect of the cross might be considered the truth that is transmitted. The vertical post of truth is placed firmly in the ground, intentionally transmitting certain knowledge on which students can build. The horizontal aspect of the cross is the transformation of individuals and society. Transformation, however, cannot occur without the vertical post of principles on which the horizontal transformation must be attached.

It is important for teachers, parents, and students to use discernment—to analyze the purpose of education that is being presented in their schools. As Nancy Pearcey (2008) states in her book *Total Truth*, "As American culture moves away from its Christian heritage, the public classroom is becoming a battleground for competing ideologies, so that one of our most important tasks is to teach students how to identify and critique worldviews." To understand and to critique all ideas is a worthy goal of education.

Understanding the Basics of Select Philosophies of Education

To grasp a basic understanding of any philosophy of education and to evaluate its degree of systematic coherence, one should examine ten aspects related to the philosophy: (1) key proponents of the philosophy; (2) metaphysics, the nature of ultimate reality; (3) epistemology, theory of truth, and knowledge acquisition; (4) axiology, ethical, and aesthetic values; (5) nature and role of the learner; (6) role of the teacher; (7) curriculum most worthy of study; (8) most effective instructional methods; and (9) main criticisms of the philosophy; and (10) key opponents. Below is an outline of prominent philosophies of education, highlighting each of these aspects.

IDEALISM: (1) Plato and Augustine are proponents of idealism. (2) Ultimate purpose and meaning are found in the realm of abstract ideas. (3) Truth is valid if it is congruent with the purpose of the cosmos, and it is acquired through the intellect. (4) The greatest value is in the propagation of a system of goodness and beauty compatible with universal moral law. (5) Learners naturally want to be good and are motivated to strive for the perfect model of goodness. (6) Teachers serve as models of goodness as represented by the abstract ideals of justice, freedom, beauty, etc. (7) The humanities are best suited for the study of abstract themes to live the good life. (8) Since abstract ideals are conveyed through language, idealism implements words and metaphors through lectures, discussions, and reading materials. (9) Idealism is perceived as an "ivory tower" perspective of life, focused more on preserving heritage rather than on learning for change. (10) Realists, pragmatists, and progressives oppose idealism; critics include Aristotle, Charles Darwin, Karl Marx, and John Dewey.

REALISM: (1) Aristotle and Thomas Aquinas are proponents of realism. (2) The physical world as it operates according to natural law is the source of meaning. (3) Knowledge is acquired through sensory perception. (4) Logic and order of the universe provide a basis for ethical judgment. (5) Learners are neutral observers. (6) Teachers are more sophisticated observers who convey object facts to students. (7) Science and math are paramount in the curriculum. (8) Instruction is primarily conducted through demonstrations, visuals, field experiences, and objective observations. (9) Students are dehumanized as programmable learning machines, and the status quo of society is maintained. (10) Idealists and constructivists oppose realism; critics include Plato, Piaget, Vygotsky, Dewey, and Alfie Kohn.

NEO-SCHOLASTICISM: (1) Thomas Aquinas, proponents of traditional Catholic schools and the classical school movement. (2) There is a dual reality of faith and reason, of natural and supernatural. (3) There is self-evident truth than can be known by human intuition, and there is synthetic truth that depends on scientific inquiry. (4) As rational beings, humans use logic to decide what is moral. (5) Learners are both rational creatures and spiritual beings; as such, they use logic to arrive at truth and practice faith when logic is incapable of arriving at truth. (6) Teachers are mental disciplinarians who lead students in exercising the power of reason; they are also spiritual leaders and role models. (7) Because neo-scholasticism is a form of realism, it emphasizes subjects with internal logic, like mathematics; it also stresses the classical languages and natural science. (8) The learning process includes catechisms, recitations, and rote memorization to strengthen mental faculties. (9) Overemphasis on the past draws criticism that it propagates the status quo and does not address current problems relevant to students. (10) Non-traditionalists, postmodernists, and existentialists oppose neo-scholasticism; critics include Martin Luther, John Calvin, and progressive educators.

PRAGMATISM: (1) John Dewey, Jane Addams, and William Heard Kilpatrick. (2) Reality depends upon human experience and, as such, is constantly changing. (3) Because truth is what works, the solving of problems through human effort is how one acquires knowledge. This knowledge is subject to change as both problems and problem-solving strategies change. (4) Values are relative, may change based upon circumstances, and are subject to democratic processes. (5) As experiential beings, learners act upon the environment to change reality by solving social problems. (6) Teachers are facilitators who guide students not through the subject area disciplines but instead through the solving of meaningful, age-appropriate problems. (7) Projects and problem-based curriculum focus the learner's attention on applying relevant knowledge to solve problems. Students have input on the curriculum. (8) In a democratic environment, students choose learning processes that tend to lean toward group collaboration. (9) Pragmatism minimizes traditional knowledge and values that have proven valuable to society. (10) Traditionalists of every stripe reject pragmatism; critics include William Chandler Bagley and Admiral Hyman Rickover.

EXISTENTIALISM: (1) Søren Kierkegaard, Friedrich Nietzsche, Jean-Paul Sartre, and A. S. Neil. (2) The individual has the authority to assign meaning and purpose; therefore, choice is the greatest action in human experience. (3) Truth and the acquisition of it is a personal matter for individuals to resolve. (4) There are no collective absolute values that society may impose on individuals; values result as individual actions and are to be personally embraced by each learner. (5) Learners, as free choosing agents, are fully responsible for their learning. (6) Teachers serve to facilitate the student's exploration of possibilities. (7) Basic literacy is valued as a means to empower students to make informed personal choices. Beyond that, the curriculum is a personal journey of understanding oneself and one's decisions. The humanities and expressive arts serve this purpose well. (8) Methods include personal goal-setting, reflection, self-assessment, and student choice. (9) Existentialism breeds moral relativity, social non-compliance, and disregard for rules. (10) Traditionalists reject existentialism; critics include Arthur Bestor, Allan Bloom, E. D. Hirsch, and supporters of the accountability movement.

PERENNIALISM: (1) Mortimer Adler and Robert M. Hutchins. (2) Reality is objective and universal to all humanity. (3) Truth is what has been tested and proven over time and embraced by consensus. Similar to idealism and neo-scholasticism, perennialism holds that learners acquire truth through rational thought. (4) Absolute values have been arrived at through rational thought and are applicable to all cultural demographics throughout time. Unlike animal instincts, human values are passed down from generation to generation. (5) Learners are rational beings who hold universal qualities of the mind in common. (6) Similar to the role of the teacher in idealism and neo-scholasticism, perennialism perceives the teacher as an authority who designs the curriculum to pass down universal truth and values. (7) Perennialists value the good aspects of the past, and—as such—emphasize the teaching of history and classical literature; the liberal arts and humanities are central. (8) Traditional methods of instruction are implemented with attention given to primary sources. (9) Perennialism focuses so much on the past that it may not properly prepare students for jobs in the future; technology is minimized; and the strong teacher-directedness may inhibit student freedom. (10) Progressive educators and those who embrace critical theory reject perennialism; critics include John Dewey, Paulo Freire, Peter McLaren, Henry Giroux, James A. Banks, and Alfie Kohn.

ESSENTIALISM: (1) William Chandler Bagley, Arthur Bestor, and E. D. Hirsch. (2) As a back-to-basics movement, essentialism is also known as cultural literacy and the core knowledge movement—not to be confused with the more recent Common Core Curriculum. Essentialism applies mostly to the United States and is not rooted metaphysically in an explicit statement of meaning and purpose. It does draw however from idealism and realism in that it claims that there are essential abstract concepts and natural laws that all learners must know to be good citizens. (3) Absolute universal truths exist and may be acquired through intellectual pursuits. (4) Similar to perennialism, essentialism holds that societal values have been determined over time and are to be taught through direct instruction. (5) The student's role is to apply effort to acquire basic knowledge, skills, and values that will result in becoming a contributing member of society. (6) As an authority on what learning is best for the student, the teacher directs the curriculum and instruction. (7) Primary grades incline to basic literacy and mathematics; secondary grades cover a comprehensive curriculum of traditional subject matter and modern languages. (8) Learning requires discipline and hard work, relying heavily on traditional methods of memorization and testing. Methods borrowed from Skinnerian behaviorism are common in essentialism. (9) Essentialism limits the curriculum to basics and traditional subjects, not leaving much room for student preference; it is often perceived as coercive. (10) Progressive educators and critical theorists oppose essentialism; critics include Alfie Kohn and James A. Banks.

BEHAVIORISM: (1) Edward L. Thorndike and B. F. Skinner. (2) Grounded in the philosophy of realism, behaviorism explains reality as a matter of natural law. Environment transcends human experience as it acts upon human behavior to condition it. (3) Truth is found in natural law, and humans acquire this truth through stimulus and response, which results in behavior that complies with the laws of matter and motion. (4) Principal values are those that promote efficiency, precision, economy, and objectivity. (5) The nature of the learner is neutral, programmable. As part of the Darwinian evolutionary process, the learner can progress best in the proper environment. (6) The teacher is the architect of an environment that acts on the learner through strategic stimuli and responses. The teacher is responsible for arranging positive and negative reinforcements for a desired outcome. (7) Behaviorism tends toward traditional subject matter and is often the preferred method to deliver the curriculum of essentialism. (8) Programmed learning involves carefully prescribed behavioral objectives strategically aligned to a menu of reinforcements. In effect, the instructional methodology of behaviorism is operant conditioning. (9) Skinnerian behaviorism dismisses free will and human choice as conditioned responses. It denies the dignity of humans above that of animals and rejects the notion of supernatural forces. (10) Constructivists, critical theorists, and many religious educators reject behaviorism; critics include John Dewey, Jean Piaget, David Elkind, Jonathon Kozol, Henry Giroux, and bell hooks.

SOCIAL RECONSTRUCTIONISM: (1) Theodore Brameld and George S. Counts. (2) Social reconstructionism is based in pragmatism and may be considered an extension of it. Reconstructionism acknowledges societal dysfunction and impending chaos unless drastic action is taken. (3) Similar to pragmatism, truth is a social construct that is in constant flux. (4) The highest values are those that result in social reform. (5) Akin to Rousseau's view of the learner, resonstructionists see the nature of individuals as being good but with the potential of being corrupted by society. Given the opportunity, learners can take action to redeem society and to prevent their own demise. (6) Teachers encourage all possible solutions as proposed by students while not withholding their own perspectives. (7) The curriculum highlights social problems in the context of the social sciences, for example, sociology, anthropology, economics, politics, and psychology. (8) Instruction occurs via dialogue, debate, analysis of current events, problem posing, and social activism. (9) Reconstructionism may place too much confidence in teachers to act as agents of social change. Its utopian outlook assumes that social change will benefit humanity. (10) Traditional educators and behaviorists typically oppose reconstructionism; critics include Arthur Bestor, E. D. Hirsch, and Allan Bloom.

CRITICAL PEDAGOGY: (1) Paulo Freire, Peter McLaren, Henry Giroux, bell hooks, Nel Noddings, and Richard Rorty. (2) The philosophical base of critical pedagogy, or "education for liberation," is similar to that of pragmatism and reconstructionism. The main difference is that critical pedagogy is strongly influenced by Marxist theory and liberation theology. Meaning is found in conscientization—becoming aware of oppression and taking social action to fight injustice. (3) Knowledge is power and power is acquired through social activism. (4) The value of justice is supreme. (5) All learners—whether among the marginalized or of the dominant class—have the potential to stand together in solidarity to transform society. (6) The main role of the teacher is to bring about conscientization of oppression. (7) Like reconstructionism, critical pedagogy is more problem-centered than subject-centered. It may draw its curriculum more from popular media, cinema, politics, and current events. (8) Active learning and reality-based situations serve as instructional methodology. With its emphasis on *praxis*, or the relationship of theory to practice, there is a strong connection between teaching and learning, beliefs, and action. Theory and practice inform each other and occur within the context of the other. (9) A main concern regarding critical pedagogy is the influence of Marxist and anti-capitalist ideology and the potential for inciting violence in the fight against oppression. Its emphasis on conscientization may diminish the development of academic skills. (10) Traditional educators and those who support capitalism and free markets generally oppose critical pedagogy; critics would include the same critics of reconstructionism.

CONSTRUCTIVISM: (1) Jerome Bruner, Jean Piaget, Lev Vygotsky, and Constance Kamii. (2) As the term constructivism indicates, individuals construct truth, meaning, and reality. Sense-making is accomplished as individuals construct rules and mental models by which to organize reality. (3) Learners construct an understanding of their experience through the processes of accommodation and assimilation. (4) Reminiscent of existentialism, constructivism presents values as constructs relative to individual learners. (5) Learners progress through natural stages of development as described by Jean-Jacque Rousseau, Jean Piaget, Erik Erikson, and other developmental stage theorists. As learners act on their environment, they periodically experience disequilibrium, which motivates them to engage in accommodation and assimilation. These actions result in the creation of schemata, which are patterns that help the learner make sense of experiences. (6) The teacher's role is to provide experiences that facilitate natural development and to engage learners in opportunities for self-discovery. The best tool for the teacher is an awareness of constructivist principles. (7) Similar to pragmatism, existentialism, and critical pedagogy, the constructivist curriculum is not subject centered. Rather, it is organized to maximize questioning, exploration, and discovery. (8) Instructional methods flow from the teacher's understanding of the constructivist model itself. Methods are personalized as much as possible for each student and structured to enhance the student's ability to make connections among concepts and experiences. (9) With standardized achievement tests and high accountability for teachers to provide evidence of student learning, many educators find the constructivist approach difficult to implement, especially in American public schools. Teachers who risk releasing autonomous learners in the classroom may be perceived as creating an environment that is permissive, unorganized, hectic, and unproductive. Because behavioral objectives are anathema to constructivists, evidence of learning may be lacking. (10) Traditionalists and behaviorists oppose constructivism; critics include Mortimer Adler, E. D. Hirsch, and Alan Bloom.

Go to www.khlearn.com to watch a video about select philosophies of education.

FORMULATING A PERSONAL PHILOSOPHY OF EDUCATION

© Triff/Shutterstock.com

Educators are often asked to articulate a personal philosophy of education. This might be for something as formal as a university course, job application, or interview. It is most frequently an informal and often spontaneous sharing of beliefs that motivate educators and ground the decision-making of their professional practice. Whatever the setting, educators should be prepared to convey their well-thought-out ideas in a coherent, logically consistent manner. Just as Christians are charged to "always be prepared to give an answer to everyone who asks you to give the reason for the hope that you have" (1 Peter 3:15, New International Version), educators should be prepared to share their personal philosophy of education to students, parents, colleagues, or the general public.

On a job application, typically a paragraph or two will suffice, and a practical approach rather than a philosophical treatise is generally preferred by administrators who will be reading these brief statements. There are exceptions to this, however; one exception is on applications for schools that are faith-based or that are driven by a particular learning theory. Christian schools, for example, may require a multiple-page document in which applicants are expected to express their views on ultimate reality (metaphysics), the nature of truth (epistemology), and values (axiology). Because these issues are indeed central to any philosophy of education, it is wise always to address them to some degree—even if the bulk of the statement centers on the practice of education rather than the theoretical foundation supporting it.

Schools that are grounded in a particular theoretical framework may also expect more than a generic statement. One of my graduate students, for example, told me that the next morning she was being interviewed for a job at a school that was based on Howard Gardner's theory of multiple intelligences. She was excited about the prospect of working at a school that was intentional about aligning its teaching and learning activities with a popular model for differentiation. "What should I say in the interview?" she asked me. It became clear in our discussion that she knew relatively little about multiple intelligence theory and did not have experience in developing lesson plans on Gardner's model. "I can't really tell you what to say in the interview," I replied, "but you should step into it fully aware that they want to hire an educator who understands multiple intelligences, wholeheartedly believes in the theory, and already practices strategies based on it." She was not offered the job.

An example with a more positive outcome is Brandon Fleming, one of my undergraduate students. Brandon was so driven by his philosophy of education that he began to implement it while he was still an undergraduate student. He collaborated with a number of organizations to gain community support for a Saturday, half-day program to tutor and motivate elementary children to succeed in school. Having struggled academically himself, Brandon was driven to help other African-American youth to excel. His philosophy of education and his practical application of it gained the attention of famed educator Ron Clark, who offered Brandon a job teaching at the Ron Clark Academy in Atlanta. It was Brandon's intentionality in connecting his theory to practice that led him to establish and coach a debate team at the Academy. Today, Brandon is a debate coach at Harvard University and is the founder and CEO of the Harvard Diversity Project, which serves as a pipeline to attract African-American students to enroll at Harvard on scholarships that Brandon raises money to help fund. In 2019, Brandon was invited to speak at the United Nations General Assembly to share his philosophy of education on International Day of Education. In 2020, Forbes included him on its "30 under 30" list. Yes, Brandon has done all of this and more at the age of just 29, all because he was driven by a philosophy of education that he articulated so well that others got behind his initiatives and supported him in them!

Unfortunately, there are many pre-service and in-service teachers who neither articulate nor intentionally carry out a personal philosophy of education. When asked to share their philosophy, they may say, "Learning should be fun!" or "Education for all!" These declarations are positive rallying cries, but they do not serve as a basis for a personal philosophy of education. For those who struggle with developing their own philosophy statement, the suggestions below may be helpful.

 Thesis Statement

Whether you will be sharing your philosophy of education in written or oral form, a thesis statement will serve as the central point on which everything else rests. Do not let this intimidate you. Consider your initial thoughts to be a preliminary thesis statement that you will revisit and revise along the way. Developing a philosophy of education is a recursive process in which you will return to your thoughts to refine them and possibly to change your ideas altogether as you see them in print.

The thesis statement should be no more than a sentence or two and should focus on the purpose, outcome, goals, and impact of education. It should not address how important it is to have a philosophy of education and should not focus on the process of instruction. Focus on the *why* instead of the *how*. If you struggle with this, consider this question: "What do you see as the long-range impact education should have on individuals and on society?"

After you have answered the above question in no more than one or two sentences, come up with a shortened coffee-mug version of your thesis statement. This abbreviated form will serve as your motto, slogan, or bumper-sticker version of your philosophy. It should be clear enough to give some idea of what you believe about the purpose or outcome of education. Avoid statements that sound vague or flippant or that focus on the process of education instead of its outcome. If you are writing your philosophy, this slogan may serve as the title. You may consider adding a subtitle, as subtitles can bring clarity to the main title.

Amy Price, a sixth-grade teacher in Florida, placed the slogan of her philosophy of education on a banner at the front of her class. On the first day of school, she explained the slogan to her students, telling them how it represented her philosophy of education, how she was driven by it every day, and how it described her intentions for her students. When she saw them outside of class, whether in the school cafeteria or out in the community, she often quizzed them, "Why do I do what I do?" While the question was offered in fun, students knew that Mrs. Price was intentional and serious about her philosophy of education. On back-to-school night, she shared the banner's meaning with parents, and at sixth-grade graduation at the end of the year, her students recited the slogan in unison to the audience. There was no question what motivated her as a teacher. No one was surprised when she was presented the Florida Teacher of the Year Award by the Association of Christian Schools International.

 Philosophy of Schools and Learning

After introducing your thesis statement, you will need to support and illustrate it. If your entire philosophy statement is just a paragraph or two, you might want to jump directly into the practical application, which would be the *how* and *what* behind the *why* of your thesis statement. However, if you are writing a more formal paper and anticipate that the reader expects to know more about your beliefs, you will want to expound on the *why* aspect a bit further. This section will help you do that.

To expound on your philosophy of schools and learning before getting into the practical application of your beliefs, consider how you would answer the questions below:

- **Metaphysics:** What is ultimately real or true, and therefore what is the purpose and meaning of life?
- **Epistemology:** Is it possible to know reality and truth? If so, how do learners come to know something? What is the nature of truth? What makes the light bulb go off in a student's mind?
- **Axiology:** What values do you see as most important to cultivate in your students and why?
- **Nature of the Learner:** What is the role of the student in the learning process? What is the human condition? Are students basically good, sinful, or neutral? What implications does this condition hold for the learning process? What diverse factors about learners should be considered in the learning process? What assumptions can you make about how individual learners are similar to each other and how they are different from others? Why might all of these questions about the nature of the learner matter in schools and classrooms?

Another question to consider is the *success* question. It will help you think in terms of the long-range impact you would like education to make on students and on society—the outcome of education. What is success in your eyes? If you fully accomplished what you intended to do as a teacher, what would success look like for your students twenty years after they had been in your classroom? When I was a school administrator, one of my favorite questions to ask in a job interview was presented as a scenario:

> After you had taught for twenty years, a woman steps through your classroom door after school is out and all the students are gone for the day. She says, 'Mrs. Watts, I don't know if you remember me, but I was in your class twenty years ago. You made such an impact on me that it influenced many of my life decisions. The person I've become today is in large part because of you.' What would she say next that would please you and cause you to feel that you succeeded at your goal as a teacher?

After the interviewee answered that question, I posed another one: "What might the former student say next that would cause you to think, 'Oh no, I failed. That's not what I intended at all for my students! Her life choices don't follow what I intended?'"

The scenario and follow-up questions above get at the issues of outcomes, intentionality, and values. Some educators claim in their philosophy of education that they have no preferred long-range outcomes for their students, that they only want their students to make life choices that result in the student's individual happiness. This claim is disingenuous. It is usually made by teachers who strive to avoid indoctrinating their students, so they opt for neutrality. It is difficult, however, to justify a philosophy of neutrality consistently and logically. For educators who are concerned about indoctrinating their students, I would encourage them not to confuse intentionality with indoctrination. An educator may be intentional about outcomes without indoctrinating students.

Some educators sense an obligation to embrace fully an established philosophy, such as those listed in Appendix B. They may sense this obligation out of pressure from a professor or someone else who hopes to encourage precision and consistency of thought. While some educators indeed philosophically align with some of the established schools of thought, most are more moderate and eclectic in their beliefs, and some are so eclectic that it seems they believe all philosophies.

First, for those who believe they truly do align with an established philosophy and want to label themselves as such, they should carefully study the philosophy, examining opposing views and criticisms of the philosophy. After close scrutiny and self-reflection, you may indeed conclude that you fit that philosophy. I found this to be true for a teacher of history who claimed that she was a perennialist. In her case, the label fit, and she was able to support how her beliefs aligned with perennialism. Conversely, many educators claim to be progressivists or constructivists, yet their own beliefs and preferred teaching methods do not consistently align strongly enough for them to adopt the label. Because of this, I encourage most educators to avoid fully adopting a philosophical label. Instead, use the labels as points of reference to situate yourself among the various philosophies, indicating which philosophy is most like your own beliefs and which is least similar to your beliefs.

In situating yourself among other educational thinkers, avoid the temptation to be too eclectic. There is a wise warning that says, "Don't be so open minded that your brains fall out." In other words, if you claim to believe everything, you actually believe nothing. Different philosophies exist because they each represent views of life that contradict one another in some way. It is therefore logically impossible to embrace all of them. To avoid this problem, you should identify no more than two philosophies that are similar to your own. Even then, if there are points of conflict in the philosophies, you should identify the conflicts and discuss your viewpoint regarding these topics. Ignoring contradictions in multiple philosophies that you claim to embrace reveals a possible misunderstanding or unawareness on your part of those philosophies.

It is acceptable simply to state what you believe. Do not feel obligated to embrace a particular philosophy or to use complicated philosophical terms. However, you should attempt to situate your beliefs among others by referring to ideas that illustrate your own or are in opposition to yours. You should draw from the knowledge base in education literature that includes psychology, philosophy, and learning theory. Do not try to cover everything; just identify one or two key theories that might illustrate your own beliefs about the purpose of schools and learning.

Instructional Practice

Once you have established the *why* of education and have clearly conveyed what you believe the long-range impact education should have on individuals and on society, it is time to move to the *what* and the *how*. This section should flow smoothly from the previous one. Address what you will implement in the classroom setting. The questions below will help to formulate your philosophy of instructional practice:

- **Teacher's Role**: What is the most effective approach the teacher should take? To what degree should the teacher provide direct instruction or guided facilitation? Should the teacher be more of a sage on the stage or a guide by the side?

© Prostock-studio/Shutterstock.com

- **Curricular Focus:** What content is most important? Though it is understood that required standards of learning will be taught, what is your perception of the purpose and significance of various subject areas? What are your perspectives regarding the intended curriculum, hidden curriculum, null curriculum, and experienced curriculum?
- **Methodology:** What pedagogical strategies are most effective at accomplishing the long-range impact you would like education to make in individuals and in society? What pedagogical practices, instructional strategies, or methods will you tend to use most frequently and why? What do you hope to accomplish by using these strategies?

A common error is for educators to disconnect the practical aspect of their philosophy from the theoretical. The two, however, should be closely connected. Theory should drive practice, and then practice should help refine theory. Your philosophy of instruction should make a distinct connection with your overall purpose of education. Instructional methods, of course, are simply tools, so it is understandable that a variety of tools—especially with the intent to differentiate—should be in every educator's proverbial bag of tricks. That said, your go-to strategies that are most prominently used in your instruction should reflect your philosophy. For example, when I was a doctoral candidate, one of my professors claimed to be a constructivist. She lectured heavily on the validity of research based on the theories of Jean Piaget, Lev Vygotsky, and Jerome Bruner. The professor's practice, however, was far from constructivist. She could have been the poster child for B. F. Skinner's behaviorism! This example is extreme, but educators, especially when articulating their philosophy of education, should meaningfully connect preferred practices with philosophy.

 Figuring It Out: What's My Philosophy?

It is common and normal for educators to be frustrated with the process of formulating a personal philosophy of education. "I am not philosophical or analytical," they say. "I just want to teach and see my students learn. That's it!" While I understand these sentiments, I would encourage educators who feel this way to continue persevering. They will be glad they did. I am convinced that the remedy for teacher burnout is confidence and intentionality in a personal philosophy of education.

If you need further guidance in solidifying your own thoughts and articulating them, consider the following:
- **Take a philosophy survey.** There are many online and can be found by searching "philosophy of education survey." I recommend taking more than one. Remember that the shorter the survey the less reliable it is in helping to identify your philosophy of education. Consider the results as a point of personal reflection and discussion with others. Surveys do not decide what you believe; only you can do that. There may be a number of factors that lead you to answer survey questions the way that you do, so avoid embracing the label simply because you scored high in a particular area.
- **Agree and disagree with quotes.** Find a number of quotes from various educational thinkers, such as the ones listed in Appendix A. You may quickly find several by doing an Internet search of "quotes on the philosophy of education." As you read them, rate each on a Likert scale of 1 to 10 regarding the degree to which you embrace or reject it. After rating several, look back at which ones had high or low ratings. By reflecting on your ratings, you are situating your own ideas among others. Notice the names of the educational thinkers who made the most poignant quotes and explore some of them further. Remember that your philosophy is made up not only of what you believe but also of what you do not believe, so the quotes you reject are as important as the ones you embrace.

- **Look again at epistemology.**[1] We touched on epistemology earlier, but if you are struggling with what you believe about the nature of truth, consider these questions:
    - **Dimensions of truth:** (a) Can truth really be known? If not, you may be a skeptic or agnostic. (b) To what degree is truth absolute or relative? Do you see all truth as absolute or relative? If so, what implications does that belief have for your thoughts on education? (c) To what degree is truth subjective or objective? If truth is subjective, it relies on the learner's experience and perception; if it is objective, it is outside the learner and does not depend on the learner's experience or perception of it. Are there certain truths that are subjective and others that are objective?
    - **Sources of truth:** (a) What are the sources of truth and which ones are most important to learning? (b) Is it accurate that there are five sources of truth and that they include authority, intuition, reason, revelation, and senses? (c) What role does each of the five sources of truth have in classroom instruction? Should all five be represented equally? If so, why? If not, which ones should be minimized?
    - **Validity of truth:** How do we know something is actually true? (a) *Correspondence validity:* If we can know one thing is true by comparing it to another thing external or outside of itself, how do I do this in my instruction? In other words, how do I encourage students to compare truth claims as they draw conclusions in their thinking? (b) *Coherence validity:* If we can know something is true because of the internal noncontradiction of the truth claim, how do I implement this into my instruction? Do I encourage students to consider the consistency of ideas as they are presented? (c) *Pragmatic validity:* If we can know something is true because it works when the principle is applied, how do I display this in the classroom? What is my response when I discover that something that has seemed to have always worked in the past no longer works that way? Finally, how do I convey to my students that the validity of truth is strengthened if it evidences all three types of validity: correspondence, coherence, and pragmatic?
- **Inductive vs. deductive.** In the way that I plan my instruction, do I typically encourage inductive or deductive learning? (a) *Inductive:* A lesson that is inductive starts with experiences or observations of examples, illustrations, experiments, or problem-solving. The lesson then guides the student to draw conclusions from those multiple observations. So the lesson begins with multiple experiences and ends with the generalization or concept. (b) *Deductive:* A lesson that is deductive starts with declaring to the student either in written or oral form a truth, principle, algorithm, rule, etc. The lesson then guides the student to practice the principle by solving a number of problems or by applying the principle in a variety of ways.
- **Metaphors and imagery.** Educational thinkers often convey their philosophy of education via metaphoric language or imagery. Plato's allegory of the cave, Horace Mann's balance wheel, Booker T. Washington's head–hands–heart, and Paulo Freire's banking system are all means of conveying a philosophy of education. To help you develop your own metaphor, complete the stems below:
    - Schools are like . . .
    - Education is similar to . . .
    - Learning could be compared to . . .
    - A teacher is kind of like . . .
    - A school system functions like . . .
    - Students remind me of . . .

If you are artistic or think in terms of images, consider sketching your beliefs about education. You may use a symbol, chart, illustration, icon, conceptual framework, or semantic map.

- **School examples.** Examine school or university statements of vision, mission, philosophy, objectives, and core values. You may start with schools with which you are familiar. Their statements are typically easy to find on their websites. Look for elements in the statements that appeal to you, but be aware that many school statements are vague enough to appeal broadly to stakeholders, so they might serve as poor examples. "Every child, every day!" is a wonderful rallying cry to remind the school community to practice equity and inclusion, but it does little to convey a specific philosophy of education.

 Go to www.khlearn.com to watch a video about formulating a personal philosophy of education.

ENDNOTES

1. The structure of this examination of epistemology is based on George R. Knight, *Philosophy & Education: An Introduction in Christian Perspective* (Berrien Springs, MI: Andrews University Press, 2006).

RELIGIOUS RIGHTS IN THE PUBLIC SCHOOL CLASSROOM

Lady Justice in front of columns of the U.S. Supreme Court

Despite the notion that First Amendment rights are established, valued, and respected in the United States, there continues to be confusion in public schools that leads to legal conflict over issues associated with freedoms of speech and expression, especially as they relate to religious issues. Navigating the religious rights of teachers and students can be a precarious undertaking, as administrators' decisions regarding the expression of religious beliefs continue to be highlighted in the media and many times are resolved in the court system at great expense to school districts.

 ## Landmark Supreme Court Case: *Engel v. Vitale*, 1962

The year of 1962 was a turning point in American public schools. It was in this year that the United States Supreme Court decided on the *Engel v. Vitale* case, ruling that state-endorsed prayers could not be required in public school classrooms. Nearly three decades later, the Court took the *Lee v. Weisman* case (1992) in which it heard arguments regarding prayer at high school commencement ceremonies. Justice Davis Souter warned during the 1991 arguments that if prayers were permitted at commencement ceremonies, the court would need to overturn the 1962 ruling. Solicitor General Ken Starr responded, "I don't think the *Engel* tradition is implicated outside the classroom."[1]

While the 1962 *Engel* case was being argued and for decades thereafter, a myth prevailed that Madalyn Murray O'Hair, a prominent atheist leader, was somehow responsible for the decision. Though she was not involved in the 1962 case regarding classroom prayers, O'Hair did file a suit shortly thereafter challenging Bible-reading in Maryland schools. Her suit was combined with a similar one in Philadelphia by Ed Schempp, resulting in the 1963 *Abington School District v. Schempp* Supreme Court ruling. Consistent with the *Engel* decision, the court declared that schools could not require devotional reading of the Bible apart from a secular academic purpose.[2]

These Supreme Court decisions of the early 1960s were made in the context of the Cold War—Soviets versus Americans, communism versus capitalism, atheism versus theism—and the popular notion was that one of them would triumph over the other. It was in this cultural milieu that the New York State Board of Education in 1951 had endorsed a prayer that stated, "Almighty God, we acknowledge our dependence on Thee, and we beg Thy blessings upon us, our parents, our teachers, and our country." It was a nondenominational prayer that the state had offered to be used voluntarily. In 1958, the New Hyde Park School District adopted the prayer, permitting parents to opt out for their children by signing a form.

A group of parents—some Jewish and others non-religious—fought the implementation of the prayer with a lawsuit. Alphabetically, the name of parent Steven Engel appeared at the top of the list of plaintiffs; therefore, the case was named after him. This notoriety generated a great deal of negative attention for Engel and his family. He received obscene phone calls. Crosses were burnt in his yard, and his children were taunted in the community.

The New York District Court heard the case in 1959, ruling against the parents. The parents then appealed to the New York Appeals Court where twenty-two states filed an *amicus* brief supporting the prayer and indicating that they did not interpret the prayer as violating the U.S. Constitution's First Amendment. Losing in the Appeals Court, the parents appealed to the New York Supreme Court where the case was rejected because it was a matter relating more to the U.S. Constitution than to the New York Constitution.

In 1962, the U.S. Supreme Court conducted a judicial review of *Engels* and decided to hear the case. During court arguments, the American Civil Liberties Union claimed that the prayer was a violation of the First Amendment establishment clause. The justices responded by voting six to one in favor of the parents. Two of the justices did not participate. Justice Hugo Black wrote the majority opinion, making this statement: "It is no part of the business of government to compose official prayers for any group of American people to recite as a part of a religious program carried on by government."[3] In the dissenting opinion, Justice Potter Stewart wrote, "The Establishment Clause was only meant to prohibit the establishment of a state-sponsored church, such as the Church of England, and not prohibit all types of government involvement with religion."[4]

The *Engel* case resulted in a landmark decision because it was the first in a series of cases that eliminated or limited religious activities in government schools. Public reaction was immediate and intense. The media sensationalized the decision, and prominent citizens spoke out both in support and in opposition to it. Evangelist Billy Graham and Cardinal Francis Spellman, along with the more liberal Episcopal Bishop James A. Pike, decried the decision. Surprisingly, the National Association of Evangelicals and the magazine *Christianity Today* were in support of the Court's decision.

The Christian Legal Society's Center for Law and Religious Freedom released the following statement: "Too many school administrators took that decision as a green light to try to eradicate religion from public schools."[5] The Beckett Fund for Religious Liberty claimed that many school administrators misunderstood Justice Black's majority opinion to mean that schools should actually take a hostile stance against religious expression in public schools. The American Association of School Administrators reported that the issue of navigating religion in public schools had become a constantly moving target that administrators were having a difficulty addressing.[6]

A positive result from the *Engel* decision was that—since schools could no longer lead in religious expression—the students became empowered to do so within certain parameters. One example is See You at the Pole, an annual student-led event in which students take control of promoting and leading in prayer before school hours begin. The emphasis among Evangelical Christian groups is now on the protection of students' rights to be involved in such constitutionally protected activities in public schools.[7]

Role of Religion in Public Schools: General Guidelines[8]

The U.S. Department of Education and many other organizations distribute literature to inform educators and parents of what is acceptable based on court decisions and laws. Some of these organizations include the First Amendment Center, American Jewish Congress, Christian Legal Society, The National Education Association, the Association for Supervision and Curriculum Development, the National PTA, and many others. The following guidelines are an amalgamation presented by these organizations.

STUDENT RELIGIOUS EXPRESSION

- Students may pray and read scriptures individually or in groups at any time they would be permitted to engage in secular noncurricular speech. Any prohibitions must be on the same terms that secular speech and reading would be prohibited. According to the Supreme Court's *Tinker* (1969) statement, the only acceptable prohibition on student speech would be when the activities "substantially interfere with the work of the school, or impinge upon the rights of other students."

© Maria Dryfhout/Shutterstock.com

Go to www.khlearn.com to watch a video showing a lawyer discussing freedom of religious practice and conscious.

- Students may choose to include their religious views in assignments, such as research papers, poems, artwork, etc., with neither academic penalty nor reward for the inclusion of the religious view. Typical standards of substance and relevance should be employed to assess the assignment.
- The 1984 Equal Access Act ensures that, to the same degree extracurricular clubs are permitted to meet either during or outside school hours, religious student-led clubs may also meet. Equal access applies not just to facilities but also to promotional forums for announcements, such as the intercom system, bulletin board, and flyer distribution. If access is denied based on religious content, it must be denied to all extracurricular clubs as well.
- All student-distributed literature must be treated the same without consideration of religious content. Policies may regulate when and where it may be distributed, but additional restrictions may not be placed on religious content.

TEACHER RELIGIOUS EXPRESSION

By the very nature of their roles as school and state representatives, teachers do not have the same religious rights on the public school campus as do students. Their words are taken as being endorsed by the school and could easily be confused as being part of the official curriculum. Therefore, only in instances when it is clear to the students that the teacher is expressing a personal belief and only when it can be done in a non-proselytizing manner should a teacher convey personal religious beliefs; this is recommended only if it is in response to a student's question about personal religious beliefs.

- Teachers may wear non-obtrusive religious jewelry, such as a cross or Star of David.
- Under no circumstances are teachers free to pray or lead in devotional scripture reading in the presence of students during the school day or during a school function.
- Outside the presence of students, teachers have the right to pray and read scriptures individually or in groups at any time they would be permitted to engage in secular speech unrelated to school matters.

Some courts have taken into account the age of the students when deciding the constitutionality of a teacher's actions, reasoning that the younger the students are, the more difficult it is for them to separate the teacher's views from those of the school.[9]

TEACHING ABOUT RELIGION

In *Abington v. Schempp* (1963) Associate Justice Tom Clark wrote,

> It might well be said that one's education is not complete without a study of comparative religion or the history of religion and its relationship to the advancement of civilization. It certainly may be said that the Bible is worthy of study for its literary and historic qualities. Nothing we have said here indicates that such study of the Bible or of religion, when presented objectively as part of a secular program of education, may not be effected consistently with the First Amendment.

Inclusion of religious content in the curriculum is constitutionally appropriate only when it is carried out in an academic, informative study with the purpose to expose students to the religion. It becomes inappropriate when the content is devotional or either promotes or denigrates religion. The major religions relevant to the subject area should be addressed as is appropriate.

GRADUATIONS AND OTHER CEREMONIES

Although U.S. Supreme Court cases apparently resolved the issue of prayers at graduation ceremonies[10] and football games,[11] conflicts have continued to arise. Evidently, some school officials continue to show preferential treatment to religious speech by planning prayers or presentations by clergy while others prohibit student speeches and guest speakers from praying or quoting scriptures. These stances are violations of the establishment and free expression clauses respectively. Repeatedly, the Supreme Court has held that the First Amendment requires neutrality of school officials, which stipulates that neither favoritism nor hostility toward religious expression should be displayed.[12] The First Amendment, therefore, forbids school-sponsored or planned prayers and Scripture readings but protects private individuals who choose religious expression as part of a public presentation. For example, school officials may not invite clergy to pray at the ceremony but may permit seniors to nominate and vote on a community member to present a brief statement appropriate to the purpose of the ceremony; the elected person may then have the freedom to share secular or religious words at his or her own choosing. Neither may school officials censor religious content from the valedictorian speech or any other student presentation. Students do not "shed their constitutional rights to freedom of speech or expression at the schoolhouse gate"[13] and neither do they shed them during the graduation ceremony.

© fongbeerredhot/Shutterstock.com

Go to www.khlearn.com to watch a video about religious rights in the public school classroom.

ENDNOTES

1. Linda Greenhouse, "Court Appears Skeptical for Argument for Prayer," *New York Times* (November 7, 1991), accessed October 3, 2017, http://www.nytimes.com/1991/11/07/us/court-appears-skeptical-of-argument-for-prayer.html?pagewanted=all.
2. Barbara Bernstein, "School Prayer Ruling," *New York Times* (December 28, 1996), accessed October 3, 2017, http://www.nytimes.com/1996/12/28/opinion/l-school-prayer-ruling-939692.html.
3. "Text of Supreme Court Decision on School Prayers: Engel v. Vitale," *A Journal of Church and State* 4, no. 2 (1962): 245.
4. Ibid.
5. Matthew Brown, "50 Years Later: High Court's School Prayer Ruling Still Fuels Religious Liberty Debate," *Deseret News* (June 24, 2012).
6. Ibid.
7. See Barton, *Four Centuries*; Bernstein, "School Prayer Ruling"; Brown, "50 Years Later"; S. Oley Cutler, *Engel v. Vitale: An Appraisal* (Syracuse, NY: Syracuse University College of Law, 1962); Greenhouse, "Court Appears Skeptical"; Corinna Barrett Lain, "God, Civic Virtue, and the American Way: Reconstructing Engel," *Stanford Law Review* 67, no. 3 (2015): 479-555; Noll, *A History of Christianity*; "Text of Supreme Court Decision on School Prayers: Engel v. Vitale."
8. From *Christian Perspectives in Education*, Volume 1, Issue 1, Fall 2007 by Samuel J. Smith. Copyright © 2007 by Samuel J. Smith.
9. Mathew D. Staver, *Eternal Vigilance: Knowing and Protecting Your Religious Freedom* (Nashville, TN: Broadman & Holman Publishers, 2005).
10. *Lee v. Weisman*, 505 U.S. 577, 599 (1992).
11. *Santa Fe Independent School District v. Doe*, 530 U.S. 290, 302 (2000).
12. *Good News Club v. Milford Central School*, 533 U.S. 98 (2001).
13. *Tinker v. Des Moines Independent Community School District*, 393 U.S. 503, 506 (1969).

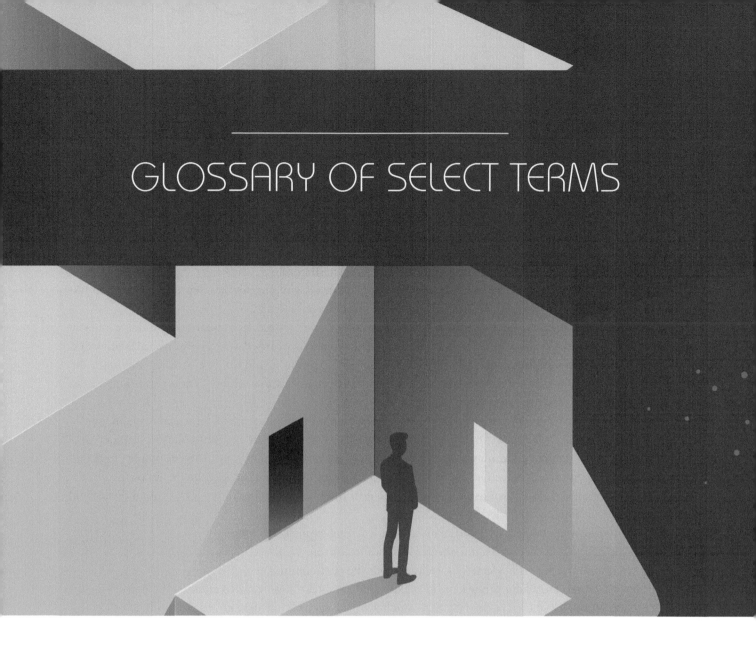

GLOSSARY OF SELECT TERMS

The definitions below are intended to bring clarity and a basic understanding to readers who are relatively new to the fields of philosophy, educational foundations, and the history of education. They are not offered as technical or comprehensive definitions but are presented to provoke readers to reflect on these concepts and their own perspectives regarding each concept.

***a posteriori*:** a description of truth perceived as being dependent upon human experience, awareness, and interaction with aspects of reality; a type of knowledge derived from human experience.

***a priori*:** a description of truth perceived as existing independently of human experience; truth that exists without anyone realizing it or acting upon it; truth that is built into the fabric of reality.

absolute mind: a Platonic notion, also referred to as the Absolute Self; the idea of a perfect existence, one that an idealist would consistently strive to reach by gaining knowledge; the source of universal forms.

aesthetics: the branch of philosophy dealing with the study of values related to the beautiful and sublime; the axiological study related to that which is pleasing to the senses.

agnosticism: the belief that one cannot know for certain that God exists; God's existence is unprovable and unknowable; a profession of ignorance, especially in reference to the existence or nonexistence of God, rather than a positive denial of any valid knowledge.

anthropocentric: human-centered; treating humans as preeminent; regarding humans as the universe's most important entity.

anthropology: the study of humankind in all its aspects, especially human culture or human development; identification of commonalities and differences among human groups and individuals.

atheism: disbelief in the existence of God or deities; nothing is God.

axiology: the study of values and value judgments regarding beauty and morality; the study of questions of value; axiology encompasses the study of ethics and aesthetics.

Calvinism: doctrine named after Protestant Reformer John Calvin; emphasizes depravity of human nature, salvation through faith alone, predestination, and eternal security.

coherence validity: places trust in the consistency of all of one's judgments; coherence validity evaluates the consistency of various truth claims within a particular work, worldview, or philosophical framework.

correspondence validity: uses agreement with fact to judge the validity of a construct; evaluates the veracity of a truth claim by comparing it with other truth claims from a variety of sources; triangulation is an example of correspondence validity.

cosmology: the study of the origin, nature, and development of the universe as an orderly system.

curriculum: subjects taught at an educational institution; elements taught in a particular subject; perspectives regarding curriculum may range from narrow (e.g., specific materials or subject matter) to broad (e.g., all experiences involved in the learning process); types of curriculum include the following:

experienced curriculum: also known as the *received curriculum*, the take-away for students from the educational experience, whether intended or not.

formal curriculum: planned activities and materials for learning explicit outcomes.

hidden curriculum: unofficial curriculum covertly promoting certain values or ideas.

null curriculum: that which is neglected or omitted from the curriculum.

deconstruction: unpacking presuppositions expressed by such things as word choices, the hidden meanings of puns, and so on; considering that which a writer, speaker, or artist chooses to include or to omit from communication; a postmodern method to analyze philosophical thought and to reorganize new constructs; reading beyond the explicitly stated message of the author to reveal new meanings; applying one's experiences, cultural settings, and historical contexts to the interpretation of text.

deism: belief in God based on reason rather than revelation; God has set the universe in motion but does not interfere with how it runs; God exists apart from, and is not interested in, humanity or the physical universe; miracles, such as the resurrection, do not exist; "warm" deists value prayer and human relationship with God while "cold" deists function in practicality as atheists.

dichotomy: separation into two divisions that differ widely from or contradict each other; examples of dichotomies include faith-reason, mind-matter, values-facts, form-function, and religion-science; an upper-story and lower-story way of thinking.

eclecticism: an approach to developing a way of believing or acting that draws individual elements from a variety of sources, systems, or styles; a risk of eclecticism is that elements from conflicting frameworks may weaken the coherence of an argument, philosophy, or theory.

emotionalism: tendency to display feelings through outward expressions; prominent during revivals of the Great Awakening.

epistemology: the study of the nature of truth and knowledge and how humans acquire them; examples of epistemological frameworks are empiricism, pragmatism, and constructivism; examples of epistemologists include B. F. Skinner, John Dewey, and Jean Piaget.

ethics: the study of moral standards and how they affect conduct; a branch of axiology relating to what is valued in human behavior; professional standards such as the Model Code of Ethics for Educators.

general revelation: the notion that God reveals himself broadly through nature, the design of the universe, and grace that is offered commonly to all; the use of logic to conclude the existence of God and what he may be communicating to humanity; presupposes a supernatural reality that breaks into the natural order.

liberal arts: academic disciplines that develop individuals as humans and good citizens; subject areas of literature, history, philosophy, mathematics, science, and languages; learning that focuses on information of general cultural concern as opposed to training for specific tasks.

limited absolutism: neither legalistic nor relativistic; relativism as limited by laws; the belief that certain truths are absolute, but others are not or that truths may be absolute in certain circumstances; sometimes referred to as "situational ethics"; universal principles that generally apply in most circumstances.

logic: a theory of reasoning; "rules" of concluding the validity of arguments that are generally agreed upon by consensus; branch of philosophy that deals with the theory of deductive and inductive arguments and aims to distinguish good from bad reasoning.

logocentrism: meaning is derived from literal text more so than from image, emotion, or intuition; focus on words and language to the exclusion of non-linguistic matters, such as personal experience or historical context; attention to the meanings of words or distinctions in their usage.

materialism: the theory that physical matter is the only reality and that psychological constructs such as emotions, reason, thought, and desire can be explained as physical functions.

meritocracy: a system in which individuals have the ability to rise from one social class to another based on effort rather than on their family of birth.

metanarrative: an overarching story by which people share common understandings about how the world works; perceived as oppressive by subcultures that may not share the metanarrative; philosophical understanding of the shape of reality that legitimizes the way things are by providing reasons for the correctness of the status quo; a prominent worldview shared by the most powerful in a society; postmodernism rejects all metanarratives; examples of metanarratives include philosophies, religions, worldviews, and collective notions like the "American dream."

metaphysics: a branch of philosophy concerned with the study of the nature of ultimate reality and truth; it includes a perspective of physical matter but transcends the physical.

modernism: understanding of the world through reason and scientific knowledge; rose to prominence in the nineteenth and twentieth centuries.

monotheism: the belief that there is only one God.

naturalism: ultimate reality consists strictly of what is found in nature; rejects all spiritual and supernatural explanations of the world and holds that science is the sole basis of what can be known.

ontology: the study of existence; questions what it means to be; René Descartes's famous quote, "I think, therefore I am," is an ontological claim.

pantheism: the belief that god and the material world are one and the same thing and that god is present in everything; all is god.

pedagogy: the science or profession of teaching; style or method of teaching.

philosophy: the study of basic questions regarding purpose, meaning, truth, existence, reality, causality, and freedom; literally, the "love of wisdom."

polytheism: worship of or believing in more than one deity.

positivism: the theory that knowledge can be acquired only through direct observation and experimentation rather than through metaphysics and theology; only that which can be quantified or experienced through the senses exists.

pragmatic validity: truth is what works; test of truth is in its utility, workability, or satisfactory consequences.

praxis: recursive interplay between theory and practice; actions that are intentionally informed by beliefs; reflective practice that results in critical evaluation of one's own beliefs.

rationalism: decisions should be based on logic and knowledge rather than on intuition or revelation; reason is a superior way of knowing than from authority, senses, or emotion.

relativism: the belief that concepts such as right and wrong, goodness and badness, or truth and falsehood are not absolute but change from culture to culture and situation to situation; because each individual holds and experiences truth differently, there are multiple realities and multiple truths that change in time and space.

republicanism: representative government in which sovereignty belongs to citizens as they choose those who will lead them.

Scottish Common Sense Realism: an Aristotelian notion that, as people perceive themselves, their environment, and society, the conclusions most common among them can be trusted as self-evident truths.

skepticism: the belief that knowledge is unattainable; people cannot make truth claims because all sources of truth (i.e., authority, intuition, reason, revelation, and senses) are unreliable.

special revelation: also known as *specific revelation*; truth that is presented to humanity directly from God, such as the Ten Commandments, the person of Jesus Christ, and the Bible; presupposes a supernatural reality that breaks into the natural order, such as a miracle.

teleology: examination of the ultimate purpose of the universe.

theism: the belief that a personal God exists who created and interacts with the world.

theology: the study of religion, especially the nature of God and how God relates to the world.

transformation: idea of drastically changing experiences of individuals and/or society into new truths rather than the imparting of knowledge by the teacher to the student.

transmission: passing down knowledge, skills, and values from one generation to another; imparting of facts from the teacher to the student.

Unitarianism: derives its name from rejection of trinitarianism; Jesus was a moral teacher but was not God incarnate.

unlimited absolutism: legalism; moral codes and laws are to be applied universally despite diverse circumstances.

utopianism: the belief that a perfect existence is possible through human effort and through specifically prescribed means; denies that humans are so flawed or sinful that society will always include injustice.

worldview: comprehensive interpretation or image of the universe and humanity; a lens through which to make sense of the world; a metanarrative.

BIBLIOGRAPHY

Alanis, Javier. "Peace and Liberation Theology." *Global Virtue Ethics Review* 7, no. 3 (2016): 34-43.

Almeida, Deirdre A. "The Hidden Half: A History of Native American Women's Education." *Harvard Educational Review* 67, no. 4 (1997): 757-71.

"American Indians Respond to the Columbian Quincentennial, 1990." In *Major Problems in Atlantic History*, edited by Alison F. Games and Adam Rothman, 456-7. Boston: Houghton Mifflin Company, 2008.

American Jewish Congress. *Public Schools & Religious Communities: A First Amendment Guide*. New York, 2018.

Anderson, Lewis Flint. *Pestalozzi*. New York: AMS Press, 1931.

Androne, Mihai. "The Influence of the Protestant Reformation on Education." *Procedia – Social and Behavioral Sciences* 137 (July 2014): 80-87.

Aquinas, Thomas. *Compendium of Theology*. Translated by Richard J. Regan. Oxford: Oxford University Press, 2009.

———. *St. Thomas Aquinas, Summa Theologica: Vol. 3 of 10*. Translated by Dominican Province. Forgotten Books, 2007.

———. *Summa Theologica*. Translated by Dominican Fathers. New York: Christian Classics, 1948.

Armitage, David. "The Varieties of Atlantic History." In *Major Problems in Atlantic History*, edited by Alison Games and Adam Rothman, 16-23. Boston: Houghton Mifflin, 2008.

Augustine. "Confessions." In *Christian Apologetics: Past & Present*, edited by William Edgar and K. Scott Oliphint, vol. 1, 210-59. Wheaton: Crossway, 2009.

———. "Instruction on the Uninstructed." In *The History and Philosophy of Education: Voices of Educational Pioneers*, by Madonna Murphy, 83-85. Upper Saddle River: Pearson Prentice Hall, 2006.

———. "On Christian Doctrine." In *A Passion for Learning*, edited by D. Bruce Lockerbie, 56-9. 2nd ed. Colorado Springs: Purposeful Design Publications, 2007.

Baker, Richard. "The Crime of Mrs. Douglass in Teaching Colored Children to Read." January 10, 1854. In *The Annals of America. Vol. 4, 1850-1857: A House Dividing*, 224-226. Chicago: Encyclopedia Britannica, 1968.

Baker-Fletcher, Garth Kasimu. "Liberation Theologies in the United States: An Introduction." *Religious Studies Review* 37, no. 4 (2011): 297-8.

Barton, David. *Four Centuries of American Education*. Aledo: Wallbuilder Press, 2004.

Bauman, Dan, and Brock Read. "A Brief History of GOP Attempts to Kill the Education Dept." *The Chronicle of Higher Education*, June 21, 2018.

Beecher, Catharine E. *Educational Reminiscences and Suggestions*. New York: J. B. Ford and Company, 1874.

———. *Religious Training of Children in the School, the Family, and the Church*. Ann Arbor: University of Michigan Library, 1864.

Beecher, Lyman. *Lyman Beecher and the Reform of Society: Four Sermons, 1804-1828*. New York: Arno Press, 1972.

———. "Resources of the Adversary, and Means of their Destruction." *The Wesleyan-Methodist Magazine* 7 (August 1828): 516-24.

Benjamin, Thomas. *The Atlantic World: Europeans, Africans, Indians and Their Shared History, 1400-1900*. Cambridge: Cambridge University Press, 2009.

Bentley, George R. *A History of the Freedmen's Bureau*. New York: Octagon Books, 1970.

Berlin, Ira. "From Creole to African: Atlantic Creoles and the Origins of African-American Society in Mainland North America." *The William and Mary Quarterly* 53, no. 2 (1996): 251-88.

Bernstein, Barbara. "School Prayer Ruling." *New York Times*, December 28, 1996. Accessed October 3, 2017. http://www.nytimes.com/1996/12/28/opinion/l-school-prayer-ruling-939692.html.

Best, John Hardin. "Education in the Forming of the American South." *History of Education Quarterly* 36, no. 1 (1996): 39-51.

Blaustien, Albert P., and Robert L. Zangrando, ed. *Civil Rights and the American Negro: A Documentary History*. New York: Washington Square Press, 1968.

Blinderman, Abraham. "Three Early Champions of Education: Benjamin Franklin, Benjamin Rush, and Noah Webster." *Phi Delta Kappa* (April 7, 1976): 5-36.

Blount, Jackie M. *Destined to Rule the Schools : Women and the Superintendency, 1873-1995*. New York: State University of New York Press, 1998.

Bonhoeffer, Dietrich. *The Cost of Discipleship*. New York: Simon & Schuster, 1959.

Brayboy, Bryan McKinley Jones. "Culture, Place, and Power: Engaging the Histories and Possibilities of American Indian Education." *History of Education Quarterly* 54, no. 3 (2014): 395-402.

Brown, Matthew. "50 Years Later: High Court's School Prayer Ruling Still Fuels Religious Liberty Debate." *Deseret News*, June 24, 2012.

Brunner, Cryss C., and Margaret Grogan. *Women Leading School Systems: Uncommon Roads to Fulfillment*. Lanham: Rowman & Littlefield Education, 2007.

Bury, J. B. *The History of Freedom of Thought*. New York: Henry Holt & Company, 1913.

Bushnell, Horace. *Christian Nurture*. New York: Scribner, 1861.

————. *Sermons for the New Life*. New York: Scribner, 1858.

Butterfield, Stephen T. "The Use of Language in the Slave Narratives." *Negro American Literature Forum* 6, no. 3 (Autumn 1972): 72-78.

Butts, Robert Freeman. *Public Education in the United States: From Revolution to Reform (1776-1976)*. New York: Holt, Rhinehart and Winston, 1978.

Cain, Mary Cathryn. "Rhetorics of Race and Freedom: The Expression of Women's Whiteness in Anti-Slavery Activism." *Studies in Popular Culture* 29, no. 2 (October 2006): 1-19.

Calvin, John. *Calvin: Theological Treatises*. Translated by J. K. S. Reid. Philadelphia: The Westminster Press, 1954.

Capers, I. Bennett. "Reading Back, Reading Black." *Hofstra Law Review* 35, no. 1 (2006): 9-22.

Carpenter, John A. "General O. O. Howard at Gettysburg." *Civil War History* 9, no. 3 (1963): 261–76.

————. *Sword and Olive Branch: Oliver Otis Howard*. New York: Fordham University Press, 1999.

Carson, Nathan P. "Passionate Epistemology: Kierkegaard on Skepticism, Approximate Knowledge, and Higher Existential Truth." *Journal of Chinese Philosophy* 40, no. 1 (2013): 29-49.

Chadwick, Henry. *Augustin of Hippo: A Life*. Oxford: Oxford University Press, 2009.

Chase, Susuan E. *Ambiguous Empowerment: The Work Narrative of Women School Superintendents*. Amherst: University of Massachusetts Press, 1995.

Child, L. Maria, ed. *The Freedmen's Book*. Boston: Ticknor and Fields, 1865.

Clarke, James Freeman. "Nullifying the Fugitive Slave Law." *The Liberator*, March 25, 1859, Accessible Archives.

Coe, George A. *The Religion of the Mature Mind*. Chicago: Revell, 1962.

Cohen, Daniel A. "The Origin and Development of the *New England Primer*." *Children's Literature* 5 (1976): 52-57.

Cohen, Ronald D. "Schooling Uncle Sam's Children: Education in the USA, 1941-1945." In *Education and the Second World War: Studies in Schooling and Social Change*, edited by Roy Lowe, 46-59. New York: Routledge, 2012.

Cornelius, Janet Duitsman. *'When I Can Read My Title Clear': Literacy, Slavery, and Religion in the Antebellum South*. Columbia: University of South Carolina Press, 1991.

Crain, Patricia. *The Story of A: The Alphabetization of America from the* New England Primer *to* The Scarlet Letter. Stanford: Stanford University Press, 2000.

Cremin, Lawrence A. *American Education: The Colonial Experience 1607-1783*. New York: Harper & Row, 1970.

————. *The Transformation of the Schools: Progressivism in American Education, 1876-1957*. New York: Vintage Books, 1961.

Cubberley, Ellwood Patterson. *Changing Conceptions of Education*. Boston: Houghton Mifflin, 1908.

Cutler, S. Oley. *Engel v. Vitale: An Appraisal*. Syracuse: Syracuse University College of Law, 1962.

Davies, Gareth. *See Government Grow: Education Politics from Johnson to Reagan*. Lawrence: University Press of Kansas, 2007.

D'Elia, Donald J. "Philosopher of the American Revolution." *Transactions of the American Philosophical Society* 64, no. 5 (1974): 1-113.

"Dinner in Honor of Gen. O. O. Howard." *New York Times* (1857-1922), November 9, 1900, 2.

Dorrien, Gary. *The Making of American Liberal Theology: Imagining Progressive Religion 1805-1900*. Louisville: Westminster John Knox Press, 2001.

Douglass, Margaret. *Educational Laws of Virginia: The Personal Narrative of Mrs. Margaret Douglass, a Southern Woman Who was Imprisoned for One Month in the Common Jail of Norfolk, Under the Laws of Virginia for the Crime of Teaching Free Colored Children to Read*. Boston: J. P. Jewitt & Co., 1854.

Dreisbach, Daniel L. "The Bible and the Political Culture of the American Founding." In *Faith and the Founders of the American Republic*, edited by Mark David Hall and Daniel L. Dreisbach, 144-173. Oxford: Oxford University Press, 2014.

Dulles, Avery Cardinal. *A History of Apologetics.* 2nd ed. San Francisco: Ignatius Press, 2005.

Dunn, Sheila G. *Philosophical Foundations of Education: Connecting Philosophy to Theory and Practice.* Upper Saddle River: Pearson, 2005.

Eavey, C. B. *History of Christian Education.* Chicago: Moody Press, 1964.

Edgar, William and Oliphint, K. Scott, eds. *Christian Apologetics: Past & Present*, vol. 1. Wheaton, IL: Crossway, 2009.

Edwards, Jonathan. "Jonathan Edwards Describes the Awakening in His Congregation in Northampton, Massachusetts, 1737." In *Major Problems in American Colonial History*, 3rd ed., edited by Karen Ordahl Kupperman, 271-2. Boston: Wadsworth, 2013.

———. *Religious Affections.* Mineola: Dover Publications, 2013.

———. "The 'Miscellanies': Number 1340." In *Christian Apologetics: Past & Present*, edited by William Edgar and K. Scott Oliphint, vol. 1, 225-38. Wheaton: Crossway, 2009.

———. *Thoughts on the Revival of Religion in New England, 1740; To Which is Prefixed, A Narrative of the Surprising Work of God in Northampton, Mass., 1735.* New York: American Tract Society, 1800.

Edwards, Sarah Pierrepont. "Sarah Pierrepont Edwards Recounts Her Religious Experience, 1742." In *Major Problems in American Colonial History*, 3rd ed., edited by Karen Ordahl Kupperman, 272-4. Boston: Wadsworth, 2013.

Erasmus, Desiderius. *The Education of a Christian Prince.* Translated by Lester K. Born. New York: Columbia University Press, 1936.

Esquith, Rafe. *Teach Like Your Hair's on Fire: The Methods and Madness Inside Room 56.* New York: Penguin Books, 2007.

Faber, Riemer. "Philipp Melanchthon on Reformed Education." *Clarion* 47, no. 18 (September 1998): 428-431.

Fărcaş, Daniel. "Thomas Aquinas: Teaching Theology in the Age of Universities." In *A Legacy of Religious Educators: Historical and Theological Introductions*, edited by Elmer L. Towns and Benjamin K. Forrest, 65-81. Lynchburg: Liberty University Press, 2017.

Ferguson, Everett. *Church History: The Rise and Growth of the Church in the Its Cultural Intellectual, and Political Context.* Vol. 1. Grand Rapids: Zondervan, 2013.

First Amendment Center. *A Parent's Guide to Religion in the Public Schools.* Nashville: Author, 2015.

Fisher, George P. "The Philosophy of Jonathan Edwards." *The North American Review* 128, no. 268 (1879): 284-303.

Fleming, Sandford. *Children and Puritanism.* New Haven: Yale University, 1933.

Folliard, Dorothy. "Sparks from the South: The Growing Impact of Liberation Theology on the United States Hispanic Church." *International Review of Mission* 78, no. 310 (1989): 150-154.

Foner, Philip S., and Josephine F. Pacheco. *Three Who Dared: Prudence Crandall, Margaret Douglass, Myrtilla Miner—Champions of Antebellum Black Education.* Westport: Greenwood Press, 1984.

Ford, Paul Leicester, ed. *The New England Primer: A History of Its Origin and Development.* New York: Dodd, Mead and Co., 1897.

Franklin, Benjamin. "Remarks Concerning the Savages of North America, 1784." *Founders Online*, National Archives.

Fraser, James W. "Abolitionism, Activism, and New Models for Ministry." *American Presbyterians* 66, no. 2 (Summer 1988): 89-103.

———. *Pedagogue for God's Kingdom: Lyman Beecher and the Second Great Awakening.* Lanham, MD: University Press of America, 1985.

———., ed. *The School in the United States: A Documentary History.* 2nd ed. New York: Routledge, 2010.

Fredriksen, John C. "Oliver O. Howard." In *The American Mosaic: The African American Experience, ABC-CLIO*, 2019. Accessed January 26, 2019.

"Freedmen's Bureau Act." In *Reconstruction Era Reference Library*, edited by Lawrence W. Baker, Bridget Hall Grumet, Kelly King Howes, and Roger Matuz, vol. 3, Primary Sources, *U.S. History in Context*, 34-45. Detroit: UXL, 2005.

Freire, Paulo. *Education for Critical Consciousness*. New York: The Seabury Press, 1973.

———. *Pedagogy of the Oppressed*. New York: Herder and Herder, 1970.

Freire, Paulo and Donaldo Mecado. *Literacy: Reading the Word and the World*. South Hadley: Bergin & Garvey, 1987.

Frey, Christopher J. "Native American Education." In *Encyclopedia of Educational Reform and Dissent*. 2 vols., edited by Thomas C. Hunt, James C. Carper, Thomas J. Lasley, and C. Daniel Raisch, 653-5. Los Angeles: Sage, 2010.

Gaither, Milton. "The History of North American Education, 15,000 BCE to 1491." *History of Education Quarterly* 54, no. 3 (2014): 323-48.

Galewski, Elizabeth. "The Strange Case for Women's Capacity to Reason: Judith Sargent Murray's Use of Irony in 'On the Equality of the Sexes' (1790)." *Quarterly Journal of Speech* 93, no. 1 (2007): 84-108.

Games, Alison, and Adam Rothman, eds. *Major Problems in Atlantic History*. Boston: Houghton Mifflin, 2008.

Gardner, Catherine Villanueva. "Heaven-Appointed Educators of Mind: Catharine Beecher and the Moral Power of Women." *Hypatia* 19, no. 2 (Spring 2004): 1-16.

Giele, Janet Zollinger, ed. *Two Paths to Women's Equality: Temperance, Suffrage, and the Origins of Modern Feminism*. New York: Twayne Publishers, 1995.

Giltner, John H. "Oliver Otis Howard: Dimensions of a Christian Soldier." *The Journal of Religious Thought* 24, no. 1 (1967): 3-13.

Giordano, Gerard. *Twentieth-Century Textbook Wars: A History of Advocacy and Opposition*. New York: Peter Lang, 2003.

Giroux, Henry A. "Curriculum, Multiculturalism, and the Politics of Identity." *NASSP Bulletin* 6 (1992): 1-11.

Gosden, P. H. J. H. *Education in the Second World War: A Study in Policy and Administration*. New York: Routledge, 1976.

Greene, Maxine. "Wide-Awakeness and the Moral Life." In *Foundations of Education: The Essential Texts*, edited by Susan F. Semel, 192-199, New York: Routledge, 2010.

Greenhouse, Linda. "Court Appears Skeptical for Argument for Prayer." *New York Times*, November 7, 1991. Accessed October 3, 2017. http://www.nytimes.com/1991/11/07/us/court-appears-skeptical-of-argument-for-prayer.html?pagewanted=all.

Gross, Magdalena. "Reclaiming the Nation: Polish Schooling in Exile during the Second World War." *History of Education Quarterly* 53, no. 3 (2013): 233-54.

Grove, DeeAnn. "White Voters, a Key Piece of the Puzzle: Education, Race, and Electoral Politics." *PS, Political Science & Politics* 51, no. 3 (2018): 517-22.

Guelzo, Allen C. *Gettysburg: The Last Invasion*. New York: Alfred A. Knopf, 2013.

Gutek, Gerald. L. *A History of the Western Educational Experience*. 2nd ed. Long Grove: Waveland Press, 1995.

———. *Historical and Philosophical Foundations of Education: A Biographical Introduction*. 5th ed. Upper Saddle River: Pearson, 2011.

———. *Pestalozzi and Education*. New York: Random House, 1968.

———. *Philosophical, Ideological, and Theoretical Perspectives on Education*. 2nd ed. Boston: Pearson, 2014.

Hagedorn, Thomas W. *Founding Zealots: How Evangelicals Created America's First Public Schools, 1783-1865*. Maitland: Xulon Press, 2013.

Harrison, Robert. "New Representations of a 'Misrepresented Bureau': Reflections of Recent Scholarship on the Freedmen's Bureau." *American Nineteenth Century History* 8, no. 2 (2007): 205-29.

Haykin, Michael A. G., and Dustin Bruce. "Jonathan Edwards: Influencing and Shaping the Heart." In *A Legacy of Religious Educators: Historical and Theological Introductions*, edited by Elmer L. Towns and Benjamin K. Forrest, 253-76. Lynchburg: Liberty University Press, 2017.

Heimert, Alan. *Religion and the American Mind: From the Great Awakening to the Revolution*. Cambridge: Harvard University Press, 1966.

Heller, Walter, and Hubert H. Humphrey. *Report on the Economy*, January 27, 1963. Minnesota Historical Society.

Higginbotham, A. Leon. "Rosa Parks: Foremother and Heroine Teaching Civility and Offering a Vision for a Better Tomorrow." *Florida State University Law Review* 22, no. 4 (1995): 899-911.

Higginbotham, A. Leon, and Anne F. Jacobs. "The 'Law Only as an Enemy': The Legitimization of Racial Powerlessness through the Colonial and Antebellum Criminal Laws of Virginia." *North Carolina Law Review* 70, no. 4 (1992): 969-1070.

Higginbotham, A. Leon, and Greer C. Bosworth. "'Rather Than the Free': Free Blacks in Colonial and Antebellum Virginia." *Harvard Civil Rights – Civil Liberties Law Review* 26, no. 1 (1991): 17-66.

Hodge, Charles. "Bushnell on Christian Nurture." *Biblical Repertory and Princeton Review* 19 (1847), 502-38.

Holder, John. J., Jr., "The Political and Educational Philosophy of Benjamin Rush." *Transactions of the Charles S. Peirce Society* 24, no. 3 (1988): 409-22.

hooks, bell. *Teaching to Transgress: Education as the Practice of Freedom*. New York: Routledge, 1994.

Hunt, Thomas C., James C. Carper, Thomas J. Lasley, and C. Daniel Raisch, eds. *Encyclopedia of Educational Reform and Dissent*. 2 vols. Los Angeles: Sage, 2010.

Ichino, Andrea, and Rudolf Winter-Ebmer. "The Long-Run Educational Cost of World War II." *Journal of Labor Economics* 22, no. 1 (2004): 57-86.

Immerwahr, John. "Augustine's Advice for College Teachers: Ever Ancient, Ever New." *Metaphilosophy* 39, no. 4 (2008): 656-65.

Jackson, Kenneth T., and David S. Dunbar, eds. *Empire City: New York Through the Centuries*. New York: Columbia University Press, 2002.

Jay, Michelle L., and Lisa Wills. "Freedmen's Bureau." In *Encyclopedia of Educational Reform and Dissent*, edited by Thomas C. Hunt, James C. Carper, Thomas J. Lasley, and C. Daniel Raisch, 387-90. Los Angeles: Sage, 2010.

Jefferson, Thomas. "A Bill of the More General Diffusion of Knowledge." In *The Papers of Thomas Jefferson*, edited by Julian P. Boyd, 526-533. Princeton: Princeton University Press, 1950.

Johnson, Lyndon B. "Johnson's Remarks on Signing the Elementary and Secondary Education Act." Johnson City, TX, April 11, 1965. Accessed May 25, 2019. http://www.lbjlibrary.org/lyndon-baines-johnson/timeline/johnsons-remarks-on-signing-the-elementary-and-secondary-education-act.

———. "The State of the Union Message to Congress, 8 January 1964." In *A Time for Action: A Selection from the Speeches and Writings of Lyndon B. Johnson*, 164-179. New York: Antheneum, 1964.

Juneau, Stan. *History and Foundation of American Indian Education*. Helena: Montana Office of Public Instruction, 2001.

Kathan, Boardman W. Horace Bushnell and the Religious Education Movement. *Religious Education* 108, no. 1 (2013), 41-57.

Keller, Tim. *The Reason for God: Belief in an Age of Skepticism*. New York: Riverhead Books, 2008.

Kenyon, Eric. "Augustine and the Liberal Arts." *Arts & Humanity in Higher Education* 12, no. 1 (2012): 105-113.

Key, E. *The Education of the Child.* New York: Knickerbocker Press, 1908.

Kienel, Paul A. *A History of Christian School Education.* Colorado Springs: Purposeful Design Publications, 2005.

Kierkegaard, Søren. *Either/Or.* Translated by Edna H. Hong and Howard V. Hong. Princeton: Princeton University Press, 1987.

———. *Fear and Trembling.* Translated by Edna H. Hong and Howard V. Hong. Princeton: Princeton University Press, 1983.

———. *Philosophical Fragments.* Translated by Edna H. Hong and Howard V. Hong. Princeton: Princeton University Press, 1985.

———. *The Sickness Unto Death. A Christian Psychological Exposition for Edification and Awakening.* Translated by Alastair Hannay. London: Penguin Books, 1989.

King, Wilma. *Stolen Childhood: Slave Youth in Nineteenth-Century America.* Bloomington: Indiana University Press, 1995.

Kirylo, James D. "Hate Won, but Love Will Have the Final Word: Critical Pedagogy, Liberation Theology, and the Moral Imperative of Resistance." *Policy Futures in Education* 15, no. 5 (2017): 590-601.

Knight, George R. *Philosophy & Education: An Introduction in Christian Perspective.* 4th ed. Berrien Springs: Andrews University Press, 2006.

Kuritz, Hyman. "Benjamin Rush: His Theory of Republican Education." *History of Education Quarterly* 7, no. 4 (1967): 432-451.

Lachmann, Richard, and Lacy Mitchell. "The Changing Face War in Textbooks: Depictions of World War II and Vietnam." *Sociology of Education* 87, no. 3 (2014): 188-203.

Lain, Corinna Barrett. "God, Civic Virtue, and the American Way: Reconstructing *Engel.*" *Stanford Law Review* 67, no. 3 (2015): 479-555.

Layman, Jack. "Modern Educational Philosophies." In *Philosophy of Christian School Education,* edited by Paul A. Kienel, Ollie E. Gibbs, and Sharron R. Berry, 72-104, Colorado Springs: Association of Christian Schools International, 1995.

Lessinger, Leon. *Every Kid a Winner: Accountability in Education.* New York: Simon & Schuster, 1970.

Lewis, John Vandenbergh. "Rhetoric and the Architecture of Empire in the Athenian Agora." Master's Thesis, Massachusetts Institute of Technology, 1995.

Lindberg, Stanley W. *The Annotated McGuffey: Selections from the McGuffey Eclectic Readers 1836-1920.* New York: Van Nostrand Reinhold, 1976.

Lockerbie, D. Bruce. *A Passion for Learning: A History of Christian Thought on Education.* 2nd ed. Colorado Springs: Purposeful Design Publications, 2007.

Luther, Martin. *Three Treatises.* Translated by Charles M. Jacobs. Minneapolis: Fortress Press, 1970.

———. *Works of Martin Luther, Volume 4.* Translated by Charles M. Jacobs. Albany: Books for the Ages, 1997.

MacCulloch, Diarmaid. *The Reformation: A History.* New York: Penguin Books, 2003.

Maddox, Samantha B. "Margaret Willis: Leading Explorers of the Past, Pioneers of the Future." Doctoral Dissertation, University of South Carolina, Columbia, 2001.

Makowski, Lee J. *Horace Bushnell on Christian Character Development.* Lanham: University Press of America, 1999.

Mangalwadi, Vishal. *The Book That Made Your World: How the Bible Created the Soul of Western Civilization.* Nashville: Thomas Nelson, 2011.

Marsden, George M. *Jonathan Edwards: A Life.* New Haven: Yale University Press, 2003.

Marshall, Peter. *The Oxford Illustrated History of the Reformation*. Oxford: Oxford University Press, 2015.

McFeely, William S. *Yankee Stepfather: General O. O. Howard and the Freedmen*. New York: W. W. Norton & Company, 1994.

McGiffert, Arthur Cushman. *The Rise of Modern Religious Ideas*. New York: Macmillan, 1915.

McGregor, Georgette F. "The Educational Career of Susan Miller Dorsey." Doctoral Dissertation, University of California, Los Angeles, 1949.

McKanan, Daniel. "Unitarianism, Universalism, and Unitarian Universalism." *Religion Compass* 7, no. 1 (2013): 15-24.

Mehta, Jal. "How Paradigms Create Politics: The Transformation of American Educational Policy, 1980-2001." *American Educational Research Journal* 50, no. 2 (2013): 285-324.

Melanchthon, Philipp. *Melanchthon: Orations on Philosophy and Education*. Edited by Sachiko Kusukawa. Cambridge: Cambridge University Press, 1999.

Meriam, Lewis. "The Problem of Indian Administration, 1928." In *The School in the United States: A Documentary History*, edited by James W. Fraser, 190-195. New York: Routledge, 2010.

Mettler, Suzanne. *Soldiers to Citizens: The G.I. Bill and the Making of the Greatest Generation*. New York: Oxford University Press, 2005.

Minkema, Kenneth P. "Jonathan Edwards on Education and His Educational Legacy." *Oxford Scholarship Online* (2017): 31-50.

Monaghan, E. Jennifer. "Reading for the Enslaved, Writing for the Free: Reflections on Liberty and Literacy." *American Antiquarian Society* 108, no. 2 (January 1998): 309-341.

Moreland, J. P., and William Lane Craig. *Philosophical Foundations for a Christian Worldview*. Downers Grove: Intervarsity Press, 2003.

Morita, Michiyo. *Horace Bushnell on Women in Nineteenth-Century America*. Lanham: University Press of America, 2004.

Mosweunyane, Dama. "The African Educational Evolution: From Traditional Training to Formal Education." *Higher Education Studies* 3, no. 4 (2013): 50-59.

Mullin, Robert Bruce. *The Puritan as Yankee: A Life of Horace Bushnell*. Grand Rapids: William B. Eerdmans, 2002.

Murphy, Madonna. M. *The History and Philosophy of Education: Voices of Educational Pioneers*. Upper Saddle River, NJ: Pearson Prentice Hall, 2006.

Muskus, Eddy. "Liberation Theology: Its Origins and Early Development." *Foundations* 29 (1992): 31-41.

National Defense Education Act of 1958. In *The School in the United States: A Documentary History*, edited by James W. Fraser, 257-258. New York: Routledge, 2010.

No Child Left Behind Act of 2001. Public Law 107-110. Government Publishing Office.

Noll, Mark A. *A History of Christianity in the United States and Canada*. Grand Rapids: William B. Eerdmans Publishing Company, 1992.

Obama, Barack. "Remarks by the President on Education." Benjamin Banneker Academic High School, Washington, DC, October 17, 2016. Accessed May 25, 2019. https://obamawhitehouse.archives.gov/the-press-office/2016/10/17/remarks-president-education.

Ornstein, Allan C., Daniel U. Levine, Gerald L. Gutek, and David E. Vocke. *Foundations of Education*. 13th ed. Boston: Cengage Learning, 2017.

Paksuniemi, Merja, Satu Uusiautti, and Kaarina Määttä. "Teacher Education in Finland during the War Years, 1939-45." *War & Society* 33, no. 1 (2014): 12-25.

Pear, Robert. "Reagan Proposes Vouchers to Give Poor a Choice of Schools." *The New York Times*, November 14, 1985.

Pearcey, Nancy. *Total Truth: Liberating Christianity from Its Cultural Captivity*. Wheaton: Crossway Books, 2008.

Pestalozzi, Johann Heinrich. *How Gertrude Teaches Her Children*. Translated by Lucy E. Holland and Francis C. Turner. Syracuse: C. W. Bardeen, 1898.

Poe, Harry Lee. *Christianity in the Academy: Teaching at the Intersection of Faith and Learning*. Grand Rapids, MI: Baker Academic, 2004.

Postman, Neil. *The End of Education: Redefining the Value of School*. New York: Vintage Books, 1995.

Purple, David E. and Svi Shapiro. *Beyond Liberation and Excellence: Reconstructing the Public Discourse on Education*. Westport, CT: Bergin & Garvey, 1995.

Reagan, Ronald. "Radio Address to the Nation on Education and Drug Abuse." Santa Barbara County, CA, September 6, 1986. Accessed May 25, 2019. https://www.reaganlibrary.gov/research/speeches/090686a.

Roberts, Peter. "Learning to Live with Doubt: Kierkegaard, Freire, and Critical Pedagogy." *Policy Futures in Education* 15, no. 7-8 (2017): 834-848.

Rocca, Risa Della, Michael Foley, and Colin Kenny. "The Educational Theory of Søren. Kierkegaard." *New Foundations*. August 18, 2011. Accessed October 15, 2018. http://www.newfoundations.com/GALLERY/Kierkegaard.html.

Rousmaniere, Kate. "Dorothy's Wars: School Leadership during the Birmingham Blitz." *Journal of Educational Administration and History* 48, no. 3 (2016): 211-224.

Rush, Benjamin. "A Defence of the Use of the Bible as a School Book. Addressed to the Rev. Jeremy Belknap, of Boston, March 10, 1791." Letter. From *Evans Early American Imprint Collection*.

———. "A Plan for the Establishment of Public Schools and the Diffusion of Knowledge in Pennsylvania; to which are Added Thoughts upon the Mode of Education, Proper in a Republic: Addressed to the Legislature and Citizens of the State, 1786." Essay. From *Evans Early American Imprint Collection*.

———. *The Selected Writings of Benjamin Rush*. Edited by Dagobert D. Runes. New York: Philosophical Library, 1947.

———. "Thoughts upon Female Education, Accommodated to the Present State of Society, Manners, and Government, in the United States of America, 1787." Essay. From *Evans Early American Imprint Collection*.

Ryan, Michael. "'The Puritans of Today': The Anti-Whig Argument of *The Scarlet Letter*." *Canadian Review of American Studies* 38, no. 2 (2008): 201-225.

Sæverot, Herner. "Kierkegaard, Seduction, and Existential Education." *Studies in Philosophy and Education* 30, no. 6 (2011): 557-572.

Schiff, Karen L. "Objects of Speculation: Early Manuscripts on Women and Education by Judith Sargent (Stevens) Murray." *Legacy: A Journal of American Women Writers* 17, no. 2 (2000): 213-228.

Schnell, Michael. "Lyman Beecher's Nativist History." *Nineteenth-Century Prose* 27, no. 1 (Spring 2000): 27-50.

Sensbach, Jon F. *Rebecca's Revival: Creating Black Christianity in the Atlantic World*. Boston: Harvard, 2005.

Senter, Mark H. "Horace Bushnell, Theodore Cuyler, and Francis Clark: A Study of How Youth Ministry Began." *Journal of Youth Ministry* 2, no 2 (2004): 31-51.

Sharfstein, Daniel J. *Thunder in the Mountains: Chief Joseph, Oliver Otis Howard, and the Nez Pierce War*. New York: W. W. Norton & Company, 2017.

Sharma, Shalika. "The Educational Philosophy of Søren Kierkegaard: The Origin of Existentialism." *Indian Journal of Research* 5, no. 5 (2016): 368-369.

Shor, Ira. *Empowering Education: Critical Teaching for Social Change*. Chicago: University of Chicago Press, 1992.

Silber, Kate. *Pestalozzi: The Man and His Work*. London: Routledge and Kegan Paul, 1960.

Sires, James W. *The Universe Next Door*. 5th ed. Downers Grove: InterVarsity Press, 2009.

Smith, Bonnie Hurd. "Judith Sargent Murray Biography." *Judith Sargent Murray Society* (2018).

Smith, David I., and Joan Dudley. "John Amos Comenius: Teaching All Things to All People." In *A Legacy of Religious Educators: Historical and Theological Introductions*, edited by Elmer L. Towns and Benjamin K. Forrest, 205-224. Lynchburg: Liberty University Press, 2017.

Smith, David I., and James K. A. Smith, eds. *Teaching and Christian Practices: Reshaping Faith & Learning*. Grand Rapids: William B. Eerdmans, 2011.

Smith, Samuel James. "Horace Bushnell: Advocate of Progressive Orthodoxy and Christian Nurture." In *A Legacy of Religious Educators: Historical and Theological Introductions*, edited by Elmer L. Towns and Benjamin K. Forrest. Lynchburg: Liberty University Press, 2017.

———. "Johann Heinrich Pestalozzi." In *Encyclopedia of Educational Theory and Philosophy*, edited by Denis. C. Phillips. Thousand Oaks: SAGE Publications, 2014.

———. "Pestalozzianism." In *Encyclopedia of Educational Reform and Dissent*, edited by Thomas C. Hunt, James C. Carper, Thomas J. Lasley, and C. Daniel Raisch, 697-699. Thousand Oaks: SAGE Publications, 2010.

———. "Margaret Douglass: Literacy Education to Freed Blacks in Antebellum Virginia." *Bound Away: The Liberty Journal of History* 2, no. 2, article 4 (2018).

———. "McGuffey Readers: Elementary School Reading Books." In Encyclopedia Britannica, 2018.

———. "Navigating Religious Rights of Teachers and Students." *Christian Perspectives in Education* 1, no. 1 (2007).

———. "*New England Primer*." *The Times of Science: Journal of Tolstoy Pedagogical University*, no. 3-4 (2018): 26-30.

———. "The Role of Controversial Issues in Moral Education: Approaches and Attitudes of Christian School Educators." Doctoral Dissertation, Oklahoma State University, 2000.

Smither, Edward L. *Augustine as Mentor: A Model for Preparing Spiritual Leaders*. Nashville, TN: B&H Academic, 2008.

———. "Augustine: Teacher as Mentor." In *A Legacy of Religious Educators: Historical and Theological Introductions*, edited by Elmer L. Towns and Benjamin K. Forrest, 21-33. Lynchburg, VA: Liberty University Press, 2017.

Soares, Judith. "A Future for Liberation Theology?" *Peace Review* 20, no. 4 (2008): 480-486.

Spring, Joel. *The American School: A Global Context from the Puritans to the Obama Era*. New York: McGraw Hill, 2011.

Stark, Rodney. *For the Glory of God: How Monotheism Led to Reformations, Science, Witch-hunts, and the End of Slavery*. Princeton: Princeton University Press, 2003.

Stenberg, Shari J. "Liberation Theology and Liberatory Pedagogies: Renewing the Dialogue." *College English* 68, no. 3 (2006): 271-290.

Stowe, Lyman Beecher. *Saints, Sinners, and Beechers*. Indianapolis: The Bobbs-Merril Company, 1934. Tehie, Janice B. *Historical Foundations of Education: Bridges from the Ancient World to the Present*. Upper Saddle River: Pearson, 2007.

Staver, Mathew D. *Eternal Vigilance: Knowing and Protecting Your Religious Freedom*. Nashville: Broadman & Holman Publishers, 2005.

Strickland, J. Steve, and Samuel James Smith. "Susan Miller Dorsey (1857-1946): Trailblazer for women school superintendents." Paper presented at the Conference of the National Council for Professors of Educational Administration, Portland, Oregon, August, 2011.

Sullivan, Dolores P. *William Holmes McGuffey: Schoolmaster to the Nation*. Rutherford: Fairleigh Dickinson University Press, 1994.

Taylor, Alan. *American Colonies: The Settling of North America*. Edited by Eric Foner. New York: Penguin Books, 2001.

Tehie, Janice B. *Historical Foundations of Education: Bridges from the Ancient World to the Present*. Upper Saddle River: Pearson, 2007.

Thomson, David. "Oliver Otis Howard: Reassessing the Legacy of the 'Christian General.'" *American Nineteenth Century History* 10, no. 3 (2009): 273-298.

Toft, Pia Pannula, Merja Paksuniemi, and Johannes Westberg. "The Challenge of Returning Home: The Role of School Teachers in the Well-being of Finnish War Children, 'Finnebørn,' during and after World War II." *Paedagogica Historica* 54, no. 6 (2018): 736-749.

Topping, Ryan N. S. "Augustine on Liberal Education: Defender and Defensive." *The Heythrop Journal* 51, no. 3 (2010): 377-387.

Towns, Elmer L. and Benjamin K. Forrest, eds., *A Legacy of Religious Educators: Historical and Theological Introductions*. Lynchburg: Liberty University Press, 2017.

"Trial of a Female at Norfolk," *The Baltimore Sun* (November 28, 1853): 1.

Troy, Gil, Arthur M. Schlesinger, Jr., and Fred Israel. *History of American Presidential Elections, 1789–2008*. 3 vols. 4th ed. New York: Facts on File, Inc., 2011.

Turley, David. "Religion and Approaches to Reform: Boston Unitarians Versus Evangelicals in the Context of the 1820s and 1830s." *American Nineteenth Century History* 10, no. 2 (June 2009): 187-209.

Urban, Wayne J., and Jennings L. Wagoner, Jr. *American Education: A History*. Boston: McGraw Hill, 2004.

Varon, Elizabeth R. *We Mean to Be Counted: White Women & Politics in Antebellum Virginia*. Chapel Hill: University of North Carolina Press, 1998.

Veith, Gene Edward, Jr. *Reading Between the Lines: A Christian Guide to Literature*. Wheaton: Crossway Books, 1990.

Venezky, R. L. "The American Reading Script and Its Nineteenth-Century Origins." *Book Research Quarterly* 6, no. 2 (1990): 16-29.

Vieth, Paul J. *The Church and Christian Education*. St. Louis: Bethany, 1947.

Warren, Donald. "American Indian Histories as Education History." *History of Education Quarterly* 54, no. 3 (2014): 255-285.

Watson, Shevaun E. "'Good Will Come of this Evil': Enslaved Teachers and the Transatlantic Politics of Early Black Literacy." *College Composition and Communication* 61, no. 1 (2009): 66-89.

Watters, David H. "'I Spake as a Child': Authority, Metaphor and the *New-England Primer*." *Early American Literature* 20, no. 3 (1985): 193-213.

Westerhoff, John H., III. *McGuffey and His Readers: Piety, Morality and Education in Nineteenth Century America*. Nashville: Abingdon, 1978.

Woodbridge, John D., and Frank A. James III. *Church History. Vol. 2, From Pre-Reformation to the Present Day*. Grand Rapids: Zondervan, 2013.

Woodson, Carter Godwin. *The Education of the Negro Prior to 1861: A History of the Education of the Colored People of the United States from the Beginning of Slavery to the Civil War*. New York: Putnam, 1915.

Yeboah, Alberta. "Education among Native Americans in the Periods before and after Contact with Europeans." Paper presented at the annual National Association of Native American Studies Conference, Houston, Texas, February 14-19, 2005.

INDEX

nurturing model, 111
optimistic view of human nature, 113
view of Christian nurture, 110

C

Calvinism, 42, 60, 98, 108–109
Calvinist theology, 105
Calvin, John, 42–43, 96
Capitalism, 39
Captain Richard Pratt, 141
Capuchin friars, 49
Carlisle Indian Industrial School, 141
Carpenter, John A., 129
Carter, Jimmy, 165
Carter, Robert "King," 53
Catechisms, 42, 60
Catholic and Protestant missionaries, 137–139
Catholic immigrants, 98
Catholicism, 188
Celebrezze, Anthony J., 168
Ceremonies, 221
Channing, William Ellery, 107
Character development, 109
Charles V, 46
Chase, Susan E., 147
Chauncy, Charles, 67–68
Chavin culture, 30
Che Guevara, 189
Cherokee, 135
Chicago City Schools, 151
Chief Red Jacket, 141
Christian/Christianity, 11, 82, 84, 138
among children, 112
curriculum, 13–14
education, 110–113
evangelism, 55
faith, 111
life, natural flow of, 110
Neoplatonism, 14
nurture, 109–110, 112
paganism with, 14
personalism, 24
and republicanism, 82
theology, 21
training, 112

Christian Nurture (Bushnell), 112
Cicero, 12, 60
style of rhetoric, 10
Civic knowledge for participation, 78
Civilization Act of 1819, 140
Civil Rights Act, 168
Civil War
Christian soldier of, 123–124
service, 124–126
Clark, Tom, 220–221
Clear expectations, 15
Clinton, Bill, 164
Clinton, DeWitt, 97
Clinton, Hillary, 164–165
Coe, George A., 112
Coherence validity, 215
College of William and Mary, 86
Colonial North America, 60
educational theory into practice, 68–70
Jonathan Edwards. *See* Edwards, Jonathan
New England Primer, 61–62
rationalism *vs.* emotionalism, 67–68
Colonization, 191
Color, 23
Columbus, Christopher, 134
Comenius, John Amos, 40, 60
Common school movement, 43, 69, 85–87, 92, 101, 111
Commonwealth of Virginia, 85
Community, learning in, 12–13
Confucius, 85
Conscientization, 188, 191
Constructivism, 207
Copernicus, 33
Correspondence validity, 215
Cotton, John, 62
Counts, George S., 158
Cremin, Lawrence A., 118, 146
Crimean War, 124
Critical pedagogy, 190
literature of, 190
proponents of, 190
Cubberley, Ellwood P., 118, 147
Cultural adjustment, 154–155
Cultural learning, 134
Cultural mandate, 39

ABOUT THE AUTHOR

Samuel James Smith serves as Professor of Education at Liberty University and is Director of School Administration Programs. He began his career as an English and history teacher and later became a school principal. His specialization is in Curriculum and Instruction with a focus on historical and philosophical foundations of education. He has worked as a teacher and administrator in Houston, Texas, and Daytona Beach, Florida. He began teaching in higher education at Mid-America Christian University in Oklahoma City while completing his doctorate at Oklahoma State University. He studied history at Houston Baptist University and Liberty University. His research pursuits involve the topics of learning theory, character education, educational leadership, and second-career teachers.

© Ellie Richardson